W9-BJE-045

Family Wisdom

Family Wisdom

The 2,000 Most Important Things Ever Said About Parenting, Children, and Family Life

Susan Ginsberg, Ed. D.

COLUMBIA UNIVERSITY PRESS NEW YORK

Columbia University Press
Publishers since 1893
New York Chichesster, West Sussex

Library of Congress Cataloging-in-Publication Data

Family Wisdom: the 2,000 most important things ever said about parenting, children and family life/[compiled by] Susan Ginsberg
p. cm.
includes biographical references.
ISBN 0-231-10376-X
1. Parenting—Quotations, maxims, etc. 2. Child rearing—Quotations, maxims, etc. 3. Children—Quotations, maxims, etc. 4. Family—Quotations, maxims, etc. I. Ginsberg, Susan.
PN6084.C48F36 1996 96-34629
808.88'2—dc20

∞

Casebound editions of Columbia University Press books are printed on permanent and durable acid-free paper.

Printed in the United States of America

c 10 9 8 7 6 5 4 3 2 1

To my wise and wonderful family
Anne and Larry
Sally and Annie
Lizzie, Katie, and Luke

Contents

Introduction

Is the family here to stay? What makes a good parent? What are the qualities of a nurturing home? How has the role of fathers changed? What is the responsibility of the community to help and support families? How can we maintain connections from one generation to the next? These and other questions about relationships between men and women, among siblings, and between families and society have been a central human concern from the earliest recorded history to the front page of today's newspaper. They are the focus of the quotations collected in this book.

As a parent and as an educator whose work has been mainly with children and families, I've searched for answers to these and other similar questions. In my professional life over the years, I've planned, evaluated, and conducted programs in a variety of settings across the country for families of different backgrounds—from Head Start parents in inner-city neighborhoods to parents who are executives at major corporations. These experiences have given me a better understanding that parents, whatever their circumstances, want the same things for their children. They want them to grow up safe and healthy, to get a good education, to realize their potential, to find their niche in the world, and to be happy and satisfied with their lives.

I've also learned how much parents grow and change through the process of parenting. Being a parent is a demanding job as well as a joyful experience—and never one for which a person can be fully prepared or accomplish entirely alone. Parents need information about child development as well as emotional sustenance and practical advice. In fact, all of us—whether or not we are parents—need emotional sustenance from the people we are closest to. And most of us also continue to need practical advice on how to keep our family relationships open and positive throughout our lives.

One of the most important things I've learned from my experiences is that no family exists apart from its community, which in turn is subject to the political climate and social policies that support or undermine it. That's why I have chosen to include in this volume quotations that go beyond the narrow focus of childrearing and child-development, placing children and families in a broader social context: the school, the neighborhood, the workplace, the community, and the larger world.

This book represents a body of family wisdom: ideas that have formed and transformed generations and societies in ways that reverberate even today. The quotations reveal recurring themes: the intertwined needs of individuals and nations, the bonds that connect one generation to another, and the universality of the coming of age experience. I have tried to bring together and organize some of this wisdom—from philosophers, poets, scholars, authors, novelists, "experts," and parents themselves—in a way that is accessible to readers. *Family Wisdom* spans the centuries and draws from many different cultures to offer a myriad of viewpoints. These include insightful statements about the condition of the family and advice for parents penned by child-development specialists:

> Attachment to a baby is a long-term process, not a single, magical moment. The opportunity for bonding at birth may be compared to falling in love—staying in love takes longer and takes more work.
>
> —T. Berry Brazelton

From journalists and essayists:

> Each day we move a little closer to the sidelines of our children's lives, which is where we belong if we do our job right.
>
> —Anna Quindlen

From politicians:

> A commonplace of political rhetoric has it that the quality of a civilization may be measured by how it cares for its elderly. Just as surely, the future of a society may be forecast by how it cares for its young.
>
> —Daniel Patrick Moynihan

Directly from the hearts of parents:

> I guess what I've really discovered is the humanizing effect of children in my life—stretching me, humbling me. Maybe my thighs aren't as thin as they used to be. Maybe my getaways aren't as glamorous. Still I like the woman that motherhood has helped me to become.
>
> —Susan Lapinski

And from the point of view of children:

> Grown-ups never understand anything for themselves, and it is tiresome for children to be always and forever explaining things to them.
>
> —Antoine de Saint-Exupéry

Some quotations snap us to attention because the content demands our response:

> The more we learn about the conditions that undergird and foster the development of human competence and character, the more we see these same conditions being eroded and destroyed in contemporary societies.
>
> —Urie Bronfenbrenner

Some offer advice that may give us a new perspective on how to handle our children:

> Even as kids reach adolescence, they need more than ever for us to watch over them. Adolescence is not about letting go. It's about hanging on during a very bumpy ride.
>
> —Ron Taffel

A few others make us laugh with self-recognition:

> Women hope men will change after marriage but they don't; men hope women won't change but they do.
>
> —Bettina Arndt

The quotations in *Family Wisdom* are categorized into four major sections: Everyday Living, Family Relationships, Ages and Stages of Life, and The Family and Society. Subgroups within each section will help you locate a particular theme, such as "Achievement" (a subtopic of Everyday Living) or "Sibling Rivalry" (under Family Relationships). Because many subjects are interrelated, I have made some arbitrary decisions about where to place each entry. If you are searching for a specific quotation or a quotation related to a topic of interest, I encourage you to scan the table of contents to determine the possible categories under which you are likely to find your choice.

My hope is that this volume will serve different readers in different ways: if you are a parent, I hope it will be a guide to a better understanding of your own children, your family, and your place in the human family; if a scholar or author, I hope it will be a resource for finding just the right quote to support your own research; and for everyone I hope it will be a springboard for inspiration, a sense of perspective, and a bit of laughter.

Acknowledgments

Reflecting back on the process of researching and drawing together the quotations for *Family Wisdom* I realize how many ties I have to Columbia University and how it plays a central role in the acknowledgments for this book.

It is the source of my academic studies and professional training; as an undergraduate at Barnard College, a graduate student in early childhood education at Teachers College, and, much later, in the unique and wonderful doctoral program called AEGIS.

It was Keith Frome, then with Columbia University Press, who initiated this project and Maxine Greene, my brilliant teacher and friend, who gave it—and me—her invaluable endorsement and enthusiastic support.

The parents I worked with during my 23 years at Bank Street College—in towns and cities all over the country, on Indian reservations and in corporate conference rooms—all influenced the choice of quotations for this book

A few of my former colleagues from Bank Street have also made important contributions to the development and production of *Family Wisdom*. Nancy Samalin opened up her library of parenting books and helped me to discover some new and wonderful sources. Kathleen Bock was an invaluable help in entering the quotations into the computer and generally keeping me on track. Anne Perryman, who works with me to write and edit the *Work & Family Life* newsletter, was and continues to be a source of spiritual sustenance and editorial help whenever I need it. Ellen Galinsky has shared many resources with me and is always in the background cheering me on.

Liz Perle McKenna gave me wonderful professional advice as well as providing the subtitle for *Family Wisdom*. Marge Kennedy, a most talented writer and editor, undertook the difficult job of reworking the categories—essentially reorganizing the book—after the quotations had been gathered. I will always be grateful for her prodigious work and her consistently positive feedback.

Thanks also to my colleagues and friends at Children First who patiently watched this project unfold and gave me words of encouragement.

"And by your children you'll be taught." I've learned and keep learning so much from my two daughters and now from their husbands and my grandchildren. They are the true inspiration for this book.

Everyday Living

Appearance/Fashion

1 There is only one pretty child in the world, and every mother has it.

CHINESE PROVERB.

2 When children dress like adults they are more likely to behave as adults do, to imitate adult actions. It is hard to walk like an adult male wearing corduroy knickers that make an awful noise. But boys in long pants can walk like men, and little girls in tight jeans can walk like women.

DAVID ELKIND, (20th-century) U.S.child psychologist and author. *The Hurried Child,* ch. 1 (1988).

3 All God's children are not beautiful. Most of God's children are, in fact, barely presentable.

FRAN LEBOWITZ, (20th-century) U.S. humorist and author. *Metropolitan Life* (1978).

4 Designer clothes worn by children are like snowsuits worn by adults. Few can carry it off successfully.

FRAN LEBOWITZ, (20th-century) U.S. humorist and author. *The Fran Lebowitz Reader,* "Parental Guidance" (1994).

5 Cuteness in children is totally an adult perspective. The children themselves are unaware that the quality exists, let alone its desirability, until the reactions of grownups inform them.

LEONTINE YOUNG, (20th-century) U.S. social worker and author. *Life Among the Giants,* ch. 12 (1965).

Bedtime/Sleep

1 Little Boy kneels at the foot of the bed
Droops on the little hands, little gold head;
Hush! Hush! Whisper who dares!
Christopher Robin is saying his prayers.

A. A. MILNE, (1882–1956) British children's author. *When We Were Very Young,* "Vespers" (1924).

2 Must we to bed, indeed? Well then,
Let us arise and go like men,
And face with an undaunted tread
The long black passage up to bed.

ROBERT LOUIS STEVENSON, (19th-century) British poet and author. *A Child's Garden of Verses,* "North-West Passage . . ." (1885).

Bonding

1 Attachment to a baby is a long-term process, not a single, magical moment. The opportunity for bonding at birth may be compared to falling in love—staying in love takes longer and demands more work.

T. Berry Brazelton, (20th-century) U.S. pediatrician and author. *Touchpoints,* ch. 3 (1992).

2 We belong to that order of mammals, the primates, distinguished by its propensity for repeated single litters, intense parental care, long life-spans, late sexual maturity, and a complex and extensive social existence. . . . Our protracted biological and psychological helplessness, which extends well into the third year of life, intensifies the bond between infant and parents, making possible a sense of generational continuity. In contrast to other primates these bonds are not obliterated after sexual maturity.

Louise Kaplan, (20th-century) U.S. psychologist and author. *Adolescence,* ch. 4 (1994).

3 Many people have an oversimplified picture of bonding that could be called the "epoxy" theory of relationships . . . if you don't get properly "glued" to your babies at exactly the right time, which only occurs very soon after birth, then you will have missed your chance.

Pamela Patrick Novotny, (20th-century) U.S. journalist and author. *The Joy of Twins,* ch. 2 (rev. 1994).

4 The bottom line on bonding with multiples seems to be that if you see bonding as a static event—a moment in time at which you must have eye contact and skin contact simultaneously with two or more infants—you may indeed be in trouble.

Pamela Patrick Novotny, (20th-century) U.S. journalist and author. *The Joy of Twins,* ch. 2 (rev. 1994).

5 Fortunately for common sense, psychological research has shown that babies with more than one attachment are less distressed when mother leaves to go to work. They are more content and playful in the presence of other adults, meaning that they feel secure with people other than Mother.

Sandra Scarr, (20th-century) U.S. developmental psychologist and author. *Mother Care/Other Care,* pt. 2, ch. 4 (1984).

6 The best way of thinking of an attachment, in my view, is to see it as the outcome of an interaction between two people, each of whom contributes to the quality of the relationship. Most parents can promote a secure relationship with a calm, pleasant, patient baby. Only particularly sensitive and patient parents can promote a secure attachment to a difficult baby.

Sandra Scarr, (20th-century) U.S. developmental psychologist and author. *Mother Care/Other Care,* pt. 2, ch. 4 (1984).

7 Instead of being a static one-time event, bonding is a process, a dynamic and continuous one. Thus, a reciprocal, loving attachment is still realizable even when early contact is delayed—as it is for many mothers and their prematurely born infants, or when illness of either the newborn or the mother intervenes.

Julius Segal, (20th-century) U.S. pediatrician. "10 Myths about Child Development," *Parents Magazine* (July 1989).

8 We have been told over and over about the importance of bonding to our children. Rarely do we hear about the skill of letting go, or, as one parent said, "that we raise our children to leave us." Early childhood, as our kids gain skills and eagerly want some distance from us, is a time to build a kind of adult-child balance which permits both of us room.

JOAN SHEINGOLD DITZION, (20th-century) U.S. parent educator. *Ourselves and Our Children,* the Boston Women's Health Book Collective, ch. 2 (1978).

Caring/Kindness/ Compassion

1 When our kids are young, many of us rush out to buy a cute little baby book to record the meaningful events of our young child's life . . . . But I've often thought there should be a second book, one with room to record the moral milestones of our child's lives. There might be space to record dates she first shared or showed compassion or befriended a new student or thought of sending Grandma a get-well card or told the truth despite its cost.

FRED G. GOSMAN, (20th-century) U.S. author. *How to Be a Happy Parent . . . In Spite or Your Children,* ch. 11 (1995).

2 [Research has found that] . . . parents whose children were "baby altruists" by two years *firmly* prohibited any child aggression against others. Adults not only restated their rule against hitting, for example, but they let the little one know that they would not tolerate the child hurting another.

ALICE STERLING HONIG, (20th-century) U.S. child psychologist. "Helping Children Become More Caring and Cooperative," *NYSAEYC (New York State Association for the the Education of Young Children) Reporter* (Winter 1994).

3 Research shows clearly that parents who have modeled nurturant, reassuring responses to infants' fears and distress by soothing words and stroking gentleness have toddlers who already can stroke a crying child's hair. Toddlers whose special adults model kindliness will even pick up a cookie dropped from a peer's high chair and return it to the crying peer rather than eat it themselves!

ALICE STERLING HONIG, (20th-century) U.S. child psychologist. "Helping Children Become More Caring and Cooperative," *NYSAEYC (New York State Association for the the Education of Young Children) Reporter* (Winter 1994).

4 Children learn to care by experiencing good care. They come to know the blessings of gentleness, or sympathy, of patience and kindness, of support and backing first through the way in which they themselves are treated.

JAMES L. HYMES, JR., (20th-century) U.S. child psychologist and author. *Teaching the Child Under Six,* ch. 3 (1968).

5 Young people . . . have more compassion and tenderness toward the elderly than most middle-aged adults. Nothing—not avarice, not pride, not scrupulousness, not impulsiveness—so disillusions a youth about her parents as the seemingly inhumane way they treat her grandparents.

LOUISE KAPLAN, (20th-century) U.S. psychologist and author. *Adolescence,* ch. 12 (1984).

6 Our most important task as parents is raising children who will be

decent, responsible, and caring people devoted to making this world a more compassionate place.

NEIL KURSHAN, (20th-century) U.S. rabbi and author. *Raising Your Child to Be a Mensch,* ch. 7 (1987).

7 The beginnings of altruism can be seen in children as early as the age of two. How then can we be so concerned that they count by the age of three, read by four, and walk with their hands across the overhead parallel bars by five, and not be concerned that they act with kindness to others?

NEIL KURSHAN, (20th-century) U.S. rabbi and author. *Raising Your Child to Be a Mensch,* ch. 3 (1987).

8 Too often I hear people say, "Well, at least so-and-so is a good person." When did being a good person become the *least* thing we can say about another? And are we raising children who will someday find that this is the *least* thing they can say about themselves?

NEIL KURSHAN, (20th-century) U.S. rabbi and author. *Raising Your Child to Be a Mensch,* ch. 1 (1987).

9 We want our children to become warm, decent human beings who reach out generously to those in need. We hope they find values and ideals to give their lives purpose so they contribute to the world and make it a better place because they have lived in it. Intelligence, success, and high achievement are worthy goals, but they mean nothing if our children are not basically kind and loving people.

NEIL KURSHAN, (20th-century) U.S. rabbi and author. *Raising Your Child to Be a Mensch,* ch. 1 (1987).

10 It has long been thought that the key to empathy is the mother-child connection—that if a mother is loving and nurturing, the child will learn by her compassionate example. But new studies suggest that it is the involvement of the father that is the most important variable in the development of empathy in children—in particular, his ability to be both warm and to set limits on unacceptable behavior.

VICTORIA SECUNDA, (20th-century) U.S. psychologist and author. *Women and Their Fathers,* ch. 5 (1992).

Character/Conscience

1 An older child, one who possesses a conscience, will be troubled with self-reproaches and feelings of shame for his naughtiness, even if he is not discovered. But our two-year-olds and our three-year-olds experience guilt feelings only when they feel or anticipate disapproval from the outside. In doing this, they have taken the first steps toward the goal of conscience, but there is a long way ahead before the policeman outside becomes the policeman inside.

SELMA H. FRAIBERG, (20th-century) U.S. child psychoanalyst and author. *The Magic Years,* ch. 4 (1959).

2 Language makes it possible for a child to incorporate his parents' verbal prohibitions, to make them part of himself. . . . We don't speak of a conscience yet in the child who is just acquiring language, but we can see very clearly how language plays an indispensable role in the formation of conscience. In fact, the moral achieve-

ment of man, the whole complex of factors that go into the organization of conscience, is very largely based upon language.

Selma H. Fraiberg, (20th-century) U.S. child psychoanalyst and author. *The Magic Years,* ch. 4 (1959).

3 Parents can only give [children] good advice or put them on their right paths, but the final forming of a person lies in their own hands.

Anne Frank, (20th-century) German diarist. *Diary of a Young Girl,* date of entry July 15, 1944 (1952).

4 Building a conscience is what discipline is all about. The goal is for a youngster to end up *believing* in decency, and acting—whether anyone is watching or not—in helpful and kind and generous, thoughtful ways.

James L. Hymes, Jr., (20th-century) U.S. child psychologist and author. "A Sensible Approach to Discipline," *Childhood* (1976).

5 Morality is not only taught; it is caught.

Neil Kurshan, (20th-century) U.S. rabbi and author. *Raising Your Child to Be a Mensch,* ch. 4 (1987).

6 You know that the beginning is the most important part of any work, especially in the case of a young and tender thing; for that is the time at which the character is being framed.

Plato, (5th-century B.C.) Greek Philosopher.

7 Children can find bottomless reserves of righteousness, moral indignation, and rigidity—when the object is another child.

Nancy Samalin, (20th-century) U.S. parent educator and author. *Love and Anger: The Parental Dilemma,* ch. 4 (1991).

8 Control cannot be called conscience until we are able to take it inside us and make it our own, until—in spite of the fact that the wrongs we have done or imagined will never be punished or known—we nonetheless feel that clutch in the stomach, that chill upon the soul, that self-inflicted misery called guilt.

Judith Viorst, (20th-century) U.S. novelist and poet. *Necessary Losses,* ch. 9 (1986).

9 There are only two reasons why any child decides to give up something he wants to do or to do something he doesn't like. One is fear, and punishment is the enforcer. The other is the wish to please someone important, and love is the enforcer. Normally in everyday life both find their place and necessarily so. The important question is which predominates and grows into the prime determiner of behavior. When it is fear, the outside rules and the power of their enforcement tell the story. When it is love, self-discipline builds the structure of consciousness.

Leontine Young, (20th-century) U.S. social worker and author. *Life Among the Giants,* ch. 16 (1965).

Preteens/Preteen Development

1 In many respects, the preteen years mimic adolescence, but without one essential ingredient: hormones.

Lawrence Balter, (20th-century) U.S. psychologist and author. *Who's in Control?* ch. 6 (1989).

2 At this age [9–12], in contrast to adolescence, girls still want to

know their parents and hear what they think. You are the influential ones if you want to be. Girls, now, want to hear your point of view and find out how you got to be what you are and what you are doing. They like their fathers and mothers to be interested in what they're doing and planning. They like to know what you think of their thoughts.

STELLA CHESS, (20th-century) U.S. psychiatrist and author. *Daughters,* ch. 6 (1978).

3 There is a parallel between the twos and the tens. Tens are trying to test their abilities again, sizing up and experimenting to discover how to fit in. They don't mean everything they do and say. They are just testing. . . . Take a good deal of your daughter's behavior with a grain of salt. Try to handle the really outrageous as matter-of-factly as you would a mistake in grammar or spelling.

STELLA CHESS, (20th-century) U.S. psychiatrist and author. *Daughters,* ch. 6 (1978).

4 When the child is twelve, your wife buys her a splendidly silly article of clothing called a training bra. To train *what*? I never had a training *jock*. And believe me, when I played football, I could have used a training jock more than any twelve-year-old needs a training bra.

BILL COSBY, (20th-century) U.S. comedian and author. *Fatherhood,* ch. 6 (1986).

5 During the latency years, American children need experiences that promote academic talents, a sense of responsibility, and most important, a belief that they can attain the goals valued by self and community. They need reassurance that these goals are attainable.

JEROME KAGAN, (20th-century) U.S. professor of developmental psychology. *In Support of Families,* ed. Michael W. Yogman and T. Berry Brazelton, ch. 3 (1986).

6 Probably more than youngsters at any age, early adolescents expect the adults they care about to demonstrate the virtues they want demonstrated. They also tend to expect adults they admire to be absolutely perfect. When adults disappoint them, they can be critical and intolerant.

THE LIONS CLUBS INTERNATIONAL AND THE QUEST NATION, *The Surprising Years,* I, ch. 4 (1985).

Children's Behavior

1 To be told that our child's behavior is "normal" offers little solace when our feelings are badly hurt, or when we worry that his actions are harmful at the moment or may be injurious to his future. It does not help me as a parent nor lessen my worries when my child drives carelessly, even dangerously, if I am told that this is "normal" behavior for children of his age. I'd much prefer him to deviate from the norm and be a cautious driver!

BRUNO BETTELHEIM, (20th-century) Austrian-born U.S. child psychologist and author. *A Good Enough Parent,* ch. 3 (1987).

2 A concern with parenting . . . must direct attention beyond behavior. This is because parenting is not simply a set of behaviors, but participation in an interpersonal, diffuse, affective relationship. Parenting is an eminently psychological

role in a way that many other roles and activities are not.

Nancy Chodorow, (20th-century) U.S. psychologist and author. *The Reproduction of Mothering: Psychoanalysis and the Sociology of Gender,* ch. 2 (1978).

3 Children, randomly at first, hit upon something sooner or later that is their mother's and/or father's Achilles' heel, a kind of behavior that especially upsets, offends, irritates or embarrasses them. One parent dislikes name-calling, another teasing . . . another bathroom jokes. For the parents, this behavior may have ties back to their childhood, may have been something not allowed, forbidden, and when it appears in the child, it causes high-voltage reaction in the parent.

Ellen Galinsky, (20th-century) U.S. child development specialist and author. *Between Generations,* ch. 3 (1981).

4 The fact that behavior is "normal," or consistent with childhood development, does not necessarily make it desirable or acceptable. . . . Undesirable impulses do not have to be embraced as something good in order to be accepted as normal. Neither does children's behavior that is unacceptable have to be condemned as "bad," in order to bring it under control.

Elaine Heffner, (20th-century) U.S. psychiatrist and author. *Mothering,* ch. 3 (1978).

5 The inability to control our children's behavior feels the same as not being able to control it in ourselves. And the fact is that primitive behavior in children does unleash primitive behavior in mothers. That's what frightens mothers most. For young children, even when out of control, do not have the power to destroy their mothers, but mothers who are out of control feel that they may destroy their children.

Elaine Heffner, (20th-century) U.S. psychiatrist and author. *Mothering,* ch. 5 (1978).

6 The psychological umbilical cord is more difficult to cut than the real one. We experience our children as extensions of ourselves, and we feel as though their behavior is an expression of something within us . . . instead of an expression of something in them. We see in our children our own reflection, and when we don't like what we see, we feel angry at the reflection.

Elaine Heffner, (20th-century) U.S. psychiatrist and author. *Mothering,* ch. 5 (1978).

7 Parents need to recognize that the negative behavior accompanying certain stages is just a small part of the total child. It should not become the main focus or be pushed into the limelight.

Saf Lerman, (20th-century) U.S. parent educator and author. *Helping Children as They Grow,* ch. 1 (1983).

8 Anytime we react to behavior in our children that we dislike in ourselves, we need to proceed with extreme caution. The dynamics of everyday family life have a way of repeating themselves.

Cathy Rindner Tempelsman, (20th-century) U.S. journalist and author. *Child-Wise,* ch. 2 (1994).

9 We often treat our children as though they are the first children in

history to exhibit such terrible behavior. In our anger, we communicate to them that "good" children don't behave in those ways when in fact good children do. Instead of acknowledging that this is appropriate developmental behavior, we think our children are doing things deliberately to drive us crazy.

NANCY SAMALIN, (20th-century) U.S. parent educator and author. *Love and Anger: The Parental Dilemma,* ch. 2 (1991).

10 Excessive attention, even if it's negative, is such a powerful "reward" to a child that it actually reinforces the undesirable behavior. You need to learn restraint, to respond to far fewer situations, to ask yourself questions like, "Is this really important?" "Could I let this behavior go?" "What would happen if I just wait?" "Could I lose by doing nothing?"

STANLEY TURECKI, (20th-century) U.S. psychiatrist and author. *The Difficult Child,* ch. 6 (1985).

11 But, children, you should never let
Such angry passions rise;
Your little hands were never made
To tear each other's eyes.

ISAAC WATTS, (1674–1748) English theologian and hymn writer. *Divine Songs for Children,* "Against Quarreling," xvi (1715).

Children's Behavior and Feelings Compared

1 If she [a mother] is confident that feeling something is not the same as acting it out, she will be able to teach this to her child. His feeling will seem less terrifying if she is sure she can control her own. It will be clear to her that respecting his feelings is not the same as giving in to his wishes or accepting his behavior; containing his behavior does not have to be the same as squelching his feelings. Since for most of us, these distinctions were never made clear in our own childhood, we need as much help as our children do in learning to distinguish between behavior and feelings, in keeping our feelings while exercising control over our actions.

ELAINE HEFFNER, (20th-century) U.S. psychiatrist and author. *Mothering,* ch. 6 (1978).

2 If your child yells at you in front of someone else, you may feel outraged and embarrassed. Even so, try to see the incident from your child's perspective and discover what compelled him to act this way ("You must have been pretty angry to speak to me that way"). If you can do this, you can put an unpleasant incident behind you and in the process gain insight into your child.

CATHY RINDNER TEMPELSMAN, (20th-century) U.S. journalist and author. *Child-Wise,* ch. 14 (1994).

3 The skill of acknowledgment applies to feelings—not to misbehavior. When a child is using the living-room wall as a mural for his Magic Markers, empathy is not in order—clear limits are. This is not the time to say, "You wish you could use Magic Marker on the walls." This is the time to state firmly, "Markers are to be used *only* on paper."

NANCY SAMALIN, (20th-century) U.S. parent educator and author. *Loving Your Child Is Not Enough,* ch. 2 (1987).

4 The confusion of emotions with behavior causes no end of unnecessary trouble to both adults and children. Behavior can be commanded; emotions can't. An adult can put controls on a child's behavior—at least part of the time—but how do you put controls on what a child feels? An adult can impose controls on his own behavior—if he's grown up—but how does he order what he feels?

LEONTINE YOUNG, (20th-century) U.S. social worker and author. *Life Among the Giants,* ch. 1 (1965).

5 When the manipulations of childhood are a little larceny, they may grow and change with the child into qualities useful and admired in the grown-up world. When they are the futile struggle for love and concern and protection, they may become the warped and ruthless machinations of adults who seek in the advantages of power what they could never win as children.

LEONTINE YOUNG, (20th-century) U.S. social worker and author. *Life Among the Giants,* ch. 9 (1965).

Children's Fears

1 A child . . . who has learned from fairy stories to believe that what at first seemed a repulsive, threatening figure can magically change into a most helpful friend is ready to believe that a strange child whom he meets and fears may also be changed from a menace into a desirable companion.

BRUNO BETTELHEIM, (20th-century) Austrian-born U.S. child psychologist and author. *The Uses of Enchantment,* "Fairy Tales vs. Myth" (1975).

2 Whenever reality reinforces a child's fantasied dangers, the child will have more difficulty in overcoming them. . . . So, while parents may not regard a spanking as a physical attack or an assault on a child's body, the child may regard it as such, and experience it as a confirmation of his fears that grown-ups under certain circumstances can really hurt you.

SELMA H. FRAIBERG, (20th-century) U.S. child psychoanalyst and author. *The Magic Years,* ch. 1 (1959).

3 Young children scare easily—a tough tone, a sharp reprimand, an exasperated glance, a peeved scowl will do it. Little signs of rejection—you don't have to hit young children to hurt them—cut very deeply.

JAMES L. HYMES, JR., (20th-century) U.S. child psychologist and author. *Teaching the Child Under Six,* ch. 2 (1968).

4 It's important to remember that children who are facing a frightening situation have three fundamental concerns: Am I safe? Are you, the people who care for me, safe? How will this affect my daily life?

LAWRENCE KUTNER, (20th-century) U.S. child psychologist and author. *Toddlers and Preschoolers,* ch. 4 (1994).

5 Many parents worry that they will reinforce a fear by being overly sympathetic. It helps to know that when children are permitted to avoid an animal or an object that frightens them, they tend to overcome a fear sooner than if parents push them to confront it.

CATHY RINDNER TEMPELSMAN, (20th-century) U.S. journalist and author. *Child-Wise,* ch. 8 (1994).

6 We've forgotten what it's like not to be able to reach the light switch. We've forgotten a lot of the monsters that seemed to live in our room at night. Nevertheless, those memories are still there, somewhere inside us, and can sometimes be brought to the surface by events, sights, sounds, or smells. Children, though, can never have grown-up feelings until they've been allowed to do the growing.

Fred Rogers, (20th-century) U.S. children's television personality and author. *Mister Rogers Talks with Parents,* ch. 1 (1983).

Children's Feelings

1 When we acknowledge a child's feelings, we do him a great service. We put him in touch with his inner reality. And once he's clear about that reality, he gathers the strength to begin to cope.

Adele Faber and Elaine Mazlish, (20th-century) U.S. parent educators. *How to Talk So Kids Will Listen and Listen So Kids Will Talk,* ch. 1 (1980).

2 If a child is feeling disappointed, angry, or afraid about something, you can be sympathetic and understanding. But you don't need to get into your child's shoes and become disappointed, angry, or afraid yourself. Parents help by standing by their children, not by taking over their children's moods and feelings.

Saf Lerman, (20th-century) U.S. parent educator and author. *Helping Children as They Grow,* ch. 1 (1983).

3 Because the young child feels with such intensity, he experiences sorrows that seem inconsolable and losses that feel unbearable. A precious toy gets broken or a good-bye cannot be endured. When this happens, words like "sad" or "disappointed" seem a travesty because they cannot possibly capture the enormity of the child's loss. He needs a loving adult presence to support him in his pain but he does not want to be talked out of it.

Alicia F. Lieberman, (20th-century) U.S. psychologist and author. *The Emotional Life of the Toddler,* ch. 3 (1993).

4 Isn't it strange that it's easier to be gentle with the feelings of people we care less about than those of our children, whom we love so much?

Stephanie Marston, (20th-century) U.S. family therapist and author. *The Magic of Encouragement,* ch. 4 (1990).

5 When our children see us expressing our emotions, they can learn that their own feelings are natural and permissible, can be expressed, and can be talked about. That's an important thing for our children to learn.

Fred Rogers, (20th-century) U.S. children's television personality and author. *Mister Rogers Talks with Parents,* ch. 10 (1983).

6 The more I read and the more I talked to other parents of children with disabilities and normal children, the more I found that feelings and emotions about children are very much the same in all families. The accident of illness or disability serves only to intensify feelings and emotions, not to change them.

Judith Weatherly, (20th-century) U.S. editor and journalist. "Meeting Parental Needs, A Never-ending Dilemma," *The Exceptional Parent* (October 1984).

7 The smaller the person, the less we worry about his dignity. Sometimes

we even find the idea a little ludicrous as if smallness and inexperience were incompatible with anything so majestic as human dignity. . . .Yet children have a great sense of their own dignity. They couldn't define what it is but they know when it has been violated.

LEONTINE YOUNG, (20th-century) U.S. social worker and author. *Life Among the Giants,* ch. 12 (1965).

8 Unfortunately the laughter of adults too often carries to the ears of the young the ring of ridicule, that annihilating enemy of human dignity. Like grownups, children enjoy participating in a joke and appreciate admiration of their wit and cleverness, but do not enjoy being the butt of the jokes.

LEONTINE YOUNG, (20th-century) U.S. social worker and author. *Life Among the Giants,* ch. 12 (1965).

Children's Needs and Wants

1 A sense of worthiness is a child's most important need.

POLLY BERRIEN BERENDS, (20th-century) U.S. author. *Whole Child/Whole Parent,* ch. 3 (rev. 1987).

2 Parents' ability to survive a child's unabating needs, wants, and demands . . . varies enormously. Some people can give and give. . . .Whether children are good or bad, brilliant or just about normal, enormously popular or born loners, they keep their cool and say just the right thing at all times . . . even when they are miserable themselves, inexhaustible springs of emotional energy, reserved just for children, keep flowing unabated.

STELLA CHESS, (20th-century) U.S. psychiatrist and author. *Daughters,* ch. 2 (1978).

3 We all enter the world with fairly simple needs: to be protected, to be nurtured, to be loved unconditionally, and to belong.

LOUISE HART, (20th-century) U.S. community psychologist and author. *On the Wings of Self-Esteem,* ch. 2 (1994).

4 A major misunderstanding of child rearing has been the idea that meeting a child's needs is an end in itself, for the purpose of the child's mental health. Mothers have not understood that this is but one step in social development, the goal of which is to help a child begin to consider others. As a result, they often have not considered their children but have instead allowed their children's reality to take precedence, out of a fear of damaging them emotionally.

ELAINE HEFFNER, (20th-century) U.S. psychiatrist and author. *Mothering,* ch. 5 (1978).

5 At each stage of development the child needs different resources from the family. During the first year, a variety of experiences and the availability of the parents for attachment are primary. During the second and third years, stimulation of language development is critical. During the years prior to school entrance, information that persuades children they are loved becomes critical, and during the school years it is important for children to believe that they can succeed at the tasks they want to master.

JEROME KAGAN, (20th-century) U.S. Professor of developmental psychology. *In Support of Families,* ed. Michel W. Yogman and T. Berry Brazelton, ch. 3 (1986).

6 I don't believe that children can develop in a healthy way unless they feel that they have value apart from anything they own or any skill that they learn. They need to feel they enhance the life of someone else, that they are needed. Who, better than parents, can let them know that?

FRED ROGERS, (20th-century) U.S. children's television personality and author. *Mister Rogers Talks with Parents,* ch. 1 (1983).

7 When we acknowledge our children's right to want things, as well as their right to be upset when they can't have what they want, it can go a long way toward defusing their anger and the tantrums that occur as a result.

NANCY SAMALIN, (20th-century) U.S. parent educator and author. *Love and Anger: The Parental Dilemma,* ch. 2 (1991).

8 Children cannot eat rhetoric and they cannot be sheltered by commissions. I don't want to see another commission that studies the needs of kids. We need to help them.

MARIAN WRIGHT EDELMAN, (20th-century) U.S. child advocate and author. As quoted in *Woman to Woman,* by Julia Gilden and Mark Riedman (1994).

9 Grownups are always saying about an irritating child, "All he's after is attention," with the implication that it is an unimportant and more, an unwarranted demand. It's a curious adult reaction because the need for attention is not exactly unknown to grownups, and it is not a need they take lightly when it concerns themselves. . . . To be ignored by those who are important to one when one is age forty-two can be devastating, but to be ignored by those who are important to one when one is age two can be annihilating.

LEONTINE YOUNG, (20th-century) U.S. social worker and author. *Life Among the Giants,* ch. 7 (1965).

Conflict, General

1 Family life is full of angry situations. That's especially true because of all the voices we have in the back of our heads telling us about the things we should be doing and should be feeling: spouses should love each other; parents should feel nothing but love for their children; children should be respectful of adults; our children shouldn't be acting the way they are; we shouldn't be feeling the way we do. The conflict each of us experiences between what we really feel and how we think we ought to feel is the cause of much guilt and frustration.

RUTH DAVIDSON BELL, (20th-century) U.S. author. *Ourselves and Our Children,* the Boston Women's Health Book Collective, ch. 3 (1978).

2 It should come as no surprise to any of us that the solution to ending bickering in families is to talk to one another more often without blaming, making judgments, or insulting one another.

DONALD C. MEDEIROS, (20th-century) U.S. psychologist and author. *Children Under Stress,* ch. 2 (1983).

3 Never assume one child is always the victim and the other the aggressor. Remember, no matter how things appear, it takes two to tango.

If you look closely enough . . . you will see how the victim subtly provokes the aggressor into attacking.

Ron Taffel, (20th-century) U.S. psychologist and author. *Why Parents Disagree,* ch. 13 (1994).

Conflict Between Parents and Children

1 If the issue doesn't matter a whole lot, just drop it. You don't have to win every fight . . . and you will not have lost any of your authority by giving in when it doesn't matter very much.

Lawrence Balter, (20th-century) U.S. psychologist and author. *Who's In Control?,* ch. 3 (1989).

2 To make life more bearable and pleasant for everybody, choose the issues that are significant enough to fight over, and ignore or use distraction for those you can let slide that day. Picking your battles will eliminate a number of conflicts, and yet will still leave you feeling in control.

Lawrence Balter, (20th-century) U.S. psychologist and author. *Who's In Control?* "Speaking of Discipline" (1989).

3 Children are intensely invested in getting their way. They will devote more emotional and intellectual energy to winning arguments than parents ever will, and are almost always better rested.

Jean Callahan, (20th-century) U.S. journalist. "Single Parents," *Parenting Magazine* (February 1992).

4 Taking the child's point of view demands good will, time, and effort on the part of parents. The child is the clear beneficiary. Parents who make the effort to understand their children's point of view are likely to treat children fairly and in an age-appropriate manner.

David Elkind, (20th-century) U.S. child psychologist and author. *Ties that Stress,* ch. 5 (1994).

5 There is no prescribed method for resolving every specific conflict a mother has with her child, and there is certainly no method that will enable her to have exactly what she wants. . . . There is, however, a larger goal, which is to establish an overall climate of reasonableness, one in which she and her child can hear each other.

Elaine Heffner, (20th-century) U.S. psychiatrist and author. *Mothering,* ch. 5 (1978).

6 We've all got to remember to pick our battles carefully, to be prepared to lose small ones, and to hold out for big ones.

Marge Kennedy, (20th-century) U.S. author. *The Single Parent Family,* ch. 1 (1994).

7 Anytime you have a difficult encounter with your child, there is a good chance that at least one of these factors is bringing out the worst in him or her: transitions, time pressure, competition for your attention, conflicting objectives.

Cathy Rindner Tempelsman, (20th-century) U.S. journalist and author. *Child-Wise,* ch. 6 (1994).

8 The daily arguments over putting away the toys or practicing the piano defeat us so easily. We see them coming yet they frustrate us time and time again. In many cases, we are mothers and fathers who have managed budgets and unruly

bosses and done difficult jobs well through sheer tenacity and dogged preparation. So why are we unable to persuade someone three feet tall to step into six inches of water at bathtime?

Cathy Rindner Tempelsman, (20th-century) U.S. journalist and author. *Child-Wise,* ch. 1 (1994).

9 We will never be able to avoid conflicts entirely because parents' needs and children's needs are so often opposed. When we need to hurry, they want to dawdle. When we crave ten minutes of solitude after a trying day, they issue eighteen demands for immediate attention. When we get a long-distance phone call, they interrupt us with a crisis.

Nancy Samalin, (20th-century) U.S. parent educator and author. *Loving Your Child Is Not Enough,* ch. 1 (1987).

Conflict Between Spouses about Children

1 Kids need to see that their parents may not always be of the same mind, that people who differ, even angrily, can continue in a loving relationship, . . . that it's okay to argue with a loved one, and that one can do so without risking the love of the other person.

Lawrence Balter, (20th-century) U.S. psychologist and author. *"Not in Front of the Children . . . ,"* ch. 4 (1993).

2 You and your spouse should consider the arguments you have, not as calamities in the history of your child's development, but as opportunities for learning. Take the opportunity to teach your children the art of and value in negotiation, and to demonstrate your ability to empathize, your willingness to compromise, and your readiness to apologize for hurt you have inflicted on others.

Lawrence Balter, (20th-century) U.S. psychologist and author. *"Not in Front of the Children . . . ,"* ch. 4 (1993).

3 Parents are led to believe that they must be consistent, that is, always respond to the same issue the same way. Consistency is good up to a point but your child also needs to understand context and subtlety. . . . Much of adult life is governed by context: what is appropriate in one setting is not appropriate in another; the way something is said may be more important than what is said. . . .

Stanley Greenspan, (20th-century) U.S. child psychiatrist and author. *First Feelings: Milestones in the Emotional Development of Your Baby and Child,* ch. 6 (1985).

4 For decades child development experts have erroneously directed parents to sing with one voice, a unison chorus of values, politics, disciplinary and loving styles. But duets have greater harmonic possibilities and are more interesting to listen to, so long as cacophony or dissonance remains at acceptable levels.

Kyle D. Pruett, (20th-century) U.S. child psychiatrist and author. *The Nurturing Father,* ch. 9 (1987).

Creativity

1 As the creative adult needs to toy with ideas, the child, to form his ideas, needs toys—and plenty of leisure and scope to play with them as he likes, and not just the way

adults think proper. This is why he must be given this freedom for his play to be successful and truly serve him well.

BRUNO BETTELHEIM, (20th-century) Austrian-born U.S. child psychologist and author. *A Good Enough Parent,* ch. 14 (1987).

2 Certainly parents play a crucial role in the lives of individuals who are intellectually gifted or creatively talented. But this role is not one of active instruction, of teaching children skills . . . rather, it is support and encouragement parents give children and the intellectual climate that they create in the home which seem to be the critical factors.

DAVID ELKIND, (20th-century) U.S. psychologist and author. *Miseducation,* ch. 1 (1987).

3 Creativity becomes more visible when adults try to be more attentive to the cognitive processes of children than to the results they achieve in various fields of doing and understanding.

LORIS MALAGUZZI, (20th-century) Italian early education specialist. As quoted in *The Hundred Languages of Children,* ch. 3, Carolyn Edwards (1993).

4 Creativity seems to emerge from multiple experiences, coupled with a well-supported development of personal resources, including a sense of freedom to venture beyond the known.

LORIS MALAGUZZI, (20th-century) Italian early education specialist. As quoted in *The Hundred Languages of Children,* ch. 3, Carolyn Edwards (1993).

5 Our task, regarding creativity, is to help children climb their own mountains, as high as possible. No one can do more.

LORIS MALAGUZZI, (20th-century) Italian early education specialist. As quoted in *The Hundred Languages of Children,* ch. 3, Carolyn Edwards (1993).

6 Every child is an artist. The problem is how to remain an artist once he grows up.

PABLO PICASSO, (1881–1973) Spanish-born artist. As quoted in *Wit and Wisdom from the Peanut Butter Gang,* H. Jackson Brown (1994).

7 They [creative children] ask more questions than most children. They're usually spontaneous and enthusiastic. Their ideas are unique and occasionally strike other kids as *weird.* They're independent. Not that they don't care at all what other kids think, but they're able to do their thing despite the fact that their peers may think it's strange. And they have lots and lots of ideas.

SILVIA RIMM, (20th-century) U.S. psychologist. "Creativity: Is it a Gift from the Gods or Can We Teach it to Our Children," Gurney Williams III. As quoted in *Working Mother* (August 1987).

8 If our entertainment culture seems debased and unsatisfying, the hope is that our children will create something of greater worth. But it is as if we expect them to create out of nothing, like God, for the encouragement of creativity is in the popular mind, opposed to instruction. There is little sense that creativity must grow out of tradition, even when it is critical of that tradition, and children are scarcely being given the materials on which their creativity could work.

C. JOHN SOMMERVILLE, (20th-century) U.S. historian and author. *The Rise and Fall of Childhood,* ch.1 (rev. 1990).

9 Teaching creativity to your child isn't like teaching good manners. No one can paint a masterpiece by bowing to another person's precepts about elbows on the table.

Gurney Williams iii, (20th-century) U.S. editor and journalist. "Creativity: Is It a Gift from the Gods or Can We Teach It To Our Children," *Working Mother* (August 1987).

Crisis/Stress

1 A family's responses to crisis or to a new situation mirror those of a child. That is to say, the way a small child deals with a new challenge (for instance, learning to walk) has certain predictable stages: regression, anxiety, mastery, new energy, growth, and feedback for future achievement. These stages can also be seen in adults coping with new life events, whether positive or negative.

T. Berry Brazelton, (20th-century) U.S. pediatrician and author. *Families: Crisis and Caring,* ch. 6 (1989).

2 If we parents accept that problems are an essential part of life's challenges, rather than reacting to every problem as if something has gone wrong with the universe that's supposed to be perfect, we can demonstrate serenity and confidence in problem solving for our kids. . . . By telling them that we know they have a problem and we know they can solve it, we can pass on a realistic attitude as well as empower our children with self-confidence and a sense of their own worth.

Barbara Coloroso, (20th-century) U.S. parent educator and author. *Kids Are Worth It,* ch. 6 (1994).

3 It is not stressful circumstances, as such, that do harm to children. Rather, it is the quality of their interpersonal relationships and their transactions with the wider social and material environment that lead to behavioral, emotional, and physical health problems. If stress matters, it is in terms of how it influences the relationships that are important to the child.

Felton Earls, (20th-century) U.S. psychiatrist. *In Support of Families,* ed. Michael W. Yogman and T. Berry Brazelton, ch. 2 (1986).

4 In the most desirable conditions, the child learns to manage anxiety by being exposed to just the right amounts of it, not much more and not much less. This optimal amount of anxiety varies with the child's age and temperament. It may also vary with cultural values. . . . There is no mathematical formula for calculating exact amounts of optimal anxiety. This is why child-rearing is an art and not a science.

Alicia F. Lieberman, (20th-century) U.S. psychologist and author. *The Emotional Life of the Toddler,* ch. 7 (1993).

5 Part of the responsibility of being a parent is to arrange situations in children's lives so they are able to meet crises with a reasonable chance of coping successfully with them. . . . Parents who believe children are unharmed by crises and will simply bounce back in time seriously misunderstand children.

Donald C. Medeiros, (20th-century) U.S. psychologist and author. *Children Under Stress,* ch. 2 (1983).

6 The symbol in Chinese for crisis is made up of two ideographs: one

means danger, the other means opportunity. This symbol is a reminder that we can choose to turn a crisis into an opportunity or into a negative experience.

VIRGINIA SATIR, (20th-century) U.S. family therapist and author. *Friends Can Be Good Medicine,* "Barriers, hurdles, and miles to go before I sleep" (1981).

Cursing/Swearing/Name Calling

1 The parent in charge is the disciplinarian. . . . I do not believe in letting discipline wait for another parent to handle it, nor do I think the father or mother should be allowed to become a shadowy figure who walks in the door and has to play the bad guy in the house.

LAWRENCE BALTER, (20th-century) U.S. psychologist and author. *Who's In Control?* ch. 1 (1989).

2 When a toddler uses profanity, don't make a big deal about it. If you do, you give the child more power. After all, it's only a word—one that won't do much harm to anybody. In fact, if you think about it, a nasty word is a step up from hitting or biting someone. So look at it as a sign of growth.

LAWRENCE BALTER, (20th-century) U.S. psychologist and author. *Who's In Control?* ch. 3 (1989).

3 Your child . . . may not call you or other people names. . . . Don't be tempted to gloss over this issue. You may be able to talk to yourself into not minding being called names, but this decision may come back to haunt you in later years. If you let a preschooler speak disrespectfully to you now, you'll have a much harder time of it when your child is a preteen and the issue resurfaces, which it is likely to do then.

LAWRENCE BALTER, (20th-century) U.S. psychologist and author. *Who's In Control?* ch. 4 (1989).

4 Nothing, neither acceptance nor prohibition, will induce a child to stop swearing overnight. Teach your child respect for himself and others, that profanity can hurt, offend, and disgust, and you'll be doing the best you can. . . . And save your parental giggling over mispronounced curses for after the children's bedtime.

JEAN CALLAHAN, (20th-century) U.S. journalist. "And Other Choice Words to Strike from Your Child's Vocabulary," *Parenting Magazine* (April 1990).

Discipline and Setting Limits

1 Our children are counting on us to provide two things: consistency and structure. Children need parents who say what they mean, mean what they say, and do what they say they are going to do.

BARBARA COLOROSO, (20th-century) U.S. parent educator and author. *Kids Are Worth It,* ch. 6 (1994).

2 Caring for children is a dance between setting appropriate limits as caretakers and avoiding unnecessary power struggles that result in unhappiness.

CHARLOTTE DAVIS KASL, (20th-century) U.S. psychologist and author. *Finding Joy,* ch. 70 (1994).

3 The job for us is to develop a way to teach children without demanding

instant perfection or without giving in to every whim.

JEANNETTE W. GALAMBOS, (20th-century) U.S. early childhood educator and author. *A Guide to Discipline,* ch. 1 (1969).

4 A child with no limits is a child who will grow to hate freedom.

FRED G. GOSMAN, (20th-century) U.S. author. *How to Be a Happy Parent . . . In Spite of Your Children,* ch. 3 (1995).

5 If you are willing to inconvenience yourself in the name of discipline, the battle is half over. Leave Grandma's early if the children are acting impossible. Depart the ballpark in the sixth inning if you've warned the kids and their behavior is still poor. If we do something like this once, our kids will remember it for a long time.

FRED G. GOSMAN, (20th-century) U.S. author. *How to Be a Happy Parent . . . In Spite of Your Children,* ch. 11 (1995).

6 Kids won't come out and thank you each and every time you make a decision they aren't totally fond of. . . . But in their hearts kids know you're doing your job, just like they are doing their job by arguing.

FRED G. GOSMAN, (20th-century) U.S. author. *How to Be a Happy Parent . . . In Spite or Your Children,* ch. 3 (1995).

7 Setting limits gives your child something to define himself against. If you are able to set limits without being overly intrusive or controlling, you'll be providing him with a firm boundary against which he can test his own ideas.

STANLEY I. GREENSPAN, (20th-century) U.S. child psychiatrist and author, and **NANCY THORNDIKE GREENSPAN,** U.S. health economist. *First Feelings: Milestones in the Emotional Development of Your Baby and Child,* ch. 5 (1985).

8 Establishing limits, structure, rules, and expectations takes self-confidence on the part of parents. Parents need to recognize that they are the legitimate authority figures in their households and feel secure in that role.

KAREN LEVINE, (20th-century) U.S. author. "Are You a Softie?" *Parents Magazine* (April 1990).

9 The message you give your children when you discipline with love is "I care too much about you to let you misbehave. I care enough about you that I'm willing to spend time and effort to help you learn what is appropriate." All children need the security and stability of food, shelter, love, and protection, but unless they also receive effective and appropriate discipline, they won't feel secure.

STEPHANIE MARSTON, (20th-century) U.S. family therapist and author. *The Divorced Parent,* ch. 1 (1994).

10 Be aware that the more often a child hears the word no, the greater his need to say no himself.

CATHY RINDNER TEMPELSMAN, (20th-century) U.S. journalist and author. *Child-Wise,* ch. 5 (1994).

11 We find it easy to set limits when the issue is safety. . . . But 99 percent of the time there isn't imminent danger; most of life takes place on more ambiguous ground, and children are experts at detecting ambivalence.

CATHY RINDNER TEMPELSMAN, (20th-century) U.S. journalist and author. *Child-Wise,* ch. 5 (1994).

12 When parents fail to set appropriate limits, children may feel more vulnerable at night: the aggressive urges that have not been "tamed" by day may be terrifying to a small child alone in the dark.

CATHY RINDNER TEMPELSMAN, (20th-century) U.S. journalist and author. *Child-Wise,* ch. 2 (1994).

13 When we approach discipline as learning, this ability to internalize moral behavior will occur in the natural course of growth. Children will make mistakes, but, given half a chance, they will learn from them. Our disappointment and displeasure give them pause—and a strong desire to do better the next time around. However, when parents are too quick to punish (or when they assume that children will not really learn from their mistakes without paying a penalty), these lessons may be lost.

CATHY RINDNER TEMPELSMAN, (20th-century) U.S. journalist and author. *Child-Wise,* ch. 7 (1994).

14 Call them rules or call them limits, good ones, I believe, have this in common: they serve reasonable purposes; they are practical and within a child's capability; they are consistent; and they are an expression of loving concern.

FRED ROGERS, (20th-century) U.S. children's television personality and author. *Mister Rogers Talks with Parents,* ch. 6 (1983).

15 I think of discipline as the continual everyday process of helping a child learn self-discipline.

FRED ROGERS, (20th-century) U.S. children's television personality and author. *Mister Rogers Talks with Parents,* ch. 6 (1983).

16 It is our continuing love for our children that makes us want them to become all they can be, and their continuing love for us that helps them accept healthy discipline—from us and eventually from themselves.

FRED ROGERS, (20th-century) U.S. children's television personality and author. *Mister Rogers Talks with Parents,* ch. 6 (1983).

17 Love is at the root of all healthy discipline. The desire to be loved is a powerful motivation for children to behave in ways that give their parents pleasure rather than displeasure. It may even be our own long-ago fear of losing our parents' love that now sometimes makes us uneasy about setting and maintaining limits. We're afraid we'll lose the love of our children when we don't let them have their way.

FRED ROGERS, (20th-century) U.S. children's television personality and author. *Mister Rogers Talks with Parents,* ch. 6 (1983).

18 It is normal for children to test our limits—both in words and actions. Establishing independence from adult authority is a healthy way for children to find their own styles. The question is how can parents walk the tricky line between allowing their children to express their feelings while still asserting their authority as parents, and setting necessary limits.

NANCY SAMALIN, (20th-century) U.S. parent educator and and author. *Love and Anger: The Parental Dilemma,* ch. 3 (1991).

19 Children need both latitude of expression and firmly enforced limits on their behaviors, in a blend that results in calm, patient management. The key to success is to tailor the rearing environment to the developmental level of the child—what she or he can handle—

and to individual differences among children.

SANDRA SCARR, (20th-century) U.S. developmental psychologist and author. *Mother Care/Other Care,* pt. 1, ch. 1 (1984).

20 Parents who are cowed by temper tantrums and screaming defiance are only inviting more of the same. Young children become more cooperative with parents who confidently assert the reasons for their demands and enforce reasonable rules. Even if there are a few rough spots, relationships between parents and young children run more smoothly when the parent, rather than the child, is in control.

SANDRA SCARR, (20th-century) U.S. developmental psychologist. *Mother Care/Other Care,* part 3, ch. 6 (1984).

21 The child supplies the power but the parents have to do the steering.

BENJAMIN SPOCK, (20th-century) U.S. pediatrician and author. *Dr. Spock's Baby and Child Care,* (rev. 1985).

22 Relying on any one disciplinary approach—time-out, negotiation, tough love, the star system—puts the parenting team at risk. Why? Because children adapt to any method very quickly; today's effective technique becomes tomorrow's worn dance.

RON TAFFEL, (20th-century) U.S. psychologist and author. *Why Parents Disagree,* ch. 7 (1994).

23 How can you tell if you discipline effectively? Ask yourself if your disciplinary methods generally produce lasting results in a manner you find acceptable. Whether your philosophy is democratic or autocratic, whatever techniques you use—reasoning, a "star" chart, time-outs, or spanking—*if it doesn't work, it's not effective.*

STANLEY TURECKI, (20th-century) U.S. psychiatrist and author. *The Emotional Problems of Normal Children,* ch. 9 (1994).

24 Children can't make their own rules and no child is happy without them. The great need of the young is for authority that protects them against the consequences of their own primitive passions and their lack of experience, that provides with guides for everyday behavior and that builds some solid ground they can stand on for the future.

LEONTINE YOUNG, (20th-century) U.S. social worker and author. *Life Among the Giants,* ch. 16 (1965).

25 No one knows better than children how much they need the authority that protects, that sets the outer limits of behavior with known and prescribed consequences. As one little boy expressed it to his mother, "You care what I do."

LEONTINE YOUNG, (20th-century) U.S. social worker and author. *Life Among the Giants,* ch. 16 (1965).

Discipline and Punishment Compared

1 Discipline isn't just punishing, forcing compliance or stamping out bad behavior. Rather, discipline has to do with teaching proper deportment, caring about others, controlling oneself and putting someone else's wishes before one's own when the occasion calls for it.

LAWRENCE BALTER, (20th-century) U.S. psychologist and author. *Who's In Control?* Ch. 1 (1989).

2 Punishment may make us obey the orders we are given, but at best it will only teach an obedience to authority, not a self-control which enhances our self-respect.

BRUNO BETTELHEIM, (20th-century) Austrian-born U.S. child psychologist and author. *A Good Enough Parent,* ch. 9 (1987).

3 What children learn from punishment is that might makes right. When they are old and strong enough, they will try to get their own back; thus many children punish their parents by acting in ways distressing to them.

BRUNO BETTELHEIM, (20th-century) Austrian-born U.S. child psychologist and author. *A Good Enough Parent,* ch. 10 (1987).

4 While criticism or fear of punishment may restrain us from doing wrong, it does not make us wish to do right. Disregarding this simple fact is the great error into which parents and educators fall when they rely on these negative means of correction. The only effective discipline is self-discipline, motivated by the inner desire to act meritoriously in order to do well in one's own eyes, according to one's own values, so that one may feel good about oneself—may "have a good conscience."

BRUNO BETTELHEIM, (20th-century) Austrian-born U.S. child psychologist and author. *A Good Enough Parent,* ch. 10 (1987).

5 Although a firm swat could bring a recalcitrant child swiftly into line, the changes were usually external, lasting only as long as the swatter remained in view. . . . Permanent transformation had to be internal. . . . The habits of self-discipline, as laborious and frustrating as they were to achieve, offered the only real possibility of keeping children safe from their own excesses as well as the omnipresent dangers of society.

MARY KAY BLAKELY, (20th-century) U.S. journalist and author. *American Mom,* ch. 4 (1994).

6 Our goal as a parent is to give life to our children's learning—to instruct, to teach, to help them develop self-discipline—an ordering of the self from the inside, not imposition from the outside. Any technique that does not give life to a child's learning and leave a child's dignity intact cannot be called discipline—it is punishment, no matter what language it is clothed in.

BARBARA COLOROSO, (20th-century) U.S. parent educator and author. *Kids Are Worth It,* ch. 1 (1994).

7 It's not appropriate to punish children under three, because they really can't evaluate or control their own actions very well. . . . To be able to follow rules, to discipline herself, a child has to understand not only the rule, but the ideas behind it. She has to be able to recognize similar but not identical situations where the same rule applies. She has to have enough self-control to stop herself from acting on impulses (a separate problem from knowing she shouldn't do something).

AMY LAURA DOMBRO, (20th-century) U.S. early childhood educator and author. *The Ordinary Is Extraordinary,* ch. 2 (1988).

8 Fences, unlike punishments, clearly mark out the perimeters of any specified territory. Young children learn where it is permissible to play,

because their backyard fence plainly outlines the safe area. They learn about the invisible fence that surrounds the stove, and that Grandma has an invisible barrier around her cabinet of antique teacups.

Jeanne Elium and Don Elium, (20th-century) U.S. family counselors and authors. *Raising a Daughter,* ch. 6 (1994).

9 Good discipline is more than just punishing or laying down the law. It is liking children and letting them see that they are liked. It is caring enough about them to provide good, clear rules for their protection.

Jeannette W. Galambos, (20th-century) U.S. early childhood educator and author. *A Guide to Discipline,* ch. 1 (1969).

10 If the child knows the rewards and punishments in advance and knows that his parents will stick to them, the parents can actually empathize with the child's plight while, at the same time, creating a firm sense of structure. . . . Your child will sense your resolve and your empathy whether you do this with words or just a sense of warmth.

Stanley I. Greenspan, (20th-century) U.S. child psychiatrist and author. *Playground Politics,* ch. 8 (1993).

11 Above and beyond paying attention to feelings before and after a separation, never threaten your child with leaving or loss of love in an effort to control her behavior. Children believe their parents' assertions that "I will send you away," "I won't love you any more," "I'll go away," and are terrified with good reason. Fear is a very poor way of disciplining a child, and it can cause severe lifelong anxiety.

Alicia F. Lieberman, (20th-century) U.S. psychologist and author. *The Emotional Life of the Toddler,* ch. 8 (1993).

12 Routine physical punishment such as spanking teaches a toddler that might makes right and that it is fine to hit when one is stronger and can get away with it.

Alicia F. Lieberman, (20th-century) U.S. psychologist and author. *The Emotional Life of the Toddler,* ch. 7 (1993).

13 Children respond to our wish for vengeance by concentrating on retaliation, not on their own misdeeds.

Nancy Samalin, (20th-century) U.S. parent educator and author. *Loving Your Child Is Not Enough,* ch. 4 (1987).

14 The best time to punish is not when we're at our maddest, but that's usually when we do it.

Nancy Samalin, (20th-century) U.S. parent educator and author. *Love and Anger: The Parental Dilemma,* ch. 3 (1991).

Family Communication

1 Children pick up words as pigeons peas,
And utter them again as God shall please.

Old English Proverb.

2 There is no end to the violations committed by children on children, quietly talking alone.

Elizabeth Bowen, (20th-century) U.S. author. *The House in Paris,* pt. 1, ch. 2 (1935).

3 It is through attentive love, the ability to ask "What are you going through?" and the ability to hear the answer that the reality of the child is both created and respected.

MARY FIELD BELENKY, (20th-century) U.S. psychologist. *Women's Ways of Knowing,* part 2, ch. 8 (1986).

4 Ultimately, it is the receiving of the child and hearing what he or she has to say that develops the child's mind and personhood. . . . Parents who enter into a dialogue with their children, who draw out and respect their opinions, are more likely to have children whose intellectual and ethical development proceeds rapidly and surely.

MARY FIELD BELENKY, (20th-century) U.S. psychologist. *Women's Ways of Knowing,* part 2, ch. 8 (1986).

5 Men especially need to communicate. To tell people years after the fact that they were the priority is the coward's way. If men can muster the courage to fire an employee, tell off a boss, or assume financial risk, they can dig deep and say the three little words their wives and children need to hear.

FRED G. GOSMAN, (20th-century) U.S. author. *How to Be a Happy Parent . . . In Spite of Your Children,* ch. 1 (1995).

6 Children who are not spoken to by live and responsive adults will not learn to speak properly. Children who are not answered will stop asking questions. They will become incurious. And children who are not told stories and who are not read to will have few reasons for wanting to learn to read.

GAIL HALEY, (20th-century) U.S. educator. As quoted in *The New Read-Aloud Handbook,* by Jim Trelease (1985).

7 A mother understands what a child does not say.

PROVERB.

8 Too-broad questions, such as "What's on your mind?" are apt to be answered "nothing" nearly one hundred percent of the time. Be careful of slipping into "psycho-speak," however. Kids pick up instantly your attempt at being a pseudo-shrink. Most resent it and are apt to tune out anything that sounds like you're reading a script from the latest child-psychology text.

MARGE KENNEDY, (20th-century) U.S. author. *The Single Parent Family,* ch. 3 (1994).

9 We cannot set aside an hour for discussion with our children and hope that it will be a time of deep encounter. The special moments of intimacy are more likely to happen while baking a cake together, or playing hide and seek, or just sitting in the waiting room of the orthodontist.

NEIL KURSHAN, (20th-century) U.S. rabbi and author. *Raising Your Child to Be a Mensch,* ch. 2 (1987).

10 With all the attention paid to your new baby, it's easy for your own feelings and needs to get lost in the shuffle. Although all parents engage in some self-sacrifice for their children, keep in mind that your goal isn't just to raise a happy, healthy child. You want that child to be part of a happy, healthy family as well.

LAWRENCE KUTNER, (20th-century) U.S. child psychologist and author. *Pregnancy and Your Baby's First Year,* ch. 8 (1993).

11 If family communication is good, parents can pick up the signs of stress in children and talk about it

before it results in some crisis. If family communication is bad, not only will parents be insensitive to potential crises, but the poor communication will contribute to problems in the family.

DONALD C. MEDEIROS, (20th-century) U.S. psychologist and author. *Children Under Stress,* ch. 2 (1983).

12 One important reason to stay calm is that calm parents hear more. Low-key, accepting parents are the ones whose children keep talking.

MARY PIPHER, (20th-century) U.S. psychologist and author. *Reviving Ophelia,* ch. 15 (1994).

13 When words fail us or, quite the opposite, when they rush from our mouths faster than we would like, we can console ourselves that if no single moment is going to define our relationship with a child, neither can a single lapse of good judgment or patience destroy it.

CATHY RINDNER TEMPELSMAN, (20th-century) U.S. journalist and author. *Child-Wise,* parting words (1994).

14 What can I do to get my kid to listen. . . ? The answer is brief: talk less.

NANCY SAMALIN, (20th-century) U.S. parent educator and author. *Loving Your Child Is Not Enough,* ch. 1 (1987).

15 Whining is like chalk scratching on a blackboard for most parents.

NANCY SAMALIN, (20th-century) U.S. parent educator and author. *Loving Your Child Is Not Enough,* ch. 1 (1987).

16 Many mothers believe that unless they're having heart-to-hearts (like those Supermoms on TV) they're doing something wrong. True, a conversation in the midst of . . . driving to pick up pizza doesn't have the same official stamp of "intimacy" as snuggling . . . or having a quiet talk at bedtime. But this is when kids naturally open up. The best you can do is accept that the most important information you'll get will be in the form of a two-minute sound bite dropped in your lap when you least expect it.

RON TAFFEL, (20th-century) U.S. psychologist and author. *Why Parents Disagree,* ch. 8 (1994).

17 Communication is a continual balancing act, juggling the conflicting needs for intimacy and independence. To survive in the world, we have to act in concert with others, but to survive as ourselves, rather than simply as cogs in a wheel, we have to act alone.

DEBORAH TANNEN, (20th-century) U.S. author. *You Just Don't Understand: Women and Men in Conversation,* Ch. 1 (1990).

18 Little pitchers have big ears.

MODERN PROVERB.

19 The child says nothing but what is heard by the fire.

MODERN PROVERB.

Family Communication as an Aspect of Development

1 Young children . . . are often uninterested in conversation. It is not that they don't have ideas and feelings, or need to express them to

others. It is simply that as one eight-year-old boy once told me, "Talking is okay, but I don't like to do it all the time the way grown-ups do; I guess you have to develop the habit."

Robert Coles, (20th-century) U.S. child psychiatrist and author. *Children of Crisis,* ch. 3 (1964).

2 Your preschool child will chatter endlessly to you. If you half-listen and half-reply the whole conversation will seem, and become, tediously meaningless for both of you. But if you really listen and really answer, he will talk more and what he says will make more sense.

Penelope Leach, (20th-century) British child development specialist and author. *Your Baby and Child,* introduction (1977).

3 Adolescents sometimes say . . . "My friends listen to me, but my parents only hear me talk." Often they are right. Familiarity breeds inattention.

Laurence Steinberg, (20th-century) U.S. professor of psychology and author. *You and Your Adolescent,* ch. 2 (1990).

4 If we always speak in the calm reflective, therapeutic tone that works very well with younger children (and it is advised in many child-rearing books), preteens look at us as if we're nuts! After a kid acts like a sarcastic pain in the you-know-what, don't you think he knows what he's been doing? He can see right through your calm, cool, collected exterior!

Ron Taffel, (20th-century) U.S. psychologist and author. *Parenting by Heart,* ch. 4 (1991).

Family Communication: Answering Children's Questions

1 Because it is not always easy for an adult to predict what inaccurate ideas a child may have, it can help to answer questions first with one of your own: "What do you think?" Once you find out what a child is really asking, you'll be in a better position to give a helpful answer based on the facts.

Joanna Cole, (20th-century) U.S. author. *How You Were Born* (1995).

2 Answering questions can be a responsibility. Children think that their parents have all the answers. In the words of one child, children are "whyers" and parents "becausers."

Ruth Formanek, (20th-century) U.S. psychologist and author. *Why? Children's Questions,* introduction (1980).

3 Think of the child's question as the start of a two-way conversation rather than a question-and-answer session. Sometimes it may be necessary to learn what children think about the subject and what misconceptions they may have before providing an answer.

Ruth Formanek, (20th-century) U.S. psychologist and author. *Why? Children's Questions,* introduction (1980).

4 Young children constantly invent new explanations to account for complex processes. And since their inventions change from week to week, furnishing the "correct" explanation is not quite so important as conveying a willingness to

discuss the subject. Become an "askable parent."

RUTH FORMANEK, (20th-century) U.S. psychologist and author. *Why? Children's Questions,* ch. 2 (1980).

Food

1 Early on, we equate being a good parent with how we feed our children. You're a "good mother" if you feed your kid food that is healthy.

GOLDIE ALFASI, (20th-century) U.S. psychologist. As quoted in *Child-Wise,* ch. 9, by Cathy Rindner Templesman (1994).

2 Kids are without a doubt the most suspicious diners in the world. They will eat mud (raw or baked) rocks, paste, crayons, ball-point pens, moving goldfish, cigarette butts, and cat food. Try to coax a little beef stew into their mouths and they look at you like a puppy when you stand over him with the Sunday paper rolled up.

ERMA BOMBECK, (20th-century) U.S. humorist and author. *Motherhood: The Second Oldest Profession,* ch. 30 (1983).

Frustration

1 Parents must not only have certain ways of guiding by prohibition and permission; they must also be able to represent to the child a deep, an almost somatic conviction that there is a meaning to what they are doing. Ultimately, children become neurotic not from frustrations, but from the lack or loss of societal meaning in these frustrations.

ERIK H. ERIKSON, (20th-century) German-born U.S. psychoanalyst and author. *Childhood and Society,* ch. 7 (1950).

2 The more we shelter children from every disappointment, the more devastating future disappointments will be.

FRED G. GOSMAN, (20th-century) U.S. author. *How to Be a Happy Parent . . . In Spite of Your Children,* ch. 1 (1995).

3 A mother wants all of life to be painless for her child. This is not a realistic goal, however. Deprivation and frustration are as much a part of life as gratification. It is some balance between these that a mother is looking for. To take the next step is always painful in part. It means relinquishing gratification on some level. If one is totally gratified where one is, why move ahead? If one is totally frustrated, why bother?

ELAINE HEFFNER, (20th-century) U.S. psychiatrist and author. *Mothering,* ch. 5 (1978).

4 Mothers often are too easily intimidated by their children's negative reactions. . . . When the child cries or is unhappy, the mother reads this as meaning that she is a failure. This is why it is so important for a mother to know . . . that the process of growing up involves by definition things that her child is not going to like. Her job is not to create a bed of roses, but to help him learn how to pick his way through the thorns.

ELAINE HEFFNER, (20th-century) U.S. psychiatrist and author. *Mothering,* ch. 5 (1978).

5 To achieve the larger goal of teaching her children consideration of others, a mother can tolerate some frustration of her own wishes, she can delay having what she wants,

she can be flexible enough to compromise. And this is exactly what her child must also learn: that it is possible to survive frustration, it is possible to wait for what he wants, it is possible to compromise without capitulating.

ELAINE HEFFNER, (20th-century) U.S. psychiatrist and author. *Mothering,* ch. 5 (1978).

6 Managing a tantrum involves nothing less than the formation of character. Even the parent's capacity to cope well with conflict can improve with this experience. When a parent knows he is right and does not give in for the sake of temporary peace, everybody wins. The parent learns that denying some pleasure does not create a neurotic child and the child learns that she can survive momentary frustration.

ALICIA F. LIEBERMAN, (20th-century) U.S. psychologist and author. *The Emotional Life of the Toddler,* ch. 2 (1993).

7 When parents take their child's vulnerabilities too seriously, they allow themselves to be cowed by them. This can create an expectation in the child that she is entitled to instant gratification because she is too fragile to withstand anything else. When frustration finally occurs (as it inevitably must), aggression becomes the only coping mechanism available to the child to fend off the feared damage to herself.

ALICIA F. LIEBERMAN, (20th-century) U.S. psychologist and author. *The Emotional Life of the Toddler,* ch. 6 (1993).

8 Every life and every childhood is filled with frustrations; we cannot imagine it otherwise, for even the best mother cannot satisfy all her child's wishes and needs. It is not the suffering caused by frustration, however, that leads to emotional illness, but rather the fact that the child is forbidden by the parents to experience and articulate this suffering, the pain felt at being wounded.

ALICE MILLER, (20th-century) German-born U.S. psychoanalyst and author. *For Your Own Good,* "Sylvia Plath: An Example of Forbidden Suffering" (trans. 1983).

Guilt

1 I respect guilt. It is a dangerous but sometimes useful beast. The guilt that made me want to solve all my children's problems meant trouble. The guilt that made me question my role in our mother-daughter squabbles proved helpful. Yes, I care about my kids' problems, and I long to make suggestions. But these days I wait for children to ask for help, and I give it sparingly. Some things can't be fixed, and I tell them so.

SUSAN FERRARO, (20th-century) U.S. journalist. "My 11-year-old Knows Just How to Get to Me," *Working Mother* (August 1988).

2 The experience of a sense of guilt for wrong-doing is necessary for the development of self-control. The guilt feelings will later serve as a warning signal which the child can produce himself when an impulse to repeat the naughty act comes over him. When the child can produce his own warning signals, independent of the actual presence of the adult, he is on the way to developing a conscience.

SELMA H. FRAIBERG, (20th-century) U.S. child psychoanalyst and author. *The Magic Years,* ch. 8 (1959).

3 Hard though it may be to accept, remember that guilt is sometimes a friendly internal voice reminding you that you're messing up.

MARGE KENNEDY, (20th-century) U.S. author. *The Single Parent Family,* ch. 6 (1994).

4 Guilt is the most destructive of all emotions. It mourns what has been while playing no part in what may be, now or in the future. Whatever you are doing, however you are coping, if you listen to your child and to your own feelings, there will be something you can actually do to make things right.

PENELOPE LEACH, (20th-century) British child development specialist and author. *Your Baby and Child,* introduction (1977).

5 The very presence of guilt, let alone its tenacity, implies imbalance: something, we suspect, is getting more of our energy than it warrants, at the expense of something else, we suspect, that deserves more of our energy than we're giving.

MELINDA M. MARSHALL, (20th-century) U.S. editor and author. *Good Enough Mothers,* ch. 4 (1993).

6 Good guilt is a product of love and responsibility. It is a natural, positive instinct that parents and good childcare providers have. If bad guilt is a monster, good guilt is a friendly fairy godmother, yakking away in your head to keep you alert to the needs of your baby.

JEAN MARZOLLO, (20th-century) U.S. author. *Your Maternity Leave,* ch. 3 (1989).

7 When the masculine mystique is pulling boys and men out into the world to growl manly noises at one another, the only power with a stronger pull on the male psyche is maternally induced guilt. The guilt is quite necessary for our moral development, but it is often uncomfortable.

FRANK PITTMAN, (20th-century) U.S. psychiatrist and family therapist. *Man Enough,* ch. 7 (1993).

8 Guilt is often an appropriate response to wrongdoing, but punishment impedes the development of a conscience by taking away the opportunity for [a child] . . . to feel guilty. He has no chance to develop inner motivation.

NANCY SAMALIN, (20th-century) U.S. parent educator and author. *Loving Your Child Is Not Enough,* ch. 4 (1987).

9 Nagging guilt is like gray paint splashed over life's sparkling moments.

SALLY SHANNON, (20th-century) U.S. journalist. "Goodbye to Guilt," *Working Mother* (November 1989).

10 Without a sense of the shame or guilt of his or her action, the child will only be hardened in rebellion by physical punishment. Shame (and praise) help the child to internalize the parent's judgment. It impresses upon the child that the parent is not only more powerful but also right. Like the Puritans, Locke (in 1690) wanted the child to adopt the parent's moral position, rather than simply bow to superior strength or social pressure.

C. JOHN SOMMERVILLE, (20th-century) U.S. historian and author. *The Rise and Fall of Childhood,* ch. 12 (rev. 1990).

11 Most people agree that men have trouble showing hurt, jealousy, and

fear but even mothers, whose wider emotional range is often taken for granted, also seem more comfortable with anger than these other "unparentlike" feelings. This is probably because several generations of mothers have now been twelve-step-programmed and pop-psychologized enough to believe that expressing hurt, fear, anxiety, or dependence will create pathological guilt in their kids.

RON TAFFEL, (20th-century) U.S. psychologist and author. *Why Parents Disagree*, ch. 4 (1994).

12 Mothers often take children's negative feelings so personally that the moment they come back from work to a moody child, a whole checklist appears before their eyes. "Was I rushed this morning? Did I forget to pack lunch right? Am I away too much?" This personalization of children's day to day moods (which I've found practically nonexistent in fathers) makes moms an easy target. . . . Within seconds, children pick up on your guilt and use it to gain special attention.

RON TAFFEL, (20th-century) U.S. psychologist and author. *Why Parents Disagree*, ch. 8 (1994).

Happiness/Joy of Living

1 No man is quick enough to enjoy life to the full.

SPANISH PROVERB.

2 The parent *is* the strongest statement that the child hears regarding what it means to be alive and real. More than what we say or do, the way we are expresses what we think it means to be alive. So the articulate parent is less a telling than a listening individual.

POLLY BERRIEN BERENDS, (20th-century) U.S. author. *Whole Child/Whole Parent*, ch. 6 (rev. 1987).

3 A child's world is fresh and new and beautiful, full of wonder and excitement. It is our misfortune that for most of us that clear-eyed vision, that true instinct for what is beautiful and awe-inspiring, is dimmed and even lost before we reach adulthood.

RACHEL CARSON, (20th-century) U.S. author. As quoted in *The Last Word*, ed. Carolyn Warner, ch. 28 (1992).

4 If I had influence with the good fairy who is supposed to preside over the christening of all children, I should ask that her gift to each child in the world be a sense of wonder so indestructible that it would last throughout life.

RACHEL CARSON, (20th-century) U.S. author. As quoted in *The Last Word*, ed. Carolyn Warner, ch. 19 (1992).

5 Seeing to it that a youngster grows up believing not just in the here and now but also in the grand maybes of life guarantees that some small yet crucial part of him remains forever a child.

ANNE CASSIDY, (20th-century) U.S. journalist and author. "The Power of Make-Believe," *Working Mother* (May 1992).

6 You can make lots of mistakes, but if you give children avenues for creativity and joy, they will have resources to carry them through. For example, if cooking together, reading, listening to music, coloring, participating in sports, or

taking a walk in the woods are paired with pleasure and closeness, throughout life doing these things will kindle old feelings of happiness and/or comfort.

CHARLOTTE DAVIS KASL, (20th-century) U.S. psychologist and author. *Finding Joy,* ch. 73 (1994).

7 We must return optimism to our parenting. To focus on the joys, not the hassles; the love, not the disappointments; the common sense, not the complexities.

FRED G. GOSMAN, (20th-century) U.S. author. *How to Be a Happy Parent . . . In Spite of Your Children,* ch. 1 (1995).

8 Everyone needs reminders that the fact of their being on this earth is important and that each life changes everything.

MARGE KENNEDY, (20th-century) U.S. author. *100 Things You Can Do to Keep Your Family Together . . . ,* pt. 1 (1994).

9 If you like to make things out of wood, or sew, or dance, or style people's hair, or dream up stories and act them out, or play the trumpet, or jump rope, or whatever you really love to do, and you love that in front of your children, that's going to be a far more important gift than anything you could ever give them wrapped up in a box with ribbons.

FRED ROGERS, (20th-century) U.S. children's television personality and author. "That Which Is Essential Is Invisible to the Eye," *Young Children* (July 1994).

10 Life is not meant to be easy, my child; but take courage: it can be delightful.

BERNARD SHAW, (1856-1950) Irish-born British playwright and author. *Back to Methuselah,* pt. 5 (1921).

Housework

1 If my sons are to become the kind of men our daughters would be pleased to live among, attention to domestic details is critical. The hostilities that arise over housework . . . are crushing the daughters of my generation. . . . Change takes time, but men's continued obliviousness to home responsibilities is causing women everywhere to expire of trivialities.

MARY KAY BLAKELY, (20th-century) U.S. journalist and author. *American Mom,* ch. 4 (1994).

2 Housework is the only activity at which men are allowed to be consistently inept because they are thought to be so competent at everything else.

LETTY COTTIN POGREBIN, (20th-century) U.S. editor and author. *Family and Politics,* ch. 7 (1983).

3 Like plowing, housework makes the ground ready for the germination of family life. The kids will not invite a teacher home if beer cans litter the living room. The family isn't likely to have breakfast together if somebody didn't remember to buy eggs, milk, or muffins. Housework maintains an orderly setting in which family life can flourish.

LETTY COTTIN POGREBIN, (20th-century) U.S. editor and author. *Family and Politics,* ch. 7 (1983).

4 There are three ways to get something done: do it yourself, hire someone, or forbid your kids to do it.

ANONYMOUS.

5 Cleaning your house while your kids are still growing up is like shoveling the walk before it stops snowing.

PHYLLIS DILLER, (20th-century) U.S. comedian. As quoted in *The Last Word,* ch. 16, ed. Carolyn Warner (1992).

6 Minimize, eliminate, delegate, and routinize. Decide what's important and forget the rest.

DONNA N. DOUGLASS, (20th-century) U.S. editor and author. *Choice and Compromise,* ch. 6 (1983).

7 After decades of unappreciated drudgery, American women just don't do housework any more—that is, beyond the minimum that is required in order to clear a path from the bedroom to the front door so they can get off to work in the morning.

BARBARA EHRENREICH, (20th-century) U.S. essayist and author. *The Snarling Citizen,* "Housework Is Obsolescent" (1995).

8 Even when couples share more equitably in the work at home, women do two-thirds of the daily jobs at home, like cooking and cleaning up—jobs that fix them into a rigid routine. Most women cook dinner and most men change the oil in the family car. But dinner needs to be prepared every evening around six o'clock, whereas the car oil needs to be changed every six months, any day around that time, any time that day. . . . Men thus have more control over when they make their contributions than women do.

ARLIE HOCHSCHILD, (20th-century) U.S. sociologist and author. *The Second Shift: Working Parents and the Revolution at Home,* ch. 1 (1989).

9 Many women cut back what had to be done at home by redefining what the house, the marriage and, sometimes, what the child needs. One woman described a fairly common pattern: "I do my half. I do half of his half, and the rest doesn't get done."

ARLIE HOCHSCHILD, (20th-century) U.S. sociologist and author. *The Second Shift: Working Parents and the Revolution at Home,* ch. 17 (1989).

10 Most women without children spend much more time than men on housework; with children, they devote more time to both housework and child care. Just as there is a wage gap between men and women in the workplace, there is a "leisure gap" between them at home. Most women work one shift at the office or factory and a "second shift" at home.

ARLIE HOCHSCHILD, (20th-century) U.S. sociologist and author. *The Second Shift: Working Parents and the Revolution at Home,* ch. 1 (1989).

11 The happiest two-job marriages I saw during my research were ones in which men and women shared the housework and parenting. What couples called good communication often meant that they were good at saying thanks to one another for small aspects of taking care of the family. Making it to the school play, helping a child read, cooking dinner in good spirit, remembering the grocery list . . . these were silver and gold of the marital exchange.

ARLIE HOCHSCHILD, (20th-century) U.S. sociologist and author. *The Second Shift: Working Parents and the Revolution at Home,* ch. 16 (1989).

12 It's sad but true that if you focus your attention on housework and

meal preparation and diapers, raising children does start to look like drudgery pretty quickly. On the other hand, if you see yourself as nothing less than your child's nurturer, role model, teacher, spiritual guide, and mentor, your days take on a very different cast.

JOYCE MAYNARD, (20th-century) U.S. journalist. "A Mother's Day," *Parenting Magazine* (June/July 1995).

13 Freud is all nonsense; the secret of neurosis is to be found in the family battle of wills to see who can refuse longest to help with the dishes. The sink is the great symbol of the bloodiness of family life.

JULIAN MITCHELL, (20th-century) U.S. author. *As Far As You Can Go,* pt. 1, ch. 1.

14 Why do otherwise sane, competent, strong men, men who can wrestle bears or raid corporations, shrink away in horror at the thought of washing a dish or changing a diaper?

FRANK PITTMAN, (20th-century) U.S. psychiatrist and family therapist. *Man Enough,* ch. 11 (1993).

15 Is it possible that my sons-in-law will do toilets? If we raise boys to know that diapers need to be changed and refrigerators need to be cleaned, there's hope for the next generation.

ANNE ROIPHE, (20th-century) U.S. author. "Raising Daughters," *Working Women* (April 1994).

16 Modern labor-saving devices eliminated drudgery, not labor. Before industrialization, women fed, clothed, and nursed their families by preparing (with the help of their husbands and children) food, clothing, and medication. In the post-industrial age, women feed, clothe, and nurse their families (without much direct assistance from anyone else) by cooking, cleaning, driving, shopping, and waiting.

RUTH SCHWARZ COWAN, (20th-century) U.S. sociologist. As quoted in: "Twentieth Century Housework: Less Drudgery, But Just As Much Work," *The Utne Reader* (April 1990).

17 Men perceive that equating love and domestic work is a trap. They fear that to get involved with housework would send them hurtling into the bottomless pit of self-sacrifice that is women's current caring role.

DEBBIE TAYLOR, (20th-century) U.S. journalist. "Domestic Chores Weren't Always Women's Work," *New Internationalist* (March 1988).

18 The growing of food and the growing of children are both vital to the family's survival. . . . Who would dare make the judgment that holding your youngest baby on your lap is less important than weeding a few more yards in the maize field? Yet this is the judgment our society makes constantly. Production of autos, canned soup, advertising copy is important. Housework—cleaning, feeding, and caring—is unimportant.

DEBBIE TAYLOR, (20th-century) U.S. journalist. "Domestic Chores Weren't Always Women's Work," *New Internationalist* (March 1988).

Imagination

1 It can be demonstrated that the child's contact with the real world is strengthened by his periodic excursions into fantasy. It becomes

easier to tolerate the frustrations of the real world and to accede to the demands of reality if one can restore himself at intervals in a world where the deepest wishes can achieve imaginary gratification.

SELMA H. FRAIBERG, (20th-century) U.S. child psychoanalyst and author. *The Magic Years,* ch. 1 (1959).

2 There must be a solemn and terrible aloneness that comes over the child as he takes those first independent steps. All this is lost to memory and we can only reconstruct it through analogies in later life. . . . To the child who takes his first steps and finds himself walking alone, this moment must bring the first sharp sense of the uniqueness and separateness of his body and his person, the discovery of the solitary self.

SELMA H. FRAIBERG, (20th-century) U.S. child psychoanalyst and author. *The Magic Years,* ch. 8 (1959).

3 A child who has never fantasized about having other parents is seriously lacking in imagination.

FRED G. GOSMAN, (20th-century) U.S. author. *How to Be a Happy Parent . . . In Spite of Your Children,* ch. 1 (1995).

4 By directing our sentiments, passions, and reason toward the common human plight, imagination grants us the advantages of a moral existence. What we surrender of innocent love of self is exchanged for the safeties and pleasures of belonging to a larger whole. We are born dependent, but only imagination can bind our passions to other human beings.

LOUISE KAPLAN, (20th-century) U.S. psychologist and author. *Adolescence,* ch. 12 (1984).

5 It is not speech or tool making that distinguishes us from other animals, it is imagination. . . . Of what use are speech sounds and tools without an inspiration toward perfectibility, without a sense that we can create or construct a history?

LOUISE KAPLAN, (20th-century) U.S. psychologist and author. *Adolescence,* ch. 12 (1984).

Independence

1 Compliant children are very easily led when they are young, because they thrive on approval and pleasing adults. They are just as easily led in their teen years, because they still seek the same two things: approval and pleasing their peers. Strong-willed children are never easily led by anybody—not by you, but also not by their peers. So celebrate your child's strength of will throughout the early years . . . and know that the independent thinking you are fostering will serve him well in the critical years to come.

BARBARA COLOROSO, (20th-century) U.S. parent educator and author. *Kids Are Worth It,* ch. 4 (1994).

2 A wise parent humours the desire for independent action, so as to become the friend and advisor when his absolute rule shall cease.

ELIZABETH GASKELL, (19th century) British novelist. Mr. Hale, in *North and South,* ch. 15 (1855).

3 In healthy families, children discover (through being listened to) that what they have to say is important and that their experiences and ideas (and they themselves) have worth. They are encouraged to

think for themselves, express opinions, and make decisions for themselves. Parents support them in standing on their own two feet and doing what they think is right. Trusting and gaining confidence in themselves, they develop an inner locus of control.

LOUISE HART, (20th-century) U.S. community psychologist and author. *On the Wings of Self-Esteem,* ch. 8 (1994).

4 Once a child has demonstrated his capacity for independent functioning in any area, his lapses into dependent behavior, even though temporary, make the mother feel that she is being taken advantage of. . . . What only yesterday was a description of the child's stage in life has become an indictment, a judgment.

ELAINE HEFFNER, (20th-century) U.S. psychiatrist and author. *Mothering,* ch. 7 (1978).

5 In a famous Middletown study of Muncie, Indiana, in 1924, mothers were asked to rank the qualities they most desire in their children. At the top of the list were conformity and strict obedience. More than fifty years later, when the Middletown survey was replicated, mothers placed autonomy and independence first. The healthiest parenting probably promotes a balance of these qualities in children.

RICHARD LOUV, (20th-century) U.S. journalist and author. *Childhood's Future,* pt. 2, ch. 4 (1991).

6 Children are as destined biologically to break away as we are, emotionally, to hold on and protect. But thinking independently comes of acting independently. It begins with a two-year-old doggedly pulling on flannel pajamas during a July heat wave and with parents accepting that the impulse is a good one. When we let go of these small tasks without anger or sorrow but with pleasure and pride we give each act of independence our blessing.

CATHY RINDNER TEMPELSMAN, (20th-century) U.S. journalist and author. *Child-Wise,* ch. 14 (1994).

7 Children crawl before they walk, walk before they run—each generally a precondition for the other. And with each step they take toward more independence, more mastery of the environment, their mothers take a step away—each a small separation, a small distancing.

LILLIAN BRESLOW RUBIN, (20th-century) U.S. sociologist and family therapist. *Women of a Certain Age,* ch. 2 (1979).

8 Contrary to popular belief, children (even adolescents) are not only pushing for independence, they are pushing for contact and connection. It is a major error to think independence is all they are after.

RON TAFFEL, (20th-century) U.S. psychologist and author. *Parenting by Heart,* ch. 1 (1991).

9 Craving that old sweet oneness yet dreading engulfment, wishing to be our mother's and yet be our own, we stormily swing from mood to mood, advancing and retreating—the quintessential model of two-mindedness.

JUDITH VIORST, (20th-century) U.S. novelist and poet. *Necessary Losses,* ch. 3 (1986).

10 The need to become a separate self is as urgent as the yearning to merge forever. And as long as we, not our mother, initiate parting, and as long as our mother remains reliably there, it seems possible to risk, and even to revel in, standing alone.

JUDITH VIORST, (20th-century) U.S. novelist and poet. *Necessary Losses,* ch. 3 (1986).

Individuality

1 The extent to which a parent is able to see a child's world through that child's eyes depends very much on the parent's ability to appreciate the differences between herself and her child and to respect those differences. Your own children need you to accept them for who they are, not who you would like them to be.

LAWRENCE BALTER, (20th-century) U.S. psychologist and author. *"Not in Front of the Children . . . ,"* Ch. 3 (1993).

2 The parent must not give in to his desire to try to create the child he would like to have, but rather help the child to develop—in his own good time—to the fullest, into what he wishes to be and can be, in line with his natural endowment and as the consequence of his unique life in history.

BRUNO BETTELHEIM, (20th-century) Austrian-born U.S. child psychologist and author. *A Good Enough Parent,* ch. 1 (1987).

3 Remember . . . that each child is a separate person, yours forever, but never fully yours. She can never be all you wished or wanted, or all you know she could be. But she will be a better human being if you can let her be herself.

STELLA CHESS, (20th-century) U.S. psychiatrist and author. *Daughters,* ch. 6 (1978).

4 Parents must begin to discover their children as individuals of developing tastes and views and so help them be, and see, themselves as thinking, feeling people. It is far too easy for a middle-years child to absorb an over-simplified picture of himself as a sloppy, unreliable, careless, irresponsible, lazy creature and not much more—an attitude toward himself he will carry far beyond these years.

DOROTHY H. COHEN, (20th-century) U.S. educator and child development specialist. *The Learning Child,* "Parent and Child During the Intermediate Years" (1972).

5 There is one thing you and I as parents cannot do, nor do we want to do if we really think about it, and that's control our children's will—that spirit that lets them be themselves apart from you and me. They are not ours to possess, control, manipulate, or even to make mind.

BARBARA COLOROSO, (20th-century) U.S. parent educator and author. *Kids Are Worth It,* epilogue (1994).

6 If a child is "free of neurotic symptoms" but values his freedom from fear so highly that he will never in his lifetime risk himself for an idea or a principle, then this mental health does not serve human welfare. If he is "secure" but never aspires to anything but personal security, then this security cannot be valued in itself. If he is "well adjusted to the group" but secures his adjustment through uncritical acceptance of and compliance with the ideas of others, then this adjustment does not serve a democratic

society. If he "adjusts well in school" but furnishes his mind with commonplace ideas and facts . . . then what civilization can value the "adjustment" of this child?

SELMA H. FRAIBERG, (20th-century) U.S. child psychoanalyst and author. *The Magic Years,* ch. 1 (1959).

7 From the beginning moments of life, the urges for each of us to become a self in the world are there—in the liveliness of our innate growth energies, in the vitality of our stiffening-away muscles, in our looking eyes, our listening ears, our reaching-out hands.

LOUISE KAPLAN, (20th-century) U.S. psychologist and author. *Adolescence,* ch. 3 (1984).

8 Schoolchildren make up their own rules and enforce their own conformities. They feel safest when leisure time is rationed and dosed. They like to wear uniforms, and they frown on personal idiosyncrasies. Deviance is the mark of an outsider.

LOUISE KAPLAN, (20th-century) U.S. psychologist and author. *Adolescence,* ch. 5 (1984).

9 Children are born as individuals. If we fail to see that, if we see them as clay to be molded in any shape we like, the tougher ones will fight back and end up spiteful and wild, while the less strong will lose that uniqueness they were born with.

MELVIN KONNER, (20th-century) U.S. professor of anthropology and psychiatry. As quoted in *Childhood,* a viewer's guide produced in collaboration with Thirteen WNET, Robert H. Wozniak (1991).

10 No parent should strive to be like another; just like our children, each of us is unique. And just as we love each of our children for being a special person, our children learn to love each of us for being a distinct parent and person.

SAF LERMAN, (20th-century) U.S. parent educator and author. *Helping Children as They Grow,* ch. 1 (1983).

11 It is neither possible nor desirable to be always attuned to the moods of children because this thwarts their need to test and enrich their individuality by standing up to adult authority. What is possible and desirable is to cultivate an attitude of partnership: to be willing to listen, acknowledge that parents and children at times have different goals, try to reconcile the differences, and agree to disagree if this is not possible.

ALICIA F. LIEBERMAN, (20th-century) U.S. psychologist and author. *The Emotional Life of the Toddler,* ch. 1 (1993).

12 Just as Michelangelo saw the "David" in the raw, unformed block of marble before he struck it with his chisel, we as parents can imagine the fine adult human beings who will emerge from our children's growing, evolving selves. By holding this image in our minds, we can, through our encouragement, nurture our children to blossom into their fullest potential.

STEPHANIE MARSTON, (20th-century) U.S. family therapist and author. *The Magic of Encouragement,* ch. 1 (1990).

13 Each child has his own individual expressions to offer to the world. That expression can take many forms, from artistic interests, a way of thinking, athletic activities, a particular style of dressing, musical

talents, different hobbies, etc. Our job is to join our children in discovering who they are.

Stephanie Marston, (20th-century) U.S. family therapist and author. *The Magic of Encouragement,* ch. 1 (1990).

14 Anyone who has ever been a mother or father and is at all honest knows from experience how difficult it can be for parents to accept certain aspects of their children. It is especially painful to have to admit this if we really love our child and want to respect his or her individuality yet are unable to do so.

Alice Miller, (20th-century) German-born U.S. psychanalyst and author. *For Your Own Good,* "Poisonous Pedagogy," (trans. 1983).

15 What strikes many twin researchers now is not how much identical twins are alike, but rather how different they are, given the same genetic makeup. . . . Multiples don't walk around in lockstep, talking in unison, thinking identical thoughts. The bond for normal twins, whether they are identical or fraternal, is based on how they, as individuals who are keenly aware of the differences between them, learn to relate to one another.

Pamela Patrick Novotny, (20th-century) U.S. journalist and author. *The Joy of Twins,* ch. 9 (rev. 1994).

16 Adolescents have the right to be themselves. The fact that you were the belle of the ball, the captain of the lacrosse team, the president of your senior class, Phi Beta Kappa, or a political activist doesn't mean that your teenager will be or should be the same. . . . Likewise, the fact that you were a wallflower, uncoordinated, and a C student shouldn't mean that you push your child to be everything you were not.

Laurence Steinberg, (20th-century) U.S. psychologist and author. *You and Your Adolescent,* ch. 1 (1990).

17 Let your child be the teenager he or she wants to be, not the adolescent you were or wish you had been.

Laurence Steinberg, (20th-century) U.S. psychologist and author. *You and Your Adolescent,* ch. 1 (1990).

Love: Conditional/ Unconditional

1 The parent who loves his child dearly but asks for nothing in return might qualify as a saint, but he will not qualify as a parent. For a child who can claim love without meeting any of the obligations of love will be a self-centered child and many such children have grown up in our time to become petulant lovers and sullen marriage partners because the promise of unconditional love has not been fulfilled.

Selma H. Fraiberg, (20th-century) U.S. child psychoanalyst and author. *The Magic Years,* ch. 8 (1959).

2 Conditional love is love that is turned off and on. . . . Some parents only show their love after a child has done something that pleases them. "I love you, honey, for cleaning your room!" Children who think they need to earn love become people pleasers, or perfectionists. Those who are raised on conditional love never really feel loved.

LOUISE HART, (20th-century) U.S. psychologist and author. *On the Wings of Self-Esteem*, ch. 6 (1994).

3 "Make love, not war," was not just a protest against the indifference and lack of humaneness in Vietnam; it was also a positive statement that love between parent and child, teacher and pupil, fiancé and fiancée, and husband and wife is an activity we should try to pursue in the house when work is not necessary. It is the one real source of truth, beauty, and salvation in a community where deceit, corruption, and impersonality seem to be rampant.

JEROME KAGAN, (20th-century) U.S professor of developmental psychology. *In Support of Families*, ed. Michael W. Yogman and T. Berry Brazelton, ch. 3 (1986).

4 Can we love our children when they are homely, awkward, unkempt, flaunting the styles and friendships we don't approve of, when they fail to be the best, the brightest, the most accomplished at school or even at home? Can we be there when their world has fallen apart and only we can restore their faith and confidence in life?

NEIL KURSHAN, (20th-century) U.S. rabbi and author. *Raising Your Child to Be a Mensch*, ch. 4 (1987).

5 All parents occasionally have ambivalent feelings toward their children. We love our kids, but there are times when we don't really like them, or at least we can't stand what our children are doing. But most of us keep those feelings to ourselves, as if it's a dirty little secret. It doesn't fit in with our images of what we should do and feel as parents.

LAWRENCE KUTNER, (20th-century) U.S. child psychologist and author. *Pregnancy and Your Baby's First Year*, ch. 7 (1993).

6 Unconditional love is loving your kids for who they are, not for what they do. . . . I don't mean that we like or accept inappropriate behavior, but with unconditional love we love the children even at those times when we dislike their behavior. Unconditional love isn't something you will achieve every minute of every day. But it is the thought we must hold in our hearts every day.

STEPHANIE MARSTON, (20th-century) U.S. family therapist and author. *The Magic of Encouragement*, ch. 3 (1990).

7 Children also need opportunities to practice being less than perfect. They can afford to be ill tempered with us because it is our love that is most constant. This is the essence of *unconditional love*. . . . Our steadfast love provides a safe haven.

CATHY RINDNER TEMPELSMAN, (20th-century) U.S. journalist and author. *Child-Wise*, ch. 5 (1994).

Love: Expressions of

1 I think it is better to show love by meeting needs than to keep telling my son that I love him. Right now he is learning to tie his shoes. He is old enough, so even though it's hard for him, sometimes I insist. But once in a while when I see he's tired I still do it for him, and I have noticed that while I am tying his shoe, he says, "I love you, Mommy." When he says,

"I love you," I know that he knows that he is loved.

Anonymous Parent, (20th-century) As quoted in *Whole Child/Whole Parent,* ch. 3, Polly Berrien Berends (rev. 1987).

2 While over Alabama earth
These words are gently spoken:
Serve—and hate will die unborn.
Love—and chains are broken.

Langston Hughes, (20th-century) U.S. poet and author. "Alabama Earth (at Booker Washington's grave)," *Golden Slippers* (1941).

3 There would have to be something wrong with someone who could throw out a child's first Valentine card saying, "I love you, Mommy."

Ginger Hutton, (20th-century) U.S. columnist. As quoted in *The Last Word,* ed. Carolyn Warner, ch. 16 (1992).

4 The real question isn't whether you love your kids or not, but how well you are able to demonstrate your love and caring so that your children really feel loved.

Stephanie Marston, (20th-century) U.S. family therapis and author. *The Magic of Encouragement,* ch. 3 (1990).

5 We may prepare food for our children, chauffeur them around, take them to the movies, buy them toys and ice cream, but nothing registers as deeply as a simple squeeze, cuddle, or pat on the back. There is no greater reassurance of their lovability and worth than to be affectionately touched and held.

Stephanie Marston, (20th-century) U.S. family therapist and author. *The Magic of Encouragement,* ch. 3 (1990).

6 The recommended daily requirement for hugs is: four per day for survival, eight per day for maintenance, and twelve per day for growth.

Virginia Satir, (20th-century) U.S. family therapist and author. As quoted in *The Winning Family,* ch. 16, Louise Hart (1987).

7 Have you hugged your child today?

Slogan, (20th-century) U.S. origin.

8 I don't mind saying in advance that in my opinion jealousy is normal and healthy. Jealousy arises out of the fact that children love. If they have no capacity to love, then they don't show jealousy.

D. W. Winnicott, (20th-century) British child psychiatrist. *Health Education Through Broadcasting,* ch. 5 (1993).

Love: Human Need for

1 It didn't take elaborate experiments to deduce that an infant would die from want of food. But it took centuries to figure out that infants can and do perish from want of love.

Louise Kaplan, (20th-century) U.S. psychologist and author. *No Voice Is Ever Wholly Lost,* ch. 1 (1995).

2 We humans, once we have become emotionally invested in a homeplace, a prized personal possession, or, especially, in another person, find it immensely difficult to give them up.... Because they were made at a time of life when we were utterly dependent on them, the love attachments of infancy have inordinate power over us, more than any other emotional investment.

Louise Kaplan, (20th-century) U.S. psychologist and author. *Adolescence,* ch. 5 (1984).

3 You know that your toddler needed love and approval but he often

seemed not to care whether he got it or not and never seemed to know how to earn it. Your pre-school child is positively asking you to tell him what does and does not earn approval, so he is ready to learn any social refinement of being human which you will teach him. . . . He knows now that he wants your love and he has learned how to ask for it.

Penelope Leach, (20th-century) British child development specialist and author. *Your Baby and Child,* ch. 6 (1977).

4 We can only learn to love by loving.

Iris Murdoch, (20th-century) Anglo-Irish writer. As quoted in *The Last Word,* ed. Carolyn Warner, ch. 26 (1992).

5 Mother love has been much maligned. An over-mothered boy may go through life expecting each new woman to love him the way his mother did. Her love may make any other love seem inadequate. But an unloved boy would be even more likely to idealize love. I don't think it's possible for a mother or father to love a child too much.

Frank Pittman, (20th-century) U.S. psychiatrist and family therapist. "How to Manage Mom and Dad," *Psychology Today* (November/December 1994).

6 The child who acts unlovable is the child who most needs to be loved.

Cathy Rindner Tempelsman, (20th-century) U.S. journalist and author. *Child-Wise,* ch. 5 (1994).

7 The roots of a child's ability to cope and thrive, regardless of circumstance, lie in that child's having had at least a small, safe place (an apartment? a room? a lap?) in which, in the companionship of a loving person, that child could discover that he or she was lovable and capable of loving in return. If a child finds this during the first years of life, he or she can grow up to be a competent, healthy person.

Fred Rogers, (20th-century) U.S. children's television personality and author. *Mister Rogers Talks with Parents,* ch. 1 (1983).

8 There is a universal truth that I have found in my work. Everybody longs to be loved. And the greatest thing we can do is let somebody know that they are loved and capable of loving.

Fred Rogers, (20th-century) U.S. children's television personality and author. As quoted in *Kids Are Worth It* by Barbara Coloroso, ch. 1 (1994).

Love: Parents' Love for Children/Children's Love for Parents

1 The greatest love is a mother's;
Then comes a dog's,
Then comes a sweetheart's.

Polish Proverb.

2 The gain is not the having of children; it is the discovery of love and how to be loving.

Polly Berrien Berends, (20th-century) U.S. author. *Whole Child/Whole Parent,* ch. 2 (rev. 1987).

3 Not only is our love for our children sometimes tinged with annoyance, discouragement, and disappointment, the same is true for the love our children feel for us.

Bruno Bettelheim, (20th-century) Austrian-born U.S. child psychologist and author. *A Good Enough Parent,* ch. 2 (1987).

4 The Fountaine of parents duties is Love. . . . Great reason there is why this affection should be fast fixed towards their children. For great is that paine, cost, and care, which parents must undergoe for their children. But if love be in them, no paine, paines, cost or care will seeme too much.

WILLIAM GOUGE, (17th-century) U.S. Puritan. As quoted in *The Rise and Fall of Childhood* by C. John Sommerville, ch. 11 (rev. 1990). Originally from *Of Domestical Duties* by William Gouge (1622).

5 Children are incurable romantics. Brimful of romance and tragedy, we whirl through childhood hopelessly in love with our parents. In our epic imagination, we love and are loved with a passion so natural and innocent we may never know its like as adults.

ROGER GOULD, (20th-century) U.S. psychotherapist and author. *Transformations,* sec. 1, ch. 1 (1978).

6 Loving a baby is a circular business, a kind of feedback loop. The more you give the more you get and the more you get the more you feel like giving.

PENELOPE LEACH, (20th-century) British child development specialist and author. *Your Baby and Child,* introduction (1977).

7 Even when they cannot be always available, the parents' fierce, unique love for their child makes them different in the child's heart and mind from all other caregivers. In spite of a long working day, a parent's passion for his or her child retains its many nuances of emotional intensity, ranging from rapture and delight to impatience and even rage, that no other relationship in the child's life can match. Even very young infants are smart enough to recognize this passionate commitment and to reciprocate it in kind.

ALICIA F. LIEBERMAN, (20th-century) U.S. psychologist and author. *The Emotional Life of the Toddler,* ch. 10 (1993).

8 By continually affirming our children's lovableness and capableness, we help them build a strong sense of self-worth. The more love you give your children, the more love you are helping them to create inside themselves. Think of love as a basic right of your kids. Give it away freely, and it will come back a thousand fold.

STEPHANIE MARSTON, (20th-century) U.S. family therapist and author. *The Magic of Encouragement,* ch. 3 (1990).

9 Give a little love to a child, and you get a great deal back.

JOHN RUSKIN, (19th-century) English essayist and critic.

10 I do not love him because he is good, but because he is my little child.

RABINDRANATH TAGORE, (1861–1941) Indian author and Nobel Prize winner. *The Crescent Moon,* "The Judge," (1913).

Lying/Dishonesty

1 A child who fears excessive retaliation for even minor offenses will learn very early on that to lie is to protect himself. . . . If your child intuits that you will react very punitively to his wrongdoing, he may be tempted to lie and may become, as time goes on, a habitual liar.

LAWRENCE BALTER, (20th-century) U.S. psychologist and author. *Who's In Control?* ch. 6 (1989).

2 One parent is enough to spoil you but deception takes two.

ANONYMOUS.

3 Three-year-olds see the world in black-and-white terms. . . . They have been told that they should be good. They want to believe that they are good. . . . Therefore, they weren't the ones who poured jam all over the sleeping cocker spaniel. Denying their culpability is neither malicious nor sneaky; it just reflects the unshaded terms in which preschoolers view the world.

LAWRENCE KUTNER, (20th-century) U.S. child psychologist and author. *Parent and Child,* ch. 7 (1991).

4 I've noticed over the years that kids who are allowed to be emotionally honest develop a genuineness that more repressed kids don't ever seem to acquire. Their words match their facial expressions. Their actions match their words, and they relate from a position of strength.

STEPHANIE MARSTON, (20th-century) U.S. family therapist, author. *The Magic of Encouragement,* ch. 1 (1990).

5 The three-year-old who lies about taking a cookie isn't really a "liar" after all. He simply can't control his impulses. He then convinces himself of a new truth and, eager for your approval, reports the version that he knows will make you happy.

CATHY RINDNER TEMPELSMAN, (20th-century) U.S. journalist and author. *Child-Wise,* ch. 2 (1994).

6 [Children] do not yet lie to themselves and therefore have not entered upon that important tacit agreement which marks admission into the adult world, to wit, that I will respect your lies if you will agree to let mine alone. That unwritten contract is one of the clear dividing lines between the world of childhood and the world of adulthood.

LEONTINE YOUNG, (20th-century) U.S. social worker and author. *Life Among the Giants,* ch. 2 (1965).

7 The point is children lie to others for good and sufficient reasons, but they don't kid themselves. They know who did what, but they feel no moral imperative to inform grownups.

LEONTINE YOUNG, (20th-century) U.S. social worker and author. *Life Among the Giants,* ch. 2 (1965).

Money/Family Finances

1 When the history of guilt is written, parents who refuse their children money will be right up there in the Top Ten.

ERMA BOMBECK, (20th-century) U.S. humorist and author. *Motherhood: The Second Oldest Profession,* ch. 38 (1983).

2 Given the choice, children who don't want for anything will not save. . . . We have an obligation as parents to give our children what they need. What they want we can give them as a special gift, or they can save their money for it.

BARBARA COLOROSO, (20th-century) U.S. parent educator and author. *Kids Are Worth It,* ch. 10 (1994).

3 The best time to start giving your children money is when they will no longer eat it. Basically, when they don't put it in their mouths,

they can start putting it in their bank.

BARBARA COLOROSO, (20th-century) U.S. parent educator and author. *Kids Are Worth It,* ch. 10 (1994).

4 What is important for kids to learn is that no matter how much money they have, earn, win, or inherit, they need to know how to spend it, how to save it, and how to give it to others in need. This is what handling money is about, and this is why we give kids an allowance.

BARBARA COLOROSO, (20th-century) U.S. parent educator and author. *Kids Are Worth It,* ch. 10 (1994).

5 It doesn't make any difference how much money a father earns, his name is always Dad-Can-I. . . . Like all other children, my five have one great talent: they are gifted beggars. Not one of them ever ran into the room, looked up at me, and said, "I'm really happy that you're my father, and as a tangible token of my appreciation, here's a dollar."

BILL COSBY, (20th-century) U.S. comedian and author. *Fatherhood,* ch. 3 (1986).

6 Our kids will develop a work ethic only if we require them to pay a portion of the cost of some of the things they want. They'll learn to defer gratification the moment we stop routinely pulling out our wallets. And they'll learn self-discipline only if we care enough to enforce reasonable limits.

FRED G. GOSMAN, (20th-century) U.S. author. *How to Be a Happy Parent . . . In Spite of Your Children,* ch. 11 (1995).

7 Taking a child to the toy store is the nearest thing to a death wish parents can have.

FRED G. GOSMAN, (20th-century) U.S. author. *How to Be a Happy Parent . . . In Spite of Your Children,* ch. 4 (1995).

8 The site of the true bottomless financial pit is the toy store. It's amazing how much a few pieces of plastic and paper will sell for if the purchasers are parents or grandparent, especially when the manufacturers claim their product improves a child's intellectual or physical development.

LAWRENCE KUTNER, (20th-century) U.S. child psychologist and author. *Pregnancy and Your Baby's First Year,* ch. 9 (1993).

9 Children need money. As they grow older they need more money. They need money for essentially the same reasons that adults need money. They need to buy stuff. . . . They need it regardless of whether they get good grades, violate a family rule, or offend a parent.

DONALD C. MEDEIROS, (20th-century) U.S. psychologist and author. *Children Under Stress,* ch. 2 (1983).

10 Children should know there are limits to family finances or they will confuse "we can't afford that" with "they don't want me to have it." The first statement is a realistic and objective assessment of a situation, while the other carries an emotional message.

JEAN ROSS PETERSON, (20th-century) U.S. author. *It Doesn't Grow on Trees,* ch. 1 (1988).

Nature vs. Nurture

1 A child is born with the potential ability to learn Chinese or Swahili, play a kazoo, climb a tree, make a strudel or a birdhouse, take pleasure

in finding the coordinates of a star. Genetic inheritance determines a child's abilities and weaknesses. But those who raise a child call forth from that matrix the traits and talents they consider important.

EMILIE BUCHWALD, (20th-century) U.S. author. "Raising Girls for the 21st Century," *Barnard Magazine,* (Summer/Fall 1993).

2 Genes and family may determine the foundation of the house, but time and place determine its form.

JEROME KAGAN, (20th-century) U.S. professor of developmental psychology. As quoted in *Childhood,* a viewer's guide produced in collaboration with Thirteen WNET, Robert H. Wozniak (1991).

3 Nature, we are starting to realize, is every bit as important as nurture. Genetic influences, brain chemistry, and neurological development contribute strongly to who we are as children and what we become as adults. For example, tendencies to excessive worrying or timidity, leadership qualities, risk taking, obedience to authority, all appear to have a constitutional aspect.

STANLEY TURECKI, (20th-century) U.S. psychiatrist and author. *The Difficult Child,* ch. 1 (1985).

4 While each child is born with his or her own distinct genetic potential for physical, social, emtional and cognitive development, the possibilities for reaching that potential remain tied to early life experiences and the parent-child relationship within the family.

BERNICE WEISSBOURD, (20th-century) U.S. family advocate and author. "Family Focus," *Children Today* (March/April 1981).

5 The route through childhood is shaped by many forces, and it differs for each of us. Our biological inheritance, the temperament with which we are born, the care we receive, our family relationships, the place where we grow up, the schools we attend, the culture in which we participate, and the historical period in which we live—all these affect the paths we take through childhood and condition the remainder of our lives.

ROBERT H. WOZNIAK, (20th-century) U.S. professor of human development and author. *Childhood,* a viewer's guide produced in collaboration with Thirteen WNET (1991).

Parenting Styles, General

1 Govern a small family as you would cook a small fish, very gently.

CHINESE PROVERB.

2 I believe that I am letting my kids see that a man can be tender, sensitive, warm, attentive to feelings, and present, just plain there. That's important to me, because I didn't get any of that from my own father, and I am realizing now how much I missed it.

ANONYMOUS FATHER, (20th-century) as quoted in *Ourselves and Our Children,* the Boston Women's Health Collective, ch. 6 (1978).

3 Parents ought, through their own behavior and the values by which they live, to provide direction for their children. But they need to rid themselves of the idea that there are surefire methods which, when well applied, will produce certain predictable results. Whatever we do

with and for our children ought to flow from our understanding of and our feelings for the particular situation and the relation we wish to exist between us and our child.

Bruno Bettelheim, (20th-century) Austrian-born U.S. child psychologist and author. *A Good Enough Parent,* ch. 2 (1987).

4 The politics of the family are the politics of a nation. Just as the authoritarian family is the authoritarian state in microcosm, the democratic family is the best training ground for life in a democracy.

Letty Cottin Pogrebin, (20th-century) U.S. editor and author. *Family and Politics,* ch. 1 (1983).

5 In the man whose childhood has known caresses and kindness, there is always a fibre of memory that can be touched by gentle issues.

George Eliot, (20th-century) British novelist. *The Last Word,* ed. Carolyn Warner, ch. 26 (1992).

6 Children must eventually train their own children, and any impoverishment of their impulse life, for the sake of avoiding friction, must be considered a possible liability affecting more than one lifetime.

Erik H. Erikson, (20th-century) German-born U.S. psychoanalyst and author. *Childhood and Society,* ch. 8 (1950).

7 A method of child-rearing is not—or should not be—a whim, a fashion or a shibboleth. It should derive from an understanding of the developing child, of his physical and mental equipment at any given stage, and, therefore, his readiness at any given stage to adapt, to learn, to regulate his behavior according to parental expectations.

Selma H. Fraiberg, (20th-century) U.S. child psychoanalyst and author. *The Magic Years,* ch. 4 (1959).

8 We find that even the parents who justify spanking to themselves are defensive and embarrassed about it. . . . I suspect that deep in the memory of every parent are the feelings that had attended his own childhood spankings, the feelings of humiliation, of helplessness, of submission through fear. The parent who finds himself spanking his own child cannot dispel the ghosts of his own childhood.

Selma H. Fraiberg, (20th-century) U.S. child psychoanalyst and author. *The Magic Years,* ch. 8 (1959).

9 Finding the perfect balance is getting harder and harder. We need to teach our children to be cautious without imparting fear, to learn right from wrong without being judgmental, to be assertive but not pushy, to stick to routines without sacrificing spontaneity, and to be determined but not stubborn.

Fred G. Gosman, (20th-century) U.S. author. *How to Be a Happy Parent . . . In Spite of Your Children,* introduction (1995).

10 Deep inside us, we know what every family therapist knows: the problems between the parents become the problems within the children.

Roger Gould, (20th-century) U.S. psychotherapist and author. *Transformations,* sec. 2 (1978).

11 A man's fatherliness is enriched as much by his acceptance of his femi-

nine and childlike strivings as it is by his memories of tender closeness with his own father. A man who has been able to accept tenderness from his father is able later in life to be tender with his own children.

LOUISE J. KAPLAN, (20th-century) U.S. psychologist and author. *Oneness and Separateness: From Infant to Individual,* ch. 1 (1978).

12 For all of us there will be those irreconcilable injuries and humiliations that persist and infiltrate into adult existence. They may become the seeds for those monotonous repetitions of hurting others and getting hurt ourselves . . . or the leftover traumas can be incentives for innovation and change . . . the opportunity to rewrite the scripts, introduce a few new characters, get rid of one or two, perhaps even change the ending, and free the lover and jester inside us all.

LOUISE KAPLAN, (20th-century) U.S. psychologist and author. *Adolescence,* ch. 6 (1984).

13 Let children know you are human. It's important for children to see that parents are human and make mistakes. When you're sorry about something you've said or done, apologize! But don't sound guilt ridden. It is best when parents apologize in a manner that is straightforward and sincere.

SAF LERMAN, (20th-century) U.S. parent educator and author. *Helping Children as They Grow,* ch. 1 (1983).

14 When we raise our children, we relive our childhood. Forgotten memories, painful and pleasurable, rise to the surface. . . . So each of us thinks, almost daily, of how our own childhood compares with our children's, and of what our children's future will hold.

RICHARD LOUV, (20th-century) U.S. journalist and author. *Childhood's Future,* pt. 1, ch. 1 (1991).

15 The knowledge that you were beaten and that this, as your parents tell you, was for your own good may well be retained (although not always), but the suffering caused by the way you were mistreated will remain unconscious and will later prevent you from empathizing with others. This is why battered children grow up to be mothers and fathers who beat their offspring.

ALICE MILLER, (20th-century) German-born psycohanalyst and author. *For Your Own Good,* "Poisonous Pedagogy" (trans. 1983).

16 The reason why parents mistreat their children has less to do with character and temperament than with the fact that they were mistreated themselves and were not permitted to defend themselves.

ALICE MILLER, (20th-century) German-born psycohanalyst and author. *For Your Own Good,* "Poisonous Pedagogy," (trans. 1983).

17 As we try to change, we will discover within us a fierce struggle between our loyalty to that battle-scarred victim of his own childhood, our father, and the father we want to be. We must meet our childhood father at close range: get to know him, learn to forgive him, and somehow, go beyond him.

AUGUSTUS Y. NAPIER, (20th-century) U.S. family therapist. *The Fragile Bond,* ch. 14 (1988).

18 This part of being a man, changing the way we parent, happens only

when we want it to. It changes because we are determined for it to change; and the motive for changing often comes out of wanting to be the kind of parent we didn't have.

AUGUSTUS Y. NAPIER, (20th-century) U.S. family therapist. *The Fragile Bond,* ch. 17 (1988).

19 It is one of the paradoxes of parenting, and often a painful paradox, that even as our children need us for love and trust, they also need us for honest differing. It's not only over limits and rules . . . [but also] about what we represent in the way of culture, traditions, and values. We owe it to our children to let them know what we believe, and if they differ with us, we owe it to them to be honest adversaries, for it is through this honest confrontation that children can grow into adults who have a firm sense of their place in the sequence of the generations.

FRED ROGERS, (20th-century) U.S. children's television personality and author. *Mister Rogers Talks with Parents,* ch. 1 (1983).

20 Most childhood problems don't result from "bad" parenting, but are the inevitable result of the growing that parents and children do together. The point isn't to head off these problems or find ways around them, but rather to work through them together and in doing so to develop a relationship of mutual trust to rely on when the next problem comes along.

FRED ROGERS, (20th-century) U.S. children's television personality and author. *Mister Rogers Talks with Parents,* ch. 2 (1983).

21 In the nurturing family . . . parents see themselves as empowering leaders not as authoritative bosses. They see their job primarily as one of teaching their children how to be truly human in all situations. They readily acknowledge to the child their poor judgment as well as their good judgment; their hurt, anger, or disappointment as well as their joy. The behavior of these parents matches what they say.

VIRGINIA SATIR, (20th-century) U.S. family therapist and author. *The New Peoplemaking,* ch. 2 (1988).

22 What lingers from the parent's individual past, unresolved or incomplete, often becomes part of her or his irrational parenting.

VIRGINIA SATIR, (20th-century) U.S. family therapist and author. As quoted in *The Winning Family,* by Louise Hart, ch. 16 (1987).

23 When I was away from home and missing my children, I asked myself why I didn't show my approval and enjoyment of them more when I was with them, when it would do them—and me—a lot of good. But I don't think I was ever able to take my own advice. The psychological explanation for this is that we crabby perfectionists were started in that direction in our own childhood by the frequent criticism of our parents; it is very difficult to overcome the compulsion to repeat what was done to us.

BENJAMIN SPOCK, (20th-century) U.S. pediatrician and author. "What Makes a Satisfying Christmas for Children and their Parents," *Redbook Magazine* (December 1981).

24 It seems to me that upbringings have themes. The parents set the theme, either explicitly or implicitly, and the children pick it up, sometimes accurately and some-

times not so accurately.... The theme may be "Our family has a distinguished heritage that you must live up to" or "No matter what happens, we are fortunate to be together in this lovely corner of the earth" or "We have worked hard so that you can have the opportunities we didn't have."

CALVIN TRILLIN, (20th-century) U.S. author. "Messages from My Father," *The New Yorker* (June 20, 1994).

Parenting Styles, Authoritarian

1 You want to prepare your child to think as he gets older. You want him to be critical in his judgments. Teaching a child, by your example, that there's never any room for negotiating or making choices in life may suggest that you expect blind obedience—but it won't help him in the long run to be discriminating in choices and thinking.

LAWRENCE BALTER, (20th-century) U.S. psychologist and author. *Dr. Balter's Child Sense,* pt. 2, ch. 26 (1985).

2 My father was frightened of his mother. I was frightened of my father and I am damned well going to see to it that my children are frightened of me.

GEORGE V, (1865-1936) King of Great Britain and Northern Ireland.

3 Authoritarian methods do not produce independence: they reinforce dependence. Independent functioning is not simply the ability to do something, but also the ability to decide what to do. It is not only the ability to take care of oneself. It is also the ability to take responsibility for oneself. Autonomy and independence do not grow out of being told what to do and when to do it. It is only by having his needs considered, by becoming a participant in the decision-making process, that a child develops the capacity for autonomy.

ELAINE HEFFNER, (20th-century) U.S. psychiatrist and author. *Mothering,* ch. 7 (1978).

4 In child-rearing it would unquestionably be easier if a child were to do something because we say so. The authoritarian method does expedite things, but it does not produce independent functioning. If a child has not mastered the underlying principles of human interactions and merely conforms out of coercion or conditioning, he has no tools to use, no resources to apply in the next situation that confronts him.

ELAINE HEFFNER, (20th-century) U.S. psychiatrist and author. *Mothering,* ch. 9 (1978).

5 We all know children who grew up in authoritarian families and have never stopped rebelling against restrictiveness wherever they find it. And they seem to be more prone than others to find it!

NEIL KURSHAN, (20th-century) U.S. rabbi and author. *Raising Your Child to Be a Mensch,* ch. 4 (1987).

6 The authoritarian child-rearing style so often found in working-class families stems in part from the fact that parents see around them so many young people whose lives are touched by the pain and delinquency that so often accompanies a life of poverty. Therefore, these

parents live in fear for their children's future—fear that they'll lose control, that the children will wind up on the streets or, worse yet, in jail.

LILLIAN BRESLOW RUBIN, (20th-century) U.S. sociologist and family therapist. *Families on the Fault Line,* ch. 3 (1994).

Parenting Styles, Permissive

1 The opposite of love is not hate, as many believe, but rather indifference. Nothing communicates disinterest more clearly than distancing. A child cannot feel valued by parents who are forever absorbed in their own affairs.

DOROTHY CORKILLE BRIGGS, (20th-century) U.S. parent educator. *Your Child's Self-Esteem,* ch. 7 (1975).

2 Because we cannot control all that our children see, hear, and play, it is tempting to throw up our hands and do nothing. Although we cannot do everything, we can do something, and this is to talk with our children and teenagers about unexpected encounters with inappropriate violence, sexuality, and profanity.

DAVID ELKIND, (20th-century) U.S. child psychologist and author. *Ties That Stress,* ch. 4 (1994).

3 Allowing children to spew forth whatever is on their minds in the name of openness only creates an illusion of family closeness.

NEIL KURSHAN, (20th-century) U.S. rabbi and author. *Raising Your Child to Be a Mensch,* ch. 4 (1987).

4 Every family should extend First Amendment rights to all its members, but this freedom is particularly essential for our kids. Children must be able to say what they think, openly express their feelings, and ask for what they want and need if they are ever able to develop an integrated sense of self. They must be able to think their own thoughts, even if they differ from ours. They need to have the opportunity to ask us questions when they don't understand what we mean.

STEPHANIE MARSTON, (20th-century) U.S. family therapist and author. *The Magic of Encouragement,* ch. 1 (1990).

5 Parents are used to being made to feel guilty about . . . their contribution to the population problem, the school tax burden, and declining test scores. They expect to be blamed by teachers and psychologists, if not by police. And they will be blamed by the children themselves. It is hardy a wonder, then, that they withdraw into what used to be called "permissiveness" but is really neglect.

C. JOHN SOMMERVILLE, (20th-century) U.S. historian and author. *The Rise and Fall of Childhood,* ch. 1 (rev. 1990).

Play

1 From a child's play, we can gain understanding of how he sees and construes the world—what he would like it to be, what his concerns are, what problems are besetting him.

BRUNO BETTELHEIM, (20th-century) Austrian-born U.S. child psychologist and author. *A Good Enough Parent,* ch. 14 (1987).

2 Play permits the child to resolve in symbolic form unsolved problems

of the past and to cope directly or symbolically with present concerns. It is also his most significant tool for preparing himself for the future and its tasks.

BRUNO BETTELHEIM, (20th-century) Austrian-born U.S. child psychologist and author. *A Good Enough Parent,* ch. 14 (1987).

3 The child knows only that he engages in play because it is enjoyable. He isn't aware of his need to play—a need which has its source in the pressure of unsolved problems. Nor does he know that his pleasure in playing comes from a deep sense of well-being that is the direct result of feeling in control of things, in contrast to the rest of his life, which is managed by his parents or other adults.

BRUNO BETTELHEIM, (20th-century) Austrian-born U.S. child psychologist and author. *A Good Enough Parent,* ch. 16 (1987).

4 Four- and five-year-olds' play is permeated with the rankest sexism. No matter what their parents do and say, they play their mom and pop roles in ultraconventional style. We've seen little girls whose mothers are doctors absolutely refuse to take the doctors' parts in their play, insisting that "only boys can be doctors," against all reason. Girls do more washing and drying of clothes, dishes, and babies than they've ever seen their own mothers do, and they turn their play husbands into TV-watching drones who do nothing but talk about money.

STELLA CHESS, (20th-century) U.S. psychiatrist and author. *Daughters,* ch. 6 (1978).

5 Playing games with agreed upon rules helps children learn to live by rules, establish the delicate balance between competition and cooperation, between fair play and justice and exploitation and abuse of these for personal gain. It helps them learn to manage the warmth of winning and the hurt of losing; it helps them to believe that there will be another chance to win the next time.

JAMES P. COMER, (20th-century) U.S. psychiatrist and author. *School Power,* ch. 10 (1980).

6 The playing adult steps sideward into another reality; the playing child advances forward to new stages of mastery. . . . Child's play is the infantile form of the human ability to deal with experience by creating model situations and to master reality by experiment and planning.

ERIK H. ERIKSON, (20th-century) German-born U.S. psychoanalyst and author. *Childhood and Society,* ch. 6 (1950).

7 Although pretend play is important, it is still the means to an end, not the end itself. Do not make the mistake of thinking a contrived, pretend drama can substitute for real interpersonal comfort in dealing with important emotional issues.

STANLEY I. GREENSPAN, (20th-century) U.S. child psychiatrist and author, and **NANCY THORNING GREENSPAN,** U.S. health economist. *First Feelings: Milestones in the Emotional Development of Your Baby and Child,* ch. 6 (1985).

8 Make-believe is the avenue to much of the young child's early understanding. He sorts out impressions and tries out ideas that are foundational to his later realistic comprehension. This private world sometimes is a quiet, solitary world. More often it is a noisy, busy,

crowded place where language grows, and social skills develop, and where perseverance and attention-span expand.

JAMES L. HYMES, JR., (20th-century) U.S. psychologist and author. *Teaching the Child Under Six,* ch. 2 (1968).

9 Play builds the kind of free-and-easy, try-it-out, do-it-yourself character that our future needs. We must become more self-conscious and more explicit in our praise and reinforcement as children use unstructured play materials: "That's good. You use your own ideas. . . ." "That's good. You did it your way. . . ." "That's good. You thought it all out yourself."

JAMES L. HYMES, JR., (20th-century) U.S. psychologist and author. *Teaching the Child Under Six,* ch. 3 (1968).

10 Play for young children is not recreation activity. . . . It is not leisure-time activity nor escape activity. . . . Play is thinking time for young children. It is language time. Problem-solving time. It is memory time, planning time, investigating time. It is organization-of-ideas time, when the young child uses his mind and body and his social skills and all his powers in response to the stimuli he has met.

JAMES L. HYMES, JR., (20th-century) U.S. psychologist and author. *Teaching the Child Under Six,* ch. 4 (1968).

11 You will always be your child's favorite toy.

VICKI LANSKY, (20th-century) U.S. author. *Trouble-Free Travel with Children,* ch. 3 (1991).

12 For a small child there is no division between playing and learning; between the things he or she does "just for fun" and things that are "educational." The child learns while living and any part of living that is enjoyable is also play.

PENELOPE LEACH, (20th-century) British child development specialist and author. *Your Baby and Child,* ch. 5 (1977).

13 Play is a major avenue for learning to manage anxiety. It gives the child a safe space where she can experiment at will, suspending the rules and constraints of physical and social reality. In play, the child becomes master rather than subject. . . . Play allows the child to transcend passivity and to become the active doer of what happens around her.

ALICIA F. LIEBERMAN, (20th-century) U.S. psychologist and author. *The Emotional Life of the Toddler,* ch. 7 (1993).

14 Although there are not real winners or losers, in games of pretending children soon learn that the game ends when mutuality ends.

JOANNE E. OPPENHEIM, (20th-century) U.S. educator and author. *Kids and Play,* ch. 5 (1984).

15 It is not an exaggeration to say that play is as basic to your child's total development as good food, cleanliness, and rest.

JOANNE E. OPPENHEIM, (20th-century) U.S. educator and author. *Kids and Play,* ch. 1 (1984).

16 Playing at make-believe, the young child becomes the all-powerful person he cannot be in reality. In pretending, the child takes control of his otherwise powerless position.

JOANNE E. OPPENHEIM, (20th-century) U.S. educator and author. *Kids and Play,* ch.4 (1984).

17 PLAYING SHOULD BE FUN! In our great eagerness to teach our children we studiously look for "educational" toys, games with built-in lessons, books with a "message." Often these "tools" are less interesting and stimulating than the child's natural curiosity and playfulness. Play is by its very nature educational. And it should be pleasurable. When the fun goes out of play, most often so does the learning.

JOANNE E. OPPENHEIM, (20th-century) U.S. educator and author. *Kids and Play,* ch. 1 (1984).

18 One way to think about play is as the process of finding new combinations for known things—combinations that may yield new forms of expression, new inventions, new discoveries, and new solutions. . . . It's exactly what children's play seems to be about and explains why so many people have come to think that children's play is so important a part of childhood—and beyond.

FRED ROGERS, (20th-century) U.S. children's television personality and author. *Mister Rogers Talks with Parents,* ch. 5 (1983).

19 Play gives children a chance to practice what they are learning. . . . They have to play with what they know to be true in order to find out more, and then they can use what they learn in new forms of play.

FRED ROGERS, (20th-century) U.S. children's television personality and author. *Mister Rogers Talks with Parents,* ch. 5 (1983).

20 The indispensable ingredient of any game worth its salt is that the children themselves play it and, if not its sole authors, share in its creation. Watching TV's ersatz battles is not the same thing at all. Children act out their emotions, they don't talk them out and they don't watch them out. Their imagination and their muscles need each other.

LEONTINE YOUNG, (20th-century) U.S. social worker and author. *Life Among the Giants,* ch. 17 (1965).

Quality Time

1 Ordinary time is "quality time" too. Everyday activities are not just necessities that keep you from serious child-rearing: they are the best opportunities for learning you can give your child . . . because her chief task in her first three years is precisely to gain command of the day-to-day life you take for granted.

AMY LAURA DOMBRO, (20th-century) U.S. early childhoodeducator and author. *The Ordinary Is Extraordinary,* ch. 1 (1988).

2 I have three kinds of "quality time." The first I call "Split-Brain Time" because only one side of my brain is with my children. . . . The second type of quality time is what I call "Timed Time" and is best characterized by declarations such as, "okay, you children have ten minutes to get in bed and fall asleep. . . ." On the really bad days I settle for the "Quality Greeting"—a brief "Hi there! or "Sleep tight"—usually uttered from a comfortable chair just before I drift off to sleep.

NEIL KURSHAN, (20th-century) U.S. rabbi and author.*Raising Your Child to Be a Mensch,* ch. 2 (1987).

3 Anybody who knows the difference between the kind of conversation you have walking in the woods and the kind of conversation you have between the segments of a show on

Nickelodeon can tell you that quality time exists. Quality time is when you and your child are together and keenly aware of each other. You are enjoying the same thing at the same time, even if it is just being in a room or going for a drive in the car. You are somehow in tune, even while daring to be silent together.

Louise Lague, (20th-century) U.S. editor and author. *The Working Mom's Book of Hints, Tips, and Everyday Wisdom,* ch. 2 (1995).

4 Weekend planning is a prime time to apply the Deathbed Priority Test: On your deathbed, will you wish you'd spent more prime weekend hours grocery shopping or walking in the woods with your kids?

Louise Lague, (20th-century) U.S. editor and author. *The Working Mom's Book of Hints, Tips, and Everyday Wisdom,* ch. 2 (1995).

5 Working parents are often told that it is the quality of time, rather than the quantity of time one spends with children, that is significant. Unfortunately, good quality time is difficult to define, to measure, and to make happen on schedule.

Joyce Portner, (20th-century) U.S. author. *Stress and the Family,* ch. 11 (1983).

Reading/Children's Literature

1 Children don't read to find their identity, to free themselves from guilt, to quench the thirst for rebellion or to get rid of alienation. They have no use for psychology. . . . They still believe in God, the family, angels, devils, witches, goblins, logic, clarity, punctuation, and other such obsolete stuff. . . . When a book is boring, they yawn openly. They don't expect their writer to redeem humanity, but leave to adults such childish illusions.

Isaac Bashevis Singer, (20th-century) Polish-born U.S. author. As quoted in the *Observer,* London (December 17, 1978).

2 A parent who from his own childhood experience is convinced of the value of fairy tales will have no difficulty in answering his child's questions; but an adult who thinks these tales are only a bunch of lies had better not try telling them; he won't be able to relate them in a way which would enrich the child's life.

Bruno Bettelheim, (20th-century) Austrian-born U.S. child psychologist and author. *The Uses of Enchantment,* "Fears of Fantasy" (1975).

3 Fairy tales are loved by the child not because the imagery he finds in them conforms to what goes on within him, but because—despite all the angry, anxious thoughts in his mind to which the fairy tale gives body and specific content—these stories always result in a happy outcome, which the child cannot imagine on his own.

Bruno Bettelheim, (20th-century) Austrian-born U.S. child psychologist and author. *The Uses of Enchantment,* "Fears of Fantasy" (1975).

4 If learning to read was as easy as learning to talk, as some writers claim, many more children would learn to read on their own. The fact that they do not, despite their being surrounded by print, suggests that learning to read is not a spontaneous or simple skill.

DAVID ELKIND, (20th-century) U.S. child psychologist and author. *The Hurried Child,* ch. 2 (1988).

5 Experts generally agree that taking all opportunities to read books and other material aloud to children is the best preparation for their learning to read. The pleasures of being read to are far more likely to strengthen a child's desire to learn to read than are repetitions of sounds, alphabet drills, and deciphering uninteresting words.

LILIAN G. KATZ, (20th-century) U.S. early childhood educator. "Should Preschoolers Learn the Three R's?" *Parents Magazine* (October 1990).

6 Just as all children's books shouldn't be read by children (nor by anyone else), neither should children read only children's books. Every young child should be exposed to poetry—good adult poetry—not only to learn to appreciate the rhythm of its sophisticated beat (as opposed to the amusing, political doggerel of *Mother Goose*) but because poetry has the scope and precision to conjure pictures that prose can seldom paint.

MARGUERITE KELLY, (20th-century) U.S. author. *The Mother's Almanac* (rev. 1992).

7 To me, nothing can be more important than giving children books. It's better to be giving books to children than drug treatment to them when they're fifteen years old. Did it ever occur to anyone that if you put nice libraries in public schools you wouldn't have to put them in prisons?

FRAN LEBOWITZ, (20th-century) U.S. humorist and author. "Words Are Easy, Books Are Not," *The New York Times* (August 10, 1994).

8 Common sense should tell us that reading is the ultimate weapon—destroying ignorance, poverty and despair before they can destroy us. A nation that doesn't read much doesn't know much. And a nation that doesn't know much is more likely to make poor choices in the home, the marketplace, the jury box and the voting booth. . . . The challenge, therefore, is to convince future generations of children that carrying a book is more rewarding than carrying guns.

JIM TRELEASE, (20th-century) U.S. educator and author. *The Read-Aloud Handbook,* introduction (1995).

9 Skill sheets, workbooks, basal reader, flash cards are not enough. To convey meaning you need someone sharing the meaning and flavor of real stories with the student.

JIM TRELEASE, (20th-century) U.S. educator and author. *The New Read-Aloud Handbook,* ch. 1 (1985).

10 You become a reader because you saw and heard someone you admired enjoying the experience, someone led you to the world of books even before you could read, let you taste the magic of stories, took you to the library, and allowed you to stay up later at night to read in bed.

JIM TRELEASE, (20th-century) U.S. educator and author. *The New Read-Aloud Handbook,* ch. 1 (1985).

Rebellion

1 I come from a long line of male chauvinists in a very traditional family. To rebel against my background, I didn't shoot dope—I married a working woman.

Joe Bologna, (20th-century) U.S. actor. As quoted in *Family and Politics,* ch. 6, Letty Cottin Pogrebin (1983).

2 The area [of toilet training] is one where a child really does possess the power to defy. Strong pressure leads to a powerful struggle. The issue then is not toilet training but who holds the reins—mother or child? And the child has most of the ammunition!

Dorothy Corkille Briggs, (20th-century) U.S. parent educator. *Your Child's Self-Esteem,* ch. 15 (1975).

3 Today so much rebellion is aimless and demoralizing precisely because children have no values to challenge. Teenage rebellion is a testing process in which young people try out various values in order to make them their own. But during those years of trial, error, embarrassment, a child needs family standards to fall back on, reliable habits of thought and feeling that provide security and protection.

Neil Kurshan, (20th-century) U.S. rabbi and author. *Raising Your Child to Be a Mensch,* ch. 4 (1987).

4 Affection, indulgence, and humor alike are powerless against the instinct of children to rebel. It is essential to their minds and their wills as exercise is to their bodies. If they have no reasons, they will invent them, like nations bound on war. It is hard to imagine families limp enough always to be at peace. Wherever there is character there will be conflict. The best that children and parents can hope for is that the wounds of their conflict may not be too deep or too lasting.

New York State Division Of Youth Newsletter, (1975).

Respect/Disrespect

1 Respect is not fear and awe; it . . . [is]the ability to see a person as he is, to be aware of his unique individuality. Respect, thus, implies the absence of exploitation. I want the loved person to grow and unfold for his own sake, and in his own ways, and not for the purpose of serving me.

Erich Fromm, (20th-century) German-born U.S. psychoanalyst and author. *The Art of Loving,* ch. 2 (1956).

2 Ignoring a child's disrespect is the surest guarantee that it will continue.

Fred G. Gosman, (20th-century) U.S. author. *How to Be a Happy Parent . . . In Spite of Your Children,* ch. 9 (1995).

3 "Walk a mile in my shoes" is good advice. Our children will learn to respect others if they are used to imagining themselves in another's place.

Neil Kurshan, (20th-century) U.S. rabbi and author. *Raising Your Child to Be a Mensch,* ch. 4 (1987).

4 When children are treated with respect, they conclude that they deserve respect and hence develop self-respect. When children are treated with acceptance, they develop self-acceptance; when they are cherished, they conclude that they deserve to be loved, and they develop self-esteem.

Stephanie Marston, (20th-century) U.S. family therapist and author. *The Magic of Encouragement,* ch. 1 (1990).

5 Wherever I look, I see signs of the commandment to honor one's parents and nowhere of a com-

mandment that calls for the respect of a child.

ALICE MILLER, (20th-century) German-born U.S. psychoanalyst and author. *For Your Own Good,* "Unlived Anger" (trans. 1983).

Rituals/Traditions

1 The greatest part of each day, each year, each lifetime is made up of small, seemingly insignificant moments. Those moments may be cooking dinner . . . relaxing on the porch with your own thoughts after the kids are in bed, playing catch with a child before dinner, speaking out against a distasteful joke, driving to the recycling center with a week's newspapers. But they are not insignificant, especially when these moments are models for kids.

BARBARA COLOROSO, (20th-century) U.S. parent educator and author. *Kids Are Worth It,* ch. 9 (1994).

2 A life-long blessing for children is to fill them with warm memories of times together. Happy memories become treasures in the heart to pull out on the tough days of adulthood.

CHARLOTTE DAVIS KASL, (20th-century) U.S. psychologist and author. *Finding Joy,* ch. 73 (1994).

3 Traditions are the "always" in life—the rituals and customs that build common memories for children, offer comfort and stability in good times and bad, and create a sense of family identity.

MARIAN EDELMAN BORDEN, (20th-century) U.S. journalist. "Rituals Kids Can Count On," *Parenting Magazine* (May 1992).

4 Boy meets girl. Boy marries girl. Boy and girl angst over which family they visit at Thanksgiving and which one in December and whether or not it's best to serve turkey or goose for the family feast. When first faced with the reality that the family you married into does things differently, the warmth of tradition can take on a chill.

MARGE KENNEDY, (20th-century) U.S. author. *100 Things You Can Do to Keep Your Family Together . . . ,* pt. 1 (1994).

5 By building relations . . . we create a source of love and personal pride and belonging that makes living in a chaotic world easier.

SUSAN LIEBERMAN, (20th-century) U.S. author. *New Traditions: Redefining Celebrations for Today's Family,* ch. 2 (1991).

6 Family traditions counter alienation and confusion. They help us define who we are; they provide something steady, reliable and safe in a confusing world.

SUSAN LIEBERMAN, (20th-century) U.S. author. *New Traditions: Redefining Celebrations for Today's Family,* ch. 2 (1991).

7 Kids are fascinated by stories about what they were like when they were babies and what they said and did as they grew. This sense of history and connectedness increases your children's feelings of security and safety, and helps them build the ability to make healthy connections in the world at large.

STEPHANIE MARSTON, (20th-century) U.S. family therapist and author. *The Magic of Encouragement,* ch. 1 (1990).

8 Family lore can be a bore, but only when you are hearing it, never when you are relating it to the ones who will be carrying it on for you. A family without a storyteller or two has no way to make sense out

of their past and no way to get a sense of themselves.

FRANK PITTMAN, (20th-century) U.S. psychiatrist and family therapist. "How to Manage Mom and Dad," *Psychology Today* (November/December 1994).

9 I like to compare the holiday season with the way a child listens to a favorite story. The pleasure is in the familiar way the story begins, the anticipation of familiar turns it takes, the familiar moments of suspense, and the familiar climax and ending.

FRED ROGERS, (20th-century) U.S. children's television personality and author. *Mister Rogers Talks with Parents,* ch. 11 (1983).

10 What will our children remember of us, ten, fifteen years from now? The mobile we bought or didn't buy? Or the tone in our voices, the look in our eyes, the enthusiasm for life—and for them—that we felt? They, and we, will remember the spirit of things, not the letter. Those memories will go so deep that no one could measure it, capture it, bronze it, or put it in a scrapbook.

SONIA TAITZ, (20th-century) U.S. journalist and author. *Mothering Heights,* introduction (1992).

Self-esteem, General

1 If self-esteem were easy to impart, everyone would have it.

FRED G. GOSMAN, (20th-century) U.S. author. *How to Be a Happy Parent . . . In Spite of Your Children,* ch. 9 (1995).

2 In order to feel good about himself, a child must be successful in his own eyes, not just in your eyes. Self-esteem is an inner feeling: sometimes it corresponds with outer reality, and sometimes it doesn't.

STANLEY I. GREENSPAN, (20th-century) U.S. child psychiatrist and author. *Playground Politics,* ch. 3 (1993).

3 Healthy parenting is nothing if not a process of empowerment. As we help to raise our children's self-esteem, we also increase their personal power. When we encourage them to be confident, self-reliant, self-directed, and responsible individuals, we are giving them power.

LOUISE HART, (20th-century) U.S. community psychologist and author. *The Winning Family,* ch. 12 (1987).

4 Self-esteem creates natural highs. Knowing that you're lovable helps you to love more. Knowing that you're important helps you to make a difference to to others. Knowing that you are capable empowers you to create more. Knowing that you're valuable and that you have a special place in the universe is a serene spiritual joy in itself.

LOUISE HART, (20th-century) U.S. community psychologist and author. *The Winning Family,* ch. 4 (1987).

5 Self-esteem is as important to our well-being as legs are to a table. It is essential for physical and mental health and for happiness.

LOUISE HART, (20th-century) U.S. community psychologist and author. *The Winning Family,* ch. 20 (1987).

6 Children's self-esteem develops in proportion to the depth of trust that is reached in the parent/child relationship.

STEPHANIE MARSTON, (20th-century) U.S. family therapist and author. *The Magic of Encouragement,* ch. 3 (1990).

7 Nurturing competence, the food of self-esteem, comes from acknowledging and appreciating the positive contributions your children make. By catching our kids doing things right, we bring out the good that is already there.

STEPHANIE MARSTON, (20th-century) U.S. family therapist and author. *The Magic of Encouragement,* ch. 4 (1990).

8 Self-esteem evolves in kids primarily through the quality of our relationships with them. Because they can't see themselves directly, children know themselves by reflection. For the first several years of their lives, you are their major influence. Later on, teachers and friends come into the picture. But especially at the beginning, you're it with a capital I.

STEPHANIE MARSTON, (20th-century) U.S. family therapist and author. *The Magic of Encouragement,* ch. 1 (1990).

9 Self-esteem is the real magic wand that can form a child's future. A child's self-esteem affects every area of her existence, from friends she chooses, to how well she does academically in school, to what kind of job she gets, to even the person she chooses to marry.

STEPHANIE MARSTON, (20th-century) U.S. family therapist and author. *The Magic of Encouragement,* ch. 1 (1990).

10 A child who thinks he is good at something even if he is not—soccer, math, violin—is likely to be more resilient than a child who is never satisfied with his efforts.

BARBARA F. MELTZ, (20th-century) U.S. journalist. "Raising Kids to Be Resilient," *Boston Globe* (July 28, 1994).

11 And those handmade presents that children often bring home from school: they have so much value! The value is that the child put whatever he or she could into making them. The way we parents respond to the giving of such gifts is very important. To the child the gift is really self, and they want so much for their selves to be acceptable, to be loved.

FRED ROGERS, (20th-century) U.S. children's television personality and author. *Mister Rogers Talks with Parents,* ch. 11 (1983).

12 No child ever has too much self-esteem. If you take every possible opportunity to point out what children do well, praise them descriptively for it and express appreciation, your child will become more cooperative, competent and confident.

NANCY SAMALIN, (20th-century) U.S. parent educator and author. *Loving Your Child Is Not Enough,* ch. 6 (1987).

Self-esteem, Parents' Input in Developing

1 The mother whose self-image is dependent on her children places on those children the responsibility for her own identity, and her involvement in the details of their lives can put great pressure on the children. A child suffers when everything he or she does is extremely important to a parent; this kind of over-involvement can turn even a small problem into a crisis.

GRACE BARUCH, U.S. developmental psychologist, **ROSALIND BARNETT,** U.S. psychologist, and **CARYL RIVERS,** U.S. journalist (20th-century). *Lifeprints: New Patterns of Love and Work for Today's Women,* ch. 5 (1983).

2 If we view our children as stupid, naughty, disturbed, or guilty of their misdeeds, they will learn to behold themselves as foolish, faulty, or shameful specimens of humanity. They will regard us as judges from whom they wish to hide, and they will interpret everything we say as further proof of their unworthiness. If we view them as innocent, or at least merely ignorant, they will gain understanding from their experiences, and they will continue to regard us as wise partners.

Polly Berrien Berends, (20th-century) U.S. author. *Whole Child/Whole Parent,* ch. 3 (rev. 1987).

3 Whoever influences the child's life ought to try to give him a positive view of himself and of his world. The child's future happiness and his ability to cope with life and relate to others will depend on it.

Bruno Bettelheim, (20th-century) Austrian-born U.S. child psychologist and author. *A Good Enough Parent,* ch. 1 (1987).

4 Ecouraging a child means that one or more of the following critical life messages are coming through, either by word or by action: I believe in you, I trust you, I know you can handle this, You are listened to, You are cared for, You are very important to me.

Barbara Coloroso, (20th-century) U.S. parent educator and author. *Kids Are Worth It,* epilogue (1994).

5 The child benefits more from being valued than evaluated.

Don Dinkmeyer, (20th-century) U.S. parent educator and author. *Raising a Responsible Child,* ch. 2 (1973).

6 Let us be different in our homes. Let us realize that along with food, shelter, and clothing, we have another obligation to our children, and that is to affirm their "rightness." The whole world will tell them what's wrong with them—out loud and often. Our job is to let our children know what's right about them.

Adele Faber and Elaine Mazlish, (20th-century) U.S. parent educators. *How to Talk So Kids Will Listen and Listen So Kids Will Talk,* ch. 4 (1980).

7 If you tell children they are bad, that's what they believe they are—and that's probably what they will become.

Louise Hart, (20th-century) U.S. community psychologist and author. *The Winning Family,* ch. 8 (1987).

8 Of course children benefit from positive feedback. But praise and rewards are not the only methods of reinforcement. More emphasis should be placed on appreciation—reinforcement related explicitly and directly to the *content* of the child's interest and efforts.

Lilian G. Katz, (20th-century) U.S. early childhood educator. "Should Preschoolers Learn the Three R's?" *Parents Magazine* (October 1990).

9 A child's self-image is more like a scrapbook than a single snapshot. As the child matures, the number and variety of images in that scrapbook may be far more important than any individual picture pasted inside it.

Lawrence Kutner, (20th-century) U.S. child psychologist and author. *Parent and Child,* ch. 4 (1991).

10 Sometimes the children who are no problem to their parents should be

looked at more closely. This is especially true if those children are extremely obedient and have few friends their own age. A good self-concept allows children to explore the world, risk engaging in conflict and failing. Children who play it safe by never disobeying or risking conflict may be telling you that they feel unqualified to face the world head-on.

Lawrence Kutner, (20th-century) U.S. child psychologist and author. *Parent and Child,* ch. 4 (1991).

11 Our children evaluate themselves based on the opinions we have of them. When we use harsh words, biting comments, and a sarcastic tone of voice, we plant the seeds of self-doubt in their developing minds. . . . Children who receive a steady diet of these types of messages end up feeling powerless, inadequate, and unimportant. They start to believe that they are bad, and that they can never do enough.

Stephanie Marston, (20th-century) U.S. family therapist and author. *The Magic of Encouragement,* ch. 4 (1990).

12 When children feel good about themselves, it's like a snowball rolling downhill. They are continually able to recognize and integrate new proof of their value as they grow and mature.

Stephanie Marston, (20th-century) U.S. family therapist and author. *The Magic of Encouragement,* ch. 1 (1990).

13 Where did we ever get the crazy idea that in order to make children do better, first we have to make them feel worse? Think of the last time you felt humiliated or treated unfairly. Did you feel like cooperating or doing better?

Jane Nelson, (20th-century) U.S. family therapist and author. *Positive Discipline,* ch. 1 (1981).

14 Every word, facial expression, gesture, or action on the part of a parent gives the child some message about self-worth. It is sad that so many parents don't realize what messages they are sending.

Virginia Satir, (20th-century) U.S. family therapist and author. As quoted in *The Winning Family,* ch. 16, Louise Hart (1987).

15 Feelings of worth can flourish only in an atmosphere in which individual differences are appreciated, love is shown openly, mistakes are used for learning, communication is open, rules are flexible, responsibility (matching promise with delivery)is modeled and honesty is practiced—the kind of atmosphere found in a nurturing family.

Virginia Satir, (20th-century) U.S. family therapist and author. As quoted in *The Winning Family,* ch. 16, Louise Hart (1987).

Self-reliance/Responsibility

1 Never miss an opportunity to allow a child to do something she can and wants to on her own. Sometimes we're in too much of a rush—and she might spill something, or do it wrong. But whenever possible she needs to learn, error by error, lesson by lesson, to do better. And the more she is able to learn by herself the more she gets the message that she's a kid who can.

Polly Berrien Berends, (20th-century) U.S. author. *Whole Child/Whole Parent,* ch. 3 (rev. 1987).

2 Therefore, as necessarily we protect our children from harm, we are nevertheless not too quick to come between them and a negative experience from which they can safely learn something on their own.

POLLY BERRIEN BERENDS, (20th-century) U.S. author. *Whole Child/Whole Parent,* ch. 4 (rev. 1987).

3 Witness the American ideal: the Self-Made Man. But there is no such person. If we can stand on our own two feet, it is because others have raised us up. If, as adults, we can lay claim to competence and compassion, it only means that other human beings have been willing and enabled to commit their competence and compassion to us—through infancy, childhood, and adolescence, right up to this very moment.

URIE BRONFENBRENNER, (20th-century) U.S. psychologist and author. Position paper for the Working Conference on Parent Education (1977).

4 Every time a child organizes and completes a chore, spends some time alone without feeling lonely, loses herself in play for an hour, or refuses to go along with her peers in some activity she feels is wrong, she will be building meaning and a sense of worth for herself and harmony in her family.

BARBARA COLOROSO, (20th-century) U.S. parent educator and author. *Kids Are Worth It,* epilogue (1994).

5 The risk for a woman who considers her helpless children her "job" is that the children's growth toward self-sufficiency may be experienced as a refutation of the mother's indispensability, and she may unconsciously sabotage their growth as a result.

LETTY COTTIN POGREBIN, (20th-century) U.S. editor and author. *Family and Politics,* ch. 5 (1983).

6 One of the important things to learn about parenting is that the more you worry about a child, the less the child will worry about him- or herself. . . . Instead of worrying, watch with fascination and wonder as your child's life unfolds, and help the child take responsibility for his or her own life.

CHARLOTTE DAVIS KASL, (20th-century) U.S. psychologist and author. *Finding Joy,* ch. 73 (1994).

7 Spoon feeding in the long run teaches us nothing but the shape of the spoon.

E. M. (EDWARD MORGAN) FORSTER, (20th-century) British novelist and essayist. As quoted in the *Observer,* London (October 7, 1951).

8 To see self-sufficiency as the hallmark of maturity conveys a view of adult life that is at odds with the human condition, a view that cannot sustain the kinds of long-term commitments and involvements with other people that are necessary for raising and educating a child or for citizenship in a democratic society.

CAROL GILLIGAN, (20th-century) U.S. psychologist and author. *Mapping the Moral Domain,* prologue (1988).

9 Occasionally, remind children tactfully that the oven is the only self-cleaning appliance.

FRED G. GOSMAN, (20th-century) U.S. author. *How to Be a Happy Parent . . . In Spite of Your Children,* ch. 8 (1995).

10 If your child is going to develop a healthy personality with the capacity to remain intact and grow, she must learn how to test reality, regulate her impulses, stabilize her moods, integrate her feelings and actions, focus her concentration and plan.

STANLEY I. GREENSPAN, (20th-century) U.S. child psychiatrist and author, and NANCY THORNDIKE GREENSPAN, U.S. health economist. *First Feelings: Milestones in the Emotional Development of Your Baby and Child,* ch. 6 (1985).

11 To be motivated to sit at home and study, instead of going out and playing, children need a sense of themselves over time—they need to be able to picture themselves in the future. . . . If they can't, then they're simply reacting to daily events, responding to the needs of the moment—for pleasure, for affiliation, for acceptance.

STANLEY I. GREENSPAN, (20th-century) U.S. child psychiatrist and author. *Playground Politics,* ch. 4 (1993).

12 Doing your child's homework is a bit like believing that they can get into shape by watching someone else exercise.

LAWRENCE KUTNER, (20th-century) U.S. child psychologist and author. *Parent and Child,* ch. 8 (1991).

13 Becoming responsible adults is no longer a matter of whether children hang up their pajamas or put dirty towels in the hamper, but whether they care about themselves and others—and whether they see everyday chores as related to how we treat this planet.

EDA J. LE SHAN, (20th-century) U.S. educator and author. As quoted in *Kids are Worth It,* ch. 9, Barbara Coloroso (1984).

14 If parents award freedom regardless of whether their children have demonstrated an ability to handle it, children never learn to see a clear link between responsible behavior and adult privileges.

MELINDA M. MARSHALL, (20th-century) U.S. editor and author. *Good Enough Mothers,* ch. 3 (1993).

15 Our challenge as parents is to be patient enough to allow our children to take ten minutes to do something that would take us two seconds. We need to allow our children to develop what I call their "struggle muscle." This is developed the same way any other muscle develops, through regular exercise.

STEPHANIE MARSTON, (20th-century) U.S. family therapist and author. *The Magic of Encouragement,* ch. 4 (1990).

16 Whether your child is 3 or 13, don't rush in to rescue him until you know he's done all he can to rescue himself.

BARBARA F. MELTZ, (20th-century) U.S. journalist. "Raising Kids to Be Resilient," *Boston Globe* (July 28, 1994).

17 Chores begin when your child can pick it up, put it away, fold it, sort it, or carry it out the door.

JEAN ROSS PETERSON, (20th-century) U.S. author. *It Doesn't Grow on Trees,* ch. 4 (1988).

18 It is important for practical and psychological reasons to call any reasonably stable group that rears children a family. . . . The advantage of this view is that traditional and nontraditional families can all be seen to serve the interests of children. Children can also feel com-

fortable with an approved family form, even if it is not traditional.

SANDRA SCARR, (20th-century) U.S. developmental psychologist and author. *Mother Care/Other Care,* pt. 2, ch. 5 (1984).

19 The process of becoming an empathetic, autonomous adult—through all the wondrous and exhilarating and challenging, even painful, transitions of emotional growth in childhood—is not unlike learning to walk; each step makes you stronger for the next one. But if your parent is doing the walking for you, you do not have the muscles even to support your own emotional weight. You cannot stand alone.

VICTORIA SECUNDA, (20th-century) U.S. psychologist and author. *When You and Your Mother Can't Be Friends,* ch. 2 (1990).

20 Unthinking people will often try to teach you how to do the things which you can *do* better than you can be *taught* to do them. If you are sure of all this, you can start to add to your value as a mother by learning the things that can be taught, for the best of our civilization and culture offers much that is of value, if you can take it without loss of what comes to you naturally.

D. W. WINNICOTT, (20th-century) British child psychiatrist. *Babies and their Mothers,* ch. 2 (1987).

Separations/Reunions, General

1 Some authority on parenting once said, "Hold them very close and then let them go." This is the hardest truth for a father to learn: that his children are continuously growing up and moving away from him (until, of course, they move back in).

BILL COSBY, (20th-century) U.S. comedian and author. *Fatherhood,* ch. 14 (1986).

2 "Letting go" . . . implies generosity, a talent a good mother needs in abundance. Separation is not loss, it is not cutting yourself off from someone you love. It is giving freedom to the other person to be herself before she becomes resentful, stunted, and suffocated by being tied too close. Separation is not the end of love. It creates love.

NANCY FRIDAY, (20th-century) U.S. author. *My Mother, My Self,* ch. 3 (1977).

3 Face your own ambivalence about letting go and you will be better able to help your children cope with their own feelings. The insight you gain through your own acceptance of change will bolster your confidence and make you a stronger college parent. The confidence you develop will be evident to your child, who will be able to move away from you without fear.

NORMAN GODDAM, (20th-century) U.S. psychologist and author. *Parenting Through the College Years,* ch. 1 (1988).

4 A separation situation is different for adults than it is for children. When we were very young children, a physical separation was interpreted as a violation of our inalienable rights. . . . As we grew older, the withdrawal of love, whether that meant being misunderstood, mislabeled or slighted, became the separation situation we responded to.

ROGER GOULD, (20th-century) U.S. psychotherapist and author. *Transformations,* sec. 1, ch. 1 (1978).

5 How selfhood begins with a walking away,
And love is proved in the letting go.

C. DAY LEWIS, (20th-century) British poet and author. "Walking Away."

6 Being apart is always experienced by the child, at some level, as the equivalent of being left. There is an unspoken belief, "If you loved me most of all, if I was the most important thing in your life, you would never leave me." The only way to reconcile the child with this unmovable conviction is to provide abundant proof, through emotional availability and responsiveness, that he does not need to be the only important thing in your life in order to be loved well enough and deeply enough.

ALICIA F. LIEBERMAN, (20th-century) U.S. psychologist and author. *The Emotional Life of the Toddler,* ch. 8 (1993).

7 Coming together again after a long day apart can be an experience where joy, relief, anger, and fatigue are all present in different degrees both for the parent and for the child. Because of their importance in marking the resumption of direct contact, reunions deserve as much attention and care as separations to enhance the relationship between parent and child.

ALICIA F. LIEBERMAN, (20th-century) U.S. psychologist and author. *The Emotional Life of the Toddler,* ch. 10 (1993).

8 On a subconscious level your child experiences separation from you as a "punishment." And if he is to be "rewarded" with your return, he must be very good. . . . Eager for you to come back, your finicky son would probably eat liver if your baby-sitter served it, and he wouldn't dream of resisting her at bathtime.

CATHY RINDNER TEMPELSMAN, (20th-century) U.S. journalist and author. *Child-Wise,* ch. 5 (1994).

9 Separation anxiety is a normal part of development, but individual reactions are partly explained by experience, that is, by how frequently children have been left in the care of others. . . . A mother who is never apart from her young child may be saying to him or her subliminally: "You are only safe when I'm with you."

CATHY RINDNER TEMPELSMAN, (20th-century) U.S. journalist and author. *Child-Wise,* ch. 3 (1994).

10 She has problems with separation; he has trouble with unity—problems that make themselves felt in our relationships with our children just as they do in our relations with each other. She pulls for connection; he pushes for separateness. She tends to feel shut out; he tends to feel overwhelmed and intruded upon. It's one of the reasons why she turns so eagerly to children—especially when they're very young.

LILLIAN BRESLOW RUBIN, (20th-century) U.S. sociologist and family therapist. *Intimate Strangers: Men and Women Together,* ch. 8 (1983).

11 To be a good parent, separation is only half the picture. In our fragmented, supercharged, fast-paced world, figuring out how to stay connected to our kids is the real

challenge—and the other half—of good parenting.

Ron Taffel, (20th-century) U.S. psychologist and author. *Parenting by Heart,* ch. 4 (1991).

12 Just as children, step by step, must separate from their parents, we will have to separate from them. And we will probably suffer . . . from some degree of separation anxiety: because separation ends sweet symbiosis. Because separation reduces our power and control. Because separation makes us feel less needed, less important. And because separation exposes our children to danger.

Judith Viorst, (20th-century) U.S. novelist and poet. *Necessary Losses,* ch. 14 (1986).

Separations/Reunions, as Developmental Milestones

1 When we sent our first child off to school I experienced a jarring moment, an epiphany. I had been teaching young children for many years, advising parents on a wide range of issues, including the best and most painless ways to separate from their youngsters at school. When my own time came, I found that all my good advice to others was impossible to follow myself. . . . I felt like a midwife friend of mine who had assisted in the births of hundreds of babies before her own first child was born. In the middle of labor she cried out, "I've told hundreds of women, 'you can do it,' and it can't be done."

William Ayers, (20th-century) U.S. educator and author. *To Teach: The Journey of a Teacher,* ch. 7 (1993).

2 The narcissistic, the domineering, the possessive woman can succeed in being a "loving" mother as long as the child is small. Only the really loving woman, the woman who is happier in giving than in taking, who is firmly rooted in her own existence, can be a loving mother when the child is in the process of separation.

Erich Fromm, (20th-century) German-born U.S. psychoanalyst and author. *The Art of Loving,* ch. 2 (1956).

3 There is nothing intrinsically better about a child who happily bounces off to school the first day and a child who is wary, watchful, and takes a longer time to separate from his parents and join the group. Neither one nor the other is smarter, better adjusted, or destined for a better life.

Ellen Galinsky, (20th-century) U.S. child development specialis and author. *The Preschool Years,* ch. 8 (1988).

4 Normally an infant learns to use his mother as a "beacon of orientation" during the first five months of life. The mother's presence is like a fixed light that gives the child the security to move out safely to explore the world and then return safely to harbor.

Louise J. Kaplan, (20th-century) U.S. psychologist and author. *Oneness and Separateness: From Infant to Individual,* introduction (1978).

5 The invisible bond that gives the baby rein to discover his place in the world also brings the creeping baby back to home base. . . . In this way he recharges himself. He refuels on the loving energies that

flow to him from his mother. Then he's off for another foray of adventure and exploration.

Louise J. Kaplan, (20th-century) U.S. psychologist and author. *Oneness and Separateness: From Infant to Individual,* ch. 4 (1978).

6 When he was a crawler he left your feet to journey to the sofa and bring you a ball. When he was a toddler he left your side to journey across the grass and bring you a leaf. When he was a pre-school child he left your yard to journey next door and bring you back a neighbor's doll. Now he will journey into school and bring you back a piece of his new world. . . . His journeys are all outwards now, into that waiting world. But he feels the invisible and infinitely elastic threads that still guide him back to you. He returns to the base that is you, seeking rest and re-charging for each new leap into life.

Penelope Leach, (20th-century) British child development specialist and author. *Your Baby and Child,* ch. 6 (1977).

7 Acknowledging separation feelings directly and sympathetically is the best way of coping with them. It is actually helpful to tell a toddler "I'll miss you," or "I will think of you during the day," or "It is hard to say goodbye," or "I can't wait to see you at the end of the day." These messages tell the child that he is important to the parent even when they are not together and that out of sight need not mean out of mind.

Alicia F. Lieberman, (20th-century) U.S. psychologist and author. *The Emotional Life of the Toddler,* ch. 10 (1993).

8 Like sleep disturbances, some worries at separation can be expected in the second year. If you accept this, then you will avoid reacting to this anxiety as if it's your fault. A mother who feels guilty will appear anxious to the child, as if to affirm the child's anxiety. By contrast, a parent who understands that separation anxiety is normal is more likely to react in a way that soothes and reassures the child.

Cathy Rindner Tempelsman, (20th-century) U.S. journalist and author. *Child-Wise,* ch. 3 (1994).

9 When we leave our child in nursery school for the first time, it won't be just our child's feelings about separation that we will have to cope with, but our own feelings as well—from our present and from our past, parents are extra vulnerable to new tremors from old earthquakes.

Fred Rogers, (20th-century) U.S. children's television personality and author. *Mister Rogers Talks With Parents,* ch. 1 (1983).

Social Skills

1 A child who is not rigorously instructed in the matter of table manners is a child whose future is being dealt with cavalierly. A person who makes an admiral's hat out of linen napkins is not going to be in wild social demand.

Fran Lebowitz, (20th-century) U.S. humorist and author. *The Fran Lebowitz Reader,* "Parental Guidance (1994).

2 If twins are believed to be less intelligent as a class than single-born children, it is not surprising that many times they are also seen as

ripe for social and academic problems in school. No one knows the extent to which these kind of attitudes affect the behavior of multiples in school, and virtually nothing is known from a research point of view about social behavior of twins over the age of six or seven, because this hasn't been studied either.

PAMELA PATRICK NOVOTNY, (20th-century) U.S. journalist and author. *The Joy of Twins,* ch. 9 (rev. 1994).

3 Most adults will do anything to avoid going to a party where they don't know anyone. But for some reason we may be impatient with the young child who hesitates on the first day of school, or who recoils from the commotion of a birthday party where there are no familiar faces.

CATHY RINDNER TEMPELSMAN, (20th-century) U.S. journalist and author. *Child-Wise,* ch. 8 (1994).

4 Although adults have a role to play in teaching social skills to children, it is often best that they play it unobtrusively. In particular, adults must guard against embarrassing unskilled children by correcting them too publicly and against labeling children as shy in ways that may lead the children to see themselves in just that way.

ZICK RUBIN, (20th-century) U.S. social psychologist and author. *Children's Friendships,* ch. 4 (1980).

5 Children, then, acquire social skills not so much from adults as from their interactions with one another. They are likely to discover through trial and error which strategies work and which do not, and later to reflect consciously on what they have learned.

ZICK RUBIN, (20th-century) U.S. social psychologist and author.*Children's Friendships,* ch. 4 (1980).

6 If you would grow great and stately,
You must try to walk sedately.

ROBERT LOUIS STEVENSON, (19th-century) British poet and author. *A Child's Garden of Verses,* "Good and Bad Children" (1885).

7 This is no argument against teaching manners to the young. On the contrary, it is a fine old tradition that ought to be resurrected from its current mothballs and put to work. . . . In fact, children are much more comfortable when they know the guide rules for handling the social amenities. It's no more fun for a child to be introduced to a strange adult and have no idea what to say or do than it is for a grownup to go to a formal dinner and have no idea what fork to use.

LEONTINE YOUNG, (20th-century) U.S. social worker and author. *Life Among the Giants,* ch. 2 (1965).

Spoiling

1 To try to control a nine-month-old's clinginess by forcing him away is a mistake, because it counteracts a normal part of the child's development. To think that the child is clinging to you because he is spoiled is nonsense. Clinginess is not a discipline issue, at least not in the sense of correcting a wrongdoing.

LAWRENCE BALTER, (20th-century) U.S. psychologist and author. *Who's In Control?* ch. 2 (1989).

2 To worry about spoiling an infant by comforting him when he cries is needless. . . . If you put the baby down and the baby cries, pick him up. His crying isn't a habit you should try to break. Your baby can't be taught not to cry.

LAWRENCE BALTER, (20th-century) U.S. psychologist and author. *Who's In Control?* ch. 2 (1989).

3 You "spoil" a child if you give in to every request, never say no, and abdicate your responsibility to decide for him what is best.

RICHARD FERBER, (20th-century) U.S. pediatrician and author. *Solve Your Child's Sleep Problems,* ch. 5 (1985).

4 In order to become spoiled . . . a child has to be able to want things as well as need them. He has to be able to see himself as a being who is separate from everyone else. . . . A baby is none of these things. He feels a need and he expresses it. He is not intellectually capable of working out involved plans and ideas like "Can I make her give me . . . ?" "If I make enough fuss he will . . . ?" "They let me do . . . yesterday and I want to do it again today so I'll. . . ."

PENELOPE LEACH, (20th-century) British child development specialist and author. *Your Baby and Child,* ch. 3 (1983).

5 True spoiling is nothing to do with what a child owns or what amount of attention he gets. He can have the major part of your income, living space and attention and not be spoiled, or he can have very little and be spoiled. It is not what he gets that is at issue. It is how and why he gets it. Spoiling is to do with the family balance of power.

PENELOPE LEACH, (20th-century) British child development specialist and author. *Your Baby and Child,* ch. 6 (1983).

6 Could it be that those who were reared in the postwar years really were spoiled, as we used to hear? Did a child-centered generation, raised in depression and war, produce a self-centered generation that resents children and parenthood?

C. JOHN SOMMERVILLE, (20th-century) U.S. historian and author. *The Rise and Fall of Childhood,* ch. 1 (rev. 1990).

Sex/Sexuality/ Sex Education at Home

1 Sexual activity, for women, has a history of vulnerability, in a way it simply does not have for men. The mother has to teach this hidden text to her daughter. The mother's warnings, her attempts to halt sexual development in her daughter, are not so much signs of disapproval or envy, but of fear.

TERRI APTER, (20th-century) British psychologist and author. *Altered Loves,* ch. 4 (1990).

2 Young men have strong passions and tend to gratify them indiscriminately. Of the bodily desires, it is the sexual by which they are most swayed and in which they show absence of control. . . . They are changeable and fickle in their desires which are violent while they last, but quickly over: their impulses are keen but not deep rooted.

ARISTOTLE, (4th century B.C.) Greek philosopher.

3 The atmosphere parents wish to create when talking with children

about birth and reproduction is warm, honest, and reassuring, one that tells children they are free to ask questions as often as they need to, and you will answer them as lovingly as you know how.

Joanna Cole, (20th-century) U.S. author. *How You Were Born,* ch. 1 (1993).

4 During the later childhood years . . . is not a time for you to stop bringing up correct information about sexuality. . . . Misinformation is flowing just as fast in the school yard, on the streets, through the media, and sometimes in your kid's head. Don't be lulled into thinking that because you've explained it, the school taught it, or your child saw it on TV, he really got it.

Barbara Coloroso, (20th-century) U.S. parent educator and author. *Kids Are Worth It,* ch. 14 (1994).

5 Having worked with many pregnant teenagers, I've yet to see one of them pregnant on information. It just doesn't happen. Kids are less likely to have intercourse in their teen years . . . if they are given good information, have open communication with their parents, and see their parents interacting in sexually healthy ways.

Barbara Coloroso, (20th-century) U.S. parent educator and author. *Kids Are Worth It,* ch. 14 (1994).

6 As a parent, you can play three important roles in teaching your children about sex. As a *model* for your child, your own comfort level can instill a sense of confidence and trust that will reinforce his or her healthy curiosity about the world. As an *information source,* you can make sure that curiosity is satisfied with clear and accurate facts about the body, the sexes, and how babies are made. Finally, as a *guide to values,* you can guarantee that the messages your child receives about sex are invested with the family values you want to instill.

Patricia Farrell, (20th-century) U.S. school administrator. "Families and Futures," *Montessori Life* (Fall 1992).

7 The family remains the main school in which the young learn about sex roles, for better and for worse. If a wider range of roles is to be available to both sexes, changes must begin within the family. The future of the family is thus bound up with the hopes for women's future liberation and for men's emancipation from the prison of male convention.

Joseph Featherstone, (20th-century) U.S. social critic. "Family Matters," *Harvard Educational Review* (February 1979).

8 Far more critical to children than learning the details of intercourse at a young age is . . . that they learn to think of themselves as worthy of the respect of others and capable of making their own decisions, for that self-concept will inoculate them against many forms of sexual exploitation when they become older.

Lawrence Kutner, (20th-century) U.S. child psychologist and author. *Parent and Child,* ch. 4 (1991).

9 Since good fathers aren't so insecure about their sexuality, they aren't preoccupied with the gender division of parental labor. . . . Their children reap the benefits of Dad's warmth and flexibility, including academically; androgynous fathers

do not have preconceptions, say, that boys alone excel in science and girls alone are good at English. Rather they encourage their children's gender-neutral talents.

VICTORIA SECUNDA, (20th-century) U.S. psychologist and author. *Women and Their Fathers,* ch. 4 (1992).

10 Gays are not liberated yet. Their struggle is just beginning in an American culture that is still essentially fearful about homosexuality. But some mothers of gays now march proudly in Gay Liberation parades—their children are just as precious to them as the children being defended by anti-gay forces. No matter how anyone feels on this explosive subject, mothers and their gay children are here to stay and everyone might as well get on with dealing with, understanding, and accepting this fact.

LIZ SMITH, (20th-century) U.S. columnist and author. *The Mother Book,* "Mothers and Gaiety," (1978).

11 Whether we see ourselves as traditional or progressive in our views about sexuality, we may not, in the end, have very much of a say over how our children will handle this aspect of their lives. . . . We can talk with them; reason with them; we can try to examine together our sense of the possible alternatives and consequences. But in the end they choose.

JEAN JACOBS SPEIZER, (20th-century) U.S. author. *Ourselves and Our Children,* the Boston Women's Health Book Collective, ch. 4 (1978).

12 Perhaps the best function of parenthood is to teach the young creature to love with *safety,* so that it may be able to venture unafraid when later emotion comes; the thwarting of the instinct of love is the root of all sorrow and not sex only but divinity itself is insulted when it is repressed.

FREYA STARK, (20th-century) British travel author. *Traveller's Prelude,* ch. 10 (1950).

13 Literature is mostly about having sex and not much about having children. Life is the other way around.

JOHN K. VAN DE KAMP, (20th-century) Attorney general of California. As quoted in *Childhood's Future,* Richard Louv, pt. 1 (1981).

14 The upshot of pervasive public belief in the uncontrollable sexuality of teenagers, and even of preteenagers, is that parents are halfhearted in their efforts to supervise and control their children, even when they are filled with anxiety as to their children's ability to cope with a full-fledged sexual relationship. "How can we buck the tide?" parents say helplessly, often without making quite certain that the ocean they see is a real one and not a mirage.

MARIE WINN, (20th-century) U.S. author. *Children Without Childhood,* ch. 1 (1981).

Temperament

1 That a good fit between parental handling and child temperament is vital to help children adapt to the imperatives of their society is a crucial concept that can be applied to other cultures.

STELLA CHESS, (20th-century) U.S. psychiatrist and author. As quoted in *The Difficult Child,* Foreword, Stanley Turecki (1985).

2 Always remember that a child doesn't have to be average to be normal. Children with very different temperaments can be equally successful.

LAWRENCE KUTNER, (20th-century) U.S. child psychologist and author. *Pregnancy and Your Baby's First Year,* ch. 8 (1993).

3 It's largely the luck of the draw as to what type of temperament your child has.

LAWRENCE KUTNER, (20th-century) U.S. child psychologist and author. *Pregnancy and Your Baby's First Year,* ch. 8 (1993).

4 Children are just *different* from one another, especially in temperament. Some are shy, others bold; some active, others quiet; some confident, others less so. Respect for individual differences is in my view the cornerstone of good parent-child relationships.

SANDRA SCARR, (20th-century) U.S. developmental psychologist and author. *Mother Care/Other Care,* pt. 2, ch. 5 (1984).

5 Temperament is the natural, inborn style of behavior of each individual. It's the how of behavior, not the why. . . . The question is not, " Why does he behave a certain way if he doesn't get a cookie?" but rather, "When he doesn't get a cookie, how does he express his displeasure. . . ?" The environment—and your behavior as a parent—can influence temperament and interplay with it, but it is not the cause of temperamental characteristics.

STANLEY TURECKI, (20th-century) U.S. psychiatrist and author. *The Difficult Child,* ch. 1 (1985).

Tolerance

1 Rarely do American parents deliberately teach their children to hate members of another racial, religious, or nationality group. Many parents, however, communicate the prevailing racial attitudes to their children in subtle and sometimes unconscious ways.

KENNETH MACKENZIE CLARK, (20th-century) U.S. psychologist and author. *Prejudice and Your Child,* ch. 2 (rev. 1955).

2 Children who begin life with an eagerness to please need to know that *not* pleasing is also all right now and then. They learn tolerance for others' faults through our tolerance of their own.

CATHY RINDNER TEMPELSMAN, (20th-century) U.S. journalist and author. *Child-Wise,* ch. 14 (1994).

3 Children who have poor self-esteem tend to be more prejudiced; those with higher self-esteem are more open-minded.

VERNA SIMPKINS, (20th-century) U.S. journalist. *The New York Times* (October 7, 1991).

4 Parents' accepting attitudes can help children learn to be open and tolerant. Parents can explain unfamiliar behavior or physical handicaps and show children that the appropriate response to differences should be interest rather than revulsion.

DIAN G. SMITH, (20th-century) U.S. author. *Parents' Guide to Raising Kids in a*

Changing World, Preschool Through Teen Years.

Values

1 To be faced with what so-and-so's mother lets him do, or what the teacher said in class today or what all the kids are wearing is to be required to reexamine some part of our belief structure. Each time we rethink our values we reaffirm them or begin to change them. Seen in this way, parenthood affords us an exceptional opportunity for growth.

RUTH DAVIDSON BELL, (20th-century) U.S. author. *Ourselves and Our Children,* the Boston Women's Health Book Collective, ch. 3 (1978).

2 Awareness of having better things to do with their lives is the secret to immunizing our children against false values—whether presented on television or in "real life." The child who finds fulfillment in music or reading or cooking or swimming or writing or drawing is not as easily convinced that he needs recognition or power or some "high" to feel worthwhile.

POLLY BERRIEN BERENDS, (20th-century) U.S. author. *Whole Child/Whole Parent,* ch. 7 (rev. 1987).

3 Our children need to be able to see us take a stand *for* a value and *against* injustices, be those values and injustices in the family room, the boardroom, the classroom, or on the city streets.

BARBARA COLOROSO, (20th-century) U.S. parent educator and author. *Kids Are Worth It,* ch. 9 (1994).

4 Family values are a little like family vacations—subject to changeable weather and remembered more fondly with the passage of time. Though it rained all week at the beach, it's often the momentary rainbows that we remember.

LESLIE DREYFOUS, (20th-century) U.S. journalist. "In a World of Cahnge, What Are Family Values?" The Associated Press, (October 25, 1992).

5 What we often take to be family values—the work ethic, honesty, clean living, marital fidelity, and individual responsibility—are in fact social, religious, or cultural values. To be sure, these values are transmitted by parents to their children and are familial in that sense. They do not, however, *originate* within the family.

DAVID ELKIND, (20th-century) U.S. child psychologist and author. *Ties that Stress,* ch. 4 (1994).

6 It is not easy to construct by mere scientific synthesis a foolproof system which will lead our children in a desired direction and avoid an undesirable one. Obviously, good can come only from a continuing interplay between that which we, as students, are gradually learning and that which we believe in, as people.

ERIK H. ERIKSON, (20th-century) German-born U.S. psychoanalyst and author. *Childhood and Society,* ch. 11 (1950).

7 Our first line of defense in raising children with values is modeling good behavior ourselves. This is critical. How will our kids learn tolerance for others if our hearts are filled with hate? Learn compassion if we are indifferent? Perceive academics as important if soccer

practice is a higher priority than homework?

FRED G. GOSMAN, (20th-century) U.S. author. *How to Be a Happy Parent . . . In Spite of Your Children,* ch. 11 (1995).

8 If mothers are to be successful in achieving their child-rearing goals, they must have the inner freedom to find their own value system and within that system to find what is acceptable to them and what is not. This means leaving behind the anxiety, but also the security, of simplistic good-bad formulations and deciding for themselves what they want to teach their children.

ELAINE HEFFNER, (20th-century) U.S. psychiatrist and author. *Mothering,* ch. 4 (1978).

9 The most powerful lessons about ethics and morality do not come from school discussions or classes in character building. They come from family life where people treat one another with respect, consideration, and love.

NEIL KURSHAN, (20th-century) U.S. rabbi and author. *Raising Your Child to Be a Mensch,* ch. 3 (1987).

10 With the breakdown of the traditional institutions which convey values, more of the burdens and responsibility for transmitting values fall upon parental shoulders, and it is getting harder all the time both to embody the virtues we hope to teach our children and to find for ourselves the ideals and values that will give our own lives purpose and direction.

NEIL KURSHAN, (20th-century) U.S. rabbi and author. *Raising Your Child to Be a Mensch,* ch. 4 (1987).

11 I describe family values as responsibility towards others, increase of tolerance, compromise, support, flexibility. And essentially the things I call the silent song of life—the continuous process of mutual accommodation without which life is impossible.

SALVADOR MINUCHIN, (20th-century) U.S. child psychiatrist and family therapist. As quoted in "On Family Therapy: A Visit with Salvador Minuchin," *Psychology Today* (March–April 1993).

12 I doubt that we can ever successfully impose values or attitudes or behaviors on our children—certainly not by threat, guilt, or punishment. But I do believe they can be induced through relationships where parents and children are growing together. Such relationships are, I believe, built on trust, example, talk, and caring.

FRED ROGERS, (20th-century) U.S. children's television personality and author. *Mister Rogers Talks With Parents,* ch. 6 (1983).

13 Two big questions present themselves to every parent in one form or another: "What kind of human being do I want my child to become?" and "How can I go about making that happen?"

VIRGINIA SATIR, (20th-century) U.S. family therapist and author. *The New Peoplemaking,* ch. 15 (1988).

Family Relationships

Birth Order

1 In families children tend to take on stock roles, as if there were hats hung up in some secret place, visible only to the children. Each succeeding child selects a hat and takes on that role: the good child, the black sheep, the clown, and so forth.

ELLEN GALINSKY, (20th-century) U.S. child development specialist and author. *Between Generations,* ch. 3 (1981).

2 Every milestone of a firstborn is scrutinized, photographed, recorded, replayed, and retold by doting parents to admiring relatives and disinterested friends. . . . While subsequent children will strive to keep pace with siblings a few years their senior, the firstborn will always have a seemingly Herculean task of emulating his adult parents.

MARIANNE E. NEIFERT, (20th-century) U.S. pediatrician and author. *Dr. Mom's Parenting Guide,* ch. 4 (1991).

3 Unfortunately, life may sometimes seem unfair to middle children, some of whom feel like an afterthought to a brilliant older sibling and unable to captivate the family's attention like the darling baby. Yet the middle position offers great training for the real world of lowered expectations, negotiation, and compromise. Middle children who often must break the mold set by an older sibling may thereby learn to challenge family values and seek their own identity.

MARIANNE E. NEIFERT, (20th-century) U.S. pediatrician and author. *Dr. Mom's Parenting Guide,* ch. 4 (1991).

4 Being in a family is like being in a play. Each birth order position is like a different part in a play, with distinct and separate characteristics for each part. Therefore, if one sibling has already filled a part, such as the good child, other siblings may feel they have to find other parts to play, such as rebellious child, academic child, athletic child, social child, and so on.

JANE NELSON, (20th-century) U.S. family therapist and author. *Positive Discipline,* ch. 3 (1981).

5 If we are the younger, we may envy the older. If we are the older, we may feel that the younger is always being indulged. In other words, no

matter what position we hold in family order of birth, we can prove beyond a doubt that we're being gypped.

JUDITH VIORST, (20th-century) U.S. novelist and poet. *Necessary Losses,* ch. 6 (1986).

Families, General

1 If the family were a container, it would be a nest, an enduring nest, loosely woven, expansive, and open. If the family were a fruit, it would be an orange, a circle of sections, held together but separable—each segment distinct. If the family were a boat, it would be a canoe that makes no progress unless everyone paddles. If the family were a sport, it would be baseball: a long, slow, nonviolent game that is never over until the last out. If the family were a building, it would be an old but solid structure that contains human history, and appeals to those who see the carved moldings under all the plaster, the wide plank floors under the linoleum, the possibilities.

LETTY COTTIN POGREBIN, (20th-century) U.S. editor and author. *Family and Politics,* ch. 2 (1983).

2 [Our family is] a wonderfully messy arrangement, in which relationships overlap, underlie, support, and oppose one another. It didn't always come together easily nor does it always stay together easily. It's known very good times and very bad ones. It has held together, often out of shared memories and hopes, sometimes out of the lure of my sisters' cooking, and sometimes out of sheer stubbornness. And like the world itself, our family is renewed by each baby.

MARGE KENNEDY, (20th-century) U.S. author. *100 Things You Can Do To Keep Your Family Together . . . , introduction* (1994).

3 Soup is a lot like a family. Each ingredient enhances the others; each batch has its own characteristics; and it needs time to simmer to reach full flavor.

MARGE KENNEDY, (20th-century) U.S. author. *100 Things You Can Do to Keep Your Family Together . . . ,* pt. 2 (1994).

4 Family life is not a computer program that runs on its own; it needs continual input from everyone.

NEIL KURSHAN, (20th-century) U.S. rabbi and author. *Raising Your Child to Be a Mensch,* ch. 4 (1987).

5 The touchstone for family life is still the legendary "and so they were married and lived happily ever after." It is no wonder that any family falls short of this ideal.

SALVADOR MINUCHIN, (20th-century) U.S. child psychiatrist and family therapist. *Families and Family Therapy,* ch. 3 (1974).

6 Families and societies are small and large versions of one another. Both are made up of people who have to work together, whose destinies are tied up with one another. Each features the components of a relationship: leaders perform roles relative to the led, the young to the old, and male to female; and each is involved with the process of decision-making, use of authority, and the seeking of common goals.

VIRGINIA SATIR, (20th-century) U.S. family therapist and author. *The New Peoplemaking,* ch. 24 (1988).

7 It is now clear to me that the family is a microcosm of the world. To understand the world, we can study the family: issues such as power, intimacy, autonomy, trust, and communication skills are vital parts underlying how we live in the world. To change the world is to change the family.

Virginia Satir, (20th-century) U.S. family therapist and author. *The New Peoplemaking,* ch. 1 (1988).

8 Children thrive in a variety of family forms; they develop normally with single parents, with unmarried parents, with multiple caretakers in a communal setting, and with traditional two-parent families. What children require is loving and attentive adults, not a particular family type.

Sandra Scarr, (20th-century) U.S. developmental psychologist and author. *Mother Care/Other Care,* pt. 2, ch. 5 (1984).

Families, Children's Role in

1 Honour thy father and thy mother: that thy days may be long upon the land which the Lord thy God giveth thee.

Bible: Hebrew *Exodus* 20:12, one of the Ten Commandments.

2 It is not a bad thing that children should occasionally, and politely, put parents in their place.

Colette [Sidonie Gabrielle Colette], (1873–1954) French novelist and author. *The Priest on the Wall* (1922).

(1922).

3 Your children are not your children.
They are the sons and daughters of Life's longing for itself.
They came through you but not from you.
And though they are with you yet they belong not to you.
You may give them your love but not your thoughts,
For they have their own thoughts.
You may house their bodies but not their souls,
For their souls dwell in the house of tomorrow, which you cannot visit, not even in your dreams.
You may strive to be like them, but seek not to make them like you,
For life goes not backward nor tarries with yesterday.
You are the bows from which your children as living arrows are sent forth.

Kahlil Gibran, (1883–1931) Lebanese-born U.S. poet and painter. "On Children," *The Prophet,* 1923.

4 Your children are not here to fill the void left by marital dissatisfaction and disengagement. They are not to be utilized as a substitute for adult-adult intimacy. They are not in this world in order to satisfy a wife's or a husband's need for love, closeness or a sense of worth. A child's task is to fully develop his/her emerging self. When we place our children in the position of satisfying our needs, we rob them of their childhood.

Aaron Hess, (20th-century) U.S. psychotherapist. *The Gift of Fatherhood,* ch. 9 (1994).

5 Our kids are not here to comfort us, to entertain us, or to validate us. Those things need to come

from ourselves and from other adults.

MARGE KENNEDY, (20th-century) U.S. author. *The Single Parent Family,* ch. 1 (1994).

6 Children can't be a center of life and a reason for being. They can be a thousand things that are delightful, interesting, satisfying, but they can't be a wellspring to live from. Or they shouldn't be.

DORIS LESSING, (20th-century) British author. As quoted in *Woman to Woman,* Julia Gilden and Mark Riedman (1994).

7 It is possible to make friends with our children—but probably not while they are children. . . . Friendship is a relationship of mutual dependence-interdependence. A family is a relationship in which some of the participants are dependent on others. It is the job of parents to provide for their children. It is not appropriate for adults to enter into parenthood recognizing they have made a decision to accept dependents and then try to pretend that their children are not dependent on them.

DONALD C. MEDEIROS, (20th-century) U.S. psychologist and author. *Children Under Stress,* ch. 1 (1983).

8 Parents have to get over the idea that their children belong just to them; children are a family affair.

FRANK PITTMAN, (20th-century) U.S. psychiatrist and family therapist. "How to Manage Mom and Dad," *Psychology Today* (November/December 1994).

9 Parents learn a lot from their children about coping with life.

MURIEL SPARK, (20th-century) British novelist. *The Comforters,* ch. 6 (1957).

Families, their Role in Development

1 The family endures because it offers the truth of mortality and immortality within the same group. The family endures because, better than the commune, kibbutz, or classroom, it seems to individualize and socialize its children, to make us feel at the same time unique and yet joined to all humanity, accepted as is and yet challenged to grow, loved unconditionally and yet propelled by greater expectations. Only in the family can so many extremes be reconciled and synthesized. Only in the family do we have a lifetime in which to do it.

LETTY COTTIN POGREBIN, (20th-century) U.S. editor and author. *Family and Politics,* ch. 2 (1983).

2 We are born into them, marry into them, even create them among the people we love. They come large and extended . . . or small and nuclear. But whatever their size or wherever they live, strong families give us the nurturance and strength we need in order to survive.

ANDREA DAVIS, (20th-century) U.S. author. Contemporary Living column, *Essence* magazine (August 1990).

3 At best the family teaches the finest things human beings can learn from one another—generosity and love. But it is also, all too often, where we learn nasty things like hate, rage and shame.

BARBARA EHRENREICH, (20th-century) U.S. essayist and author. *The Snarling Citizen,* "Oh, Those Family Values" (1995).

4 Our conversation begins to look like the last scene in Eugene

O'Neill's great family drama, *Long Day's Journey Into the* [sic] *Night.* Sitting together in a dwindling pool of light, the family talks on. Fathers, mothers, brothers, sisters are trying to explain: not understanding, but comprehending; loving one another, but hating and hurting each other; tangling and untangling like badly cast fishing lines, a group of inviolate, wounded selves. O'Neill's characters, like the rest of us, are speaking about the family in order to explain their attitudes toward life itself.

JOSEPH FEATHERSTONE, (20th-century) U.S. social critic. "Family Matters," *Harvard Educational Review,* (February 1979).

5 The family is both a biological and a cultural group. It is biological in sense that it is the best arrangement for begetting children and protecting them while they are dependent. It is a cultural group because it brings into intimate association persons of different age and sex who renew and reshape the folkways of the society into which they are born. The household serves as a "cultural workshop" for the transmission of old traditions and for the creation of new social values.

ARNOLD GESELL, (20th-century) U.S. child development specialist. *Infant and Child in the Culture of Today,* ch. 1 (1943).

6 Children belong in families, which, ideally, serve as a sanctuary and a cushion from the world at large. Parents belong to society and are a part of that greater world. Sometimes parents are a channel to the larger society, sometimes they are a shield from it. Ideally they act as filters, guiding their children and teaching them to avoid the tempting trash.

LOUISE HART, (20th-century) U.S. community psychologist and author. *On the Wings of Self-Esteem,* ch. 3 (1994).

7 In truth a family is what you make it. It is made strong, not by the number of heads counted at the dinner table, but by the rituals you help family members create, by the memories you share, by the commitment of time, caring, and love you show to one another, and by the hopes for the future you have as individuals and as a unit.

MARGE KENNEDY, (20th-century) U.S. author. *The Single Parent Family,* introduction (1994).

8 The informality of family life is a blessed condition that allows us all to become our best while looking our worst.

MARGE KENNEDY, (20th-century) U.S. author. *100 Things You Can Do to Keep Your Family Together . . . ,* pt. 2 (1994).

9 Far from being the basis of the good society, the family, with its narrow privacy and tawdry secrets, is the source of all our discontents.

SIR EDMUND LEACH, (20th-century) British author. *Listener* (November 30, 1967). From the BBC *Reith Lectures.*

10 In all cultures, the family imprints its members with selfhood. Human experience of identity has two elements; a sense of belonging and a sense of being separate. The laboratory in which these ingredients are mixed and dispensed is the family, the matrix of identity.

SALVADOR MINUCHIN, (20th-century) U.S. child psychiatrist and family therapist. *Families and Family Therapy,* ch. 3 (1974).

11 The institution of the family is decisive in determining not only if a person has the capacity to love another individual but in the larger social sense whether he is capable of loving his fellow men collectively. The whole of society rests on this foundation for stability, understanding and social peace.

DANIEL PATRICK MOYNIHAN, (20th-century) U.S. senator and historian. *Family and Nation,* ch. 1 (1986).

12 The family is both the fundamental unit of society as well as the root of culture. It represents a child's initial source of unconditional love and acceptance and provides lifelong connectedness with others. The family is the first setting in which socialization takes place and where children learn to live with mutual respect for one another. A family is where a child learns to display affection, control his temper, and pick up his toys. Finally, a family is a perpetual source of encouragement, advocacy, assurance, and emotional refueling that empowers a child to venture with confidence into the greater world and to become all that he can be.

MARIANNE E. NEIFERT, (20th-century) U.S. pediatrician and author. *Dr. Mom's Parenting Guide,* ch.1 (1991).

13 But however the forms of family life have changed and the number expanded, the role of the family has remained constant and it continues to be the major institution through which children pass en route to adulthood.

BERNICE WEISSBOURD, (20th-century) U.S. family advocate and author. "Family Focus," *Children Today,* vol 10, no. 2 (March/April 1981).

Fathers/Fathers' Roles

1 Fathers have a special excitement about them that babies find intriguing. At this time in his life an infant counts on his mother for rootedness and anchoring. He can count on his father to be just different enough from a mother. Fathers embody a delicious mixture of familiarity and novelty. They are novel without being strange or frightening.

LOUISE J. KAPLAN, (20th-century) U.S. psychologist and author. *Oneness and Separateness: From Infant to Individual,* ch. 4 (1978).

2 Fathers represent another way of looking at life—the possibility of an alternative dialogue.

LOUISE J. KAPLAN, (20th-century) U.S. psychologist and author. *Oneness and Separateness: From Infant to Individual,* ch. 4 (1978).

3 Important as fathers are, their influence on children shouldn't be exaggerated just because they were ignored so long. There is no evidence that there is something especially good about fathers as caretakers. There are no areas where it can be said that fathers must do certain things in order to achieve certain outcomes in children. The same goes for mothers.

MICHAEL LAMB, (20th-century) U.S. professor of psychology and pediatrics. "Report on Greater New York Area Fatherhood Forum," June 17 and 18, 1983, in *Growing Child Research Review* (November 1983).

4 Even if fathers are more benignly helpful, and even if they spend time with us teaching us what they know, rarely do they tell us what they feel. They stand apart emo-

tionally: strong perhaps, maybe caring in a nonverbal, implicit way; but their internal world remains mysterious, unseen, "What are they really like?" we ask ourselves. "What do they feel about us, about the world, about themselves?"

AUGUSTUS Y. NAPIER, (20th-century) U.S. family therapist. *The Fragile Bond,* ch. 14 (1988).

5 It is much easier to become a father than to be one.

KENT NERBURN, (20th-century) U.S. theologian and author. *Letters to My Son,* ch. 25 (1994).

6 A man doesn't have to have all the answers—children will teach him how to parent them, and in the process will teach him everything he needs to know about life.

FRANK PITTMAN, (20th-century) U.S. psychiatrist and family therapist. *Man Enough,* ch. 12 (1993).

7 Becoming Father the Nurturer rather than just Father the Provider enables a man to fully feel and express his humanity and his masculinity. Fathering is the most masculine thing a man can do.

FRANK PITTMAN, (20th-century) U.S. psychiatrist and family therapist. *Man Enough,* ch. 12 (1993).

8 Fathering makes a man, whatever his standing in the eyes of the world, feel strong and good and important, just as he makes his child feel loved and valued.

FRANK PITTMAN, (20th-century) U.S. psychiatrist and family therapist. *Man Enough,* ch. 12 (1993).

9 Fathers who compete hard with their kids are monstrous. The father, for a throw-away victory, is sacrificing the very heart of his child's sense of being good enough. He may believe he is making his son tough, as he was made tough by a similarly contending father, but he is only making his child desperate and mean like himself. Fathers must let their sons (and daughters) have their victories.

FRANK PITTMAN, (20th-century) U.S. psychiatrist and family therapist. *Man Enough,* ch. 3 (1993).

10 If fathers who fear fathering and run away from it could only see how little fathering is enough. Mostly, the father just needs to be there.

FRANK PITTMAN, (20th-century) U.S. psychiatrist and family therapist. *Man Enough,* ch. 6 (1993).

11 In colonial America, the father was the primary parent. . . . Over the past two hundred years, each generation of fathers has had less authority than the last. . . . Masculinity ceased to be defined in terms of domestic involvement, skills at fathering and husbanding, but began to be defined in terms of making money. Men had to leave home to work. They stopped doing all the things they used to do.

FRANK PITTMAN, (20th-century) U.S. psychiatrist and family therapist. *Man Enough,* ch. 6 (1993).

12 The guys who fear becoming fathers don't understand that fathering is not something perfect men do, but something that perfects the man. The end product of child raising is not the child but the parent.

FRANK PITTMAN, (20th-century) U.S. psychiatrist and family therapist. *Man Enough,* ch. 12.

13 So often, as the septuagenarian reflects on life's rewards, we hear that, "in the final analysis" of money, power, prestige, and marriage, fathering alone was what "mattered."

KYLE D. PRUETT, (20th-century) U.S. child psychiatrist and author. *The Nurturing Father,* ch. 15 (1987).

14 We have seen that men are learning that work, productivity, and marriage may be very important parts of life, but they are not its whole cloth. The rest of the fabric is made of nurturing relationships, especially those with children—relationships which are intimate, trusting, humane, complex, and full of care.

KYLE D. PRUETT, (20th-century) U.S. child psychiatrist and author. *The Nurturing Father,* ch. 15 (1987).

15 But whether a child is male or female, fathers are needed for their "otherness," to put a healthy wedge between mother and child, to be a haven from real or imagined maternal injustice or excessive hovering.

VICTORIA SECUNDA, (20th-century) U.S. psychologist and author. *Women and Their Fathers,* ch. 1 (1992).

16 If mothers are to their children the domestic world, the humdrum, the predictable, the familiar and routine, fathers are the other—periodic, bigger, stronger, strange, different. Mothers represent the day, fathers the night—and the weekend, the holiday, the special dinner out.

VICTORIA SECUNDA, (20th-century) U.S. psychologist and author. *Women and Their Fathers,* ch. 1 (1992).

17 Since it is fathers, much more than mothers, who are absent, it is not surprising that children often seem to prefer their fathers, because they so desperately crave Dad's longed-for, reassuring presence. In the delicate balance of a child's emotional negotiation, it makes perfect sense to impart to fathers heroic qualities. Surely, they think, Daddy would be here if he could; he must be doing something very important out there.

VICTORIA SECUNDA, (20th-century) U.S. psychologist and author. *Women and Their Fathers,* ch. 2 (1992).

18 The good-enough father is not simply a knight in shining armor galloping to the occasional rescue; he is there through good times and bad, insisting on and delighting in his paternity every pleasurable and painful step of the way.

VICTORIA SECUNDA, (20th-century) U.S. psychologist and author. *Women and Their Fathers,* ch. 4 (1992).

Fathers/Fathers' Roles, Historical Perspectives

1 Defining and celebrating the New Father are by far the most popular ideas in our contemporary discourse on fatherhood. Father as close and nurturing, not distant and authoritarian. Fatherhood as more than bread winning. Fatherhood as new-and-improved masculinity. Fathers unafraid of feelings. Fathers without sexism.

Fatherhood as fifty-fifty parenthood, undistorted by arbitrary gender divisions or stifling social roles.

David Blankenhorn, (20th-century) U.S. editor and author. *Fatherless America,* ch. 6 (1995).

2 More broadly across time and cultures, it seems, one perennial piece of advice to father has been the importance of acting tenderly toward their children. The New Father, it turns out, is an old story.

David Blankenhorn, (20th-century) U.S. editor and author. *Fatherless America,* ch. 6 (1995).

3 The most important domestic challenge facing the U.S. at the close of the twentieth century is the re-creation of fatherhood as a vital social role for men. At stake is nothing less than the success of the American experiment. For unless we reverse the trend of fatherlessness, no other set of accomplishments—not economic growth or prison construction or welfare reform or better schools—will succeed in arresting the decline of child well-being and the spread of male violence. To tolerate the trend of fatherlessness is to accept the inevitability of continued social recession.

David Blankenhorn, (20th-century) U.S. editor and author. *Fatherless America,* ch. 12 (1995).

4 To recover the fatherhood idea, we must fashion a new cultural story of fatherhood. The moral of today's story is that fatherhood is superfluous. The moral of the new story must be that fatherhood is essential.

David Blankenhorn, (20th-century) U.S. editor and author. *Fatherless America,* ch. 12 (1995).

5 The traditional husband/father has always made choices concerning career, life-styles, values, and directions for the whole family, but he generally had another person on the team—called a wife. And his duties were always clear: Bring home the bacon and take out the garbage.

Donna N. Douglass, (20th-century) U.S. editor and author. *Choice and Compromise,* ch. 1 (1983).

On Being a Father

1 We have to give ourselves—men in particular—permission to really be with and get to know our children. The premise is that taking care of kids can be a pain in the ass, and it is frustrating and agonizing, but also gratifying and enjoyable. When a little kid says, "I love you, Daddy," or cries and you comfort her or him, life becomes a richer experience.

Anonymous Father, as quoted in *Ourselves and Our Children,* the Boston Women's Health Book Collective, ch. 3 (1978).

2 Parenting is the one area of my life where I can feel incompetent, out of control and like a total failure all of the time.

Attorney Father, as quoted in *Reviving Ophelia,* Mary Pipher, ch. 4 (1994).

3 Then I discovered that my son had learned something new. For the first time, he was able to give a

proper kiss, puckering up his lips and enfolding my face in his arms. "Kees Dada," he said as he bussed me on the nose and cheeks. No amount of gratification at work could have compensated for that moment.

Donald H. Bell, U.S. journalist. "Conflicting Interests," *The New York Times Magazine* (July 31, 1983).

4 The meaningful role of the father of the bride was played out long before the church music began. It stretched across those years of infancy and puberty, adolescence and young adulthood. That's when she needs you at her side.

Tom Brokaw, (20th-century) U.S. broadcast journalist. "Supporting Role," *The New York Times Magazine* (December 5, 1993).

5 A new father quickly learns that his child invariably comes to the bathroom at precisely the times when he's in there, as if he needed company. The only way for this father to be certain of bathroom privacy is to shave at the gas station.

Bill Cosby, (20th-century) U.S. comedian and author. *Fatherhood,* ch. 3 (1986).

6 "Do you like being a parent—you know, being a father, having children and all?" Linnet once asked me. "Yes," I said, after a moment. "It's like dancing with a partner. It takes a lot of effort to do it well. But when it's done well it's a beautiful thing to see."

Gerald Early, (20th-century) U.S. author. *Daughters,* preface (1994).

7 I looked at my daughters, and my boyhood picture, and appreciated the gift of parenthood, at that moment, more than any other gift I have ever been given. For what person, except one's own children, would want so deeply and sincerely to have shared your childhood? Who else would think your insignificant and petty life so precious in the living, so rich in its expressiveness, that it would be worth partaking of what you were, to understand what you are?

Gerald Early, (20th-century) U.S. author. *Daughters,* pt. 2 (1994).

8 As a father I had some trouble finding the words to separate the person from the deed. Usually, when one of my sons broke the rules or a window, I was too angry to speak calmly and objectively. My own solution was to express my feelings, but in an exaggerated, humorous way: "You do that again and you will be grounded so long they will call you Rip Van Winkle II," or "If I hear that word again, I'm going to braid your tongue."

David Elkind, (20th-century) U.S. child psychologist and author. *Ties That Stress,* ch. 5 (1994).

9 Not only do our wives need support, but our children need our deep involvement in their lives. If this period [the early years] of primitive needs and primitive caretaking passes without us, it is lost forever. We can be involved in other ways, but never again on this profoundly intimate level.

Augustus Y. Napier, (20th-century) U.S. family therapist. *The Fragile Bond,* ch. 13 (1988).

10 Being a father
Is quite a bother
. . . .
You improve them mentally
And straighten them dentally,
. . . .
They're no longer corralable
Once they find that you're fallible
. . . .
But after you've raised them and
educated them and
gowned them,
They just take their little fingers
and wrap you around
them.
Being a father
Is quite a bother,
But I like it, rather.

OGDEN NASH, (20th-century) U.S. poet. "Soliloquy in Circles," *Versus* (1949).

11 I thought I never wanted to be a father. A child seemed to be a series of limitations and responsibilities that offered no reward. But when I experienced the perfection of fatherhood, the rest of the world remade itself before my eyes.

KENT NERBURN, (20th-century) U.S. theologian and author. *Letters to My Son,* ch. 25 (1993).

12 The power of this experience [fatherhood] can never be explained. It is one of those joyful codings that rumbles in the species far below understanding. When it is experienced it makes you one with all men in a way that fills you with warmth and harmony.

KENT NERBURN, (20th-century) U.S. theologian and author. *Letters to My Son,* ch. 25 (1993).

13 This is not to say that becoming a father automatically makes you a good father. Fatherhood, like marriage, is a constant struggle against your limitations and self-interests. But the urge to be a perfect father is there, because your child is a perfect gift.

KENT NERBURN, (20th-century) U.S. theologian and author. *Letters to My Son,* ch. 25 (1993).

14 [Fatherhood] is the single most creative, complicated, fulfilling, frustrating, engrossing, enriching, depleting endeavor of a man's adult life.

KYLE D. PRUETT, (20th-century) U.S. child psychiatrist and author. *The Nurturing Father,* ch. 15 (1987).

15 Dad, if you really want to know what happened in school, then you've got to know exactly who's in the class, who rides the bus, what project they're working on in science, and how your child felt that morning. . . . Without these facts at your fingertips, all you can really think to say is "So how was school today?" And you've got to be prepared for the inevitable answer—"Fine." Which will probably leave you wishing that you'd never asked.

RON TAFFEL, (20th-century) U.S. psychologist and author. *Why Parents Disagree,* ch. 8 (1994).

16 Men just don't "get" that the reason to become involved is for ourselves. Doing more with our children won't simply make women happier or keep them "off our backs," but will create a deeper, more positive connection with the kids.

RON TAFFEL, (20th-century) U.S. psychologist and author. *Why Parents Disagree,* ch. 3 (1994).

Fathers and Daughters

1 There's something like a line of gold thread running through a man's words when he talks to his daughter, and gradually over the years it gets to be long enough for you to pick up in your hands and weave into a cloth that feels like love itself. It's another thing, though, to hold up that cloth for inspection.

JOHN GREGORY BROWN, (20th-century) U.S. novelist. Catherine in *Decorations in a Ruined Cemetery*, ch. 4 (1994).

2 Fathers are still considered the most important "doers" in our culture, and in most families they are that. Girls see them as the family authorities on careers, and so fathers' encouragement and counsel is important to them. When fathers don't take their daughters' achievements and plans seriously, girls sometimes have trouble taking themselves seriously.

STELLA CHESS, (20th-century) U.S. psychiatrist and author. *Daughters*, ch. 6 (1978).

3 Fathers can seem powerful and overwhelming to their daughters. Let her see your soft side. Express your feelings and reactions. Tell her where you came from and how you got there. Let her see that you have had fears, failures, anxious times, hurts, just like hers, even though you may look flawless to her.

STELLA CHESS, (20th-century) U.S. psychiatrist and author. *Daughters*, ch. 6 (1978).

4 Women's childhood relationships with their fathers are important to them all their lives. Regardless of age or status, women who seem clearest about their goals and most satisfied with their lives and personal and family relationships usually remember that their fathers enjoyed them and were actively interested in their development.

STELLA CHESS, (20th-century) U.S. psychiatrist and author. *Daughters*, ch. 6 (1978).

5 The father of a daughter is nothing but a high-class hostage. A father turns a stony face to his sons, berates them, shakes his antlers, paws the ground, snorts, runs them off into the underbrush, but when his daughter puts her arm over his shoulder and says, "Daddy, I need to ask you something," he is a pat of butter in a hot frying pan.

GARRISON KEILLOR, (20th-century) U.S. humorist and author. *The Book of Guys*, introduction (1993).

6 When it comes to little girls, God the father has nothing on father, the god. It's an awesome responsibility.

FRANK PITTMAN, (20th-century) U.S. psychiatrist and family therapist. As quoted in *Women and Their Fathers*, Victoria Secunda, ch. 4 (1992).

7 A daughter needs a loving, available, predictable father or father figure who can be counted on, whether divorced or at home. She needs his best paternal intentions, even if his efforts occasionally fall short. She needs his maturity and limit setting and sexual oppositeness, so that she can function with confidence in the wider world of adult love and work.

VICTORIA SECUNDA, (20th-century) U.S. psychologist and author. *Women and Their Fathers*, ch. 1 (1992).

8 A doting father is not simply surprised when his little girl grows up, he is crushed. His love may have an invisible price tag that sounds a shrill alarm when she edges toward independence, planting the notion that without his vigilant ardor she can never feel safe. He will always be there for her—as long as she still worships him, still turns only to him for solace and wisdom.

VICTORIA SECUNDA, (20th-century) U.S. psychologist and author. *Women and Their Fathers,* ch. 5 (1992).

9 A father is available to help his daughter balance both her love and her anger toward her mother, to moderate the inevitable emotional extremes in the intense mother-daughter equation. With Daddy's steadying influence daughters can learn to be comfortable with healthy anger, rather than feeling that they must be eternal good girls who must at all costs conceal it.

VICTORIA SECUNDA, (20th-century) U.S. psychologist and author. *Women and Their Fathers,* ch. 3 (1992).

10 Idealizing Daddy is grand when you're five; it's crippling when you're twenty-five or thirty-five. For if you still believe in Daddy's miracles, you may not believe that you can make your own dreams come true. Worse, you may not even be able to formulate them without his guidance.

VICTORIA SECUNDA, (20th-century) U.S. psychologist and author. *Women and Their Fathers,* ch. 5 (1992).

11 If Daddy must be dethroned for daughter to begin to accept him as merely mortal, so, too, must a father give up the idea that his daughter will forever be his worshipping little girl—a process that can be peaceful or, more often than not, turbulent.

VICTORIA SECUNDA, (20th-century) U.S. psychologist and author. *Women and Their Fathers,* ch. 4 (1992).

12 It is from her father that she begins to infer messages that will linger a lifetime—"I am, or am not, considered by men to be pretty, desirable, valuable, dependent, weak, strong, dim-witted, brilliant"; "Men are, or are not, trustworthy, loving, predatory, dependable, available, dangerous."

VICTORIA SECUNDA, (20th-century) U.S. psychologist and author. *Women and Their Fathers,* ch. 1 (1992).

13 Mommy is still the front-line parent, and Daddy is still the "other." Daddy is still "different." Daddy is still a daughter's defender, her hero, the first man in her life—no matter how old she is.

VICTORIA SECUNDA, (20th-century) U.S. psychologist and author. *Women and Their Fathers,* ch. 1 (1992).

14 Most fathers don't see the war within the daughter, her struggles with conflicting images of the idealized and flawed father, her temptation both to retreat to Daddy's lap and protection and to push out of his embrace to that of beau and the world beyond home.

VICTORIA SECUNDA, (20th-century) U.S. psychologist and author. *Women and Their Fathers,* ch. 1 (1992).

15 The daughter who is her father's indulged "little princess" may spend the rest of her life stamping her foot when she doesn't get her

way, or pulling away when a love affair hits rough waters, or becoming a fair-weather friend who detaches when a chum asks too much of her.

VICTORIA SECUNDA, (20th-century) U.S. psychologist and author. *Women and Their Fathers,* ch. 5 (1992).

16 The daughters of distant fathers, when they're little, don't know about biology and cultural bias and incest taboos and gender role and economic downturns and all the buzz words of sociological, anthropological and psychological mitigation. All they know is that Daddy isn't there as much as Mommy . . . Daddy is simply the silent partner.

VICTORIA SECUNDA, (20th-century) U.S. psychologist and author. *Women and Their Fathers,* ch. 2 (1992).

17 When a father gives his daughter an emotional visa to strike out on her own, he is always with her. Such a daughter has her encouraging, understanding daddy in her head, cheering her on—not simply as a woman but as a whole, unique human being with unlimited possibilities.

VICTORIA SECUNDA, (20th-century) U.S. psychologist and author. *Women and Their Fathers,* ch. 1 (1992).

18 Our father presents an optional set of rhythms and responses for us to connect to. As a second home base, he makes it safer to roam. With him as an ally—a love—it is safer, too, to show that we're mad when we're mad at our mother. We can hate and not be abandoned, hate and still love.

JUDITH VIORST, (20th-century) U.S. novelist and poet. *Necessary Losses,* ch. 5 (1986).

Fathers and Sons

1 A wise son maketh a glad father: but a foolish son is the heaviness of his mother.

BIBLE: HEBREW, *Proverbs* 10:1.

2 Prizing a male child, although seemingly an old fashioned notion, is still widespread. . . . This strong desire for boys in the family translates into a difference in fathering. Studies show that men play with boy babies more than girl babies and in general are more involved with their families if they have at least one son. Marriages, on average, last longer if there is a son. Even divorced fathers tend to see their sons more than their daughters (at least until adolescence).

ELYSE ZORN KARLIN, (20th-century) U.S. journalist and author. *Sons: A Mother's Manual,* ch. 1 (1994).

3 It is the same for all men. None of us can escape this shadow of the father, even if that shadow fills us with fear, even if it has no name or face. To be worthy of that man, to prove something to that man, to exorcise the memory of that man from every corner of our life—however it affects us, the shadow of that man cannot be denied.

KENT NERBURN, (20th-century) U.S. theologian and author. *Letters to My Son,* ch. 1 (1994).

4 My fatherhood made me understand my parents and honor them more for the love they gave. My sonhood was revealed to me in its own perfection and I understood the reason the Chinese so value fil-

iality, the responsibility of the son to honor the parents.

KENT NERBURN, (20th-century) U.S. theologian and author. *Letters to My Son,* ch. 25 (1994).

5 Until you have a son of your own . . . you will never know the joy, the love beyond feeling that resonates in the heart of a father as he looks upon his son. You will never know the sense of honor that makes a man want to be more than he is and to pass something good and hopeful into the hands of his son. And you will never know the heartbreak of the fathers who are haunted by the personal demons that keep them from being the men they want their sons to be.

KENT NERBURN, (20th-century) U.S. theologian and author. *Letters to My Son,* prologue (1993).

6 Every boy was supposed to come into the world equipped with a father whose prime function was to be our father and show us how to be men. He can escape us, but we can never escape him. Present or absent, dead or alive, real or imagined, our father is the main man in our masculinity.

FRANK PITTMAN, (20th-century) U.S. psychiatrist and family therapist. *Man Enough,* ch. 5 (1993).

7 Many people now believe that if fathers are more involved in raising children than they were, children and sons in particular will learn that men can be warm and supportive of others as well as be high achievers. Thus, fathers' involvement may be beneficial not because it will help support traditional male roles, but because it will help break them down.

JOSEPH H. PLECK, (20th-century) U.S. professor of psychology. "Prisoners of Manliness," *Psychology Today* (September 1981).

8 For a boy to reach adulthood feeling that he knows his father, his father must allow his emotions to be visible—hardly an easy task when most males grow up being either subtly or openly taught that this is not acceptable behavior. A father must teach his son that masculinity and feelings can go hand in hand.

KYLE D. PRUETT, (20th-century) U.S. child psychiatrist and author. *The Nurturing Father,* ch. 9 (1987).

9 Having a child ends forever a man's boyhood, if not his boyishness. Having a child means that the son has, in a real sense, become his father. Sons are for fathers the twice-told tale.

VICTORIA SECUNDA, (20th-century) U.S. psychologist and author. *Women and Their Fathers,* ch. 1 (1992).

10 What thing, in honor, had my
father lost,
That need to be revived and
breathed in me?

WILLIAM SHAKESPEARE, (1564–1616) English playwright and poet. *Henry IV, pt. II.*

11 What strikes me as odd now is how much my father managed to get across to me without those heart-to-hearts which I've read about fathers and sons having in the study or in the rowboat or in the car. . . . Somehow I understood completely how he expected me to behave, in small matters as well as large, even though I can't remember being

given any lectures about it beyond the occasional, undramatic "You might as well be a mensch."

CALVIN TRILLIN, (20th-century) U.S. author. "Messages from My Father," *The New Yorker* (June 20, 1994).

12 When I was a boy of fourteen, my father was so ignorant I could hardly stand to have the old man around. But when I got to be twenty-one, I was astonished at how much he had learned in seven years.

MARK TWAIN [SAMUEL LANGHORNE CLEMENS], (1835–1910) U.S. author. "Old Times on the Mississippi," *Atlantic Monthly* (1874).

Grandparents/ Grandparenting

1 The men who are grandfathers should be the fathers. Grandpas get to do it right with their grandchildren.

ANONYMOUS GRANDPARENT, as quoted in *Women and Their Fathers,* Victoria Secunda, ch. 2 (1992).

2 Another appealing aspect to having grandparents is that they do help to give [your child] a sense of continuity—of his place in the world and in the generations. Not only do grandparents help him intellectually to comprehend that there are parents of parents, but they also aid him in understanding where he fits in the succession of things. Even a very young child can begin to feel a sense of rootedness and history.

LAWRENCE BALTER, (20th-century) U.S. psychologist and author. *Dr. Balter's Child Sense,* pt. 3, ch. 62 (1985).

3 A grandchild is a miracle, but a renewed relationship with your own children is even a greater one.

T. BERRY BRAZELTON, (20th-century) U.S. pediatrician and author. *Touchpoints,* ch. 3 (1992).

4 Grandparents who want to be truly helpful will do well to keep their mouths shut and their opinions to themselves until these are requested.

T. BERRY BRAZELTON, (20th-century) U.S. pediatrician and author. *Touchpoints,* ch. 44 (1992).

5 Although my parents have never been the kind to hint around about grandchildren, I can think of no better tribute to them than giving them some. . . . I can't help thinking that the cycle is not complete until I can introduce them to a child of their child. And I can think of no better comfort when they are gone than to know that something of them lives on, not only in me but in my children.

ANNE CASSIDY, (20th-century) U.S. journalist and author."Every Child Should Have a Father But. . . . ," *McCall's* (March 1985).

6 Why do grandparents and grandchildren get along so well? The mother.

CLAUDETTE COLBERT, (20th-century) U.S. actress. As quoted in *Wit and Wisdom from the Peanut Butter Gang,* by H. Jackson Brown (1994).

7 I love this child. Red-haired—patient and gentle like her mother—fey and funny like her father. When she giggles I can hear him when he and I were young. I am part of this child. It may be only because we share genes and therefore smell familiar to each other. . . . It may be that a part of me lives in her in some important way. . . . But for now, it's jelly beans and "Old MacDonald" that unite us.

ROBERT FULGHUM, (20th-century) U.S. author. *Uh-Oh: Some Observations from Both Sides of the Refrigerator Door . . .* (1991).

8 Even young grandparents seem enormously old to a small child, although the child may politely deny it. One small girl, feeling proud of reaching the monumental age of four, turned to her young-looking grandmother and asked, "How come I'm so old if you're so new?"

ALISON JUDSON RYERSON, (20th-century) U.S. author. *Ourselves and Our Children,* the Boston Women's Health Book Collective, ch. 5 (1978).

9 Glance in the mirror, and you see a person who doesn't "look like a grandparent." But listen to your inner urges and you will find that your "grandparent hunger," your biological need to be a grandparent and to do the best job possible in that vital role, is as insistent as it has been for all people in all places and in all times.

ARTHUR KORNHABER, (20th-century) U.S. child psychiatrist. *Grandparent Power,* afterword (1994).

10 The very fact that you don't look or act or feel like the grandparents of even a generation ago does not mean that you are less, but that you are more—in effect, an evolved form of grandparents, primed to do a bigger and more challenging job than any group before you.

ARTHUR KORNHABER, (20th-century) U.S. child psychiatrist. *Grandparent Power,* afterword (1994).

11 Becoming more flexible, open-minded, having a capacity to deal with change is a good thing. But it is far from the whole story. Grandparents, in the absence of the social institutions that once demanded civilized behavior, have their work cut out for them. Our grandchildren are hungry for our love and approval, but also for standards being set.

EDA LE SHAN, (20th-century) U.S. educator and author. *Grandparenting in a Changing World,* ch. 1 (1993).

12 Grandparents can be role models about areas that may not be significant to young children directly but that can teach them about patience and courage when we are ill or handicapped by problems of aging. Our attitudes toward retirement, marriage, recreation, even our feelings about death and dying may make much more of an impression than we realize.

EDA LE SHAN, (20th-century) U.S. educator and author. *Grandparenting in a Changing World,* ch. 3 (1993).

13 If grandparents want to have a meaningful and constructive role, the first lesson they must learn is that becoming a grandparent is not having a second chance at parenthood!

EDA LE SHAN, (20th-century) U.S. educator and author. *Grandparenting in a Changing World,* ch. 3 (1993).

14 It is strange but true that although we may have learned all sorts of important facts while raising our own children, when we become grandparents we still tend to forget a whole lot of things we knew.

EDA LE SHAN, (20th-century) U.S. educator and author. *Grandparenting in a Changing World,* ch. 4 (1993).

15 Something magical happens when parents turn into grandparents.

Their attitude changes from "money-doesn't-grow-on-trees" to spending it like it does.

PAULA LINDEN, (20th-century) U.S. author. *Taking Care of Mommy* (1983).

16 While grandma looks forward to special moments with her grandchild, she must now schedule those moments in between her other engagements, like working, working out, and being worked over (nails and hair).

PAULA LINDEN, (20th-century) U.S. author. *Taking Care of Mommy* (1983).

17 The best thing about Sassy Seats is that grandmothers cannot figure out how they work and are in constant fear of the child's falling. This often makes them forget to comment on other aspects of the child's development, like why he is not yet talking or is still wearing diapers. Some grandmothers will spend an entire meal peering beneath the table and saying, "Is that thing steady?" rather than, "Have you had a doctor look at that left hand?"

ANNA QUINDLEN, (20th-century) U.S. journalist and novelist. *Living Out Loud,* "Baby Gear" (1988).

18 The presence of a grandparent confirms that parents were, indeed, little once, too, and that people who are little can grow to be big, can become parents, and one day even have grandchildren of their own. So often we think of grandparents as belonging to the past; but in this important way, grandparents, for young children, belong to the future.

FRED ROGERS, (20th-century) U.S. children's television personality and author. *Mister Rogers Talks With Parents,* ch. 11 (1983).

19 A mother becomes a true grandmother the day she stops noticing the terrible things her children do because she is so enchanted with the wonderful things her grandchildren do.

LOIS WYSE, (20th-century) U.S. author. *Funny, You Don't Look Like a Grandmother,* introduction (1990).

20 Grandchildren are the dots that connect the lines from generation to generation.

LOIS WYSE, (20th-century) U.S. author. *Funny, You Don't Look Like a Grandmother,* "Age-Old Conversations" (1990).

21 Grandmothers are to life what the Ph.D. is to education. There is nothing you can feel, taste, expect, predict, or want that the grandmothers in your family do not know about in detail.

LOIS WYSE, (20th-century) U.S. author. *Funny, You Don't Look Like a Grandmother,* "Listen to Your Grandmother" (1990).

Home

1 Home is the place where, when you have to go there, they have to take you in.

ROBERT FROST, (1874–1963) U.S. poet. "The Death of the Hired Man" (1914).

2 Parents offer an open womb. More than anyone else in your life, mothers, and sometimes fathers, can kiss it, and make it well when their grown children need to regress and repair. More than anyone else in your life, mothers, and sometimes fathers, can catch you when you start to fall. When you are in disgrace, defeat, and despair, home may be the safest place to hide.

Frank Pittman, (20th-century) U.S. psychiatrist and family therapist. "How to Manage Mom and Dad," *Psychology Today* (November/December 1994).

3 Whatever brawls disturb the street
There should be peace at home.

Isaac Watts, (1674–1748) English theologian and hymn writer. *"Love Between Brothers and Sisters,"* xvii.

Marriage, General

1 Marriage is our last, best chance to grow up.

Joseph Barth, (20th-century) U.S. clergyman. *Ladies Home Journal* (April 1961).

2 If you feed a man, and wash his clothes, and borne his children, you and that man are married, that man is yours. If you sweep a house, and tend its fires and fill its stoves, and there is love in you all the years you are doing this, then you and that house are married, that house is yours.

Truman Capote, (20th-century) U.S. novelist. Catherine Creek, in *The Grass Harp* (1945).

3 Who of us is mature enough for offspring before the offspring themselves arrive? The value of marriage is not that adults produce children but that children produce adults.

Peter De Vries, (20th-century) U.S. author. *Tunnel of Love,* ch. 8 (1954).

4 One of the silliest lines ever said in a feature film came from *Love Story*, the 1970s hit, which immortalized the phrase, "Love means never having to say you're sorry." There are few people who would actually want to share a life with someone who held that concept near and dear.

Marge Kennedy, (20th-century) U.S. author. *100 Things You Can Do to Keep Your Family Together . . . ,* pt. 4 (1994).

5 Good marriages are built on respectful disagreement and back-and-forth cooperation. We learn to cue each other, fill in for each other, forgive each other's fumbles, celebrate small victories. We revel in the realization that we're working on something bigger than both of us, and that parenthood is not only incredibly challenging but also incredibly enriching.

Susan Lapinski, (20th-century) U.S. journalist. "Parenting Passages," *Child* (June–July 1992).

Marriage, Historical Perspectives

1 Traditionally, marriage involved a kind of bartering, rather than mutual inter-dependence or role sharing. Husbands financially and economically supported wives, while wives emotionally, psychologically and socially supported husbands. He brought home the bacon, she cooked it. He fixed the plumbing, she the psyche.

Bettina Arndt, (20th-century) Australian journalist and author. *Private Lives,* ch. 2 (1986).

2 A two-parent family based on love and commitment can be a wonderful thing, but historically speaking the "two-parent paradigm" has left an extraordinary amount of room for economic inequality, violence and male dominance.

Stephanie Coontz, (20th-century) U.S. historian. *Washington Post* (May 9, 1993).

3 Few stories are written about what happens to the princess after the wedding. Reading between the lines of other stories, we can sketch out her "happily ever after": the princess gets pregnant and hopes for sons. As long as she is faithful and bears sons, she is considered to be a good wife. We don't hear whether or not she's a good mother, unless something goes wrong with her children. . . . All of history has been written about the subsequent adventures in the chapters of his life.

ELIZABETH DEBOLD, IDELISSE MALAVE, AND MARIE WILSON, (20th-century) U.S. pychologists and authors. *Mother Daughter Revolution,* ch. 3 (1993).

4 As long as one sex was helped and one sex the helper, the system worked well. There was a balanced organizational structure. . . . Then one day the helpmate rebelled and wanted out of the subservient role. That movement caused nothing less than a total social revolution, one that will take generations to resolve.

DONNA N. DOUGLASS, (20th-century) U.S. editor and author. *Choice and Compromise,* ch. 1 (1983).

5 We attempt to remember our collective American childhood, the way it was, but what we often remember is a combination of real past, pieces reshaped by bitterness and love, and, of course, the video past—the portrayals of family life on such television programs as "Leave it to Beaver" and "Father Knows Best" and all the rest.

RICHARD LOUV, (20th-century) U.S. journalist and author. *Childhood's Future,* pt. 1, ch. 3 (1991).

6 Mothers have not always had the most important role in their children's upbringing, when they had other economic roles to play. In past centuries, fathers were the key parent in the upbringing of the next generation, because moral training, not emotional sensitivity, was thought to be central to successful child-rearing. Mothers were thought to corrupt their little ones with too much affection and not enough stern training.

SANDRA SCARR, (20th-century) U.S. developmental psychologist and author. *Mother Care/Other Care,* ch. 1 (1984).

7 It was palpable, all that wanting: Mother wanting something more, Dad wanting something more, everyone wanting something more. This wasn't going to do for us fifties girls; we were going to have to change the equation even if it meant . . . abstaining from motherhood, because clearly that was where Mother got caught.

ANNE TAYLOR FLEMING, (20th-century) U.S. author and essayist. *Motherhood Deferred,* ch. 4 (1994).

8 That, of course, was the thing about the fifties with all their patina of familial bliss: a lot of the memories were not happy, not mine, not my friends.' That's probably why the myth so endures, because of the dissonance in our lives between what actually went on at home and what went on up there on those TV screens where we were allegedly seeing ourselves reflected back.

ANNE TAYLOR FLEMING, (20th-century) U.S. author and essayist. *Motherhood Deferred,* ch. 4 (1994).

9 You watched and you saw what happened and in the accumulation

of episodes you saw the pattern: Daddy ruled the roost, called the shots, made the money, made the decisions, so you signed up on his side, and fifteen years later when the women's movement came along with its incendiary manifestos telling you to avoid marriage and motherhood, it was as if somebody put a match to a pile of dry kindling.

ANNE TAYLOR FLEMING, (20th-century) U.S. author and essayist. *Motherhood Deferred,* ch. 4 (1994).

Marriage, Husbands and Wives at Home

1 Women hope men will change after marriage but they don't; men hope women won't change but they do.

BETTINA ARNDT, (20th-century) Australian journalist and author. *Private Lives,* ch. 2 (1986).

2 Being a husband is a whole-time job. That is why so many husbands fail. They cannot give their entire attention to it.

ARNOLD BENNETT, (1867–1931) British playwright. *The Title,* act I (1918).

3 Summer is different. We now have breakfast together, for example . . . it hasn't happened in so long that we're not sure how to go about it. So we bump into each other in the kitchen. I never saw Ozzie and Harriet bump into each other in the kitchen—not once. Ozzie knew his place was at the table, while Harriet knew that her place was at the stove.

NATHAN COBB, (20th-century) U.S. journalist. "Call Us the Cleavers," *Boston Globe* (August 16, 1994).

4 Any man today who returns from work, sinks into a chair, and calls for his pipe is a man with an appetite for danger.

BILL COSBY, (20th-century) U.S. comedian and author. *Fatherhood,* ch. 5 (1986).

5 A married guy is responsible for everything, no matter what. Women, thanks to their having been oppressed all these years, are blameless, free as birds, and all the dirt they do is the result of premenstrual syndrome or postmenstrual stress or menopause or emotional disempowerment by their fathers or low expectations by their teachers or latent unspoken sexual harassment in the workplace, or some other airy excuse. The guy alone is responsible for every day of marriage that is less than marvelous and meaningful.

GARRISON KEILLOR, (20th-century) U.S. humorist and author. *The Book of Guys* (1993).

6 Our ability to fall in love requires enough comfort with our masculinity to join it with someone's femininity and feel enhanced. . . . If our mother made us feel secure and proud in our masculinity, then we want to find that again in our wife. If we are really comfortable with our mother, we can even marry a woman who is a friend rather than an adversary, and form a true partnership.

FRANK PITTMAN, (20th-century) U.S. psychiatrist and family therapist. *Man Enough,* ch. 5 (1993).

7 We know how powerful our mother was when we were little, but is our wife that powerful to us now? Must we relive our great deed of

escape from Mama with every other woman in our life?

Frank Pittman, (20th-century) U.S. psychiatrist and family therapist. *Man Enough,* ch. 7 (1993).

8 A man in the house is worth two in the street.

Mae West, (20th-century) U.S. actress. As quoted in *Woman to Woman,* Julia Gilden and Mark Riedman (1994).

9 Commuter—one who spends his life
In riding to and from his wife;
A man who shaves and takes a train,
And then rides back to shave again.

E. B. White, (20th-century) U.S. journalist and author. "The Commuter," *Poems and Sketches* (1982).

10 The only time a woman really succeeds in changing a man is when he is a baby.

Natalie Wood, (20th-century) U.S. actress. As quoted in *The Joys of Having a Child,* Bill and Gloria Adler (1993).

Mothers/Mothers' Roles

1 Who takes the child by the hand takes the mother by the heart.

Danish Proverb.

2 Mothers have as powerful an influence over the welfare of future generations as all other causes combined.

John Abbott, as quoted in *Worlds Apart,* Sara Lawrence Lightfoot, ch. 2 (1978).

3 Don't poets know it
Better than others
God can't be always everywhere; and so,
Invented Mothers.

Sir Edward Arnold, as quoted in *The Future of Motherhood,* Jessie Bernard (1974).

4 The good enough mother, owing to her deep empathy with her infant, reflects in her face his feelings; this is why he sees himself in her face as if in a mirror and finds himself as he sees himself in her. The not good enough mother fails to reflect the infant's feelings in her face because she is too preoccupied with her own concerns, such as her worries over whether she is doing right by her child, her anxiety that she might fail him.

Bruno Bettelheim, (20th-century) Austrian-born U.S. child psychologist and author. *A Good Enough Parent,* ch. 1 (1987).

5 It's the biggest on-the-job training program in existence today.

Erma Bombeck, (20th-century) U.S. humorist and author. *Motherhood, the Second Oldest Profession,* introduction (1983).

6 Motherhood is the second oldest profession in the world. It never questions age, height, religious preference, health, political affiliation, citizenship, morality, ethnic background, marital status, economic level, convenience, or previous experience.

Erma Bombeck, (20th-century) U.S. humorist and author. *Motherhood, the Second Oldest Profession,* introduction (1983).

7 Mothers are not the nameless, faceless stereotypes who appear once a year on a greeting card with their virtues set to prose, but women who have been dealt a hand for life and play each card one at a time the best way they know how. No mother is all good or all bad, all laughing or all serious, all loving or

all angry. Ambivalence rushes through their veins.

ERMA BOMBECK, (20th-century) U.S. humorist and author. *Motherhood, the Second Oldest Profession,* introduction (1983).

8 A mother is not a person to lean on but a person to make leaning unnecessary.

DOROTHY CANFIELD FISHER, (20th-century) U.S. author. As quoted in *Woman to Woman,* Julia Gilden and Mark Riedman (1994).

9 The most consistent gift and burden of motherhood is advice.

SUSAN CHIRA, (20th-century) U.S. journalist. "Still Guilty After All These Years: A Bouquet of Advice Books for the Working Mom," *The New York Times Book Review* (May 8, 1994).

10 The art of living is to function in society without doing violence to one's own needs or to the needs of others. The art of mothering is to teach the art of living to children.

ELAINE HEFFNER, (20th-century) U.S. psychiatrist and author. *Mothering,* ch. 3 (1978).

11 Mother's arms are made of tenderness,
And sweet sleep blesses the child who lies therein.

VICTOR HUGO, (1802–1885) French novelist. As quoted in *The Future of Motherhood,* Jessie Bernard (1974).

12 No mother is so wicked but she desires to have good children.

ITALIAN PROVERB.

13 The only thing that seems eternal and natural in motherhood is ambivalence.

JANE LAZARRE, (20th-century) U.S. educator and author. *The Last Word,* ed. Carolyn Warner, ch. 16. (1992)

14 Even though fathers, grandparents, siblings, memories of ancestors are important agents of socialization, our society focuses on the attributes and characteristics of mothers and teachers and gives them the ultimate responsibility for the child's life chances.

SARA LAWRENCE LIGHTFOOT, (20th-century) U.S. educator and author. *Worlds Apart,* ch. 2 (1978).

15 But while being a mother is admittedly a lifelong preoccupation, it cannot, should not, must not be a lifelong occupation. . . .

MELINDA M. MARSHALL, (20th-century) U.S. editor and author. *Good Enough Mothers,* ch. 3 (1993).

16 Motherhood in all its guises and permutations is more art than science.

MELINDA M. MARSHALL, (20th-century) U.S. editor and author. *Good Enough Mothers,* ch. 3 (1993).

17 Mothers who are strong people, who can pursue a life of their own when it is time to let their children go, empower their children of either gender to feel free and whole. But weak women, women who feel and act like victims of something or other, may make their children feel responsible for taking care of them, and they can carry their children down with them.

FRANK PITTMAN, (20th-century) U.S. psychiatrist and family therapist. *Man Enough,* ch. 7 (1993).

18 But a mother is like a broomstick or like the sun in the heavens, it does

not matter which as far as one's knowledge of her is concerned: the broomstick is there and the sun is there; and whether the child is beaten by it or warmed and enlightened by it, it accepts it as a fact in nature, and does not conceive it as having had youth, passions, and weaknesses, or as still growing, yearning, suffering, and learning.

BERNARD SHAW, (1856–1950) Irish-born British playwright and author. *Misalliance,* preface.

19 Hence the spiritual weariness of the conscientious mother: you're always finding out just one more vital tidbit.

SONIA TAITZ, (20th-century) U.S. journalist and author. *Mothering Heights,* ch. 8 (1992).

20 However, it can't be helped; mothers, if they do their job properly, are the representatives of the hard, demanding world and it is they who gradually introduce reality which is so often the enemy of impulse. There is anger with mother and hatred is somewhere even when there is absolutely no doubt of love that is mixed with adoration.

D. W. WINNICOTT, (20th-century) British child psychiatrist. *Health Education Through Broadcasting,* ch. 2 (1993).

21 It's only too easy to idealise a mother's job. We know well that every job has its frustrations and its boring routines and its times of being the last thing anyone would choose to do. Well, why shouldn't the care of babies and children be thought of that way too?

D. W. WINNICOTT, (20th-century) British child psychiatrist. *Health Education Through Broadcasting,* ch. 6 (1993).

22 Good mothers know that their relationship with each of their children is like a movable feast, constantly changing and evolving.

SUE WOODMAN, (20th-century) U.S. broadcaster and journalist. "Seven Habits of Smart Moms," *McCalls* (1995).

23 We honor motherhood with glowing sentimentality, but we don't rate it high on the scale of creative occupations.

LEONTINE YOUNG, (20th-century) U.S. social worker and author. *Life Among the Giants,* introduction (1965).

Mothers/Mothers' Roles, Historical Perspectives

1 Unpleasant questions are being raised about Mother's Day. Is this day necessary? . . . Isn't it bad public policy? . . . No politician with half his senses, which a majority of politicians have, is likely to vote for its abolition, however. As a class, mothers are tender and loving, but as a voting bloc they would not hesitate for an instant to pull the seat out from under any Congressman who suggests that Mother is not entitled to a box of chocolates each year in the middle of May.

RUSSELL BAKER, (20th-century) U.S. journalist and humorist. As quoted in *The Mother Book,* Liz Smith (1978).

2 No one who traces the history of motherhood, of the home, of child-rearing practices will ever assume the eternal permanence of our own way of institutionalizing them.

JESSIE BERNARD, (20th-century) U.S. sociologist and author. *The Future of Motherhood,* foreword (1974).

3 Fashions change, and with the new psychoanalytical perspective of the postwar period [WWII], child rearing became enshrined as the special responsibility of mothers. . . . Any shortcoming in adult life was now seen as rooted in the failure of mothering during childhood.

SYLVIA ANN HEWLETT, (20th-century) U.S. economist. *A Lesser Life,* ch. 11 (1986).

4 What is sad for women of my generation is that they weren't supposed to work if they had families. What were they to do when the children were grown—watch raindrops coming down the windowpane?

JACQUELINE KENNEDY ONASSIS, (20th-century) U.S. First Lady and editor. *The Last Word,* ed. Carolyn Warner, ch. 40 (1992).

5 Most women of [the WWII] generation have but one image of good motherhood—the one their mothers embodied. . . . Anything done "for the sake of the children" justified, even ennobled the mother's role. Motherhood was tantamount to martyrdom during that unique era when children were gods. Those who appeared to put their own needs first were castigated and shunned—the ultimate damnation for a gender trained to be wholly dependent on the acceptance and praise of others.

MELINDA M. MARSHALL, (20th-century) U.S. editor and author. *Good Enough Mothers,* pt. II (1993).

6 The women of my mother's generation had, in the main, only one decision to make about their lives: who they would marry. From that, so much else followed: where they would live, in what sort of conditions, whether they would be happy or sad or, so often, a bit of both. There were roles and there were rules.

ANNA QUINDLEN, (20th-century) U.S. journalist and novelist. *Living Out Loud,* "In the Beginning," (1988).

7 Ideas about mothers have swung historically with the roles of women. When women were needed to work the fields or shops, experts claimed that children didn't need them much. Mothers, who might be too soft and sentimental, could even be bad for children's character development. But when men left home during the Industrial Revolution to work elsewhere, women were "needed" at home. The cult of domesticity and motherhood became a virtue that kept women in their place.

SANDRA SCARR, (20th-century) U.S. developmental psychologist and author. *Mother Care/Other Care,* pt. 2, ch. 3 (1984).

8 The Depression-era generation of mothers, reared on the values of flag, Mom, and apple pie, believed in self-sacrifice and commitment to others. For them, the worst fate was to be *independent*: a spinster, or married to a man who couldn't support his family on his salary alone, and *have* to work. Their daughters, jolted by Vietnam, the sexual revolution, and feminism, were largely committed to themselves. For them, the worst fate was to be *dependent.*

VICTORIA SECUNDA, (20th-century) U.S. psychologist and author. *When You and Your Mother Can't Be Friends,* ch. 4 (1990).

9 Let's just call what happened in the eighties the reclamation of mother-

hood . . . by women I knew and loved, hard-driving women with major careers who were after not just babies per se or motherhood per se, but after a reconciliation with their memories of their own mothers. So having a baby wasn't just having a baby. It became a major healing.

ANNE TAYLOR FLEMING, (20th-century) U.S. author and essayist. *Motherhood Deferred,* ch. 4 (1994).

10 We were the daughters of the post-World War II American dream, the daughters of those idealized fifties sitcom families in which father knew best and mother knew her place and a kind of disappointment, and tense, unspoken sexuality rattled around like ice cubes in their nightly cocktails.

ANNE TAYLOR FLEMING, (20th-century) U.S. author and essayist. *Motherhood Deferred,* ch. 2 (1994).

On Being a Mother

1 Most days I feel like an acrobat high above a crowd out of which my own parents, my in-laws, potential employers, phantoms of "other women who do it" and a thousand faceless eyes stare up.

ANONYMOUS MOTHER, as quoted in *Ourselves and Our Children,* the Boston Women's Health Book Collective, ch. 2 (1978).

2 Being constantly with children was like wearing a pair of shoes that were expensive and too small. She couldn't bear to throw them out, but they gave her blisters.

BERYL BAINBRIDGE, (20th-century) British novelist. *Injury Time,* ch. 4 (1977).

3 I know how to do anything—I'm a mom.

ROSEANNE BARR ARNOLD, (20th-century) U.S. actress and comedian. As quoted in *The Last Word,* ed. Carolyn Warner, ch. 1 (1992).

4 Every one of my friends had a bad day somewhere in her history she wished she could forget but couldn't. A very bad mother day changes you forever. Those were the hardest stories to tell. . . . "I could still see the red imprint of his little bum when I changed his diaper that night. I stared at my hand, as if they were alien parts of myself . . . as if they had betrayed me. From that day on, I never hit him again."

MARY KAY BLAKELY, (20th-century) U.S. journalist and author. *American Mom,* prologue (1994).

5 However diligent she may be, however dedicated, no mother can escape the larger influences of culture, biology, fate . . . until we can actually live in a society where mothers and children genuinely matter, ours is an essentially powerless responsibility. Mothers carry out most of the work orders, but most of the rules governing our lives are shaped by outside influences.

MARY KAY BLAKELY, (20th-century) U.S. journalist and author. *American Mom,* prologue (1994).

6 However global I strove to become in my thinking over the past twenty years, my sons kept me rooted to an utterly pedestrian view, intimately involved with the most inspiring and fractious passages in human development. However unconsciously by now, motherhood informs every thought I have, influ-

encing everything I do. More than any other part of my life, being a mother taught me what it means to be human.

Mary Kay Blakely, (20th-century) U.S. journalist and author. *American Mom,* prologue (1994).

7 In motherhood, where seemingly opposite realities can be simultaneously true, the role of nurturer invariably conflicts with the role of socializer. When trouble came as it surely must, was I the good cop who understood, the bad cop who terrorized, or both?

Mary Kay Blakely, (20th-century) U.S. journalist and author. *American Mom,* ch. 4 (1994).

8 Today, only a fool would offer herself as the singular role model for the Good Mother. Most of us know not to tempt the fates. The moment I felt sure I had everything under control would invariably be the moment right before the principal called to report that one of my sons had just driven somebody's motorcycle through the high school gymnasium.

Mary Kay Blakely, (20th-century) U.S. journalist and author. *American Mom,* prologue (1994).

9 With two sons born eighteen months apart, I operated mainly on automatic pilot through the ceaseless activity of their early childhood. I remember opening the refrigerator late one night and finding a roll of aluminum foil next to a pair of small red tennies. Certain that I was responsible for the refrigerated shoes, I quickly closed the door and ran upstairs to make sure I had put the babies in their cribs instead of the linen closet.

Mary Kay Blakely, (20th-century) U.S. journalist and author. *American Mom,* prologue (1994).

10 As a mother I am often confused about how to help my children make wise decisions for themselves. One day I extol the virtues of a free and open education and the next I tell them they can't watch TV until they finish their homework. One day I tell them to eat what they like, their bodies know intuitively what they need; and the next I say, "Okay, that's it—no more junk food in this house!" I flounder like this because I have no training and very little support for this work and there are days when I'm the one who needs the parenting, even more than they do.

Martha Boesing, (20th-century) U.S. author. *Mother Journeys,* ed. Maureen T. Reddy, Martha Roth, Amy Sheldon, sec. 3 (1994).

11 I have always felt that too much time was given before the birth, which is spent learning things like how to breathe in and out with your husband (I had my baby when they gave you a shot in the hip and you didn't wake up until the kid was ready to start school), and not enough time given to how to mother after the baby is born.

Erma Bombeck, (20th-century) U.S. humorist and author. *Motherhood, the Second Oldest Profession,* ch. 1 (1983).

12 I was a closet pacifier advocate. So were most of my friends. Unknown to our mothers, we owned thirty or forty of those little suckers that were placed strategically around the

house so a cry could be silenced in less than thirty seconds. Even though bottles were boiled, rooms disinfected, and germs fought one on one, no one seemed to care where the pacifier had been.

ERMA BOMBECK, (20th-century) U.S. humorist and author. *Motherhood, the Second Oldest Profession,* ch. 7 (1983).

13 Mothers who have little sense of their own minds and voices are unable to imagine such capacities in their children. Not being fully aware of the power of words for communicating meaning, they expect their children to know what is on their minds without the benefit of words. These parents do not tell their children what they mean by "good" much less why. Nor do they ask the children to explain themselves.

MARY FIELD BELENKY, (20th-century) U.S. psychologist. *Women's Ways of Knowing,* pt. 2, ch. 8 (1986).

14 The central paradox of motherhood is that while our children become the absolute center of our lives, they must also push us back out in the world. . . . But motherhood that can narrow our lives can also broaden them. It can make us focus intensely on the moment and invest heavily in the future.

ELLEN GOODMAN, (20th-century) U.S. journalist. *Value Judgments* (1993).

15 I guess what I've really discovered is the humanizing effect of children in my life—stretching me, humbling me. Maybe my thighs aren't as thin as they used to be. Maybe my getaways aren't as glamorous. Still I like the woman that motherhood has helped me to become.

SUSAN LAPINSKI, (20th-century) U.S. journalist. "As Mom Turns Forty," *American Baby* (July 1989).

16 *Life is crazy.* Now, maybe you knew this all along. But before I had children, I actually held on to the illusion that there was some sense of order to the universe. . . . I am now convinced that we are all living in a Chagall painting—a world where brides and grooms and cows and chickens and angels and sneakers are all mixed up together, sometimes floating in the air, sometimes upside down and everywhere.

SUSAN LAPINSKI, (20th-century) U.S. journalist. "As Mom Turns Forty," *American Baby* (July 1989).

17 I have often felt that I cheated my children a little. I was never so totally theirs as most mothers are. I gave to audiences what belonged to my children, got back from audiences the love my children longed to give me.

ELEANOR ROOSEVELT, (1884–1962) U.S. First Lady and humanitarian. As quoted in *The Mother Book,* Liz Smith (1978).

18 Sometimes the laughter in mothering is the recognition of the ironies and absurdities. Sometimes, though, it's just pure, unthinking delight.

BARBARA SCHAPIRO, (20th-century) U.S. author. *Mother Journeys,* ed. Maureen T. Reddy, Martha Roth, Amy Sheldon, sec. 3 (1994).

Mothers and Daughters

1 As is the mother, so is her daughter.

BIBLE: HEBREW, *Ezekiel* 16:44.

2 The myth of independence from the mother is abandoned in mid-

life as women learn new routes around the mother—both the mother without and the mother within. A mid-life daughter may reengage with a mother or put new controls on care and set limits to love. But whatever she does, her child's history is never finished.

TERRI APTER, (20th-century) British psychologist and author. *Secret Paths,* ch. 9 (1995).

3 When a mother quarrels with a daughter, she has a double dose of unhappiness—hers from the conflict, and empathy with her daughter's from the conflict with her. Throughout her life a mother retains this special need to maintain a good relationship with her daughter.

TERRI APTER, (20th-century) British psychologist and author. *Altered Loves,* ch. 3 (1990).

4 I love my mother for all the times she said absolutely nothing. . . . Thinking back on it all, it must have been the most difficult part of mothering she ever had to do: knowing the outcome, yet feeling she had no right to keep me from charting my own path. I thank her for all her virtues, but mostly for never once having said, "I told you so."

ERMA BOMBECK, (20th-century) U.S. humorist and author. *Motherhood, the Second Oldest Profession,* ch. 42 (1983).

5 I would have gone home to my mother, but I'm not that crazy about my mother.

CHER, (20th-century) U.S. entertainer and actress. As quoted in *The Mother Book,* Liz Smith (1978).

6 We mothers are learning to mark our mothering success by our daughters' lengthening flight. When they need us, we are fiercely there. But we do not need them to need us—or to become us.

LETTY COTTIN POGREBIN, (20th-century) U.S. editor and author. *Family and Politics,* ch. 5 (1983).

7 Generation after generation of women have pledged to raise their daughters differently, only to find that their daughters grow up and fervently pledge the same thing.

ELIZABETH DEBOLD, IDELISSE MALAYE, AND MARIE WILSON, (20th-century) U.S. psychologists and authors. *Mother Daughter Revolution,* ch. 1 (1993).

8 Raising a daughter is an extremely political act in this culture. Mothers have been placed in a no-win situation with their daughters: if they teach their daughters simply how to get along in a world that has been shaped by men and male desires, then they betray their daughters' potential But, if they do not, they leave their daughters adrift in a hostile world without survival strategies.

ELIZABETH DEBOLD, IDELISSE MALAYE, AND MARIE WILSON, (20th-century) U.S. psychologists and authors. *Mother Daughter Revolution,* introduction (1993).

9 Suddenly, through birthing a daughter, a woman finds herself face to face not only with an infant, a little girl, a woman-to-be, but also with her own unresolved conflicts from the past and her hopes and dreams for the future . . . . As though experiencing an earthquake, mothers of daughters may find their lives shifted, their deep

feelings unearthed, the balance struck in all relationships once again off kilter.

ELIZABETH DEBOLD, IDELISSE MALAYE, AND MARIE WILSON, (20th-century) U.S. psychologists and authors. *Mother Daughter Revolution,* ch. 1 (1993).

10 The tension to mother the "right" way can leave a peculiar silence within mother daughter relationships—the silence of a mother's own truth and experience. Within this silence, a daughter's authentic voice can also fall silent. This is the silence of perfection. This silence of perfection prevents mothers from listening and learning from their daughters.

ELIZABETH DEBOLD, IDELISSE MALAYE, AND MARIE WILSON, (20th-century) U.S. psychologists and authors. *Mother Daughter Revolution,* ch. 5 (1993).

11 Because mothers and daughters can affirm and enjoy their commonalities more readily, they are more likely to see how they might advance their individual interests in tandem, without one having to be sacrificed for the other.

MARY FIELD BELENKY, (20th-century) U.S. psychologist. *Women's Ways of Knowing,* pt. 2, ch. 8 (1986).

12 What the daughter does, the mother did.

JEWISH PROVERB.

13 What I would like to give my daughter is freedom. And this is something that must be given by example, not by exhortation. Freedom is a loose leash, a license to be different from your mother and still be loved. . . . Freedom is . . . not insisting that your daughter share your limitations. Freedom also means letting your daughter reject you when she needs to and come back when she needs to. Freedom is unconditional love.

ERICA JONG, (20th-century) U.S. author. *Fear of Fifty,* ch. 2 (1994).

14 So I begin to understand why my mother's radar is so sensitive to criticism. She still treads the well-worn ruts of her youth, when her impression of mother was of a woman hard to please, frequently negative, and rarely satisfied with anyone—least of all herself.

MELINDA M. MARSHALL, (20th-century) U.S. editor and author. *Good Enough Mothers,* ch. 3 (1993).

15 Having children can smooth the relationship, too. Mother and daughter are now equals. That is hard to imagine, even harder to accept, for among other things, it means realizing that your own mother felt this way, too—unsure of herself, weak in the knees, terrified about what in the world to do with you. It means accepting that she was tired, inept, sometimes stupid; that she, too, sat in the dark at 2:00 A.M. with a child shrieking across the hall and no clue to the child's trouble.

ANNA QUINDLEN, (20th-century) U.S. journalist and novelist. *Living Out Loud,* "Mother's Day," (1988).

16 How deep is our desire to do better than our mothers—to bring daughters into adulthood strong and fierce yet loving and gentle, adventurous and competitive but still

nurturing and friendly, sweet yet sharp. We know as working women that we can't quite have it all, but that hasn't stopped us from wanting it all for them.

ANNE ROIPHE, (20th-century) U.S. author. "Raising Daughters," *Working Woman* (April 1994).

17 If I wanted a special doll, and I begged my mother for it, she would give me a speech about how I had three dolls at home and I didn't need another one, and remind me of how fortunate I was compared to all the poor little girls all over the world who didn't have dolls. And when she finished telling me why I shouldn't want what I wanted, I still wanted it just as badly—only I felt ashamed of myself for wanting it.

NANCY SAMALIN, (20th-century) U.S. parent educator and author. *Love and Anger: The Parental Dilemma,* ch. 2 (1991).

18 A daughter is a mother's gender partner, her closest ally in the family confederacy, an extension of her self. And mothers are their daughters' role model, their biological and emotional road map, the arbiter of all their relationships.

VICTORIA SECUNDA, (20th-century) U.S. psychologist and author. *Women and Their Fathers,* ch. 3 (1992).

19 A mother sets the tone for her daughter's life, provides a roadmap and role model, continues through the daughter's middle and old age to be her example.

VICTORIA SECUNDA, (20th-century) U.S. psychologist and author. *When You and Your Mother Can't Be Friends,* ch. 1 (1990).

20 Mothers are not simply models of femininity to their daughters but also examples of how a woman reacts to a man. Daughters learn about fathers, and men, not only by being with Dad but also by observing their parents' marital relationship—or its unraveling.

VICTORIA SECUNDA, (20th-century) U.S. psychologist and author. *Women and Their Fathers,* ch. 1 (1992).

21 Of all the haunting moments of motherhood, few rank with hearing your own words come out of your daughter's mouth.

VICTORIA SECUNDA, (20th-century) U.S. psychologist and author. *Women and Their Fathers,* ch. 3 (1992).

22 One of the largely unproductive chores of maternity is helping daughters figure out what Daddy is all about, rather than letting daughters experience Daddy for themselves. If men are mysterious to women, not the least reason is because mothers are the self-appointed code breakers of fathers' cryptic messages, an expertise that, at best, is so much guesswork.

VICTORIA SECUNDA, (20th-century) U.S. psychologist and author. *Women and Their Fathers,* ch. 3 (1992).

23 Unlike the mother-son relationship, a daughter's relationship with her mother is something akin to bungee diving. She can stake her claim in the outside world in what looks like total autonomy—in some cases, even "divorce" her mother in a fiery exit from the family—but there is an invisible emotional cord that snaps her back. For always there is the memory of mother, whose judgments are so completely absorbed into the daughter's identity that she may

wonder where Mom leaves off and she begins.

Victoria Secunda, (20th-century) U.S. psychologist and author. *Women and Their Fathers,* ch. 3 (1992).

24 Whether our relationship is strained or easy, hostile or amiable, we need [our mother] if only in memory or fantasy, to conjugate our history, validate our femaleness, and guide our way. We need to know she's there if we stumble, to love us *no matter what,* to nurture the child that resides within us even now without infantalizing us.

Victoria Secunda, (20th-century) U.S. psychologist and author. *When You and Your Mother Can't Be Friends,* ch. 1 (1990).

25 No mother-in-law ever remembers that she was once a daughter-in-law.

Anonymous.

26 I thought about all of us women and how we spend half our lives rebelling against our mothers and the next half rebelling against our daughters.

Lois Wyse, (20th-century) U.S. author. *"Diary of a Mad Grandmother"* (1990).

27 A mother-in-law and a daughter-in-law in one house are like two cats in a bag.

Yiddish Proverb.

Mothers and Sons

1 It takes twenty or so years before a mother can know with any certainty how effective her theories have been—and even then there are surprises. The daily newspapers raise the most frightening questions of all for a mother of sons: Could my once sweet babes ever become violent men? Are my sons really who I think they are?

Mary Kay Blakely, (20th-century) U.S. journalist and author. *American Mom,* prologue (1994).

2 Raising boys has made me a more generous woman than I really am. Undoubtedly, there are other routes to learning the wishes and dreams of the presumably opposite sex, but I know of none more direct, or more highly motivating, than being the mother of sons.

Mary Kay Blakely, (20th-century) U.S. journalist and author. *American Mom,* prologue (1994).

3 With boys you always know where you stand. Right in the path of a hurricane. It's all there. The fruit flies hovering over their waste can, the hamster trying to escape to cleaner air, the bedrooms decorated in Early Bus Station Restroom.

Erma Bombeck, (20th-century) U.S. humorist and author. *Motherhood, the Second Oldest Profession,* ch. 8 (1983).

4 1946: I go to graduate school at Tulane in order to get distance from a "possessive" mother. I see a lot of a red-haired girl named Maude-Ellen. My mother asks one day: "Does Maude-Ellen have warts? Every girl I've known named Maude-Ellen has had warts." Right: Maude-Ellen had warts.

Bill Bourke, (20th-century) U.S. psychologist. As quoted in *The Mother Book,* "Mothers and Sons" Liz Smith, 1978.

5 As the mother of a son, I do not accept that alienation from me is

necessary for his discovery of himself. As a woman, I will not cooperate in demeaning womanly things so that he can be proud to be a man. I like to think the women in my son's future are counting on me.

Letty Cottin Pogrebin, (20th-century) U.S. editor and author. *Family and Politics,* ch. 5 (1983).

6 When Mabelle Webb died, Clifton began the mourning that lasted until his own death. Noel Coward noted in a letter, . . . "Poor Clifton . . . is still, after two months, wailing and sobbing over Mabelle's death. As she was well over ninety, gaga, and driving him mad for years, this seems excessive and over indulgent. . . ." The most famous remark to go the rounds of Clifton Webb's friends was Noel Coward's final, acerbic one to him: "It must be tough to be orphaned at seventy-one!"

Liz Smith, (20th-century) U.S. columnist and author. As quoted in *The Mother Book,* "Sing Out Louise" (1978).

7 A man loves his sweetheart the most, his wife the best, but his mother the longest.

Irish Proverb.

8 The good mother knows that frustration teaches tolerance and that instant gratification is not always best; the too good mother meets all of her son's needs instantly. The good enough mother knows that a son needs to have ownership of his actions. She stands on the sidelines and cheers him on but lets him run past her in the race. The too good mother keeps her child from becoming independent; she mothers in a way that benefits herself, not her son.

Elyse Zorn Karlin, (20th-century) U.S. journalist and author. *Sons: A Mother's Manual,* ch. 5 (1994).

9 Remember that every son had a
mother
whose beloved son he was,
and every woman had a mother
whose beloved son she wasn't.

Marge Piercy, (20th-century) U.S. author. "Doing It Differently," *Circles on the Water* (1992).

10 A boy is not free to find a partner of his own as long as he must be the partner to his mother.

Frank Pittman, (20th-century) U.S. psychiatrist and family therapist. *Man Enough,* ch. 7 (1993).

11 A real man doesn't have to run from his mother, and may even have to face the reality that no great deed is going to be great enough for him to ransom himself completely, and he may always be in his mother's debt. If he understands that . . . he won't have to feel guilty, and he won't have to please her completely. He can go ahead and be nice to her and let her be part of his life.

Frank Pittman, (20th-century) U.S. psychiatrist and family therapist. *Man Enough,* ch. 7 (1993).

12 Breaking free from the delicious security of mother love can be a painful rupture for either mother or son. Some boys can't do it. Some mothers can't let it happen because they know the boy is not ready to leave her; others are simply not ready to give up their sons.

Frank Pittman, (20th-century) U.S. psychiatrist and family therapist. *Man Enough,* ch. 7 (1993).

13 However patriarchal the world, at home the child knows that his mother is the source of all power. The hand that rocks the cradle rules his world. . . . The son never forgets that he owes his life to his mother, not just the creation of it but the maintenance of it, and that he owes her a debt he cannot conceivably repay, but which she may call in at any time.

Frank Pittman, (20th-century) U.S. psychiatrist and family therapist. *Man Enough,* ch. 7 (1993).

14 Nothing is quite so horrifying and paralyzing as to win the Oedipal struggle and to be awarded your mother as the prize.

Frank Pittman, (20th-century) U.S. psychiatrist and family therapist. *Man Enough,* ch. 7 (1993).

15 The mother must teach her son how to respect and follow the rules. She must teach him how to compete successfully with the other boys. And she must teach him how to find a woman to take care of him and finish the job she began of training him how to live in a family. But no matter how good a job a woman does in teaching a boy how to be a man, he knows that she is not the real thing, and so he tends to exaggerate the differences between men and women that she embodies.

Frank Pittman, (20th-century) U.S. psychiatrist and family therapist. *Man Enough,* ch. 1 (1993).

16 I would rather be the child of a mother who has all the inner conflicts of the human being than be mothered by someone for whom all is easy and smooth, who knows all the answers, and is a stranger to doubt.

D. W. Winnicott, (20th-century) British child psychiatrist. *Health Education Through Broadcasting,* ch. 2 (1993).

Mothers as Bearers of Blame

1 We are seeing an increasing level of attacks on the "selfishness" of women. There are allegations that all kinds of social ills, from runaway children to the neglected elderly, are due to the fact that women have left their "rightful" place in the home. Such arguments are simplistic and wrongheaded but women are especially vulnerable to the accusation that if society has problems, it's because women aren't nurturing enough.

Grace Baruch, U.S. developmental psychologist, **Rosalind Barnett,** U.S. psychologist, and **Caryl Rivers,** U.S. journalist (20th-century). *Life Prints,* ch. 2 (1983).

2 "Mother" is the first word that occurs to politicians and columnists and popes when they raise the question, "Why isn't life turning out the way we want it?"

Mary Kay Blakely, (20th-century) U.S. journalist and author. *American Mom,* prologue (1994).

3 Mothers are likely to have more bad days on the job than most other professionals, considering the hours: round-the-clock, seven days a week, fifty-two weeks a year. . . . You go to work when you're sick, maybe even clinically depressed,

because motherhood is perhaps the only unpaid position where failure to show up can result in arrest.

MARY KAY BLAKELY, (20th-century) U.S. journalist and author. *American Mom,* prologue (1994).

4 When trouble comes no mother should have to plead guilty alone. The pediatricians, psychologists, therapists, goat herders, fathers, and peer groups should all be called to the bench as well. . . .

MARY KAY BLAKELY, (20th-century) U.S. journalist and author. *American Mom,* ch. 1 (1994).

5 Somewhere it is written that parents who are critical of other people's children and publicly admit they can do better are asking for it.

ERMA BOMBECK, (20th-century) U.S. humorist and author. *Motherhood, the Second Oldest Profession,* ch. 21 (1983).

6 She [the mother] deals with the world of child-rearing, where hundreds of experts give contradictory advice; the outcome can't be measured for fifteen to twenty years. She has to process this advice through her intuition and a constant stream of her own childhood memories dredged up by her child's dilemmas. And she must do all this with others—mother, mother-in-law, neighbors and schoolteachers—looking over her shoulder, marking her report card, measuring her against their own standards.

ROGER GOULD, (20th-century) U.S. psychotherapist and author. *Transformations,* sec. 4, ch. 2 (1978).

7 The ease with which problems are understood and solved on paper, in books and magazine articles, is never matched by the reality of the mother's experience. . . . Her child's behavior often does not follow the storybook version. Her own feelings don't match the way she has been told she ought to feel. . . . There is something wrong with either her child or her, she thinks. Either way, she accepts the blame and guilt.

ELAINE HEFFNER, (20th-century) U.S. psychiatrist and author. *Mothering,* ch. 2 (1978).

8 Unfortunately, mothers interpret the fact that they feel guilty to mean that they are guilty. Professionals have simply confirmed this interpretation by telling mothers why they are guilty.

ELAINE HEFFNER, (20th-century) U.S. psychiatrist and author. *Mothering,* ch. 2 (1978).

9 So long as the source of our identity is external—vested in how others judge our performance at work, or how others judge our children's performance, or how much money we make—we will find ourselves hopelessly flawed, forever short of the ideal.

MELINDA M. MARSHALL, (20th-century) U.S. editor and author. *Good Enough Mothers,* ch. 4 (1993).

10 Like those before it, this decade takes on the marketable subtleties of a private phenomenon: parenthood. Mothers are being teased out of the home and into the agora for a public trial. Are we doing it right? Do we have the right touch? The right toys? The right lights? Is our child going to grow up tall, thin and bright? Something private, and precious, has become public, vul-

garized—and scored by impersonal judges.

SONIA TAITZ, (20th-century) U.S. journalist and author. *Mothering Heights,* introduction (1992).

11 You have got to prepare for a lifetime of the pillory, for whatever you do will be seen as wrong by total strangers, up until and including the time when whatever your child does will be seen as wrong by total strangers.

SONIA TAITZ, (20th-century) U.S. journalist and author. *Mothering Heights,* ch. 3 (1992).

12 If you could choose your parents, . . . we would rather have a mother who felt a sense of guilt—at any rate who felt responsible, and felt that if things went wrong it was probably her fault—we'd rather have that than a mother who immediately turned to an outside thing to explain everything, and said it was due to the thunderstorm last night or some quite outside phenomenon and didn't take responsibility for anything.

D. W. WINNICOTT, (20th-century) British child psychiatrist. *Health Education Through Broadcasting,* ch. 8 (1993).

Mothers' Reproductive Years

1 In the nineteenth century . . . explanations of who and what women were focused primarily on reproductive events—marriage, children, the empty nest, menopause. You could explain what was happening in a woman's life, it was believed, if you knew where she was in this reproductive cycle.

GRACE BARUCH, U.S. developmental psychologist, **ROSALIND BARNETT,** U.S. psychologist, and **CARYL RIVERS,** U.S. journalist (20th-century). *Life Prints,* ch. 12 (1983).

2 All of women's aspirations—whether for education, work, or any form of self-determination—ultimately rest on their ability to decide whether and when to bear children. For this reason, reproductive freedom has always been the most popular item in each of the successive feminist agendas—and the most heavily assaulted target of each backlash.

SUSAN FALUDI, (20th-century) U.S. author. *Backlash: The Undeclared War Against American Women,* ch. 14 (1993).

3 If women's role in life is limited solely to housewife/mother, it clearly ends when she can no longer bear more children and the children she has borne leave home.

BETTY FRIEDAN, (20th-century) U.S. feminist and author. *The Fountain of Age,* ch. 4 (1993).

4 What had really caused the women's movement was the *additional years of human life.* At the turn of the century women's life expectancy was forty-six; now it was nearly eighty. Our groping sense that we couldn't live all those years in terms of motherhood alone was "the problem that had no name." Realizing that it was not some freakish personal fault but our common problem as women had enabled us to take the first steps to change our lives.

BETTY FRIEDAN, (20th-century) U.S. feminist and author. *The Fountain of Age,* preface (1993).

5 The child-rearing years are relatively short in our increased life span. It is hard for young women caught between diapers and formulas to believe, but there are years and years of freedom ahead. I regret my impatience to get on with my career. I wish I'd relaxed, allowed myself the luxury of watching the world through my little girl's eyes.

EDA LE SHAN, (20th-century) U.S. educator and author. As quoted in *Mister Rogers Talks With Parents,* Fred Rogers, ch. 1 (1983).

6 If I get the forty additional years statisticians say are likely coming to me, I could fit in at least one, maybe two new lifetimes. Sad that only one of those lifetimes can include being the mother of young children.

ANNA QUINDLEN, (20th-century) U.S. journalist and novelist. *Living Out Loud,* "Blind Ambition" (1988).

Parents/Parents' Roles

1 The joys of parents are secret, and so are their griefs and fears.

FRANCIS BACON, (1561–1626) British philosopher and essayist. "Of Parents and Children," *Essays* (1625).

2 Especially with our first child, we tend to take too much responsibility—both credit and blame—for everything. The more we want to be good parents, the more we tend to see ourselves as making or breaking our children.

POLLY BERRIEN BERENDS, (20th-century) U.S. author. *Whole Child/Whole Parent,* ch. 3 (rev. 1987).

3 Among the most valuable but least appreciated experiences parenthood can provide are the opportunities it offers for exploring, reliving, and resolving one's own childhood problems in the context of one's relation to one's child.

BRUNO BETTELHEIM, (20th-century) Austrian-born U.S. child psychologist and author. *A Good Enough Parent,* ch. 11 (1987).

4 To be a good enough parent one must be able to feel secure in one's parenthood, and one's relation to one's child . . . The security of the parent about being a parent will eventually become the source of the child's feeling secure about himself.

BRUNO BETTELHEIM, (20th-century) Austrian-born U.S. child psychologist and author. *A Good Enough Parent,* ch. 1 (1987).

5 Parents don't make mistakes because they don't care, but because they care so deeply.

T. BERRY BRAZELTON, (20th-century) U.S. pediatrician and author. *Touchpoints,* introduction (1992).

6 Without our being especially conscious of the transition, the word "parent" has gradually come to be used as much as a verb as a noun. Whereas we formerly thought mainly about "being a parent," we now find ourselves talking about learning how "to parent." . . . It suggests that we may now be concentrating on action rather than status, on what we do rather than what or who we are.

BETTYE M. CALDWELL, (20th-century) U.S. child development specialist. *In Support of Families,* ed. Michael W. Yogman and T. Berry Brazelton, ch. 13 (1986).

7 Parenthood is not an object of appetite or even desire. It is an object of will. There is no appetite

for parenthood; there is only a purpose or intention of parenthood.

R.G. [ROBIN GEORGE] COLLINGWOOD, (20th-century) British philosopher. *The New Leviathan,* pt. 2, ch. 23 (1942).

8 There are times when parenthood seems nothing but feeding the mouth that bites you.

PETER DE VRIES, (20th-century) U.S. author. *The Tunnel of Love,* ch. 5 (1954).

9 Parenting is not logical. If it were, we would never have to read a book, never need a family therapist, and never feel the urge to call a close friend late at night for support after a particularly trying bedtime scene. . . . We have moments of logic, but life is run by a much larger force. Life is filled with disagreement, opposition, illusion, irrational thinking, miracle, meaning, surprise, and wonder.

JEANNE ELIUM AND DON ELIUM, (20th-century) U.S. family counselors and authors. *Raising a Daughter,* ch. 8 (1994).

10 The job of a parent is to eventually do himself out of a job.

ALICE FREEDMAN, (20th-century) U.S. parent educator. As stated to the author.

11 Parenthood brings profound pleasure and satisfactions—the unparalleled pleasure of caring so intensely for another human being, of watching growth, of reliving childhood, of seeing oneself in a new perspective, and of understanding more about life.

ELLEN GALINSKY, (20th-century) U.S. child development specialist and author. *Between Generations,* ch. 2 (1981).

12 There are three main parenting jobs: getting your kid to go to sleep without bedtime problems, getting your kid to eat without being finicky, and getting your kid toilet trained. Nobody I know has scored three out of three.

KEISHA, (20th-century) U.S. clothing designer. As quoted in *Your Maternity Leave* by Jean Marzollo, ch. 8 (1989).

13 Our idealized images of successful parents are filled with contradictions. We expect them (and therefore ourselves) to be young—but not too young. They must be mature as well. We want them to be financially secure—but not working long hours to achieve that security. We expect them to be loving and devoted, but not smothering and all-absorbed with their child. Such a vision is impossible to achieve.

LAWRENCE KUTNER, (20th-century) U.S. child psychologist and author. *Pregnancy and Your Baby's First Year,* ch. 2 (1993).

14 Your responsibility as a parent is not as great as you might imagine. You need not supply the world with the next conqueror of disease or a major movie star. If your child simply grows up to be someone who does not use the word "collectible" as a noun, you can consider yourself an unqualified success.

FRAN LEBOWITZ, (20th-century) U.S. humorist and author. *The Fran Lebowitz Reader,* "Parental Guidance" (1994).

15 Here is the beginning of understanding: most parents are doing their best, and most children are doing their best, and they're doing pretty well, all things considered.

RICHARD LOUV, (20th-century) U.S. journalist and author. *Childhood's Future,* introduction (1991).

16 Children aren't happy with nothing
to ignore,

And that's what parents were created for.

OGDEN NASH, (20th-century) U.S. poet. "The Parent," *Happy Days* (1933).

17 It's 10 p.m. Do you know where your children are?

U.S. PUBLIC SERVICE ANNOUNCEMENT.

18 I regard [parenting] as the hardest, most complicated, anxiety-ridden, sweat-and-blood-producing job in the world. Succeeding requires the ultimate in patience, common sense, commitment, humor, tact, love, wisdom, awareness, and knowledge. At the same time, it holds the possibility for the most rewarding, joyous experience of a lifetime, namely, that of being successful guides to a new and unique human being.

VIRGINIA SATIR, (20th-century) U.S. family therapist and author. *The New Peoplemaking,* ch. 15 (1988).

19 Parents teach in the toughest school in the word: The School for Making People. You are the board of education, the principal, the classroom teacher, and the janitor, all rolled into two. . . . There are few schools to train you for your job, and there is no general agreement on the curriculum. . . . You are on duty, or at least on call, twenty-four hours a day, 365 days a year, for at least eighteen years for each child you have. Besides that, you have to contend with an administration that has two leaders or bosses, whichever the case may be.

VIRGINIA SATIR, (20th-century) U.S. family therapist and author. *The New Peoplemaking,* ch. 15 (1988).

20 So much is asked of parents, and so little is given.

VIRGINIA SATIR, (20th-century) U.S. family therapist and author. *The New Peoplemaking,* ch. 15 (1988).

21 Parentage is a very important profession; but no test of fitness for it is ever imposed in the interest of children.

BERNARD SHAW, (1856–1950) Irish-born British playwright and author. *Everybody's Political What's What,* ch.10 (1944).

22 The desire of most parents is first and foremost to do what is best for their children. Every interview with a mother or father confirms this, every letter written by a parent breathes this deep-seated wish, "I hope I am doing the right thing for my child." This is real and honest, and at the very base of parenthood.

IRMA SIMONTON BLACK, (20th-century) U.S. author. "What to Expect of a Young Child," *Bank Street College of Education Reprint* (1941).

23 Being a parent is too complicated and emotional a task for magical techniques and miracle cures.

RON TAFFEL, (20th-century) U.S. psychologist and author. *Parenting by Heart,* preface (1991).

24 No test tube can breed love and affection. No frozen packet of semen ever read a story to a sleepy child.

SHIRLEY WILLIAMS, (20th-century) British Liberal-Democrat politician. *Daily Mirror* (March 2, 1978).

25 We do the same thing to parents that we do to children. We insist that they are some kind of categorical abstraction because they pro-

duced a child. They were people before that, and they're still people in all other areas of their lives. But when it comes to the state of parenthood they are abruptly heir to a whole collection of virtues and feelings that are assigned to them with a fine arbitrary disregard for individuality.

LEONTINE YOUNG, (20th-century) U.S. social worker and author. *Life Among the Giants,* introduction (1965).

26 Being a parent is a form of leadership. . . . Parents make a mistake, along with leaders of organizations, when they are unwilling to recognize the power inherent in the positions they occupy and when they are unwilling to use this power. . . . I do not mean a figure who is irrational, autocratic, or sadistic. I mean leaders who have the strength of character to stand up for what they believe.

ABRAHAM ZALEZNIK, (20th-century) U.S. psychologist. *In Support of Families,* ed. Michael W. Yogman and T. Berry Brazelton, ch. 8 (1986).

Siblings

1 Behold how good and how pleasant it is for brothers and sisters to dwell together in unity.

BIBLE: HEBREW *Book of Psalms.*

2 It goes without saying that you should never have more children than you have car windows.

ERMA BOMBECK, (20th-century) U.S. humorist. As quoted in *Woman to Woman,* Julia Gilden and Mark Riedman (1994).

3 It is with our brothers and sisters that we learn to love, share, negotiate, start and end fights, hurt others, and save face. The basis of healthy (or unhealthy) connections in adulthood is cast during childhood.

JANE MERSKY LEDER, (20th-century) U.S. author. *Brothers and Sisters,* ch. 3 (1991).

4 How then do you love each of your multiple children, *if* not the best or even *equally*? The answer is, you love them *uniquely.*

MARIANNE E. NEIFERT, (20th-century) U.S. pediatrician and author. *Dr. Mom's Parenting Guide,* ch. 4 (1991).

5 Your children don't have equal talents now and they won't have equal opportunities later in life. You may be able to divide resources equally in childhood, but your best efforts won't succeed in shielding them from personal or physical crises. . . . Your heart will be broken a thousand times if you really expect to equalize your children's happiness by striving to love them equally.

MARIANNE E. NEIFERT, (20th-century) U.S. pediatrician and author. *Dr. Mom's Parenting Guide,* ch. 4 (1991).

6 Just because multiples can turn to each other for companionship, and at times for comfort, don't be fooled into thinking you're not still vital to them. Don't let or make multiples be parents as well as siblings to each other. . . . Parent interaction with infants and young children has everything to do with how those children develop on every level, including how they develop their identities.

PAMELA PATRICK NOVOTNY, (20th-century) U.S. journalist and author. *The Joy of Twins,* ch. 9 (rev. 1994).

7 One internationally known twin researcher sees similarities between

twins' relationships and those of couple who have been married a long time. Fifteen-year-old twins, as well as spouses approaching their fortieth anniversary, each know their partners' likes, dislikes, habits, and idiosyncracies as well as they know their own.

Pamela Patrick Novotny, (20th-century) U.S. journalist and author. *The Joy of Twins,* ch. 9 (rev. 1994).

8 One of your biggest jobs as a parent of multiples is no bigger than simply talking to your children individually and requiring that they respond to you individually as well. The benefits of this kind of communication can be enormous, in terms of the relationship you develop with each child, in terms of their language development, and eventually in terms of their sense of individuality, too.

Pamela Patrick Novotny, (20th-century) U.S. journalist and author. *The Joy of Twins,* ch. 8 (rev. 1994).

9 We sometimes think that if we treat each child fairly and equally—and make them see that we're being fair—they will stop arguing about who gets more, who gets something first, who's our favorite. But as hard as we try to be fair, we can never succeed. Even if we believe we're completely fair, children will never agree with us. Since no one wins the fairness game, the best thing to do is avoid playing it.

Nancy Samalin, (20th-century) U.S. parent educator and author. *Loving Your Child Is Not Enough,* ch. 8 (1987).

10 A gorgeous example of denial is the story about the little girl who was notified that a baby brother or sister was on the way. She listened in thoughtful silence, then raised her gaze from her mother's belly to her eyes and said, "Yes, but who will be the new baby's mommy?"

Judith Viorst, (20th-century) U.S. novelist and poet. *Necessary Losses,* ch. 6 (1986).

11 Birds in their little nests agree
And 'tis a shameful sight
When children of one family
Fall out, and childe, and fight.

Isaac Watts, (1674–1748) English theologian and hymn writer. *"Love Between Brothers and Sisters,"* xvii.

On Being a Parent

1 Fifty years from now, it will not matter what kind of car you drove, what kind of house you lived in, how much you had in your bank account, or what your clothes looked like. But the world may be a little better because you were important in the life of a child.

Anonymous, as quoted in *The Winning Family,* Louise Hart, ch. 1 (1987).

2 Being a parent is unlike any previous job—the results of any one action are not clearly visible for a long time, if at all.

Anonymous Mother, as quoted in *Between Generations,* Ellen Galinsky, ch. 2 (1981).

3 Once you've been launched into parenthood, you'll need all your best skills, self-control, good judgment and patience. But at the same time there is nothing like the thrill and exhilaration that come from watching that bright, cheerful, inquisitive, creative, eccentric and even goofy child you have raised flourish and shine. That's what

keeps you going, and what, in the end, makes it all worthwhile.

Lawrence Balter, (20th-century) U.S. psychologist and author. *Dr. Balter's Child Sense,* afterword (1985).

4 My list of things I never pictured myself saying when I pictured myself as a parent has grown over the years.

Polly Berrien Berends, (20th-century) U.S. author. *Whole Child/Whole Parent,* ch. 2 (rev. 1987).

5 The good enough parent, in addition to being convinced that whatever his child does, he does it because at that moment he is convinced this is the best he can do, will also ask himself: "What in the world would make me act as my child acts at this moment? And if I felt forced to act this way, what would make me feel better about it?"

Bruno Bettelheim, (20th-century) Austrian-born U.S. child psychologist and author. *A Good Enough Parent,* ch. 6 (1987).

6 One of the things I've discovered in general about raising kids is that they really don't give a damn if you walked five miles to school. They want to deal with what's happening now.

Patty Duke, (20th-century) U.S. actress. As quoted in *Woman to Woman,* Julia Gilden and Mark Riedman (1994).

7 I could be, I discovered, by turns stern, loving, wise, silly, youthful, aged, racial, universal, indulgent, strict, with a remarkably easy and often cunning detachment . . . various ways that an adult, spurred by guilt, by annoyance, by condescension, by loneliness, deals with the prerogatives of power and love.

Gerald Early, (20th-century) U.S. author. *Daughters,* pt. 1 (1994).

8 I was a wonderful parent before I had children. I was an expert on why everyone else was having problems with theirs. Then I had three of my own.

Adele Faber and Elaine Mazlish, (20th-century) U.S. parent educators. *How to Talk So Kids Will Listen and Listen So Kids Will Talk,* ch. 1 (1980).

9 Being a parent is such serious business that we dare not take it too seriously. Children are inherently funny. So are parents. We all are at our funniest when we are desperately struggling to appear to be in control of a new situation.

Lawrence Kutner, (20th-century) U.S. child psychologist and author. *Parent and Child,* introduction (1991).

10 The pressures of being a parent are equal to any pressure on earth. To be a conscientious parent, and really look to that little being's mental and physical health, is a responsibility which most of us, including me, avoid most of the time because it's too hard.

John Lennon, (20th-century) British rock musician. As quoted in *Playboy* (September 1980).

11 For a parent, it's hard to recognize the significance of your work when you're immersed in the mundane details. Few of us, as we run the bath water or spread the peanut butter on the bread, proclaim proudly, "I'm making my contribution to the future of the planet." But with the exception of global hunger, few jobs in the world of paychecks and promotions com-

pare in significance to the job of parent.

JOYCE MAYNARD, (20th-century) U.S. author. "A Mother's Day," *Parenting* (June/July 1995).

12 One of the sad realities of being a parent is that the same stuff you know is exciting, educational, and enriching in your child's life is often messy, smelly and exhausting to deal with.

JOYCE MAYNARD, (20th-century) U.S. author. "The Call of the Wild," *Parenting* (August 1994).

13 The truth is, most of our alleged superheroes make meals, make beds, make ends meet, make mistakes, make amends, make love, make up, and mostly make do.

MARIANNE E. NEIFERT, (20th-century) U.S. pediatrician and author. *Dr. Mom's Parenting Guide*, ch. 2 (1991).

14 My children have taught me things. Things I thought I knew. The most profound wisdom they have given me is a respect for human vulnerability. I have known that people are resilient, but I didn't appreciate how fragile they are. Until children learn to hide their feelings, you read them in their faces, gestures, and postures. The sheer visibility of shyness, pain, and rejection let me recognize and remember them.

SHIRLEY NELSON GARNER, (20th-century) *Mother Journeys*, ed. Maureen T. Reddy, Martha Roth, Amy Sheldon, sec. 1 (1994).

15 I am aghast to find myself in such a position of power over two other people. Their father and I have them in thrall simply by having produced them. We have the power to make them feel good or bad about themselves, which is the greatest power in the world. Ours will not be the only influence, but it is the earliest, the most ubiquitous, and potentially the most pernicious. Lovers and friends will make them blossom and bleed, but they may move on to other lovers and friends. We are the only parents they will have.

ANNA QUINDLEN, (20th-century) U.S. journalist and novelist. *Living Out Loud*, "Power" (1988).

16 This is what no one warns you about, when you decide to have children. There is so much written about the cost and the changes in your way of life, but no one ever tells you that what they are going to hand you in the hospital is power, whether you want it or not. . . . I should have known, but somehow overlooked for a time, that parents become, effortlessly, just by showing up, the most influential totems in the lives of their children.

ANNA QUINDLEN, (20th-century) U.S. journalist and novelist. *Living Out Loud*, "Power" (1988).

17 Parenting forces us to get to know ourselves better than we ever might have imagined we could—and in many new ways. . . . We'll discover talents we never dreamed we had and fervently wish for others at moments we feel we desperately need them. As time goes on, we'll probably discover that we have more to give and can give more than we ever imagined. But we'll also find that there are limits to our giving, and that may be hard for us to accept.

FRED ROGERS, (20th-century) U.S. children's television personality and author. *Mister Rogers Talks With Parents,* ch. 1 (1983).

18 The very best reason parents are so special . . . is because we are the holders of a priceless gift, a gift we received from countless generations we never knew, a gift that only we now possess and only we can give to our children. That unique gift, of course, is the gift of ourselves. Whatever we can do to give that gift, and to help others receive it, is worth the challenge of all our human endeavor.

FRED ROGERS, (20th-century) U.S. children's television personality and author. *Mister Rogers Talks With Parents,* ch. 11 (1983).

19 Here is the paradox: what children take from us, they give. When we are not totally "free," we learn how to cope with a smaller world, less time, less luxury. . . . We become people who feel more deeply, question more deeply, hurt more deeply and love more deeply.

SONIA TAITZ, (20th-century) U.S. journalist and author. *Mothering Heights,* ch. 27 (1992).

20 When I turned into a parent, I experienced a real and total personality change that slowly shifted back to the "normal" me, yet has not completely vanished. I believe the two levels are now superimposed, with an additional sprinkling of mortality intimations.

SONIA TAITZ, (20th-century) U.S. journalist and author. *Mothering Heights,* ch. 6 (1992).

21 It seems to me that since I've had children, I've grown richer and deeper. They may have slowed down my writing for a while, but when I did write, I had more of a self to speak from.

ANNE TYLER, (20th-century) U.S. author. As quoted in *Woman to Woman,* Julia Gilden and Mark Riedman (1994).

Parents as Role Models

1 A young branch takes on all the bends that one gives it.

CHINESE PROVERB.

2 Train up a child in the way he should go: and when he is old, he will not depart from it.

BIBLE: HEBREW, *Proverbs 22:6.*

3 As a parent, you will often serve as an inadvertent example to your child. A child will model himself after you in many areas: how you deal with frustration, settle disagreements and cope with not being able to have the things that you want, to name just three.

LAWRENCE BALTER, (20th-century) U.S. psychologist and author. *Who's In Control?* (1989).

4 The best way to teach a child restraint and generosity is to be a model of those qualities yourself. If your child sees that you want a particular item but refrain from buying it, either because it isn't practical or because you can't afford it, he will begin to understand restraint. Likewise, if you donate books or clothing to charity, take him with you to distribute the items to teach him about generosity.

LAWRENCE BALTER, (20th-century) U.S. psychologist and author. *Who's In Control?* Ch. 5 (1989).

5 It's frightening to think that you mark your children merely by being yourself. . . . It seems unfair. You can't assume the responsibility for everything you do—or don't do.

SIMONE DE BEAUVOIR, (20th-century) French novelist and author. *Les Belles Images,* ch. 3 (1966).

6 You don't hit a child when you want him to stop hitting. You don't yell at children to get them to stop yelling. Or spit at a child to indicate that he should not spit. Of course, you want children to know how to sympathize with others and to "know how it feels," but you . . . have to show them *how to act*—not how *not* to act.

JEANNETTE W. GALAMBOS, (20th-century) U.S. early childhood educator and author. *A Guide to Discipline,* ch. 4 (1969).

7 When things turn out pretty much as expected, parents give little thought to how much they have influenced the outcome. When things don't turn out as expected, parents give a great deal of thought to the role they play.

ARLENE HARDER, (20th-century) U.S. psychotherapist. *Letting Go of Our Adult Children,* ch. 3 (1994).

8 One of the most important things we adults can do for young children is to model the kind of person we would like them to be.

CAROL B. HILLMAN, (20th-century) U.S. early childhood educator. *Teaching Four-Year-Olds: A Personal Journey,* "Friendship: Teacher to Teacher," sec. 17 (1988).

9 Family is the first school for young children, and parents are powerful models.

ALICE STERLING HONIG, (20th-century) U.S. child psychologist. "Helping Children Become More Caring and Cooperative," *NYSAEYC Reporter* (Winter 1994).

10 If there is anything that we wish to change in the child, we should first examine it and see whether it is not something that could better be changed in ourselves.

C.G. JUNG, (1875–1961) Swiss psychologist. *Integration of the Personality* (1939).

11 There must be a profound recognition that parents are the first teachers and that education begins before formal schooling and is deeply rooted in the values, traditions, and norms of family and culture.

SARA LAWRENCE LIGHTFOOT, (20th-century) U.S. educator and author. *Worlds Apart,* ch. 1 (1978).

12 Everything our children hear, see, and feel is recorded onto a cassette. Guess who is the big star in their movie? You are. What you say and, more important, what you do, is recorded there for them to replay over and over again. We all have videocassettes. Adults just have larger libraries of tapes available.

STEPHANIE MARSTON, (20th-century) U.S. family therapist and author. *The Magic of Encouragement,* ch. 1 (1990).

13 Even if society dictates that men and women should behave in certain ways, it is fathers and mothers who teach those ways to children—not just in the words they say, but in the lives they lead.

AUGUSTUS Y. NAPIER, (20th-century) U.S. family therapist. *The Fragile Bond,* introduction (1988).

14 That anger can be expressed through words and non-destructive activities; that promises are intended to be

kept; that cleanliness and good eating habits are aspects of self-esteem; that compassion is an attribute to be prized—all these lessons are ones children can learn far more readily through the living example of their parents than they ever can through formal instruction.

FRED ROGERS, (20th-century) U.S. children's television personality and author. *Mister Rogers Talks With Parents,* ch. 6 (1983).

15 You can never really live anyone else's life, not even your child's. The influence you exert is through your own life, and what you've become yourself.

ELEANOR ROOSEVELT, (1884–1962) U.S. First Lady and humanitarian. As quoted in *Woman to Woman,* Julia Gilden and Mark Riedman (1994).

Parents' Needs

1 Some fear that if parents start listening to their own wants and needs they will neglect their children. It is our belief that children are in fact far less likely to be neglected when their parents' needs—for support, for friendship, for decent work, for health care, for learning, for play, for time alone—are being met.

WENDY COPPEDGE SANFORD, (20th-century) U.S. editor and author. *Ourselves and Our Children,* the Boston Women's Health Book Collective, introduction (1978).

2 To get time for civic work, for exercise, for neighborhood projects, reading or meditation, or just plain time to themselves, mothers need to hold out against the fairly recent but surprisingly entrenched myth that "good mothers" are constantly with their children. They will have to speak out at last about the demoralizing effect of spending day after day with small children, no matter how much they love them.

WENDY COPPEDGE SANFORD, (20th-century) U.S. editor and author. *Ourselves and Our Children,* the Boston Women's Health Book Collective, introduction (1978).

3 However strongly they resist it, our kids have to learn that as adults we need the companionship and love of other adults. The more direct we are about our needs, the easier it may be for our children to accept those needs. Their jealousy may come from a fear that if we adults love each other we might not have any left for them. We have to let them know that it's a different kind of love.

RUTH DAVIDSON BELL, (20th-century) U.S. author. *Ourselves and Our Children,* the Boston Women's Health Book Collective, ch. 3 (1978).

4 Over and over again, her own direct experience teaches a woman that when she does enough for herself, she feels better and better about her child. When she does too much for too long for her child, she feels harassed and drained. But over and over again, she lapses into doing too much.

ROGER GOULD, (20th-century) U.S. psychotherapist and author. *Transformations,* sec. 4, ch. 2 (1978).

5 Babies don't need fathers, but mothers do. Someone who is taking care of a baby needs to be taken care of.

AMY HECKERLING, (20th-century) U.S. film director. As quoted in *The Last Word,* ed. Carolyn Warner, ch. 16 (1992).

6 The emotional stress of mothering . . . is intensified by a mother's idea that her own feelings are suspect, and by her fear that they will erupt into negative, aggressive behavior toward her child. She needs the confidence of knowing that she can experience these feelings without expressing them in destructive behavior toward her child. Her goal is gradually to help her child become aware that she is another person whose needs must be considered. She can only do this if she believes it herself.

ELAINE HEFFNER, (20th-century) U.S. psychiatrist and author. *Mothering*, ch. 3 (1978).

7 In the event of an oxygen shortage on airplanes, mothers of young children are always reminded to put on their own oxygen mask first, to better assist the children with theirs. The same tactic is necessary on terra firma. There's no way of sustaining our children if we don't first rescue ourselves. I don't call that selfish behavior. I call it love.

JOYCE MAYNARD, (20th-century) U.S. journalist. "The Finishing Touches," *Parenting Magazine* (November 1992).

8 All mothers need instruction, nurturing, and an understanding mentor after the birth of a baby, but in this age of fast foods, fast tracks, and fast lanes, it doesn't always happen. While we live in a society that provides recognition for just about every life event—from baptisms to bar mitzvahs, from wedding vows to funeral rites—the entry into parenting seems to be a solo flight, with nothing and no one to mark formally the new mom's entry into motherhood.

SALLY PLACKSIN, (20th-century) U.S. producer and author. *Mothering the New Mother*, ch. 2 (1994).

9 Feeling needy—mistaking vulnerability for weakness—doesn't fit in with our image of what being a mother is all about. If we are needy, how can we care well for a much needier baby? There is a widespread feeling that we have to do it all alone, and if we don't know something, or can't manage it, or, heaven forbid, don't want to, there is something lacking in our makeup.

SALLY PLACKSIN, (20th-century) U.S. producer and author. *Mothering the New Mother*, ch. 1 (1994).

10 It is easy after a day full of hassles to experience a child as being just one more hassle, one more person who wants to sap our strength. We feel emotionally fragile and put upon. We long to have someone take care of us and soothe our emotions. Instead, we are required to take care of a child who might be exhausted and needy as well, and who is acting unreasonable.

NANCY SAMALIN, (20th-century) U.S. parent educator and author. *Love and Anger: The Parental Dilemma*, ch. 2 (1991).

11 We can't nourish our children if we don't nourish ourselves. . . . Parents who manage to stay married, sane, and connected to each other share one basic characteristic: the ability to protect even small amounts of time together no matter what else is going on in their lives.

RON TAFFEL, (20th-century) U.S. psychologist and author. *Why Parents Disagree*, ch. 14 (1994).

12 Living by basic good-mothering guidelines enables a mom to blend the responsibilities of parenthood with its joys; to know when to stand her ground and when to be flexible; and to absorb the lessons of the parenting gurus while also trusting her inner voice when it reasons that another cookie isn't worth fighting over, or that her child won't suffer irreparable trauma if, once in a while, Mom puts her own needs first.

SUE WOODMAN, (20th-century) U.S. broadcaster and journalist. "Seven Habits of Smart Moms," *McCalls* (1995).

"Perfect Parents"

1 We all have bad days, of course, a secret that only makes us feel more guilty. But once my friends and I started telling the truth about how far we deviated from perfection, we couldn't stop. . . . One mother admitted leaving the grocery store without her kids—"I just forgot them. The manager found them in the frozen foods aisle, eating Eskimo Pies."

MARY KAY BLAKELY, (20th-century) U.S. journalist and author. *American Mom,* prologue (1994).

2 "Mother" has always been a generic term synonymous with love, devotion, and sacrifice. There's always been something mystical and reverent about them. They're the Walter Cronkites of the human race . . . infallible, virtuous, without flaws and conceived without original sin, with no room for ambivalence.

ERMA BOMBECK, (20th-century) U.S. humorist and author. *Motherhood, the Second Oldest Profession,* introduction (1983).

3 The art of never making a mistake is crucial to motherhood. To be effective and to gain the respect she needs to function, a mother must have her children believe she has never engaged in sex, never made a bad decision, never caused her own mother a moment's anxiety, and was never a child.

ERMA BOMBECK, (20th-century) U.S. humorist and author. *Motherhood, the Second Oldest Profession,* ch. 1 (1983).

4 If I could summarize my suggestions to parents over the past twenty-five years it would be: worry less, criticize less, preach less, listen more, have more fun, be more honest with your own feelings, develop your own joys and friendships, and don't sweat the small stuff (which is nearly everything). The goal is not to be a perfect parent, because no such thing exists. The hope is to be a good enough parent so that your child leaves home a responsible adult who can take care of him or herself.

CHARLOTTE DAVIS KASL, (20th-century) U.S. psychologist and author. *Finding Joy,* ch. 72 (1994).

5 Uncertainty about the outcome is a given in child-rearing and not a reflection of a mother's inadequacy. She should not be misled by her wish to be omnipotent, all-powerful, all-giving, the perfect mother, who will right all the wrongs and make up for all the deprivations of her own childhood. She is simply an imperfect human being with needs of her own.

ELAINE HEFFNER, (20th-century) U.S. psychiatrist and author. *Mothering,* ch. 2 (1978).

6 Fortunately, children do not need "perfect" parents. They do need mothers and fathers who will think on their feet and who will be thoughtful about what they have done. They do need parents who can be flexible, and who can use a variety of approaches to discipline.

JAMES L. HYMES, JR., (20th-century) U.S. child psychologist and author. "A Sensible Approach to Discipline," *Childhood* (1976).

7 There is an anecdote passed around in psychoanalytical circles, about a boy who for no apparent reason reached the age of six without ever speaking. One night he suddenly said, "Please pass the mashed potatoes." The boy had never spoken before because his mother had always met every one of his needs without him saying a word. This is the epitome of the too-good mother.

ELYSE ZORN KARLIN, (20th-century) U.S. journalist and author. *Sons: A Mother's Manual,* ch. 5 (1994).

8 It will help us and our children if we can laugh at our faults. It will help us tolerate our shortcomings, and it will help our children see that the goal is to be a human, not perfect.

NEIL KURSHAN, (20th-century) U.S. rabbi and author. *Raising Your Child to Be a Mensch,* ch. 4 (1987).

9 Our children do not want models of perfection, neither do they want us to be buddies, friends, or confidants who never rise above their own levels of maturity and experience. We need to walk that middle ground between perfection and peerage, between intense meddling and apathy—the middle ground where our values, standards, and expectations can be shared with our children.

NEIL KURSHAN, (20th-century) U.S. rabbi and author. *Raising Your Child to Be a Mensch,* ch. 5 (1987).

10 Feeling that you have to be the perfect parent places a tremendous and completely unnecessary burden on you. If we've learned anything from the past half-century's research on child development, it's that children are remarkably resilient. You can make lots of mistakes and still wind up with great kids.

LAWRENCE KUTNER, (20th-century) U.S. child psychologist and author. *Pregnancy and Your Baby's First Year,* ch. 7 (1993).

11 One of the main things that interfere with our joy is the belief that if we try hard enough, read the right books, follow the right advice, and buy the right things, we could be perfect parents. If we are good enough as parents, our children will be perfect too. . . . Unfortunately, what comes from trying to live out this philosophy is not perfect children but worried parents.

LAWRENCE KUTNER, (20th-century) U.S. child psychologist and author. *Parent and Child,* ch. 1 (1991).

12 Keep telling yourself and others there are no supermoms, there are only wonderful mothers.

JEAN MARZOLLO, (20th-century) U.S. author. *Your Maternity Leave,* ch. 3 (1989).

13 The attempt to be an ideal parent, that is, to behave correctly toward the child, to raise her correctly, not to give too little or too much, is in

essence an attempt to be the ideal child—well behaved and dutiful—of one's own parents. But as a result of these efforts the needs of the child go unnoticed. I cannot listen to my child with empathy if I am inwardly preoccupied with being a good mother; I cannot be open to what she is telling me.

ALICE MILLER, (20th-century) German-born psychoanalyst and author. *For Your Own Good,* "Sylvia Plath: An Example of Forbidden Suffering" (trans. 1983).

14 There are great advantages to seeing yourself as an accident created by amateur parents as they practiced. You then have been left in an imperfect state and the rest is up to you. Only the most pitifully inept child requires perfection from parents.

FRANK PITTMAN, (20th-century) U.S. psychiatrist and family therapist. "How to Manage Mom and Dad," *Psychology Today* (November/December 1994).

15 Very early in our children's lives we will be forced to realize that the "perfect" untroubled life we'd like for them is just a fantasy. In daily living, tears and fights and doing things we don't want to do are all part of our human ways of developing into adults.

FRED ROGERS, (20th-century) U.S. children's television personality and author. *Mister Rogers Talks With Parents,* ch. 11 (1983).

16 In our minds lives the madonna image—the all-embracing, all-giving tranquil mother of a Raphael painting, one child at her breast, another at her feet; a woman fulfilled, one who asks nothing more than to nurture and nourish. This creature of fantasy, this myth, is the model—the unattainable ideal against which women measure, not only their performance, but their feelings about being mothers.

LILLIAN BRESLOW RUBIN, (20th-century) U.S. sociologist and family therapist. *Women of a Certain Age,* ch. 2 (1979).

17 The good father does not have to be perfect. Rather, he has to be good enough to help his daughter to become a woman who is reasonably self-confident, self-sufficient, and free of crippling self-doubt, and to feel at ease in the company of men.

VICTORIA SECUNDA, (20th-century) U.S. psychologist and author. *Women and Their Fathers,* ch. 4 (1992).

18 We will have to give up the hope that, if we try hard, we somehow will always do right by our children. The connection is imperfect. We will sometimes do wrong.

JUDITH VIORST, (20th-century) U.S. novelist and poet. *Necessary Losses,* ch. 14 (1986).

Parents Sharing the Parenting Role

1 Sometimes my wife complains that she's overwhelmed with work and just can't take one of the kids, for example, to a piano lesson. I'll offer to do it for her, and then she'll say, "No, I'll do it." We have to negotiate how much I trespass into that mother role—it's not given up easily.

ANONYMOUS FATHER, as quoted in *Women and their Fathers,* Victoria Secunda, ch. 3 (1992).

2 The ideal of men and women sharing equally in parenting and working is a vision still. What would it

be like if women and men were less different from each other, if our worlds were not so foreign? A male friend who shares daily parenting told me that he knows at his very core what his wife's loving for their daughter feels like, and that this knowing creates a stronger bond between them.

ANONYMOUS MOTHER, as quoted in *Ourselves and Our Children,* the Boston Women's Health Book Collective, ch. 6 (1978).

3 The good husbands understand and offer to help. "All you have to do is ask" they say. But even helpful husbands have to be thanked, their contributions acknowledged, credit given. All those pleases and thank yous. Being grateful takes time and energy. It's often easier to do it yourself.

BETTINA ARNDT, (20th-century) Australian journalist and author. *Private Lives,* ch. 2 (1986).

4 The mother may be doing ninety percent of the disciplining, but the father still must have a full-time acceptance of all the children. He never must say, "Get these kids out of here; I'm trying to watch TV." If he ever does start saying this, he is liable to see one of his kids on the six o'clock news.

BILL COSBY, (20th-century) U.S. comedian and author. *Fatherhood,* ch. 14 (1986).

5 The frequent failure of men to cultivate their capacity for listening has a profound impact on their capacity for parenting, for it is mothers more than fathers who are most likely to still their own voices so they may hear and draw out the voices of their children.

MARY FIELD BELENKY, (20th-century) U.S. psychologist. *Women's Ways of Knowing,* pt. 2, ch. 8 (1986).

6 When men achieve the fruits of their material success, they often become aware of an emptiness—an incompleteness—in their lives; the hollowness of having, but not raising, children, of not making true commitments to them. Which, sadly, does not mean that they weren't capable of it.

WILLARD GAYLIN, (20th-century) U.S. psychiatrist and author. As quoted in *Women and their Fathers* , Victoria Secunda, ch. 2 (1992).

7 It may be tempting to focus on the fact that, even among those who support equality, men's involvement as fathers remains a far distance from what most women want and most children need. Yet it is also important to acknowledge how far and how fast many men have moved towards a pattern that not long ago virtually all men considered anathema.

KATHERINE GERSON, (20th-century) U.S. sociologist and author. *No Man's Land,* ch. 6 (1993).

8 You may, or may not, have better child care instincts than your husband; but his can certainly be developed. If you don't respect the natural parenting talents that each of you has, you may inadvertently cast the two of you into the skewed but complementary roles of the Expert and the Dumb Apprentice.

JEAN MARZOLLO, (20th-century) U.S. author. *Your Maternity Leave,* ch. 7 (1989).

9 Just as men must give up economic control when their wives share the responsibility for the family's finan-

cial well-being, women must give up exclusive parental control when their husbands assume more responsibility for child care.

AUGUSTUS Y. NAPIER, (20th-century) U.S. family therapist. *The Fragile Bond,* ch. 13 (1988).

10 The loosening, for some people, of rigid role definitions for men and women has shown that dads can be great at calming babies—if they take the time and make the effort to learn how. It's that time and effort that not only teaches the dad how to calm the babies, but also turns him into a parent, just as the time and effort the mother puts into the babies turns her into a parent.

PAMELA PATRICK NOVOTNY, (20th-century) U.S. journalist and author. *The Joy of Twins,* ch. 6 (1988 rev. 1994).

11 As they move into sharing parenting, men often are apprentices to women because they are not yet as skilled in child care. Mothers have to be willing to teach fathers—both by stepping in and showing and by stepping back and letting them learn.

NANCY PRESS HAWLEY, U.S. author. *Ourselves and Our Children,* the Boston Women's Health Book Collective, ch. 6 (1978).

12 In a number of other cultures, fathers are not relegated to babysitter status, nor is their ability to be primary nurturers so readily dismissed. . . . We have evidence that in our own society men can rear and nurture their children competently and that men's methods, although different from those of women, are imaginative and constructive.

KYLE D. PRUETT, (20th-century) U.S. child psychiatrist and author. *The Nurturing Father,* ch. 2 (1987).

13 Such joint ownership creates a place where mothers can "father" and fathers can "mother." It does *not* encourage mothers and fathers to compete with one another for "first-place parent." Such competition is not especially good for marriage and furthermore drives kids nuts.

KYLE D. PRUETT, (20th-century) U.S. child psychiatrist and author. *The Nurturing Father,* ch. 13 (1987).

14 Women had to deal with the men's response when the women wanted more time "out" of the home; men now must deal with the women's response as men want more time "in."

KYLE D. PRUETT, (20th-century) U.S. child psychiatrist and author. *The Nurturing Father,* ch. 1 (1987).

15 The stereotypical five o'clock dad belongs in a diorama with his "Ask your mother" and his "Don't be a cry baby." The father who believes hugs and kisses are sex-blind and a dirty diaper requires a change, not a woman, is infinitely preferable.

ANNA QUINDLEN, (20th-century) U.S. journalist and novelist. *Thinking Out Loud,* "Men at Work," February 18, 1992 (1993).

16 Rearing a family is probably the most difficult job in the world. It resembles two business firms merging their respective resources to make a single product. All the potential headaches of that opera-

tion are present when an adult male and an adult female join to steer a child from infancy to adulthood.

VIRGINIA SATIR, (20th-century) U.S. family therapist and author. *The New Peoplemaking,* ch. 2 (1988).

17 Mothers and fathers act in mostly similar ways toward their young children. Psychologists are still highlighting small differences rather than the overwhelming similarities in parents' behaviors. I think this is a hangover from the 1950s re-emergence of father as a parent. He has to be special. The best summary of the evidence on mothers and fathers with their babies is that young children of both sexes, in most circumstances, like both parents equally well. Fathers, like mothers, are good parents first and gender representatives second.

SANDRA SCARR, (20th-century) U.S. developmental psychologist and author. *Mother Care/Other Care,* pt. 2, ch. 5 (1984).

18 Most men have not had much incentive to "add on" to their skills a talent for love. They already have cultural status and power, the trade-off for being relative strangers to their children. And in view of the object lesson of working mothers' struggles, it's a trade-off they are loath to relinquish.

VICTORIA SECUNDA, (20th-century) U.S. psychologist and author. *Women and their Fathers,* ch. 3 (1992).

19 Of all the stereotypes of parenthood, one of the most destructive is the assumption that all mothers are cut out for Donna Reed kind of maternal love and that fathers are biologically incapable of it.

VICTORIA SECUNDA, (20th-century) U.S. psychologist and author. *Women and Their Fathers,* ch. 4 (1992).

20 Most American children suffer too much mother and too little father.

GLORIA STEINEM, (20th-century) U.S. feminist and author. *New York Times* (August 26, 1971).

21 And when discipline is concerned, the parent who has to make it to the end of an eighteen-hour day—who works at a job and then takes on a second shift with the kids every night—is much more likely to adopt the survivor's motto: "If it works, I'll use it." From this perspective, dads who are even slightly less involved and emphasize firm limits or character-building might as well be talking a foreign language. They just don't get it.

RON TAFFEL, (20th-century) U.S. psychologist and author. *Why Parents Disagree,* ch. 4 (1994).

22 Since mothers are more likely to take children to their activities—the playground, ballet or karate class, birthday parties—they get a chance to see other children in action. . . . Fathers usually don't spend as much time with other people's kids; because of this, they have a narrower view of what constitutes "normal" behavior, and therefore what should or shouldn't require parental discipline.

RON TAFFEL, (20th-century) U.S. psychologist and author. *Why Parents Disagree,* ch. 4 (1994).

23 The research on gender and morality shows that women and men

look at the world through very different moral frameworks. Men tend to think in terms of "justice" or absolute "right and wrong," while women define morality through the filter of how relationships will be affected. Given these basic differences, why would men and women suddenly agree about disciplining children?

RON TAFFEL, (20th-century) U.S. psychologist and author. *Why Parents Disagree,* ch. 4 (1994).

24 Apart from the fact that women possess the equipment for lactation, mothers seem no more predisposed to, or innately skilled at, child care than are fathers, siblings or nonparents. Besides, women obviously come in a variety of shapes, sizes, talents and temperaments. Why shouldn't they vary in degrees of motherhood?

SHARI THURER, (20th-century) U.S. psychologist. *The Myths of Motherhood,* ch. 6 (1994).

25 Could kinder, more altruistic words come from the mouth of man than "Sure, I'll help"? They sure could. They would be "It's my turn to take charge."

MARY-LOU WEISMAN, (20th-century) U.S. journalist. "Hers," *The New York Times* (October 13, 1983).

Parents Sharing the Parenting Role: Difficulties with

1 Parenting can be established as a time-share job, but mothers are less good at "switching off" their parent identity and turning to something else. Many women envy the father's ability to set clear boundaries between home and work, between being an on-duty and an off-duty parent. . . . Women work very hard to maintain a closeness to their child. Fathers value intimacy with a child, but often do not know how to work to maintain it.

TERRI APTER, (20th-century) British psychologist and author. *Altered Loves,* ch. 2 (1990).

2 Many women are reluctant to allow men to enter their domain. They don't want men to acquire skills in what has traditionally been their area of competence and one of their main sources of self-esteem. So while they complain about the male's unwillingness to share in domestic duties, they continually push the male out when he moves too confidently into what has previously been their exclusive world.

BETTINA ARNDT, (20th-century) Australian journalist and author. *Private Lives,* ch. 2 (1986).

3 All adults who care about a baby will naturally be in competition for that baby. . . . Each adult wishes that he or she could do each job a bit more skillfully for the infant or small child than the other.

T. BERRY BRAZELTON, (20th-century) U.S. pediatrician and author. *Touchpoints,* ch. 1 (1992).

4 It is of course, entirely possible that men (or anyone who is relatively privileged) are most defensive, most obstinate and unseeing when they are worried about losing privileges. . . . In the reactions of husbands, I detect a haunting worry

about what they will lose when true gender equality arrives.

FAYE J. CROSBY, (20th-century) U.S. psychologist and author. *Juggling,* ch. 6 (1991).

5 The traditional American husband and father had the responsibilities—and the privileges—of playing the role of primary provider. Sharing that role is not easy. To yield exclusive access to the role is to surrender some of the potential for fulfilling the hero fantasy—a fantasy that appeals to us all. The loss is far from trivial.

FAYE J. CROSBY, (20th-century) U.S. psychologist and author. *Juggling,* ch. 6 (1991).

6 A father who will pursue infant care tasks with ease and proficiency is simply a father who has never been led to believe he couldn't.

MICHAEL K. MEYERHOFF, (20th-century) U.S. researcher and parent educator. "Of Baseball and Babies: Are You Unconsciously Discouraging Father Involvement in Infant Care?" *Young Children* (May 1994).

7 Let's face it. With the singular exception of breast-feeding, there is nothing about infant care that a mother is innately better qualified to do than a father. Yet we continue to unconsciously perpetuate the myth that men just don't have what it takes to be true partners in the process.

MICHAEL K. MEYERHOFF, (20th-century) U.S. researcher and parent educator. "Of Baseball and Babies: Are You Unconsciously Discouraging Father Involvement in Infant Care?" *Young Children* (May 1994).

8 The glorious dream of full father involvement in infant care will not become a widespread reality overnight. But it can happen, and it eventually will happen, . . . A lot of progress may take place in a short period of time if we just lighten up, step back, and give the guys a decent chance.

MICHAEL K. MEYERHOFF, (20th-century) U.S. researcher and parent educator. "Of Baseball and Babies: Are You Unconsciously Discouraging Father Involvement in Infant Care?" *Young Children* (May 1994).

9 When Dad can't get the diaper on straight, we laugh at him as though he were trying to walk around in high-heel shoes. Do we ever assist him by pointing out that all you have to do is lay out the diaper like a baseball diamond, put the kid's butt on the pitcher's mound, bring home plate up, then fasten the tapes at first and third base?

MICHAEL K. MEYERHOFF, (20th-century) U.S. researcher and parent educator. "Of Baseball and Babies: Are You Unconsciously Discouraging Father Involvement in Infant Care?" *Young Children* (May 1994).

10 The greatest impediments to changes in our traditional roles seem to lie not in the visible world of conscious intent, but in the murky realm of the unconscious mind.

AUGUSTUS Y. NAPIER, (20th-century) U.S. family therapist. *The Fragile Bond,* ch. 4 (1988).

11 Mothers risk alienating their mates if they expect them to hold or care for the baby exactly as they do. Fathers who are constantly criticized or corrected may lose interest in handling the baby, and this is a loss for everyone. The cycle is a dangerous one. Now the same mother feels bitter because she is no longer getting any help at home.

CATHY RINDNER TEMPELSMAN, (20th-century) U.S. journalist and author. *Child-Wise,* ch. 9 (1994).

12 Women may give lip service to wanting husbands who take on an equal role in raising children, but many will pull rank when an important decision, like how to discipline or what baby sitter to hire, has to be made.

PEPPER SCHWARTZ, (20th-century) U.S. sociologist and author. "When Dads Participate, Families Benefit," *The New York Times* (August 18, 1994).

13 As fathers, men often feel either like guests in their own homes or clumsy bulls in china shops, deferring to their wives as the "emotional experts" and squelching their own wish to be fully involved.

RON TAFFEL, (20th-century)U.S. psychologist and author. *Parenting by Heart,* ch. 1 (1991).

14 Our culture still holds mothers almost exclusively responsible when things go wrong with the kids. Sensing this ultimate accountability, women are understandably reluctant to give up control or veto power. If the finger of blame was eventually going to point in your direction, wouldn't you be?

RON TAFFEL, (20th-century) U.S. psychologist and author. *Why Parents Disagree,* ch. 2 (1994).

Parents Raising Children

1 Raising children is a creative endeavor, an art rather than a science.

BRUNO BETTELHEIM, (20th-century) Austrian-born U.S. child psychologist and author. *A Good Enough Parent,* ch. 1 (1987).

2 The goal in raising one's child is to enable him, first, to discover who he wants to be, and then to become a person who can be satisfied with himself and his way of life. Eventually he ought to be able to do in his life whatever seems important, desirable, and worthwhile to him to do; to develop relations with other people that are constructive, satisfying, mutually enriching; and to bear up well under the stresses and hardships he will unavoidably encounter during his life.

BRUNO BETTELHEIM, (20th-century) Austrian-born U.S. child psychologist and author. *A Good Enough Parent,* ch. 4 (1987).

3 How can one explain all the time and thought that goes into raising a child, all the opportunities for mistakes, all the chances to recover and try again? How does one break the news that nothing permanent can be formed in an instant—children are not weaned, potty trained, taught manners, introduced to civilization in one or two tries—as everyone imagined.

MARY KAY BLAKELY, (20th-century) U.S. journalist and author. *American Mom,* ch. 3 (1994).

4 Since civilizing children takes the better part of two decades—some twenty years of nonstop thinking, nurturing, teaching, coaxing, rewarding, forgiving, warning, punishing, sympathizing, apologizing, reminding, and repeating, not to mention deciding what to do when—I now understand that one wrong move is invariably followed by hundreds of opportunities to be wrong again.

MARY KAY BLAKELY, (20th-century) U.S. journalist and author. *American Mom,* ch. 4 (1994).

5 If it is to be done well, child-rearing requires, more than most activities of life, a good deal of decentering from one's own needs and perspectives. Such decentering is relatively easy when a society is stable and when there is an extended, supportive structure that the parent can depend upon.

DAVID ELKIND, (20th-century) U.S. child psychologist and author. *The Hurried Child,* ch. 2 (1988).

6 It's my feeling that God lends you your children until they're about eighteen years old. If you haven't made your points with them by then, it's too late.

BETTY FORD, (20th-century) U.S. First Lady. As quoted in *The Last Word,* ed. Carolyn Warner, ch. 16 (1992).

7 To nourish children and raise them against odds is in any time, any place, more valuable than to fix bolts in cars or design nuclear weapons.

MARILYN FRENCH, (20th-century) U.S. author. As quoted in *Woman to Woman,* Julia Gilden and Mark Riedman (1994).

8 The "universal moments" of child-rearing are in fact nothing less than a confrontation with the most basic problems of living in society: a facing through one's children of all the conflicts inherent in human relationships, a clarification of issues that were unresolved in one's own growing up. The experience of child-rearing not only can strengthen one as an individual but also presents the opportunity to shape human relationships of the future.

ELAINE HEFFNER, (20th-century) U.S. psychiatrist and author. *Mothering,* preface (1978).

9 I'd often heard that having pets prepares a person for parenthood. That, of course, is ridiculous. . . . I have never worried about [the cat's] grades or ability to make friends.

MARGE KENNEDY, (20th-century) U.S. author. *100 Things You Can Do to Keep Your Family Together . . . ,* pt. 3 (1994).

10 It is at once the most overwhelmingly frustrating and exasperating task and the most joyous and rewarding experience to make human beings out of children.

NEIL KURSHAN, (20th-century) U.S. rabbi and author. *Raising Your Child to Be a Mensch,* ch. 4 (1987).

11 Raising human beings is a process of teaching children right from wrong and turning them into responsible individuals.

NEIL KURSHAN, (20th-century) U.S. rabbi and author. *Raising Your Child to Be a Mensch,* ch. 1 (1987).

12 Parents decide to accept the responsibility of raising children. Any thanks they get for doing that is gravy. Grateful children are a blessing, but they aren't a necessity.

DONALD C. MEDEIROS, (20th-century) U.S. psychologist and author. *Children Under Stress,* ch. 2 (1983).

13 In considering the ledger equal, understand the greatest gift you have given your parents is the opportunity to raise you. The things a child gets from parents

can't compare to the things a parent gets from raising a child. Only by experiencing this can you understand the degree to which children give meaning to parents' lives.

FRANK PITTMAN, (20th-century) U.S. psychiatrist and family therapist. "How to Manage Mom and Dad," *Psychology Today* (November/December 1994).

14 The end product of child raising is not only the child but the parents, who get to go through each stage of human development from the other side, and get to relive the experiences that shaped them, and get to rethink everything their parents taught them. They get, in effect, to reraise themselves and become their own person.

FRANK PITTMAN, (20th-century) U.S. psychiatrist and family therapist. "How to Manage Mom and Dad," *Psychology Today* (November/December 1994).

15 The person who designed a robot that could act and think as well as your four-year-old would deserve a Nobel Prize. But there is no public recognition for bringing up several truly human beings.

C. JOHN SOMMERVILLE, (20th-century) U.S. historian and author. *The Rise and Fall of Childhood,* ch. 1 (rev. 1990).

Parents Raising Girls and Boys Differently

1 My son and daughter tell me where they are in very different ways. I know where my son is because I hear him. I know where my daughter is because she tells me.

ANONYMOUS FATHER, as quoted in *Raising a Daughter* by Jeanne Elium and Don Elium, ch. 1 (1994).

2 A father . . . knows exactly what those boys at the mall have in their depraved little minds because he once owned such a depraved little mind himself. In fact, if he thinks enough about the plans that he used to have for young girls, the father not only will support his wife in keeping their daughter home but he might even run over to the mall and have a few of those boys arrested.

BILL COSBY, (20th-century) U.S. comedian and author. *Fatherhood,* ch. 6 (1986).

3 There are two kinds of fathers in traditional households: the fathers of sons and the fathers of daughters. These two kinds of fathers sometimes co-exist in one and the same man. For instance, Daughter's Father kisses his little girl goodnight, strokes her hair, hugs her warmly, then goes into the next room where he becomes Son's Father, who says in a hearty voice, perhaps with a light punch on the boy's shoulder: "Goodnight, Son, see ya in the morning."

LETTY COTTIN POGREBIN, (20th-century) U.S. editor and author. *Family and Politics,* ch. 5 (1983).

4 Mothers tend to encourage their sons to run away and romp. . . . Mothers of little boys often complain that "There's no controlling him." "He's all over the place. . . ." The complaints are tinged with more than a little pride at the boy's marvelous independence and masculine bravado. It's almost as though the mother enjoyed being overwhelmed by her spectacular conquering hero.

LOUISE J. KAPLAN, (20th-century) U.S. psychologist and author. *Oneness and Sepa-*

rateness: From Infant to Individual, ch. 5 (1978).

5 We're not always aware of subliminal messages we send, like "Big boys don't cry" or "Stop whining," which are reflections of society's credo that men should not show their emotions. Boys and men are not inherently less emotional than women; they are taught to be that way, which means that mothers and fathers have an important responsibility in raising sons who are aware of their emotions.

Elyse Zorn Karlin, (20th-century) U.S. journalist and author. *Sons: A Mother's Manual,* ch. 5 (1994).

6 Girls . . . were allowed to play in the house . . . and boys were sent outdoors. . . . Boys ran around in the yard with toy guns going kksshh-kksshh, fighting wars for made-up reasons and arguing about who was dead, while girls stayed inside and played with dolls, creating complex family groups and learning how to solve problems through negotiation and role-playing. Which gender is better equipped, on the whole, to live an adult life, would you guess?

Garrison Keillor, (20th-century) U.S. humorist and author. *The Book of Guys* (1993).

7 When it comes to toys, however, fathers tighten the gender-based screws: there will be no unisexuality, especially with their sons. While mothers generally allow both boys and girls to choose from an array of playthings, it is fathers who most often decree what is considered "appropriate" for sons and daughters.

Victoria Secunda, (20th-century) U.S. psychologist and author. *Women and Their Fathers,* ch. 1 (1992).

The Link Between Generations

1 The fathers have eaten sour grapes, and the children's teeth are set on edge.

Bible: Hebrew, *Ezekiel* 18:2.

2 I've begun to appreciate the generational patterns that ripple out from our lives like stones dropped in water, pulsing outward even after we are gone. Although we have but one childhood, we relive it first through our children's and then our grandchildren's eyes.

Anne Cassidy, (20th-century) U.S. journalist and author. "Circular Living in a Linear Work," *Christian Science Monitor* (February 23, 1989).

3 Raising children is an incredibly hard and risky business in which no cumulative wisdom is gained: each generation repeats the mistakes the previous one made.

Bill Cosby, (20th-century) U.S. comedian and author. *Fatherhood,* ch. 1 (1986).

4 Every generation rediscovers and re-evaluates the meaning of infancy and childhood.

Arnold Gesell, (20th-century) U.S. child development specialist. *Infant and Child in the Culture of Today,* ch. 24 (1943).

5 Before I had my first child, I never really looked forward in anticipation to the future. As I watched my son grow and learn, I began to imagine the world this generation of children would live in. I thought

of the children they would have, and of their children. I felt connected to life both before my time and beyond it. Children are our link to future generations that we will never see.

LOUISE HART, (20th-century) U.S. community psychologist and author. *The Winning Family,* ch. 26 (1987).

6 The Golden Rule of Parenting is: Do unto your children as you wish your parents had done unto you!

LOUISE HART, (20th-century) U.S. community psychologist and author. *The Winning Family,* ch. 8 (1987).

7 That children link us with the future is hardly news. . . . When we participate in the growth of children, a sense of wonder must take hold of us, providing for us a sense of future. Without the intimation of concrete individual futures, it is hardly worth bothering with social change and improvement.

GRETA HOFMANN NEMIROFF, (20th-century) U.S. author. As quoted in *Mother Journeys,* ed. Maureen T. Reddy, Martha Roth, Amy Sheldon, sec. 3 (1994).

8 Rather than accepting the drifting separation of the generations, we might begin to define a more complex and interesting set of life stages and parenting passages, each emphasizing the connections to the generations ahead and behind. As I grow older, for example, I might first see my role as a parent in need of older, mentoring parents, and then become a mentoring parent myself. When I become a grandparent, I might expect to seek out older mentoring grandparents, and then later become a mentoring grandparent.

RICHARD LOUV, (20th-century) U.S. journalist and author. *Childhood's Future,* pt. 1, ch. 3 (1991).

9 I call it our collective inheritance of isolation. We inherit isolation in the bones of our lives. It is passed on to us as sure as the shape of our noses and the length of our legs. When we are young, we are taught to keep to ourselves for reasons we may not yet understand. As we grow up we become the "men who never cry" and the "women who never complain." We become another generation of people expected not to bother others with our problems.

PAULA C. LOWE, (20th-century) U.S. family educator and author. *Care Pooling,* ch. 5 (1993).

10 Each generation's job is to question what parents accept on faith, to explore possibilities, and adapt the last generation's system of values for a new age.

FRANK PITTMAN, (20th-century) U.S. psychiatrist and family therapist. "How to Manage Mom and Dad," *Psychology Today* (November/December 1994).

11 The child who would be an adult must forgive the parents for all the ways they didn't raise him or her just right, whether their errors were in loving too much or too little. All parents, as parents of adults, do deflating things that make you feel like a child. If you have children, you'll do those things too and eventually laugh about them.

FRANK PITTMAN, (20th-century) U.S. psychiatrist and family therapist. "How to Manage Mom and Dad," *Psychology Today* (November/December 1994).

12 Parents are like shuttles on a loom. They join the threads of the past

with threads of the future and leave their own bright patterns as they go.

FRED ROGERS, (20th-century) U.S. children's television personality and author. *Mister Rogers Talks With Parents,* ch. 1 (1983).

13 The world is never the same as it was. . . . And that's as it should be. Every generation has the obligation to make the preceding generation irrelevant. It happens in little ways: no longer knowing the names of bands or even recognizing their sounds of music; no longer implicitly understanding life's rules: wearing plaid Bermuda shorts to the grocery and not giving it another thought.

JIM SHAHIN, (20th-century) U.S. magazine editor. "Parenting in the Nineties," *American Way* (March 1, 1994).

14 Americans are notorious for looking to their children for approval. How our children turn out and what they think of us has become the "final judgment" on our lives. . . . We imagine that the rising generation is rendering history's verdict on us. We may resent children simply because we expect a harsh judgment from them.

C. JOHN SOMMERVILLE, (20th-century) U.S. historian and author. *The Rise and Fall of Childhood,* ch. 1 (rev. 1990).

15 Because we believe ourselves to be better parents than our parents, we expect to produce "better" children than they produced.

JUDITH VIORST, (20th-century) U.S. novelist and poet. *Necessary Losses,* ch. 14 (1986).

16 Children begin by loving their parents. After a time they judge them. Rarely, if ever, do they forgive them.

OSCAR WILDE, (19th-century) Anglo-Irish playwright and author. Lord Illingworth in *A Woman of No Importance,* act 2.

17 You didn't have a choice about the parents you inherited, but you do have a choice about the kind of parent you will be.

MARIAN WRIGHT EDELMAN, (20th-century) U.S. child advocate and author. *The Measure of Our Success: A Letter to My Child and Yours,* IV, p. 71 (1992).

Separation and Divorce

1 Divorce is the psychological equivalent of a triple coronary bypass.

MARY KAY BLAKELY, (20th-century) U.S. journalist and author. *American Mom,* ch. 6 (1994).

2 Three factors—the belief that child care is female work, the failure of ex-husbands to support their children, and higher male wages at work—have taken the economic rug from under that half of married women who divorce.

ARLIE HOCHSCHILD, (20th-century) U.S. sociologist and author. *The Second Shift,* ch. 16 (1989).

3 Guilty, guilty, guilty is the chant divorced parents repeat in their heads. This constant reminder remains just below our consciousness. Nevertheless, its presence clouds our judgment, inhibits our actions, and interferes in our relationship with our children. Guilt is a major roadblock to building a new life for yourself and to being an effective parent.

STEPHANIE MARSTON, (20th-century) U.S. family therapist and author. *The Divorced Parent,* ch. 10 (1994).

4 You can't change what happened between you and your ex-spouse,

but you can change your attitude about it. Forgiveness doesn't mean that what your ex did was right or that you condone what he or she did; it simply means that you no longer want to hold a grudge. Forgiveness is not a gift for the other person; it is a purely selfish act that allows you to put the past behind you.

STEPHANIE MARSTON, (20th-century) U.S. family therapist and author. *The Divorced Parent,* ch. 3 (1994).

5 You have many choices. You can choose forgiveness over revenge, joy over despair. You can choose action over apathy. . . . You hold the key to how well you make the emotional adjustment to your divorce and consequently how well your children will adapt.

STEPHANIE MARSTON, (20th-century) U.S. family therapist and author. *The Divorced Parent,* ch. 3 (1994).

6 Adolescence is a time when children are supposed to move away from parents who are holding firm and protective behind them. When the parents disconnect, the children have no base to move away from or return to. They aren't ready to face the world alone. With divorce, adolescents feel abandoned, and they are outraged at that abandonment. They are angry at both parents for letting them down. Often they feel that their parents broke the rules and so now they can too.

MARY PIPHER, (20th-century) U.S. psychologist and author. *Reviving Ophelia,* ch. 7 (1994).

7 Adolescents' immature thinking makes it difficult for them to process the divorce. They tend to see things in black-and-white terms and have trouble putting events into perspective. They are absolute in their judgments and expect perfection in parents. They are likely to be self-conscious about their parent's failures and critical of their every move. They have the expectations that parents will keep them safe and happy and are shocked by the broken covenant. Adolescents are unforgiving.

MARY PIPHER, (20th-century) U.S. psychologist and author. *Reviving Ophelia,* ch. 7 (1994).

8 For a couple with young children, divorce seldom comes as a "solution" to stress, only as a way to end one form of pain and accept another.

FRED ROGERS, (20th-century) U.S. children's television personality and author. *Mister Rogers Talks With Parents,* ch. 10 (1983).

9 There are many things children accept as "grown-up things" over which they have no control and for which they have no responsibility—for instance, weddings, having babies, buying houses, and driving cars. Parents who are separating really need to help their children put divorce on that grown-up list, so that children do not see themselves as the cause of their parents' decision to live apart.

FRED ROGERS, (20th-century) U.S. children's television personality and author. *Mister Rogers Talks With Parents,* ch. 10 (1983).

Adult Siblings

1 Sisters is probably the most competitive relationship within the family, but once the sisters are

grown, it becomes the strongest relationship.

MARGARET MEAD, (20th-century) U.S. anthropologist and author. As quoted in *Woman to Woman,* Julia Gilden and Mark Riedman (1994).

2 As siblings we were inextricably bound, even though our connections were loose and frayed. . . . And each time we met, we discovered to our surprise and dismay how quickly the intensity of childhood feelings reappeared. . . . No matter how old we got or how often we tried to show another face, reality was filtered through yesterday's memories.

JANE MERSKY LEDER, (20th-century) U.S. author. *Brothers and Sisters,* prologue (1991).

3 The quickness with which all the "stuff" from childhood can reduce adult siblings to kids again underscores the strong and complex connections between brothers and sisters. . . . It doesn't seem to matter how much time has elapsed or how far we've traveled. Our brothers and sisters bring us face to face with our former selves and remind us how intricately bound up we are in each other's lives.

JANE MERSKY LEDER, (20th-century) U.S. author. *Brothers and Sisters,* ch. 1 (1991).

4 Whether changes in the sibling relationship during adolescence create long-term rifts that spill over into adulthood depends upon the ability of brothers and sisters to constantly redefine their connection. Siblings either learn to accept one another as independent individuals with their own sets of values and behaviors or cling to the shadow of the brother and sister they once knew.

JANE MERSKY LEDER, (20th-century) U.S. author. *Brothers and Sisters,* ch. 3 (1991).

Sibling Rivalry

1 The question that's probably uppermost in the child's mind is: Why do my parents want to have a baby? Don't they love me? And if they love me, why do they need another one? Aren't I enough? Imagine for a minute yourself in a similar situation. Your husband comes home and says: "Honey I love you so much, I've decided to go get another wife so I can have two." How would you feel?

LAWRENCE BALTER, (20th-century) U.S. psychologist and author. *Dr. Balter's Child Sense,* pt. 3, ch. 42 (1985).

2 As parents it is well to be aware of the tendency to equate energetic activity with contest. Our children's worth does not depend on their ability to trounce one another. And surely we can find ways of frolicking and being healthy and active together in some joyful, free way that is not an adversary relationship.

POLLY BERRIEN BERENDS, (20th-century) U.S. author. *Whole Child/Whole Parent,* ch. 4 (rev. 1987).

3 The surest route to breeding jealousy is to compare. Since jealousy comes from feeling "less than" another, comparisons only fan the fires.

DOROTHY CORKVILLE BRIGGS, (20th-century) U.S. parent educator. *Your Child's Self-Esteem,* ch. 7 (1975).

4 No matter how calmly you try to referee, parenting will eventually

produce bizarre behavior, and I'm not talking about the kids.

BILL COSBY, (20th-century) U.S. comedian and author. *Fatherhood,* ch. 4 (1986).

5 From their struggles to establish dominance over each other, siblings become tougher and more resilient. From their endless rough-housing with each other, they develop speed and agility. From their verbal sparring they learn the difference between being clever and being hurtful. From the normal irritations of living together, they learn how to assert themselves, defend themselves, compromise. And sometimes, from their envy of each other's special abilities they become inspired to work harder, persist and achieve.

ADELE FABER, (20th-century) U.S. parent educator. *Siblings Without Rivalry,* introduction (1987).

6 Take two kids in competition for their parents' love and attention. Add to that the envy that one child feels for the accomplishments of the other; the resentment that each child feels for the privileges of the other; the personal frustrations that they don't dare let out on anyone else but a brother or sister, and it's not hard to understand why in families across the land, the sibling relationship contains enough emotional dynamite to set off rounds of daily explosions.

ADELE FABER, (20th-century) parent educator. *Siblings Without Rivalry,* introduction (1987).

7 The mere existence of an additional child or children in the family could signify Less. Less time alone with parents. Less attention for hurts and disappointments. Less approval for accomplishments. . . . No wonder children struggle so fiercely to be first or best. No wonder they mobilize all their energy to have more or most. Or better still, all.

ADELE FABER, (20th-century) U.S. parent educator. *Siblings Without Rivalry,* introduction (1987).

8 Sisters define their rivalry in terms of competition for the gold cup of parental love. It is never perceived as a cup which runneth over, rather a finite vessel from which the more one sister drinks, the less is left for the others.

ELIZABETH FISHEL, (20th-century) U.S. author. As quoted in *Woman to Woman,* Julia Gilden and Mark Riedman (1994).

9 It seems to me that we have to draw the line in sibling rivalry whenever rivalry goes out of bounds into destructive behavior of a physical or verbal kind. The principle needs to be this: Whatever the reasons for your feelings you will have to find civilized solutions.

SELMA H. FRAIBERG, (20th-century) U.S. child psychoanalyst and author. *The Magic Years,* ch. 8 (1959).

10 Not all conflicts between siblings are good, of course. A child who is repeatedly humiliated or made to feel insignificant by a brother or sister is learning little except humiliation and shame.

LAWRENCE KUTNER, (20th-century) U.S. child psychologist and author. *Parent and Child,* ch. 10 (1991).

11 The more parents intervene, the more siblings fight. And the bigger role parents assume in settling

arguments, the less chance siblings have to learn how to resolve conflicts for themselves.

JANE MERSKY LEDER, (20th-century) U.S. author. *Brothers and Sisters,* ch. 3 (1991).

12 Most parents aren't even aware of how often they compare their children. . . . Comparisons carry the suggestion that specific conditions exist for parental love and acceptance. Thus, even when one child comes out on top in a comparison she is left feeling uneasy about the tenuousness of her position and the possibility of faring less well in the next comparison.

MARIANNE E. NEIFERT, (20th-century) U.S. pediatrician and author. *Dr. Mom's Parenting Guide,* ch. 4 (1991).

13 Trying to love your children equally is a losing battle. Your children's scorecards will never match your own. No matter how meticulously you measure and mete out your love and attention, and material gifts, it will never feel truly equal to your children. . . . Your children will need different things at different times, and true equality won't really serve their different needs very well, anyway.

MARIANNE E. NEIFERT, (20th-century) U.S. pediatrician and author. *Dr. Mom's Parenting Guide,* ch. 4 (1991).

14 It's a fact of life: Children will naturally seek to gain the upper hand in a family, often at the expense of a younger or more vulnerable sibling. They will observe one another closely and take advantage of any edge they can achieve.

NANCY SAMALIN, (20th-century) U.S. parent educator and author. *Love and Anger: the Parental Dilemma,* ch. 4 (1991).

15 Sibling rivalry is inevitable. The only sure way to avoid it is to have one child.

NANCY SAMALIN, (20th-century) U.S. parent educator and author. *Loving Your Child Is Not Enough,* ch. 8 (1987).

16 When children are physically hurting each other, we can't let them "work it out themselves." Just as we stop a child from touching a hot stove or running in the street, we need to protect one child from the other—for the sake of both.

NANCY SAMALIN, (20th-century) U.S. parent educator and author. *Loving Your Child Is Not Enough,* ch. 8 (1987).

17 Eventually we will learn that the loss of indivisible love is another of our necessary losses, that loving extends beyond the mother-child pair, that most of the love we receive in this world is love we will have to share—and that sharing begins at home, with our sibling rivals.

JUDITH VIORST, (20th-century) U.S. novelist and poet. *Necessary Losses,* ch. 6 (1986).

18 My mom says I'm her sugarplum.
My mom says I'm her lamb.
My mom says I'm completely perfect
Just the way I am.
My mom says I'm a super-special wonderful terrific little guy.
My mom just had another baby.
Why?

JUDITH VIORST, (20th-century) U.S. novelist and poet. *If I Were in Charge of the World and Other Worries* (1981).

19 We have to divide mother love with our brothers and sisters. Our parents can help us cope with the loss of our dream of absolute love. But

they cannot make us believe that we haven't lost it.

JUDITH VIORST, (20th-century) U.S. novelist and poet. *Necessary Losses,* ch. 6 (1986).

20 When mother boasts cheerfully, "Johnny is just crazy about his new little sister. . . . You love her, don't you, dear?" Johnny hasn't much choice but to lie like a gentleman . . . and then he begins to worry that something terrible may happen to little sister. She might get eaten by a stray tiger or fall into a tub of scalding water. . . . It doesn't often occur to that grownup to wonder why tigers and tubs of scalding water are all of a sudden wandering around the house waiting for an unwary moment.

LEONTINE YOUNG, (20th-century) U.S. social worker and author. *Life Among the Giants,* ch. 14 (1965).

Single Parents/Single Parenting

1 Many single parents say that they feel they have to be both a mother and a father to the child. This is impossible, so you may as well rule out that idea. . . . As a single parent, you cannot be both a man and a woman. Who you are is a parent.

LAWRENCE BALTER, (20th-century) U.S. psychologist and author. *Who's In Control?* ch. 7 (1989).

2 Forget dating. Forget striking a balance between work and family. Most single parents, whether they are divorced, widowed, or single by choice, report that discipline is by far the toughest issue.

JEAN CALLAHAN, (20th-century) U.S. journalist. "Single Parents," *Parenting Magazine* (February 1992).

3 For most women who are considering it, single motherhood is not their first choice, but it's not their last one either. They would *prefer* a husband in their family, but they'd rather have a family without one than no family at all.

ANNE CASSIDY, (20th-century) U.S. journalist and author. "Every Child Should Have a Father But. . . .," *McCall's* (March 1985).

4 Single mothers have as much to teach their children as married mothers and as much love to share—maybe more. Yet their motives are often labeled selfish and single-minded—never mind all the babies brought into the world to snag husbands, "save" faltering marriages or produce heirs.

ANNE CASSIDY, (20th-century) U.S. journalist and author. "Every Child Should Have a Father But. . . .," *McCall's* (March 1985).

5 It's important for all single parents to remember that not everything that goes wrong, from your son's bad attitude toward school to the six holes in your teenage daughter's ear, is because you live in a single-parent home. Every family has its problems.

MARGE KENNEDY, (20th-century) U.S. author. *The Single Parent Family,* ch. 6 (1994).

6 No matter how children came to be living with just one parent, they need to be told, again and again, that your family's configuration is the result of an adult decision or an act of fate that has nothing whatsoever to do with them.

MARGE KENNEDY, (20th-century) U.S. author. *The Single Parent Family,* ch. 3 (1994).

7 Single parents in particular may have trouble maintaining themselves as authority figures because of underlying guilt; they feel a continuing sense that they have deprived their kids of the second parent, and so they tend to give in to the children's requests, even when unreasonable.

Marge Kennedy, (20th-century) U.S. author. *The Single Parent Family,* ch. 3 (1994).

8 Yes, single-parent families are different from two-parent families. And urban families are different from rural ones, and families with six kids and a dog are different from one-child, no-pet households. But even if there is only one adult presiding at the dinner table, yours is every bit as much a real family as are the Waltons.

Marge Kennedy, (20th-century) U.S. author. *The Single Parent Family,* ch. 2 (1994).

Stepfamilies

1 For better or worse, stepparenting is self-conscious parenting. You're damned if you do, and damned if you don't.

Anonymous Parent, as quoted in *Making It as a Stepparent,* Claire Berman, introduction (1980).

2 The role of the stepmother is the most difficult of all, because you can't ever just be. You're constantly being tested—by the children, the neighbors, your husband, the relatives, old friends who knew the children's parents in their first marriage, and by yourself.

Anonymous Stepparent, as quoted in *Making It as a Stepparent,* Claire Berman, introduction (1980).

3 It is best for all parties in the combined family to take matters slowly, to use the crock pot instead of the pressure cooker, and not to aim for a perfect blend but rather to recognize the pleasures to be enjoyed in retaining some of the distinct flavors of the separate ingredients.

Claire Berman, (20th-century) U.S. author. *Making It as a Stepparent,* ch. 4 (1980).

4 Most important is the recognition that stepparenting is different from primary parenting. It can be just as satisfying, it can be a reciprocally loving and caring relationship between parent and child, and it can provide some very good moments when it works, but it is different.

Claire Berman, (20th-century) U.S. author. *Making It as a Stepparent,* introduction (1980).

5 Two myths must be shattered: that of the evil stepparent . . . and the myth of instant love, which places unrealistic demands on all members of the blended family. . . . Between the two opposing myths lies reality. The recognition of reality is, I believe, the most important step toward the building of a successful second family.

Claire Berman, (20th-century) U.S. author. *Making It as a Stepparent,* introduction (1980).

6 Compared to other parents, remarried parents seem more desirous of their child's approval, more alert to the child's emotional state, and more sensitive in their parent-child relations. Perhaps this is the result of heightened empathy for the child's suffering, perhaps it is a guilt

reaction; in either case, it gives the child a potent weapon—the power to disrupt the new household and come between parent and the new spouse.

LETTY COTTIN POGREBIN, (20th-century) U.S. editor and author. *Family and Politics,* ch. 5 (1983).

7 For even the most nurturing, devoted, loving stepfather has, with a stepdaughter, an uphill battle. The relationship can test the mettle of the sturdiest marriage, the sanity of the most circumspect husband.

VICTORIA SECUNDA, (20th-century) U.S. psychologist and author. *Women and their Fathers,* ch. 2 (1992).

8 From the adolescent's perspective, it's like discovering that another layer of management (the stepparent) is being thrust between you and the boss (parent) you've reported to for twelve, fourteen, or even sixteen years. Or worse, that the business (the home) has been bought out from under you. From the teenager's perspective, remarriage can feel like a hostile takeover.

LAURENCE STEINBERG, (20th-century) U.S. professor of psychology and author. *You and Your Adolescent,* ch. 3 (1990).

Ages and Stages of Life

Infants/Babies

1 We can see that the baby is as much an instrument of nourishment for us as we are for him.

Polly Berrien Berends, (20th-century) U.S. author. *Whole Child/Whole Parent,* ch. 2 (rev. 1987).

2 Babies are beautiful, wonderful, exciting, enchanting, extraordinary little creatures—who grow up into ordinary folk like us.

Doris Dyson, as quoted in *What Is a Baby?,* Richard and Helen Exley.

3 Babies control and bring up their families as much as they are controlled by them; in fact . . . the family brings up baby by being brought up by him.

Erik H. Erikson, (20th-century) German-born U.S. psychoanalyst and author. *Childhood and Society* (1950).

4 Loving a baby is a circular business, a kind of feedback loop. The more you give the more you get and the more you get the more you feel like giving.

Penelope Leach, (20th-century) British child development specialist and author. *Your Baby and Child,* introduction (1983).

5 Of all the joys that lighten suffering on earth, what joy is welcomed like a newborn child?

Dorothy L. Nolte, (20th-century) U.S. poet. As quoted in *The Last Word,* ed. Carolyn Warner, ch. 16 (1992).

6 Parents sometimes think of newborns as helpless creatures, but in fact parents' behavior is much more under the infant's control than the reverse. Does he come running when you cry?

Sandra Scarr, (20th-century) U.S. developmental psychologist and author. *Mother Care/Other Care,* pt. 3, ch. 6 (1984).

7 A baby is a blank cheque made payable to the human race.

Barbara Christine Seifert, as quoted in *What Is a Baby?,* Richard and Helen Exley.

8 A baby is God's way of saying the world should go on.

Doris Smith, as quoted in *What Is a Baby?,* Richard and Helen Exley.

Infant Development

1 The truth is, no matter how trying they become, babies two and under don't have the ability to make

moral choices, so they can't be "bad." That category only exists in the adult mind.

ANNE CASSIDY, (20th-century) U.S. journalist and author. "Babies Have Bad Days Too," *Working Mother* (November 1988).

2 For infants and toddlers learning and living are the same thing. If they feel secure, treasured, loved, their own energy and curiosity will bring them new understanding and new skills.

AMY LAURA DOMBRO, (20th-century) U.S. early childhood educator and author. *The Ordinary Is Extraordinary,* ch. 1 (1988).

3 The books may say that nine-month-olds crawl, say their first words, and are afraid of strangers. Your exuberantly concrete and special nine-month-old hasn't read them. She may be walking already, not saying a word and smiling gleefully at every stranger she sees. . . . You can support her best by helping her learn what she's trying to learn, not what the books say a typical child ought to be learning.

AMY LAURA DOMBRO, (20th-century) U.S. early childhood educator and author. *The Ordinary Is Extraordinary,* ch. 2 (1988).

4 The infant's first social achievement, then, is his willingness to let the mother out of sight without undue anxiety or rage, because she has become an inner certainty as well as an outer predictability.

ERIK H. ERIKSON,(20th-century) German-born U.S. psychoanalyst and author. *Childhood and Society,* ch. 7 (1950).

5 As your baby progresses from one milestone to the next, remember that he doesn't really leave any of them behind. In order to grow and develop to his full potential he must continually build on and strengthen all of the steps that have gone before.

STANLEY I. GREENSPAN, (20th-century) U.S. child psychiatrist and author, and **NANCY THORNDIKE GREENSPAN,** U.S. health economist. *First Feelings: Milestones in the Emotional Development of Your Baby and Child,* ch. 3 (1985).

6 It is a human circumstance that when we are born we have not yet come into existence. We are lured into our special human existence by a mothering presence that gratifies our innate urges to be suckled, held, rocked, caressed. But that same gratifying presence puts limits on desire and rations satisfaction. In this sense the mother is also the first lawgiver.

LOUISE KAPLAN, (20th-century) U.S. psychologist and author. *Adolescence,* ch. 5 (1984).

7 A two-week-old infant cries an average of one and a half hours every day. This increases to approximately three hours per day when the child is about six weeks old. By the time children are twelve weeks old, their daily crying has decreased dramatically and averages less than one hour. This same basic pattern of crying is present among children from a wide range of cultures throughout the world. It appears to be wired into the nervous system of our species.

LAWRENCE KUTNER, (20th-century) U.S. child psychologist and author. *Parent and Child,* ch. 7 (1991).

8 As one child psychologist friend of mine explains it with tongue in cheek, your baby only needs a lot of

light at night if he's reading or he's entertaining guests.

LAWRENCE KUTNER, (20th-century) U.S. child psychologist and author. *Pregnancy and Your Baby's First Year,* ch. 10 (1993).

9 I've always been impressed by the different paths babies take in their physical development on the way to walking. It's rare to see a behavior that starts out with such wide natural variation, yet becomes so uniform after only a few months.

LAWRENCE KUTNER, (20th-century) U.S. child psychologist and author. *Pregnancy and Your Baby's First Year,* ch. 9 (1993).

10 Our day you will find that you have stopped regarding your baby as a totally unpredictable and therefore rather alarming novelty, and have begun instead to think of him as a person with tastes, preferences and characteristics of his own. When that happens you will know that he has moved on from being a "newborn" and has got himself settled into life.

PENELOPE LEACH, (20th-century) British child development specialist and author. *Your Baby and Child,* ch. 3 (1977).

11 In order for an individual to partake of the world and contribute to it in a healthy way, he first needs to view that world as a basically kind, friendly, and supportive place. Such an outlook begins to be formed during infancy. It's essential that the baby establish a fundamental trust in his environment. The infant needs to learn that the world is a nurturing place where his needs will be met.

SAF LERMAN, (20th-century) U.S. parent educator and author. *Helping Children as They Grow,* ch. 1 (1983).

12 Babies learn most of what they know from interactions with their parents, but not of the formal, instructional variety. Babies learn from spontaneous, everyday events—the mailman at the door with a package to open . . . all of which need adult interpretation. They are real events of interest and concern to babies and young children. . . . By contrast, infant education is artificial and out of context.

SANDRA SCARR, (20th-century) U.S. developmental psychologist and author. *Mother Care/Other Care,* pt. 3, ch. 7 (1984).

13 Babies need social interactions with loving adults who talk with them, listen to their babblings, name objects for them, and give them opportunities to explore their worlds.

SANDRA SCARR, (20th-century) U.S. developmental psychologist and author. *Mother Care/Other Care,* ch. 1 (1984).

14 Not until Freud's writings became popular did descriptions of infants center on relationships with their mothers. The idea that children have feelings of any lasting importance for their development is a very recent invention (or insight if you wish).

SANDRA SCARR, (20th-century) U.S. developmental psychologist and author. *Mother Care/Other Care,* pt. 2, ch. 3 (1984).

15 But it is a myth to assume that the larger amount of early stimulation you provide, the more beneficial it will be. The truth is that babies can be overstimulated—which is what many parents, intent on beginning

to groom their progeny for college in the cradle, end up doing.

JULIUS SEGAL, (20th-century) U.S. pediatrician. "10 Myths About Child Development," *Parents* (July 1989).

Toddlerhood/Toddlers

1 Toddlers are impulsive. One- and two-year-olds have not yet developed control over their actions. What they see, they want. What they feel, they express. What they think, they do.

NANCY BALABAN, (20th-century) U.S. professor of infancy and early childhood. "Toddlers Need Understanding," *Working Mother* (October 1990).

2 A toddler believes that if you love a person, you stay with that person 100 percent of the time.

LAWRENCE BALTER, (20th-century) U.S. psychologist and author. *Who's In Control?* ch. 3 (1989).

3 In a toddler's mind, agreeing with you means that he is indistinguishable from you. . . . The adamant little tot is fighting hard to solidify a personal sense of Self. Selfhood sometimes requires great sacrifice and often precludes cooperation.

LAWRENCE BALTER, (20th-century) U.S. psychologist and author. *Who's In Control?* ch. 3 (1989).

4 Self-centeredness is a natural outgrowth of one of the toddler's major concerns: What is me and what is mine. . . ? This is why most toddlers are incapable of sharing . . . to a toddler, what's his is what he can get his hands on. . . . When something is taken away from him, he feels as though a piece of him—an integral piece—is being torn from him.

LAWRENCE BALTER, (20th-century) U.S. psychologist and author. *Who's In Control?* ch. 3 (1989).

5 If we allow our one-and-a-half-year-old to "help" us fold laundry he will learn something about buttons, zippers, snaps, where things go, the physical properties of cloth, what happens when you drop it, how easy or hard it is to carry compared with everything else he has ever carried, what clean clothes smell like, how a big towel can turn into a small bundle, how the small bundle you just folded can turn into a big towel again, plus any songs we care to sing or stories or related or unrelated facts we care to pass on.

POLLY BERRIEN BERENDS, (20th-century) U.S. author. *Whole Child/Whole Parent,* ch. 3 (rev. 1987).

6 Once we begin to appreciate that the apparent destructiveness of the toddler in taking apart a flower or knocking down sand castles is in fact a constructive effort to understand unity, we are able to revise our view of the situation, moving from reprimand and prohibition to the intelligent channeling of his efforts and the fostering of discovery.

POLLY BERRIEN BERENDS, (20th-century) U.S. author. *Whole Child/Whole Parent,* ch. 5 (rev. 1987).

7 The child does not begin to fall until she becomes seriously interested in walking, until she actually begins learning. Falling is thus more an indication of learning than a sign of failure.

POLLY BERRIEN BERENDS, (20th-century) U.S. author. *Whole Child/Whole Parent,* ch. 4 (rev. 1987).

8 As Anna Freud remarked, the toddler who wanders off into some other aisle, feels lost, and screams anxiously for his mother never says "I got lost," but accusingly says "You lost me!" It is a rare mother who agrees that she lost him! She expects her child to stay with her; in her experience it is the child who has lost track of the mother, while in the child's experience it is the mother who has lost track of him. Each view is entirely correct from the perspective of the individual who holds it .

BRUNO BETTELHEIM, (20th-century) Austrian-born U.S. child psychologist and author. *A Good Enough Parent,* ch. 4 (1987).

9 The toddler craves independence, but he fears desertion.

DOROTHY CORKVILLE BRIGGS, (20th-century) U.S. parent educator. *Your Child's Self-Esteem,* ch. 15 (1975).

10 A two-year-old can be taught to curb his aggressions completely if the parents employ strong enough methods, but the achievement of such control at an early age may be bought at a price which few parents today would be willing to pay. The slow education for control demands much more parental time and patience at the beginning, but the child who learns control in this way will be the child who acquires healthy self-discipline later.

SELMA H. FRAIBERG, (20th-century) U.S. child psychoanalyst and author. *The Magic Years,* ch. 5 (1959).

11 If we can find a principle to guide us in the handling of the child between nine and eighteen months, we can see that we need to allow enough opportunity for the handling and investigation of objects to further intellectual development and just enough restriction required for family harmony and for the safety of the child.

SELMA H. FRAIBERG, (20th-century) U.S. child psychoanalyst and author. *The Magic Years,* ch. 3 (1959).

12 Parents who want a fresh point of view on their furniture are advised to drop down on all fours and accompany the nine- or ten-month-old on his rounds. It is probably many years since you last studied the underside of a dining room chair. The ten-month-old will study this marvel with as much concentration and reverence as a tourist in the Cathedral of Chartres.

SELMA H. FRAIBERG, (20th-century)U.S. child psychoanalyst and author. *The Magic Years,* ch. 2 (1959).

13 The two-year-old . . . loves, deeply, tenderly, extravagantly and he holds the love of his parents more dearly than anything in the world. . . . He wants to be good in order to earn their love and approval; he wants to be good so that he can love himself. (This is what we mean, later, by self-esteem.)

SELMA H. FRAIBERG, (20th-century) U.S. child psychoanalyst and author. *The Magic Years,* ch. 4 (1959).

14 We find that the child who does not yet have language at his command, the child under two-and-a-half, will be able to cooperate with our education if we go easy on the "blocking" techniques, the outright prohibitions, the "no's" and go heavy on "substitution" techniques, that is, the redirection or certain impulses

and the offering of substitute satisfactions.

SELMA H. FRAIBERG, (20th-century) U.S. child psychoanalyst and author. *The Magic Years,* ch. 5 (1959).

15 We have good reason to believe that memories of early childhood do not persist in consciousness because of the absence or fragmentary character of language covering this period. Words serve as fixatives for mental images.... Even at the end of the second year of life when word tags exist for a number of objects in the child's life, these words are discrete and do not yet bind together the parts of an experience or organize them in a way that can produce a coherent memory.

SELMA H. FRAIBERG, (20th-century) U.S. child psychoanalyst and author. *The Magic Years,* ch. 3 (1959).

16 We must remember when we speak of the "negativism" of the toddler that this is also the child who is intoxicated with the discoveries of the second year, a joyful child who is firmly bound to his parents and his new-found world through ties of love. The so-called negativism is one of the aspects of this development, but under ordinary circumstances it does not become anarchy. It's a kind of declaration of independence, but there is no intention to unseat the government.

SELMA H. FRAIBERG, (20th-century) U.S. child psychoanalyst and author. *The Magic Years,* ch. 2 (1959).

17 Even if you find yourself in a heated exchange with your toddler, it is better for your child to feel the heat rather than for him to feel you withdraw emotionally.... Active and emotional involvement between parent and child helps the child make the limits a part of himself.

STANLEY I. GREENSPAN, (20th-century) U.S. child psychiatrist and author, and **NANCY THORNDIKE GREENSPAN,** U.S. health economist. *First Feelings: Milestones in the Emotional Development of Your Baby and Child,* ch. 4 (1985).

18 As he walks away on his own two feet—the toddler's body-mind has reached its moment of perfection. The world is his and he the mighty conqueror of all he beholds.... As long as mother sticks around in the wings, the mighty acrobat confidently performs his trick of twirling in circles, walking on tiptoe, jumping, climbing, staring, naming. He is joyous, filled with his grandeur and wondrous omnipotence.

LOUISE KAPLAN, (20th-century) U.S. psychologist and author. *Adolescence,* ch. 3 (1984).

19 Paradoxically, the toddler's "No" is also a preliminary to his saying yes. It is a sign that he is getting ready to convert his mother's restrictions and prohibitions into the rules for behavior that will belong to him.

LOUISE J. KAPLAN, (20th-century) U.S. psychologist and author. *Oneness and Separateness: From Infant to Individual,* ch. 6 (1978).

20 The toddler is struggling to make sense of his parents' "No." No-saying is the helpless child's way of acting as though he had the power and authority of his parents. The more their "no's" make him feel vulnerable, the more he has to say "No" himself.

LOUISE J. KAPLAN, (20th-century) U.S. psychologist and author. *Oneness and Separateness: From Infant to Individual,* ch. 6 (1978).

21 Giving toddlers and preschoolers limited choices over such things as what they will wear ("Would you prefer your red pants or your blue pants?") and what they will eat ("For a snack, would you like some apple or some banana?") is so important. By giving your child a choice, you're addressing her growing need for power and control. By limiting her choices to selections you'd find acceptable, you're eliminating some potential arguments.

LAWRENCE KUTNER, (20th-century) U.S. child psychologist and author. *Toddlers and Preschoolers,* ch. 2 (1994).

22 The fundamental job of a toddler is to rule the universe.

LAWRENCE KUTNER, (20th-century) U.S. child psychologist and author. *Toddlers and Preschoolers,* ch. 1 (1994).

23 The word *infant* derives from Latin words meaning "not yet speaking." It emphasizes what the child cannot do and reflects the baby's total dependence on adults. The word toddler, however, demonstrates our change in perspective, for it focuses on the child's increased mobility and burgeoning independence.

LAWRENCE KUTNER, (20th-century) U.S. child psychologist and author. *Toddlers and Preschoolers,* introduction (1994).

24 Grown-up people do very little and say a great deal. . . . Toddlers say very little and do a great deal. . . . With a toddler you cannot explain, you have to show. You cannot send, you have to take. You cannot control with words, you have to use your body.

PENELOPE LEACH, (20th-century) British child development specialist and author. *Your Baby and Child,* ch. 6 (1977).

25 It is not [the toddler's] job yet to consider other people's feelings, he has to come to terms with his own first. If he hits you and you hit him back to "show him what it feels like," you will have given a lesson he is not ready to learn. He will wail as if hitting was a totally new idea to him. He makes no connections between what he did to you and what you then did to him; between your feelings and his own.

PENELOPE LEACH, (20th-century) British child development specialist and author. *Your Baby and Child,* ch. 5 (1977).

26 Your toddler is no longer a baby feeling himself as part of you, using you as his controller, facilitator, his mirror for himself and the world. But he is not yet a child either; ready to see you as a person in your own right and to take responsibility for himself and his own actions in relation to you.

PENELOPE LEACH, (20th-century) British child development specialist and author. *Your Baby and Child,* ch. 5 (1977).

27 Your toddler will be "good" if he feels like doing what you happen to want him to do and does not happen to feel like doing anything you would dislike. With a little cleverness you can organize life as a whole, and issues in particular, so that you both want the same thing most of the time.

PENELOPE LEACH, (20th-century) British child development specialist and author. *Your Baby and Child,* ch. 5 (1977).

28 Much of the emotional turmoil in the second year revolves around the difficult task of integrating the child's will into the family constellation. The child learns that her personal wishes (so cherished,

seemingly so right) need to fit reasonably well with what others want. The parents learn that they, too, have to say "no" with firmness and conviction but hopefully without harshness.

ALICIA F. LIEBERMAN, (20th-century) U.S. psychologist and author. *The Emotional Life of the Toddler,* ch. 2 (1993).

29 The most important emotional accomplishment of the toddler years is reconciling the urge to become competent and self-reliant with the longing for parental love and protection.

ALICIA F. LIEBERMAN, (20th-century) U.S. psychologist and author. *The Emotional Life of the Toddler,* ch. 1 (1993).

30 The toddler's wish to please . . . is a powerful aid in helping the child to develop a social awareness and, eventually, a moral conscience. The child's love for the parent is so strong that it causes him to change his behavior: to refrain from hitting and biting, to share toys with a peer, to become toilet trained. This wish for approval is the parent's most reliable ally in the process of socializing the child.

ALICIA F. LIEBERMAN, (20th-century) U.S. psychologist and author. *The Emotional Life of the Toddler,* ch. 2 (1993).

31 Toddlers who don't learn gradually about disappointment lose their resilience through lack of practice in give-and-take with other people's needs. They can become self-centered, demanding, and difficult to like or to be with.

ALICIA F. LIEBERMAN, (20th-century) U.S. psychologist and author. *The Emotional Life of the Toddler,* ch. 3 (1993).

32 When the toddler does something and there are consequences for his action—civilization begins.

ALICIA F. LIEBERMAN, (20th-century) U.S. psychologist and author. *The Emotional Life of the Toddler* (1993).

33 When toddlers are unable to speak about urgent matters, they must resort to crying or screaming. This happens even with adults. The voice is the carrier of emotion, and when speech fails us, we need to cry out in whatever form we can to convey our meaning. Often, what passes for negativism is really the toddler's desperate effort to make herself understood.

ALICIA F. LIEBERMAN, (20th-century) U.S. psychologist and author. *The Emotional Life of the Toddler,* ch. 2 (1993).

34 Parents find many different ways to work their way through the assertiveness of their two-year-olds, but seeing that assertiveness as positive energy being directed toward growth as a competent individual may open up some new possibilities.

FRED ROGERS, (20th-century) U.S. children's television personality and author. *Mister Rogers Talks With Parents,* ch. 2 (1983).

35 Two-year-olds are not "terrible"—but their reputation is.

BERNICE WEISSBOURD, (20th-century) U.S. family advocate and author. "Encouraging Independence," *Parents Magazine* (August 1989).

Preschooler/Preschool Development

1 Preschool children are more sophisticated than toddlers. . . .

Your goal as a parent is to nurture the child's desire to be a self-starter and help him begin to adopt some of your attitudes and values, but without humiliating the child or suppressing his newfound assertiveness.

Lawrence Balter, (20th-century) U.S. psychologist and author. *Who's In Control?* (1989).

2 The wisest thing a parent can do is let preschool children figure out themselves how to draw the human figure, or solve a whole range of problems, from overcoming Saturday-morning boredom to dealing with a neighborhood bully. But even while standing on the sidelines, parents can frequently offer support ın helping children discover what they want to accomplish.

John F. Clabby, (20th-century) U.S. journalist and author. "Teach Your Child Decision Making," *Working Mother* (August 1987).

3 Preschoolers think and talk in concrete, literal terms. When they hear a phrase such as "losing your temper," they may wonder where the lost temper can be found. Other expressions they may hear in times of crisis—"raising your voice," "crying your eyes out," "going to pieces," falling apart, "picking on each other," "you follow in your father's footsteps"—may be perplexing.

Ruth Formanek, (20th-century) U.S. psychologist and author. *Why? Children's Questions,* ch. 3 (1980).

4 Added man-made failure really hurts young children [under six]. No one has to contrive lessons for these youngsters so that they will learn how to lose—they are losers too much of the time. No one has to put them in their place—they know all too well in their hearts the little place they are in. No one has to cut them down to size—their size is painfully small. At this stage in their development we are wise to stay away from competition, from games and races and contests with winners and losers. It matters too much to each child to come in first—they cannot stand the risk of competition.

James L. Hymes, Jr., (20th-century) U.S. child psychologist and author. *Teaching the Child Under Six,* ch. 2 (1968).

5 Success matters very much to the under-six age group. These children want so desperately to be able to hold their heads high. They sound exceedingly boastful: "I can count up to five. . . ." "I can tie my shoes. . . ." "I know how old I am. Do you want to see. . . ?" Each child maintains his own public relations office. He is continuously concerned with getting his name and his skill and his knowledge and his power into the "headlines." But we mustn't be misled by this drumbeating. The bombast is as much for the child's benefit as for ours—he can't quite believe his own importance.

James L. Hymes, Jr., (20th-century) U.S. child psychologist and author. *Teaching the Child Under Six,* ch. 2 (1968).

6 We are playing with fire when we skip the years of three, four, and five to hurry children into being age six. . . . Every child has a right

to his fifth year of life, his fourth year, his third year. He has a right to live each year with joy and self-fulfillment. No one should ever claim the power to make a child mortgage his today for the sake of tomorrow.

JAMES L. HYMES, JR., (20th-century) U.S. child psychologist and author. *Teaching the Child Under Six,* ch. 2 (1968).

7 A young child is no longer simply a child; he or she is a preschooler, poised at the starting gate in the race of life.

NEIL KURSHAN, (20th-century) U.S. rabbi and author. *Raising Your Child to Be a Mensch,* ch. 3 (1987).

8 The term preschooler signals another change in our expectations of children. While toddler refers to physical development, preschooler refers to a social and intellectual activity: going to school. That shift in emphasis is tremendously important, for it is at this age that we think of children as social creatures who can begin to solve problems.

LAWRENCE KUTNER, (20th-century) U.S. child psychologist and author. *Toddlers and Preschoolers,* introduction (1994).

9 A preschool child does not emerge from your toddler on a given date or birthday. He becomes a child when he ceases to be a wayward, confusing, unpredictable and often balky person-in-the-making, and becomes a comparatively cooperative, eager-and-easy-to-please real human being—at least 60 per cent of the time.

PENELOPE LEACH, (20th-century) British child development specialist and author. *Your Baby and Child,* ch. 6 (1977).

10 The prime purpose of being four is to enjoy being four—of secondary importance is to prepare for being five.

JIM TRELEASE, (20th-century) U.S. educator and author. *The Read-Aloud Handbook,* introduction (1985).

Children and Childhood, Defined

1 A child is like a precious stone, but also a heavy burden.

SWAHILI PROVERB.

2 Children are poor men's riches.

ENGLISH PROVERB.

3 Children should be seen and not heard.

ENGLISH PROVERB.

4 Little children disturb your sleep, big ones your life.

YIDDISH PROVERB.

5 Mankind owes to the child the best it has to give.

UNITED NATIONS CONVENTION ON THE RIGHTS OF THE CHILD, (1989).

6 Small children give you headache; big children heartache.

RUSSIAN PROVERB.

7 Suffer the little children to come unto me, and forbid them not; for of such is the Kingdom of God.

BIBLE: NEW TESTAMENT, *Mark* 10:14.

8 The house with no child in it is a house with nothing in it.

WELSH PROVERB, as quoted in *The Joys of Having a Child,* Bill and Gloria Adler (1993).

9 The wolf also shall dwell with the lamb, and the leopard shall lie down with the kid; and the calf and the young lion and a little child shall lead them.

Bible: Hebrew, *Isaiah* 11:6.

10 Young children step on your feet, older children step on your heart.

Modern Proverb.

11 Children sweeten labours, but they make misfortunes more bitter.

Francis Bacon, (1561–1626) British philosopher and essayist. "Of Parents and Children," *Essays* (1625).

12 Here all mankind is equal: rich and poor alike, they love their children.

Euripides, (c. 484–406 b.c.) Greek dramatist. As quoted in *The Joys of Having a Child,* Bill and Gloria Adler (1993).

13 Childhood is not from birth to a
certain age and at a certain age.
The child is grown, and puts away
childish things.
Childhood is the kingdom where
nobody dies.
Nobody that matters, that is.

Edna St. Vincent Millay, (1892–1950) U.S. poet and author. "Childhood Is the Kingdom Where Nobody Dies," *Wine From the Grapes* (1934).

14 How sharper than a serpent's tooth
it is
To have a thankless child.

William Shakespeare, (1564–1616) English playwright and poet. King Lear in *King Lear,* act I, scene 5.

15 The child that is not clean and neat,
With lots of toys and things to eat,
He is a naughty child, I'm sure—
Or else his dear Papa is poor.

Robert Louis Stevenson, (1850–1894) British poet and author. "System," *A Child's Garden of Verses* (1885).

16 Familiarity breeds contempt—and children.

Mark Twain [Samuel Langhorne Clemens], (1835–1910) U.S. author and humorist. *Notebooks* (1935).

17 It is [children] who are God's presence, promise and hope for mankind.

Marian Wright Edelman, (20th–century) U.S. child advocate and author. *The Measure of Our Success: A Letter to My Child and Yours,* I, p. 11 (1992).

Children and Childhood, Parents' Perspectives

1 Children make your life important.

Erma Bombeck, (late 20th–century) U.S. humorist and author. *Motherhood, the Second Oldest Profession,* ch. 25 (1983).

2 God sent children for another purpose than merely to keep up the race—to enlarge our hearts; and to make us unselfish and full of kindly sympathies and affections; to give our souls higher aims; to call out all our faculties to extended enterprise and exertion; and to bring round our firesides bright faces, happy smiles, and loving, tender hearts.

Mary Botham Howitt, (20th-century) British author. As quoted in *The Last Word,* ed. Carolyn Warner, ch. 16 (1992).

3 One of the luckiest things that can happen to you in life is, I think, to have a happy childhood.

Agatha Christie, (1890–1976) British mystery author. As quoted in *Wit and Wisdom for the Peanut Butter Gang,* H. Jackson Brown (1994).

4 For me, the child is a veritable image of becoming, of possibility, poised to reach towards what is not yet, towards a growing that cannot be predetermined or prescribed. I see her and I fill the space with others like her, risking, straining, wanting to find out, to ask their own questions, to experience a world that is shared.

MAXINE GREENE, (20th-century) U.S. philosopher and educator. Commencement address, Bank Street College (1987).

5 Children are like a mirror. They help you see yourself and all the flaws that you and your partner might have avoided looking at earlier.

VIRGINIA KELLY, (20th-century) Philadelphia mother. As quoted in "Parenting Passages," *Child* (June-July 1992).

6 Childhood is an adventure both for children and for their parents. There should be freedom to explore and joy in discovery. The important discoveries for both parents and children seldom come at the points where the path is smooth and straight. It is the curves in that path to adventure that make the trip interesting and worthwhile.

LAWRENCE KUTNER, (20th-century) U.S. child psychologist and author. *Parent and Child,* introduction (1991).

7 We like the idea of childhood but are not always crazy about the kids we know. We like it, that is, when we are imagining our own childhoods. So part of our apparent appreciation of youth is simply envy.

C. JOHN SOMMERVILLE, (20th-century) U.S. historian and author. *The Rise and Fall of Childhood,* ch. 1 (rev. 1990).

8 There are only two things a child will share willingly—communicable diseases and his mother's age.

BENJAMIN SPOCK, (20th-century) U.S. pediatrician and author. *Dr. Spock's Baby and Child Care* (1945, rev. 1985).

Child Development, General

1 Development, it turns out, occurs through this process of progressively more complex exchange between a child and somebody else—especially somebody who's crazy about that child.

URIE BRONFENBRENNER, (20th-century) U.S. psychologist and author. As quoted in *Childhood,* Robert H. Wozniak (1991).

2 Indeed, there are no easy correlations between parental ideology, class or race and "successful" child development. Many children the world over have revealed a kind of toughness and plasticity that make the determined efforts of some parents to spare their children the slightest pain seem ironic.

ROBERT COLES, (20th-century) U.S. child psychiatrist and author. *Children of Crisis,* ch. 9 (1964).

3 Every child has an inner timetable for growth—a pattern unique to him. . . . Growth is not steady, forward, upward progression. It is instead a switchback trail; three steps forward, two back, one around the bushes, and a few simply standing, before another forward leap.

DOROTHY CORKVILLE BRIGGS, (20th-century) U.S. parent educator. *Your Child's Self-Esteem,* ch. 13 (1975).

4 It no longer makes sense to speak of "feeding problems" or "sleep problems" or "negative behavior" as if they were distinct categories, but to speak of "problems of development" and to search for the meaning of feeding and sleep disturbances or behavior disorders in the developmental phase which has produced them.

SELMA H. FRAIBERG, (20th-century) U.S. child psychoanalyst and author. *The Magic Years,* ch. 3 (1959).

5 The child begins life as a pleasure-seeking animal; his infantile personality is organized around his own appetites and his own body. In the course of his rearing the goal of exclusive pleasure seeking must be modified drastically, the fundamental urges must be subject to the dictates of conscience and society, urges must be capable of postponement and in some instances of renunciation completely.

SELMA H. FRAIBERG, (20th-century) U.S. child psychoanalyst and author. *The Magic Years,* ch. 1 (1959).

6 The child's personality is a product of slow gradual growth. His nervous system matures by stages and natural sequences. He sits before he stands; he babbles before he talks; he fabricates before he tells the truth; he draws a circle before he draws a square; he is selfish before he is altruistic; he is dependent on others before he achieves dependence on self. All of his abilities, including his morals, are subject to laws of growth. The task of child care is not to force him into a predetermined pattern but to guide his growth.

ARNOLD GESELL, (20th-century) U.S. child development specialist. *Infant and Child in the Culture of Today,* ch. 1 (1943).

7 Children allowed to develop at their own speed will usually win the race of life.

FRED O. GOSMAN, (20th-century) U.S. author. *How to Be a Happy Parent . . . in Spite of Your Children,* ch. 2 (1995).

8 There is always one moment in childhood when the door opens and lets the future in.

GRAHAM GREENE, (20th-century) British author. *The Power and the Glory,* pt. 1, ch. 1 (1940).

9 Young children make only the simple assumption: "This is life—you go along. . . ." He stands ready to go along with whatever adults seem to want. He stands poised, trying to figure out what they want. The young child is almost at the mercy of adults—it is so important to him to please.

JAMES L. HYMES, JR., (20th-century) U.S. child psychologist and author. *Teaching the Child Under Six,* ch. 2 (1968).

10 There's one basic rule you should remember about development charts that will save you countless hours of worry. . . . The fact that a child passes through a particular developmental stage is always more important than the age of that child when he or she does it. In the long run, it really doesn't matter whether you learn to walk at ten months or fifteen months—as long as you learn how to walk.

LAWRENCE KUTNER, (20th-century) U.S. child psychologist and author. *Pregnancy and Your Baby's First Year,* ch. 6 (1993).

11 If nature has commanded that of all the animals, infancy shall last longest in human beings—it is because nature knows how many rivers there are to cross and paths to retrace. Nature provides time for mistakes to be corrected (by both children and adults), for prejudices to overcome, and for children to catch their breath and restore their image of themselves, peers, parents, teachers, and the world.

Loris Malaguzzi, (1920–1994) Italian early childhood education specialist. As quoted in *The Hundred Languages of Children,* ch. 3, Carolyn Edwards (1993).

12 A child becomes an adult when he realizes that he has a right not only to be right but also to be wrong.

Thomas Szasz, (20th-century) U.S. psychologist. "Childhood" *The Second Sin* (1973).

Child Development, Parents' Understanding of

1 It's a rare parent who can see his or her child clearly and objectively. At a school board meeting I attended . . . the only definition of a gifted child on which everyone in the audience could agree was "mine."

Jane Adams, (20th-century) U.S. author. *I'm Still Your Mother,* ch. 4 (1994).

2 I know that each stage is not going to last forever. I used to think that when he was little. Whenever he was in a bad stage I thought that he was going to be like that for the rest of his life and that I'd better do something to shape him up. When he was in a good state, I thought he was going to be a perfect child and I would never have to worry; he was always going to stay that way.

Anonymous Parent Of An Eight-Year-Old, as quoted in *Between Generations,* Ellen Galinsky, ch. 4 (1981).

3 Much of what contrives to create critical moments in parenting stems from a fundamental misunderstanding as to what the child is capable of at any given age. If a parent misjudges a child's limitations as well as his own abilities, the potential exists for unreasonable expectations, frustration, disappointment and an unrealistic belief that what the child really needs is to be punished.

Lawrence Balter, (20th-century) U.S. psychologist and author. *Who's In Control?* ch. 2 (1989).

4 Even the most normal and unavoidable problems can take on ominous proportions when one believes that one's child's entire future is decided by the way one handles a certain situation.

Bruno Bettelheim, (20th-century) Austrian-born U.S. child psychologist and author. *A Good Enough Parent,* ch. 1 (1987).

5 Good enough parents endeavor to evaluate and respond to matters both from their adult perspective and from the quite different one of the child, and to base their actions on a reasonable integration of the two, while accepting that the child, because of his immaturity, can understand matters only from his point of view.

Bruno Bettelheim, (20th-century) Austrian-born U.S. child psychologist and author. *A Good Enough Parent,* ch. 4 (1987).

6 Those feelings of envy are familiar to many of us. We see our children accomplishing things that we've always been afraid to try, or we give

them opportunities that we never had, and we find ourselves feeling jealousy mixed with our pride, or we feel resentful when they take it all for granted.

Ruth Davidson Bell, (20th-century) U.S. author. *Ourselves and Our Children,* the Boston Women's Health Book Collective, ch. 3 (1978).

7 When you take a light perspective, it's easier to step back and relax when your child doesn't walk until fifteen months, . . . is not interested in playing ball, wants to be a cheerleader, doesn't want to be a cheerleader, has clothes strewn in the bedroom, has difficulty making friends, hates piano lessons, is awkward and shy, reads books while you are driving through the Grand Canyon, gets caught shoplifting, flunks Spanish, has orange and purple hair, or is lesbian or gay.

Charlotte Davis Kasl, (20th-century) U.S. psychologist and author. *Finding Joy,* ch. 72 (1994).

8 Often, when there is a conflict between parent and child, at its very hub is an expectation that the child should be acting differently. Sometimes these expectations run counter what is known about children's growth. They stem from remembering oneself, but usually at a slightly older age.

Ellen Galinsky, (20th-century) U.S. child development specialist and author. *Between Generations,* ch. 3 (1981).

9 The colicky baby who becomes calm, the quiet infant who throws temper tantrums at two, the wild child at four who becomes serious and studious at six all seem to surprise their parents. It is difficult to let go of one's image of a child, say goodbye to the child a parent knows, and get accustomed to this slightly new child inhabiting the known child's body.

Ellen Galinsky, (20th-century) U.S. child development specialist and author. *Between Generations,* ch. 5 (1981).

10 Understanding child development takes the emphasis away from the child's character—looking at the child as good or bad. The emphasis is put on behavior as communication. Discipline is thus seen as problem-solving. The child is helped to learn a more acceptable manner of communication.

Ellen Galinsky, (20th-century) U.S. child development specialist and author. *Between Generations,* ch. 3 (1981).

11 It's funny how you never meet a parent who rushes his child. That's what other parents do. All we are doing is reacting to our child's "natural" ability.

Fred G. Gosman, (20th-century) U.S. author. *How to Be a Happy Parent . . . in Spite of Your Children,* ch. 2 (1995).

12 Gaining a better understanding of how children's minds work at different ages will allow you to make more sense of their behaviors. With this understanding come decreased stress and increased pleasure from being a parent. It lessens the frustrations that come from expecting things that a child simply cannot do or from incorrectly interpreting a child's behavior in adult terms.

Lawrence Kutner, (20th-century) U.S. child psychologist and author. *Parent and Child,* introduction (1991).

13 I tell people that when my son was this age, all of the things he did that

really aggravated me and got me upset were things that, from the standpoint of healthy child development, I wanted him to do. I just didn't want him to do them to me, or at those particular moments!

LAWRENCE KUTNER, (20th-century) U.S. psychologist and author. *Toddlers and Preschoolers,* ch. 5 (1994).

14 In some ways being a parent is like being an anthropologist who is studying a primitive and isolated tribe by living with them. . . . To understand the beauty of child development, we must shed some of our socialization as adults and learn how to communicate with children on their own terms, just as an anthropologist must learn how to communicate with that primitive tribe.

LAWRENCE KUTNER, (20th-century) U.S. child psychologist and author. *Parent and Child,* ch. 1 (1991).

15 Numerous studies have shown that those adults who feel the most frustrated by children—and the least competent as parents—usually have one thing in common. . . . They don't know what behaviors are normal and appropriate for children at different stages of development. This leads them to misinterpret their children's natural behaviors and to have inappropriate expectations, both for their children and themselves.

LAWRENCE KUTNER, (20th-century) U.S. child psychologist and author. *Toddlers and Preschoolers,* ch. 1 (1994).

16 But parents can be understanding and accept the more difficult stages as necessary times of growth for the child. Parents can appreciate the fact that these phases are not easy for the child to live through either; rapid growth times are hard on a child. Perhaps it's a small comfort to know that the harder-to-live-with stages do alternate with the calmer times,so parents can count on getting periodic breaks.

SAF LERMAN, (20th-century) U.S. parent educator and author. *Helping Children as They Grow,* ch. 1 (1983).

17 Oh, what a tangled web do parents weave/When they think that their children are naive.

OGDEN NASH, (20th-century) U.S. poet. *Baby, What Makes the Sky Blue?*

18 What had I expected of the first child? Everything. Rocket scientist. Neurosurgeon. Designated hitter. We talked wisely at cocktail parties about the sad mistake our mothers had made in pinning all their hopes and dreams on us. We were full of it.

ANNA QUINDLEN, (20th-century) U.S. journalist and novelist. *Living Out Loud,* "The Second Child" (1988).

19 Parents of young children should realize that few people, and many no one, will find their children as enchanting as they do.

BARBARA WALTERS, (20th-century) U.S. journalist. *How to Talk With Practically Anybody about Practically Anything,* ch. 4 (1970).

20 Information about child development enhances parents' capacity to respond appropriately to their children. Informed parents are better equipped to problem-solve, more confident of their decisions, and more likely to respond sensitively to their children's developmental needs.

L. P. Wandersman, (20th-century) U.S. educator. *America's Family Support Programs,* "New Directions for Parent Education," eds. S. L. Kagan, et al. (1987).

21 It's likely that adults from the caveman on have created their own fantasies of what children ought to be like and naturally have been convinced that's precisely how as children they themselves were.

Leontine Young, (20th-century) U.S. social worker and author. *Life Among the Giants,* introduction (1965).

Child Development, Intellectual

1 Helping children at a level of genuine intellectual inquiry takes imagination on the part of the adult. Even more, it takes the courage to become a resource in unfamiliar areas of knowledge and in ones for which one has no taste. But parents, no less than teachers, must respect a child's mind and not exploit it for their own vanity or ambition, or to soothe their own anxiety.

Dorothy H. Cohen, (20th-century) U.S. educator and child development specialist. *The Learning Child,* "Parent and Child During the Intermediate Years" (1972).

2 The child to be concerned about is the one who is actively unhappy, [in school]. . . . In the long run, a child's emotional development has a far greater impact on his life than his school performance or the curriculum's richness, so it is wise to do everything possible to change a situation in which a child is suffering excessively.

Dorothy H. Cohen, (20th-century) U.S. educator and child development specialist. *The Learning Child,* "Parent and Child During the Intermediate Years" (1972).

3 Children's view of the world and their capacity to understand keep expanding as they mature, and they need to ask the same questions over and over, fitting the information into their new level of understanding.

Joanna Cole, (20th-century) U.S. author. *How You Were Born,* p. 7 (1993).

4 The child whose impulsiveness is indulged, who retains his primitive-discharge mechanisms, is not only an ill-behaved child but
a child whose intellectual development is slowed down. No matter how well he is endowed intellectually, if direct action and immediate gratification are the guiding principles of his behavior, there will be less incentive to develop the higher mental processes, to reason, to employ the imagination creatively.

Selma H. Fraiberg, (20th-century) U.S. child psychoanalyst and author. *The Magic Years,* ch. 5 (1959).

5 Parents, whether or not we believe in a deity, know that to witness a child's mind searching for meaning is a miracle.

Marge Kennedy, (20th-century) U.S. author. *100 Things You Can Do to Keep Your Family Together . . .,* pt. 1, (1994).

6 I never met anyone who didn't have a very smart child. What happens to these children, you wonder, when they reach adulthood?

Fran Lebowitz, (20th-century)U.S. humorist and author. "Words Are Easy, Books Are Not," *The New York Times* (August 10, 1994).

7 My mother made me a scientist without ever intending to. Every other Jewish mother in Brooklyn would ask her child after school: So? Did you learn anything today? But not my mother. "Izzy," she would say, "did you ask a good *question* today?" That difference—asking good questions—made me become a scientist.

ISIDOR ISAAC RABI, (20th-century) U.S. physicist. As quoted in "Great Minds Start with Questions," *Parents Magazine* (September 1993).

8 Whenever parents become overly invested in a particular skill or accomplishment, a child's fear of failure multiplies. This is why some children refuse to get into the pool for a swimming lesson, or turn their back on Daddy's favorite sport.

CATHY RINDNER TEMPELSMAN, (20th-century) U.S. journalist and author. *Child-Wise,* ch. 2 (1994).

9 One of the great privileges of being a parent is witnessing, close up, the flourishing of a young mind. But that's not the only benefit. In trying to make the world a more interesting and comprehensible place for their child, parents often find their own intellectual interests rekindled.

MICHAEL SCHULMAN, (20th-century) U.S. psychologist and author. "Great Minds Start with Questions," *Parents Magazine* (September 1993).

•

Child Development, How Children Learn

1 Learn young, learn fair; learn old, learn more.

SCOTTISH PROVERB.

2 If you think of learning as a path, you can picture yourself walking beside her rather than either pushing or dragging or carrying her along.

POLLY BERRIEN BERENDS, (20th-century) U.S. author. *Whole Child/Whole Parent,* ch. 3 (rev. 1987).

3 We do not have to get our children to learn; only to allow and encourage them in their learning. We do not have to dictate what they should learn; only to discern and respond to what it is that they are learning. Such responsiveness is at once the most educational and the most loving.

POLLY BERRIEN BERENDS, (20th-century) U.S. author. *Whole Child/Whole Parent,* ch. 3 (rev. 1987).

4 There is a very important and fundamental relation between learning and personality development.... The two interact in a "circular process." Thus, mastery of symbol systems (letters, words, numbers), reasoning, judging, problem-solving, acquiring and organizing information and all such intellectual functions are fed by and feed into varied aspects of the personality—feelings about oneself, identity, potential for relatedness, autonomy, creativity, and integration.

BARBARA BIBER, (20th-century) U.S. developmental psychologist. "Learning and Personality Development: A Point of View," introduction, *Bank Street College of Education Publication* (March 1961).

5 Always and everywhere children take an active role in the construction and acquisition of learning and understanding. To learn is a satisfying experience, but also, as the psy-

chologist Nelson Goodman tells us, to understand is to experience desire, drama, and conquest.

Carolyn Edwards, (20th-century) U.S. professor of human environmental sciences. *The Hundred Languages of Children,* ch. 3, eds. Lella Gandini and George Forman (1993).

6 Learning first occurs as a part of emotional interactions; it involves the split-second initiatives that children take as they try to engage other people, interact with them, communicate and reason with them.

Stanley I. Greenspan, (20th-century) U.S. child psychiatrist and author. *Playground Politics,* ch. 4 (1993).

7 Learning starts with failure; the first failure is the beginning of education.

John Hersey, (20th-century) U.S. author. *The Child Buyer,* "Monday, October 28, 1960," (1960).

8 They [children] are autonomously capable of making meaning from their daily life experiences through mental acts involving planning, coordination of ideas, and abstraction. . . . The central act of adults, therefore, is to activate, especially indirectly, the meaning-making competencies of children as a basis of all learning. They must try to capture the right moments, and then find the right approaches, for bringing together, into a fruitful dialogue, their meanings and interpretations with those children.

Loris Malaguzzi, (1920–1994) Italian early childhood education specialist. As quoted in *The Hundred Languages of Children,* ch. 3, Carolyn Edwards (1993).

9 Learning is a result of listening, which in turn leads to even better listening and attentiveness to the other person. In other words, to learn from the child, we must have empathy, and empathy grows as we learn.

Alice Miller, (20th-century) German-born psychoanalyst and author. *For Your Own Good,* "Is There a Harmless Pedagogy?" (trans. 1983).

10 Parents sometimes feel that if they don't criticize their child, their child will never learn. Criticism doesn't make people want to change; it makes them defensive.

Laurence Steinberg, (20th-century) U.S. professor of psychology and author. *You and Your Adolescent,* ch. 2 (1990).

11 Children require guidance and sympathy far more than instruction.

Anne Sullivan, U.S. educator of the deaf and blind. As quoted in *The Last Word,* ed. Carolyn Warner, ch. 16 (1992).

Children's Friendships and Peer Groups

1 Friends don't snatch or act snobby, and they don't argue or disagree. If you're nice to them, they'll be nice to you.

Julie, (20th-century) U.S. child, age eight. As quoted in *Children's Friendships,* by Zick Rubin, ch. 3 (1980).

2 [Convey to your child] that you understand how hard it can be to lose a friend, that under the circumstances feeling sad, angry, hurt or rejected is perfectly normal, that the friendship had some good things and some bad things to it and that neither aspect should be overlooked. . . . Children should be helped to realize that in time

they'll find other friends—but they mustn't expect a new friend to "replace" a former one.

Myron Brenton, (20th-century) As quoted in *Children's Friendships,* Zick Rubin, ch. 6 (1980).

3 Friendship is learned by watching and listening to you. If she sees that your friends are people you like and trust and don't pretend with—people who suit you—she probably won't pick friends who just pass by, or people who can help her or improve her status. If you treat friends in a special way, if you are kinder, more generous, more sympathetic, more forgiving with friends, she probably will be, too.

Stella Chess, (20th-century) U.S. psychiatrist and author. *Daughters,* ch. 6 (1978).

4 Children of eight and nine who love their mothers dearly will cross to the other side of the street when they see her coming, if they happen to be with friends, because to greet or be greeted by their mothers in the presence of peers is to acknowledge having been (and perhaps still being) a baby.

Dorothy H. Cohen, (20th-century) U.S. educator and child development specialist. *The Learning Child,* "Parent and Child During the Intermediate Years" (1972).

5 The frantic search of five-year-olds for friends can thus be seen to forecast the beginnings of a basic shift in the parent-child relationship, a shift which will occur gradually over many long years, and in which a child needs not only the support of child allies engaged in the same struggle but also the understanding of his parents.

Dorothy H. Cohen, (20th-century) U.S. educator and child development specialist. *The Learning Child,* "Developmental Aspects of Five-year-olds" (1972).

6 A new world of complex relationships and feelings opens up when the peer group takes its place alongside the family as the emotional focus of the child's life. Early peer relationships contribute significantly to the child's ability to participate in a group (and in that sense, society), deal with competition and disappointment, enjoy the intimacy of friendships, and intuitively understand social relationships as they play out at school, in the neighborhood, and later in the workplace and adult family.

Stanley I. Greenspan, (20th-century) U.S. child psychiatrist and author. *Playground Politics,* afterword (1993).

7 Children treat their friends differently than they treat the other people in their lives. A friendship is a place for experimenting with new ways of handling anger and aggression. It is an arena for practicing reciprocity, testing assertiveness, and searching for compromise in ways children would not try with parents or siblings.

Lawrence Kutner, (20th-century) U.S. child psychologist and author. *Toddlers and Preschoolers,* ch. 6 (1994).

8 Belonging to a group can provide the child with a variety of resources that an individual friendship often cannot—a sense of collective participation, experience with organizational roles, and group support in the enterprise of growing up. Groups also pose for the child some of the most acute problems of

social life—of inclusion and exclusion, conformity and independence.

ZICK RUBIN, (20th-century) U.S. social psychologist and author. *Children's Friendships,* ch. 7 (1980).

9 Friends serve central functions for children that parents do not, and they play a critical role in shaping children's social skills and their sense of identity. . . . The difference between a child with close friendships and a child who wants to make friends but is unable to can be the difference between a child who is happy and a child who is distressed in one large area of life.

ZICK RUBIN, (20th-century) U.S. social psychologist and author. *Children's Friendships,* ch. 1 (1980).

10 Whereas children can learn from their interactions with their parents how to get along in one sort of social hierarchy—that of the family—it is from their interactions with peers that they can best learn how to survive among equals in a wide range of social situations.

ZICK RUBIN, (20th-century) U.S. social psychologist and author. *Children's Friendships,* ch. 1 (1980).

11 Grown-ups love figures. When you tell them that you have made a new friend, they never ask you any questions about essential matters. They never say to you "What does his voice sound like? What games does he love best? Does he collect butterflies?" Instead they demand: "How old is he? How many brothers has he? How much money does his father make?" Only from these figures do they think they have learned anything about him.

ANTOINE DE SAINT-EXUPERY, (20th-century) French author. *The Little Prince,* p. 16 (1943).

12 There is a delicate balance of putting yourself last and not being a doormat and thinking of yourself first and not coming off as selfish, arrogant, or bossy. We spend the majority of our lives attempting to perfect this balance. When we are successful, we have many close, healthy relationships. When we are unsuccessful, we suffer the natural consequences of damaged and sometimes broken relationships. Children are just beginning their journey on this important life lesson.

CINDY L. TEACHEY, (20th-century) U.S. educator. "Building Lifelong Relationships—School Age Programs at Work," *Child Care Exchange* (January 1994).

Children in the Middle Years

1 Life begins at six—at least in the minds of six-year-olds. . . . In kindergarten you are the baby. In first grade you put down the baby. . . . Every first grader knows in some osmotic way that this is real life. . . . First grade is the first step on the way to a place in the grown-up world.

STELLA CHESS, (20th-century) U.S. psychiatrist and author. *Daughters,* ch. 5 (1978).

2 Life with a daughter of nine through twelve is a special experience for parents, particularly mothers. In a daughter's looks, actions, attitudes, passions, loves, and hates,

in her fears and her foibles, a mother will see herself at the same age. You are far enough away to have some perspective on what your daughter is going through. Still, you are close enough, if reminded, to feel it all again.

Stella Chess, (20th-century) U.S. psychiatrist and author. *Daughters,* ch. 6 (1978).

3 The trick, which requires the combined skills of a tightrope walker and a cordon bleu chef frying a plain egg, is to take your [preteen] daughter seriously without taking everything she says and does every minute seriously.

Stella Chess, (20th-century) U.S. psychiatrist and author. *Daughters,* ch. 6 (1978).

4 Children of the middle years do not do their learning unaffected by attendant feelings of interest, boredom, success, failure, chagrin, joy, humiliation, pleasure, distress and delight. They are whole children responding in a total way, and what they feel is a constant factor that can be constructive or destructive in any learning situation.

Dorothy H. Cohen, (20th-century) U.S. educator and child development specialist. *The Learning Child,* "How Much Can They Learn?" (1972).

5 In the middle years of childhood, it is more important to keep alive and glowing the interest in finding out and to support this interest with skills and techniques related to the process of finding out than to specify any particular piece of subject matter as inviolate.

Dorothy H. Cohen, (20th-century) U.S. educator and child development specialist. *The Learning Child,* "What Shall They Learn in the Intermediate Grades?" (1972).

6 The middle years are ones in which children increasingly face conflicts on their own . . . One of the truths to be faced by parents during this period is that they cannot do the work of living and relating for their children. They can be sounding boards and they can probe with the children the consequences of alternative actions.

Dorothy H. Cohen, (20th-century) U.S. educator and child development specialist. *The Learning Child,* "Parent and Child During the Intermediate Years" (1972).

7 The responsibilities of parenthood take on a more subtle cast during the middle years. . . . Our child is becoming a more conscious partner in his or her growth. . . . Each time our children take a new step, each time we allow them to move ahead to try something they've never tried before, we go through a period of doubt and questioning and ambivalent feelings until the new skill is mastered or the new rules are established. It is one of the most common experiences of parenthood, and it is also one of the most challenging.

Ruth Davidson Bell, (20th-century) U.S. author. *Ourselves and Our Children,* the Boston Women's Health Book Collective, ch. 3 (1978).

8 It may comfort you to know that if your child reaches the age of eleven or twelve and you have a good bond or relationship, no matter how dramatic adolescence becomes, your children will probably turn out all right and want some form of connection to you in adulthood.

Charlotte Davis Kasl, (20th-century) U.S. psychologist and author. *Finding Joy,* ch. 73 (1994).

9 A girl in the middle years also becomes more centered in her soul-life, the feelings of her heart, and she needs our guidance to learn to express her uniqueness, those small seeds that will someday sprout into gifts, talents, and resources.

Jeanne Elium and Don Elium, (20th-century) U.S. family counselors and authors. *Raising a Daughter,* ch. 10 (1994).

10 In everything from athletic ability to popularity to looks, brains, and clothes, children rank themselves against others. At this age [7 and 8], children can tell you with amazing accuracy who has the coolest clothes, who tells the biggest lies, who is the best reader, who runs the fastest, and who is the most popular boy in the third grade.

Stanley I. Greenspan, (20th-century) U.S. child psychiatrist and author. *Playground Politics,* ch. 1 (1993).

11 The real dividing line between early childhood and middle childhood is not between the fifth year and the sixth year—it is more nearly when children are about seven or eight, moving on toward nine. Building the barrier at six has no psychological basis. It has come about only from the historic-economic-political fact that the age of six is when we provide schools for all.

James L. Hymes, Jr., (20th-century) U.S. child psychologist and author. *Teaching the Child Under Six,* ch. 2 (1968).

12 We humans undergo two major growth spurts: one during infancy and another from eleven to twelve until fifteen or sixteen—pubescence. Between the two is a relatively quiescent growth period in which most of the body takes a rest from growing while the brain continues to mature. This period of life is general referred to as childhood or, sometimes, latency.

Louise Kaplan, (20th-century) U.S. psychologist and author. *Adolescence,* ch. 4 (1984).

Adolescence/Adolescents

1 Teenagers are like people who express a burning desire to be different by dressing exactly alike.

Anonymous, as quoted in *The Last Word,* ed. Carolyn Warner, ch. 3 (1992).

2 Adolescence is society's permission slip for combining physical maturity with psychological irresponsibility.

Terri Apter, (20th-century) British psychologist and author. *Altered Loves,* ch. 3 (1990).

3 The first typical adolescent of modern times was Wagner's Siegfried: the music of *Siegfried* expressed for the first time that combination of (provisional) purity, physical strength, naturism, spontaneity and joie de vivre which was to make the adolescent the hero of our twentieth century, the century of adolescence.

Philippe Ariés, (20th-century) French historian. *Centuries of Childhood,* pt. 1, ch. 1 (1962).

4 Adolescence is the conjugator of childhood and adulthood.

Louise Kaplan, (20th-century) U.S. psychologist and author. *Adolescence,* ch. 3 (1984).

5 Adolescence represents an inner emotional upheaval, a struggle between the eternal human wish to cling to the past and the equally powerful wish to get on with the future.

LOUISE KAPLAN, (20th-century) U.S. psychologist and author. *Adolescence,* introduction (1984).

6 Adolescents are the bearers of cultural renewal, those cycles of generation and regeneration that link our limited individual destinies with the destiny of the species.

LOUISE KAPLAN, (20th-century) U.S. psychologist and author. *Adolescence,* ch. 12 (1984).

7 Remember that as a teenager you are at the last stage in your life when you will be happy to hear that the phone is for you.

FRAN LEBOWITZ, (20th-century) U.S. humorist and author. As quoted in *Woman to Woman,* Julia Gilden and Mark Riedman (1994).

8 O Adolescence, O Adolescence
I wince before thine incandescence
. . . .
When anxious elders swarm about
Crying "Where are you going?,"
thou answerest "Out,"
. . . .
Strewn! All is lost and nothing found
Lord, how thou leavest things around!
. . . .
Ah well, I must not carp and cavil
I'll chew the spinach, spit out the gravel,
Remembering how my heart has leapt
At times when me thou didst accept
Still, I'd like to be present, I must confess,
When thine own adolescents adolesce.

OGDEN NASH, (20th-century) U.S. poet. "Tarkington, Thou Should'st Be Living in This Hour," *Versus* (1949).

9 Adolescence is a border between childhood and adulthood. Like all borders, it's teeming with energy and fraught with danger.

MARY PIPHER, (20th-century) U.S. psychologist and author. *Reviving Ophelia,* ch. 15 (1994).

10 Adolescents are travelers, far from home with no native land, neither children nor adults. They are jetsetters who fly from one country to another with amazing speed. Sometimes they are four years old, an hour later they are twenty-five. They don't really fit anywhere. There's a yearning for place, a search for solid ground.

MARY PIPHER, (20th-century) U.S. psychologist and author. *Reviving Ophelia,* ch. 3 (1994).

11 Adolescents are not monsters. They are just people trying to learn how to make it among the adults in the world, who are probably not so sure themselves.

VIRGINIA SATIR, (20th-century) U.S. family therapist and author. *The New Peoplemaking,* ch. 20 (1988).

12 A normal adolescent is so restless and twitchy and awkward that he can mange to injure his knee—not playing soccer, not playing football—but by falling off his chair in the middle of French class.

JUDITH VIORST, (20th-century) U.S. novelist and poet. *Necessary Losses,* ch. 10 (1986).

13 Adolescence involves our nutty-desperate-ecstatic-rash psychologi-

cal efforts to come to terms with new bodies and outrageous urges.

JUDITH VIORST, (20th-century) U.S. novelist and poet. *Necessary Losses,* ch. 10 (1986).

Adolescent Development

1 Adolescence has been recognised as a stage of human development since medieval times—long, long before the industrial revolution—and, as it is now, has long been seen as a phase which centers on the fusion of sexual and social maturity. Indeed, adolescence as a concept has as long a history as that of puberty, which is sometimes considered more concrete, and hence much easier to name and to recognize.

TERRI APTER, (20th-century) British psychologist and author. *Altered Loves,* ch. 1 (1990).

2 Adolescents, for all their self-involvement, are emerging from the self-centeredness of childhood. Their perception of other people has more depth. They are better equipped at appreciating others' reasons for action, or the basis of others' emotions. But this maturity functions in a piecemeal fashion. They show more understanding of their friends, but not of their teachers.

TERRI APTER, (20th-century) British psychologist and author. *Altered Loves,* ch. 2 (1990).

3 Adolescents swing from euphoric self-confidence and a kind of narcissistic strength in which they feel invulnerable and even immortal, to despair, self-emptiness, self-deprecation. At the same time they seem to see an emerging self that is unique and wonderful, they suffer an intense envy which tears narcissism into shreds, and makes other people's qualities hit them like an attack of lasers.

TERRI APTER, (20th-century) British psychologist and author. *Altered Loves,* ch. 4 (1990).

4 One of the main tasks of adolescence is to achieve an identity—not necessarily a knowledge of who we are, but a clarification of the range of what we might become, a set of self-references by which we can make sense of our responses, and justify our decisions and goals.

TERRI APTER, (20th-century) British psychologist and author. *Altered Loves,* ch. 3 (1990).

5 Adolescent development is characterized throughout by oscillating progressions, regressions, and standstills.

PETER BLOS, (20th-century) U.S. psychoanalyst. *On Adolescence,* ch. 5 (1962).

6 The limitless future of childhood shrinks to realistic proportions, to one of limited chances and goals; but, by the same token, the mastery of time and space and the conquest of helplessness afford a hitherto unknown promise of self-realization. This is the human condition of adolescence.

PETER BLOS, (20th-century) U.S. psychoanalyst. *On Adolescence,* introduction (1962).

7 Adolescents may be, almost simultaneously, overconfident and riddled with fear. They are afraid of their overpowering feelings, of losing control, of helplessness, of failure. Sometimes they act bold, to

counteract their imperious yearnings to remain children. They are impulsive, impetuous, moody, disagreeable, overdemanding, underappreciative. If you don't understand them, remember, they don't understand themselves most of the time.

STELLA CHESS, (20th-century) U.S. psychiatrist and author. *Daughters,* ch. 7 (1978).

8 Many children grow through adolescence with no ripples whatever and land smoothly and predictably in the adult world with both feet on the ground. Some who have stumbled and bumbled through childhood suddenly burst into bloom. Most shake, steady themselves, zigzag, fight, retreat, pick up, take new bearings, and finally find their own true balance.

STELLA CHESS, (20th-century) U.S. psychiatrist and author. *Daughters,* ch. 7 (1978).

9 Young people of high school age can actually feel themselves changing. Progress is almost tangible. It's exciting. It stimulates more progress. Nevertheless, growth is not constant and smooth. Erik Erikson quotes an aphorism to describe the formless forming of it. "I ain't what I ought to be. I ain't what I'm going to be, but I'm not what I was."

STELLA CHESS, (20th-century) U.S. psychiatrist and author. *Daughters,* ch. 7 (1978).

10 Adolescence is a time of active deconstruction, construction, reconstruction—a period in which past, present, and future are rewoven and strung together on the threads of fantasies and wishes that do not necessarily follow the laws of linear chronology.

LOUISE KAPLAN, (20th-century) U.S. psychologist and author. *Adolescence,* introduction (1984).

11 Adolescence is the time to enlarge the natural sentiments of pity, friendship, and generosity, the time to develop an understanding of human nature and the varieties of human character, the time to gain insight into the strengths and weaknesses of all men and to study the history of mankind.

LOUISE KAPLAN, (20th-century) U.S. psychologist and author. *Adolescence,* ch. 2 (1984).

12 During adolescence imagination is boundless. The urge toward self-perfection is at its peak. And with all their self-absorption and personalized dreams of glory, youth are in pursuit of something larger than personal passions, some values or ideals to which they might attach their imaginations.

LOUISE KAPLAN, (20th-century) U.S. psychologist and author. *Adolescence,* ch. 9 (1984).

13 If they are to arrive at psychological adulthood, all adolescents must face the loneliness and heartbreak of bidding "farewell to childhood." To arrive at an adult identity, all adolescents must reconcile their newly awakened genital desires with the moral authority of society in which they live.

LOUISE KAPLAN, (20th-century) U.S. psychologist and author. *Adolescence,* ch. 4 (1984).

14 Infancy is the realm conveyed to us in dreams which look backward to the past. Adolescence, more like a work of art, is a prospective symbol of personal synthesis and of the

future of humankind. Like a work of art that sets us on the pathway to new discoveries, adolescence promotes new meanings by mobilizing energies that were initially invested in the past.

Louise Kaplan, (20th-century) U.S. psychologist and author. *Adolescence,* ch. 4 (1984).

15 It is an odd fact that what we now know of the mental and emotional life of infants surpasses what we comprehend about adolescents.... That they do not confide in us is hardly surprising. They use wise discretion in disguising themselves with the caricatures we design for them. And unfortunately for us, as for them, too often adolescents retain the caricatured personalities they had merely meant to try on for size.

Louise Kaplan, (20th-century) U.S. psychologist and author. *Adolescence,* introduction (1984).

16 The most significant change wrought by adolescence is the taming of the ideals by which a person measures himself.... Love of oneself becomes love of the species. Conscience is pointed to the future, whispering permission to reach beyond the safety net of our ordinary and finite human existence.

Louise Kaplan, (20th-century) U.S. psychologist and author. *Adolescence,* ch. 4 (1984).

17 The purpose of adolescence is to revise the past, not to obliterate it. ... Adolescence entails the deployment of family passions to the passions and ideals that bind individuals to new family units, to their communities, to the species, to nature, to the cosmos. Therefore, given half a chance, the revolution at issue in adolescence becomes a revolution of transformation, not of annihilation.

Louise Kaplan, (20th-century) U.S. psychologist and author. *Adolescence,* ch. 12 (1984).

18 While the onset of puberty can vary by as much as six years, every adolescent wants to be right on the 50-yard line, right in the middle of the field. One is always too tall, too short, too thin, too fat, too hairy, too clear-skinned, too early, too late. Understandably, problems of self-image are rampant.

Joan Lipsitz, (20th-century) U.S. educator. "Easing the Transition From Child to Adult," *Education Week* (May 16, 1984).

19 No one thinks anything silly is suitable when they are an adolescent. Such an enormous share of their own behavior is silly that they lose all proper perspective on silliness, like a baker who is nauseated by the sight of his own eclairs. This provides another good argument for the emerging theory that the best use of cryogenics is to freeze all human beings when they are between the ages of twelve and nineteen.

Anna Quindlen, (20th-century) U.S. novelist and journalist. *Living Out Loud,* "Silly," (1988).

20 I feel that adolescence has served its purpose when a person arrives at adulthood with a strong sense of self-esteem, the ability to relate intimately, to communicate congruently, to take responsibility, and to take risks. The end of adolescence is the beginning of adulthood. What hasn't been finished then will have to be finished later.

Virginia Satir, (20th-century) U.S. family therapist and author. *The New Peoplemaking,* ch. 20 (1988).

21 At a stage when young people want more than anything to be like everyone else, they find themselves the least alike. Everyone their age is growing and changing, but each at his or her own pace.

Laurence Steinberg, (20th-century) U.S. professor of psychology and author. *You and Your Adolescent,* ch. 4 (1990).

22 On an abstract level, young adolescents understand that playing with drugs can lead to addiction or an overdose, sex without contraception, to pregnancy; . . . But they do not have the intellectual wherewithal to integrate this abstract knowledge into everyday life. [One mother said her teenager] "actually believes that he won't break out into acne because he is philosophically opposed to pimples."

Laurence Steinberg, (20th-century) U.S. professor of psychology and author. *You and Your Adolescent,* ch. 7 (1990).

23 Some adolescents are troubled and some get into trouble. But the great majority (almost nine out of ten) do not. . . . The bottom line is that good kids don't suddenly go bad in adolescence.

Laurence Steinberg, (20th-century) U.S. professor of psychology and author. *You and Your Adolescent,* introduction (1990).

Adolescent Development in Girls

1 [In early adolescence] she becomes acutely aware of herself as a being perceived by others, judged by others, though she herself is the harshest judge, quick to list her physical flaws, quick to undervalue and under-rate herself not only in terms of physical appearance but across a wide range of talents, capacities and even social status, whereas boys of the same age will cite their abilities, their talents and their social status pretty accurately.

Terri Apter, (20th-century) British psychologist and author. *Altered Loves,* ch. 1 (1990).

2 The most important gift anyone can give a girl is a belief in her own power as an individual, her value without reference to gender, her respect as a person with potential.

Emilie Buchwald, (20th-century) U.S. author. *Raising Girls for the 21st Century* (1993).

3 An actress reading a part for the first time tries many ways to say the same line before she settles into the one she believes suits the character and situation best. There's an aspect of the rehearsing actress about the girl on the verge of her teens. Playfully, she is starting to try out ways to be a grown-up person.

Stella Chess, (20th-century) U.S. psychiatrist and author. *Daughters,* ch. 6 (1978).

4 While girls [age 9–12] appear to have much more social know-how, they are characteristically cliquey, disloyal, cruel, insecure, and a bit bitchy now. Today's best friend becomes tomorrow's discard. Parents watch in horror at what seem to be total personality changes in previously lovely, upright little girls. Sometimes girls are just as unsettled by their behavior as the

disapproving elders who watch them. Sometimes they are unregenerate, relishing their freewheeling and dealing.

Stella Chess, (20th-century) U.S. psychiatrist and author. *Daughters,* ch. 6 (1978).

5 Another reason for the increased self-centeredness of an adolescent is her susceptibility to humiliation. This brazen, defiant creature is also something tender, raw, thin-skinned, poignantly vulnerable. Her entire sense of personal worth can be shattered by a frown. An innocuous clarification of facts can be heard as a monumental criticism.

Louise Kaplan, (20th-century) U.S. psychologist and author. *Adolescence,* ch. 8 (1984).

6 The adolescent frequently supposes that she is breaking out of the confines of her mundane, schoolgirl existence simply in order to break rules and defy authority. . . . She rids herself of the "oughts" and "musts" that convert every minor infraction into a sin of omission or commission. It certainly does not occur to her or to her family that by questioning the moral standards she erected as a child she is taking the first steps in her journey toward a firmer, more reasonable, less harsh, more ethical form of conscience.

Louise Kaplan, (20th-century) U.S. psychologist and author. *Adolescence,* ch. 8 (1984).

7 Girls tend to attribute their failures to factors such as lack of ability, while boys tend to attribute failure to specific factors, including teachers' attitudes. Moreover, girls avoid situations in which failure is likely, whereas boys approach such situations as a challenge, indicating that failure differentially affects self-esteem.

Michael Lewis, (20th-century) Professor of pediatrics and psychiatry. *Shame, The Exposed Self,* ch. 5 (1992).

8 Adolescence is when girls experience social pressure to put aside their authentic selves and to display only a small portion of their gifts.

Mary Pipher, (20th-century) U.S. psychologist and author. *Reviving Ophelia,* ch. 1 (1994).

9 Teenage girls are extremists who see the world in black-and-white terms, missing shades of gray. Life is either marvelous or not worth living. School is either pure torment or is going fantastically. Other people are either great or horrible, and they themselves are wonderful or pathetic failures. One day a girl will refer to herself as "the goddess of social life" and the next day she'll regret that she's the "ultimate in nerdosity."

Mary Pipher, (20th-century) U.S. psychologist and author. *Reviving Ophelia,* ch. 3 (1994).

Adolescent Development of Girls, Influence of Parents on

1 Adolescent girls were fighting a mother's interference because they wanted her to acknowledge their independence. Whatever resentment they had was not towards a mother's excessive concern, or even excessive control, but towards her

inability to see, and appreciate, their maturing identity.

TERRI APTER, (20th-century) British psychologist and author. *Altered Loves,* ch. 2 (1990).

2 Insults from an adolescent daughter are more painful, because they are seen as coming not from a child who lashes out impulsively, who has moments of intense anger and of negative feelings which are not integrated into that large body of responses, impressions and emotions we call "our feelings for someone," but instead they are coming from someone who is seen to know what she does.

TERRI APTER, (20th-century) British psychologist and author. *Altered Loves,* ch. 3 (1990).

3 The adolescent does not develop her identity and individuality by moving outside her family. She is not triggered by some magic unconscious dynamic whereby she rejects her family in favour of her peers or of a larger society. . . . She continues to develop in relation to her parents. Her mother continues to have more influence over her than either her father or her friends.

TERRI APTER, (20th-century) British psychologist and author. *Altered Loves,* ch. 3 (1990).

4 This is the hope of many adolescent girls—to capture a parent's heart with love for them as they are, as people. They reject the notion of being loved just because they are the child of the parent. They want the parent to fall in love with them all over again, because being new, they deserve a new love.

TERRI APTER, (20th-century) British psychologist and author. *Altered Loves,* ch. 3 (1990).

5 A child is more than the sum of her parts. So are you. What you feel about life, about each other, about being parents—if it's on the positive side—is probably transcendent. If you enjoy your daughter, enjoy the whims and fancies, funny quirks, blind spots, and special abilities that define her, and show a decent sensitivity to her needs from year to year, that will compensate for all the inevitable false moves and sins of commission and omission and have a dominant influence on your relationship.

STELLA CHESS, (20th-century) U.S. psychiatrist and author. *Daughters,* ch. 3 (1978).

6 Listening to learn isn't about giving advice—at least not until asked—but about trying to understand exactly what someone means, how it is that someone looks at and feels about her particular situation. . . . Listening to learn from a daughter in adolescence, conspiring with her thoughts and feelings, keeps a mother in touch with a daughter's growing and changing self.

ELIZABETH DEBOLD, IDELISSE MALAYE, AND MARIE WILSON, (20th-century) U.S. psychologists and authors. *Mother Daughter Revolution,* ch. 5 (1993).

7 With a balanced combination of the two principal energies from mother and father, a girl can both be in touch with her womanly strengths and be a powerful force in the world—strong and nurturing, decisive and caring, goal-oriented and aware of the needs of others. She has the courage to voice what she thinks and feels and the strength to follow her destiny.

JEANNE ELIUM AND DON ELIUM, (20th-century) U.S. family counselors and authors. *Raising a Daughter,* ch. 2 (1994).

8 The social forces that operate on a family during the daughter's formative years continue to shape her experience. Thus the families, schools, and jobs that involve poor women are likely to be very hierarchically arranged, demanding conformity, passivity, and obedience—all unsupportive of continued intellectual growth.

Mary Field Belenky, (20th-century) U.S. psychologist. *Women's Ways of Knowing* (1986).

9 It's important for parents to watch for trouble and convey to their daughters that, if it comes, they are strong enough to deal with it. Parents who send their [adolescent] daughters the message that they'll be overwhelmed by problems aren't likely to hear what's really happening.

Mary Pipher, (20th-century) U.S. psychologist and author. *Reviving Ophelia,* ch. 15 (1994).

10 Most parents of adolescent girls have the goal of keeping their daughters safe while they grow up and explore the world. The parents' job is to protect, the daughter's job is to explore.

Mary Pipher, (20th-century) U.S. psychologist and author. *Reviving Ophelia,* ch. 1 (1994).

11 Some [adolescent] girls are depressed because they have lost their warm, open relationship with their parents. They have loved and been loved by people whom they now must betray to fit into peer culture. Furthermore, they are discouraged by peers from expressing sadness at the loss of family relationships—even to say they are sad is to admit weakness and dependency.

Mary Pipher, (20th-century) U.S. psychologist and author. *Reviving Ophelia,* ch. 8 (1994).

12 The normal family triangle, then, provides the daughter with a stage upon which to rehearse her separate identity. When the parents' marriage is relatively free of conflict, the daughter can go from one parent to the other for an emotional safety valve, to let off steam. Having equal, unambivalent access to both parents—and spared their competition for her loyalty—she can then concentrate not so much on dual allegiance as on simply growing up.

Victoria Secunda, (20th-century) U.S. psychologist and author. *Women and their Fathers,* ch. 3 (1992).

Adolescent Development in Boys

1 What eleven- to thirteen-year-old boys fear is passivity of any kind. When they do act passively we can be fairly certain that it is an act of aggression designed to torment a parent or teacher. . . . Mischief at best, violence at worst is the boy's proclamation of masculinity.

Louise Kaplan, (20th-century) U.S. psychologist and author. *Adolescence,* ch. 7 (1984).

2 Adolescence hits boys harder than it does girls. Girls bleed a little and their breasts pop out, big deal, but adolescence lands on a guy with both feet. . . . Your body is engulfed by chemicals of rage and despair, you pound, you shriek, you batter

your head against the trees. You come away wounded, feeling that life is unknowable, can never be understood, only endured and sometimes cheated.

Garrison Keillor, (20th-century) U.S. humorist and author. *The Book of Guys,* introduction (1993).

3 We carry adolescence around in our bodies all our lives. We get through the Car Crash Age alive and cruise through our early twenties as cool dudes, wily, dashing, winsome . . . shooting baskets, the breeze, the moon, and then we try to become caring men, good husbands, great fathers, good citizens.

Garrison Keillor, (20th-century) U.S. humorist and author. *The Book of Guys,* introduction (1993).

4 As a guy develops and practices his masculinity, he is accompanied by an invisible male chorus of all the other guys, who hiss or cheer as he attempts to approximate the masculine ideal, who push him to sacrifice more of his humanity for the sake of his masculinity, and who ridicule him when he holds back. The chorus is made up of all the guy's comrades and rivals, his buddies and bosses, his male ancestors and his male cultural heroes—and above all, his father, who may have been a real person in his life, or may have existed only as the myth of the man who got away.

Frank Pittman, (20th-century) U.S. psychiatrist and family therapist. *Man Enough,* introduction (1993).

5 At the heart of male bonding is this experience of boys in early puberty: they know they must break free from their mothers and the civilized world of women, but they are not ready yet for the world of men, so they are only at home with other boys, equally outcast, equally frightened, and equally involved in posturing what they believe to be manhood.

Frank Pittman, (20th-century) U.S. psychiatrist and family therapist. *Man Enough,* ch. 8 (1993).

6 Early on, girls begin to menstruate, which is dramatic but not obvious to their playmates. They grow taller and rounder, but underneath their makeup they are still recognizably themselves. For boys it is far more disorienting. Puberty comes later, sometimes much later, and its delay is humiliating. While the tall round girls are getting themselves up like grown women, the prepubertal boys, with their featureless, hairless bodies, are just dirty little kids who could pass for the children of the hypermature girls.

Frank Pittman, (20th-century) U.S. psychiatrist and family therapist. *Man Enough,* ch. 5 (1993).

7 I'm not suggesting that all men are beautiful, vulnerable boys, but we all started out that way. What happened to us? How did we become monsters of feminist nightmares? The answer, of course, is that we underwent a careful and deliberate process of gender training, sometimes brutal, always dehumanizing, cutting away large chunks of ourselves. Little girls went through something similarly crippling.
If the gender training was successful, we each ended up being half a person.

Frank Pittman, (20th-century) U.S. psychiatrist and family therapist. *Man Enough,* ch. 1 (1993).

8 Our father has an even more important function than modeling manhood for us. He is also the authority to let us relax the requirements of the masculine model: if our father accepts us, then that declares us masculine enough to join the company of men. We, in effect, have our diploma in masculinity and can go on to develop other skills.

Frank Pittman, (20th-century) U.S. psychiatrist and family therapist. *Man Enough,* ch. 5 (1993).

9 We long for our father. We wear his clothes, and actually try to fill his shoes. . . . We hang on to him, begging him to teach us how to do whatever is masculine, to throw balls or be in the woods or go see where he works. . . . We want our fathers to protect us from coming too completely under the control of our mothers. . . . We want to be seen with Dad, hanging out with men and doing men things.

Frank Pittman, (20th-century) U.S. psychiatrist and family therapist. *Man Enough,* ch. 5 (1993).

10 By school age, many boys experience pressure to reveal inner feelings as humiliating. They think their mothers are saying to them, "You must be hiding something shameful." And shucking clams is a snap compared to prying secrets out of a boy who's decided to "clam up."

Ron Taffel, (20th-century) U.S. psychologist and author. *Why Parents Disagree,* ch. 8 (1994).

Adolescent Development in Boys, Influence of Parents on

1 Unfortunately there is still a cultural stereotype that it's all right for girls to be affectionate but that once boys reach six or seven, they no longer need so much hugging and kissing. What this does is dissuade boys from expressing their natural feelings of tenderness and affection. It is important that we act affectionately with our sons as well as our daughters.

Stephanie Marston, (20th-century) U.S. family therapist and author. *The Magic of Encouragement,* ch. 3 (1990).

2 At the heart of the matter of masculine excess is a great longing for the love and approval of a father, a man who can tell another man that his masculinity is splendid enough and he can now relax.

Frank Pittman, (20th-century) U.S. psychiatrist and family therapist. *Man Enough,* ch. 1 (1993).

3 It's not that we have too much mother, but too little father. We can't forgive our mothers for taking the place of our fathers until we are ready to see that the point of a man's life is to be a father and a mentor, and we can't do that because we don't know how we would be a father or a mentor when we never had one.

Frank Pittman, (20th-century) U.S. psychiatrist and family therapist. *Man Enough,* ch. 6 (1993).

4 Most of us have felt barriers between ourselves and our fathers and had thought that going it alone

was part of what it meant to be a man. We tried to get close to our children when we became fathers, and yet the business of practicing masculinity kept getting in the way. We men have begun to talk about that.

Frank Pittman, (20th-century) U.S. psychiatrist and family therapist. *Man Enough,* introduction (1993).

5 What we men share is the experience of having been raised by women in a culture that stopped our fathers from being close enough to teach us how to be men, in a world in which men were discouraged from talking about our masculinity and questioning its roots and its mystique, in a world that glorified masculinity and gave us impossibly unachievable myths of masculine heroics, but no domestic models to teach us how to do it.

Frank Pittman, (20th-century) U.S. psychiatrist and family therapist. *Man Enough,* introduction (1993).

Adolescent and Adult Relationships, General

1 Adolescents do get very angry with their parents, and acknowledging this anger is part of acknowledging them. If the anger is not acknowledged then its expression is increased. The parent seems super-strong. The adolescent tries to become the super-attacker.

Terri Apter, (20th-century) British psychologist and author. *Altered Loves,* ch. 3 (1990).

2 Parents are never forgiven for not giving just the right response at the appropriate moment. Or, rather, there are particular times in the adolescent's or young adult's life, when a certain response is needed, and this need is not met, and the failure to meet this need is forever remembered, and is never forgiven.

Terri Apter, (20th-century) British psychologist and author. *Altered Loves,* ch. 3 (1990).

3 Preoccupied with her self, the adolescent sees enormous changes, whereas the parent sees the child she knew all along. For the parent, new developments are superficial and evanescent. For the adolescent, they are thrilling and profound.

Terri Apter, (20th-century) British psychologist and author. *Altered Loves,* introduction (1990).

4 [As a teenager], the trauma of near-misses and almost-consequences usually brings us to our senses. We finally come down someplace between our parents' safety advice, which underestimates our ability, and our own unreasonable disregard for safety, which is our child-like wish for invulnerability. Our definition of acceptable risk becomes a product of our own experience.

Roger Gould, (20th-century) U.S. psychotherapist and author. *Transformations,* sec. 2, ch. 3 (1978).

5 Every human society endeavors to preserve itself by inventing the adolescence it requires. . . . Adults are prone to create myths about the meaning of adolescence. Whatever their political or personal inclinations, whether they glorify nature or revere society, whether they are identified with youth or they are

detractors of youth, most adults find it imperative to defuse the awesome vitalities of these monsters, saints, and heroes.

LOUISE KAPLAN, (20th-century) U.S. psychologist and author. *Adolescence,* ch. 1 (1984).

6 Now that adolescence is accessible to the multitude and not restricted to gentlemen and lords, many adults are taking alarm at what seems to be a barbaric horde of scruffy girls and boys out to dismantle the structure of society. It is hard to see any virtue in it at all. What the grown-ups see in its stead is considerable evidence of pride, covetousness, anger, gluttony, envy, sloth, and a great deal of lust.

LOUISE KAPLAN, (20th-century) U.S. psychologist and author. *Adolescence,* ch. 1 (1984).

7 Though they themselves might be as surprised as their parents and teachers to hear it said, adolescents—these poignantly thin-skinned and vulnerable, passionate and impulsive, starkly sexual and monstrously self-absorbed creatures—are, in fact, avid seekers of moral authenticity. They wish above all to achieve some realistic power over the real world in which they live while at the same time remaining true to their values and ideals.

LOUISE KAPLAN, (20th-century) U.S. psychologist and author. *Adolescence,* introduction (1984).

8 Traditionally parents have wondered what their teens were doing, but now teens are much more likely to be doing things that can get them killed.

MARY PIPHER, (20th-century) U.S. psychologist and author. *Reviving Ophelia,* ch. 1 (1994).

9 Adolescence is a tough time for parent and child alike. It is a time between: between childhood and maturity, between parental protection and personal responsibility, between life stage-managed by grown-ups and life privately held.

ANNA QUINDLEN, (20th-century) U.S. journalist and novelist. *Thinking Out Loud,* "Parental Rites," (1993).

10 Adolescents need to be reassured that nothing—neither their growing maturity, their moods, their misbehavior, nor your anger at something they have done—can shake your basic commitment to them.

LAURENCE STEINBERG, (20th-century) U.S. professor of psychology and author. *You and Your Adolescent,* ch. 1 (1990).

11 Most adults would not dream of belittling, humiliating, or bullying (verbally or physically) another adult. But many of the same adults think nothing of treating their adolescent child like a nonperson. . . . Adolescents deserve the same civility their parents routinely extend to total strangers.

LAURENCE STEINBERG, (20th-century) U.S. professor of psychology and author. *You and Your Adolescent,* ch. 1 (1990).

12 The parent-adolescent relationship is like a partnership in which the senior partner (the parent) has more expertise in many areas but looks forward to the day when the junior partner (the adolescent) will

take over the business of running his or her own life.

LAURENCE STEINBERG, (20th-century) U.S. professor of psychology and author. *You and Your Adolescent,* introduction (1990).

13 What causes adolescents to rebel is not the assertion of authority but the arbitrary use of power, with little explanation of the rules and no involvement in decision-making. . . . Involving the adolescent in decisions doesn't mean that you are giving up your authority. It means acknowledging that the teenager is growing up and has the right to participate in decisions that affect his or her life.

LAURENCE STEINBERG, (20th-century) U.S. professor of psychology and author. *You and Your Adolescent,* ch. 1 (1990).

14 Even as kids reach adolescence, they need more than ever for us to watch over them. . . . Adolescence is not about letting go. It's about hanging on during a very bumpy ride.

RON TAFFEL, (20th-century) U.S. psychologist and author. "The Reason Mothers Should Never Let Go," *McCalls* (July 1994).

15 If you expect complete honesty, you'll be disappointed. And don't expect gratitude for your parenting efforts. Do expect that you'll feel like you're on a yo-yo—intimate with your child one day, distant the next. As long as she's safe, don't invade her world. Remember: most teens end up being closer to their parents after adolescence than they were before.

RON TAFFEL, (20th-century) U.S. psychologist and author. *"How to Not Go Nuts Over the Little Things," McCalls* (July 1993).

16 [As we say], "When you get to be 18 you're out of here." No wonder teenagers start to distance themselves from us.

JERRY TELLO, (20th-century) U.S. educator. Speech for NAEYC (National Asssociation for the Education of Young Children) Conference. Nov. 13, 1993.

17 Children . . . after a certain age do not welcome parental advice. Occasionally, they may listen to another adult, which is why perhaps people should switch children with their neighbors and friends for a while in the teen years!

MARIAN WRIGHT EDELMAN, (20th-century) U.S. child advocate and author. *The Measure of Our Success: A Letter to My Child and Yours,* II, p. 19 (1992).

Adolescents and Toddlers Compared

1 Suddenly we have a baby who poops and cries, and we are trying to calm, clean up, and pin things together all at once. Then as fast as we learn to cope—so soon—it is hard to recall why diapers ever seemed so important. The frontiers change, and now perhaps we have a teenager we can't reach.

POLLY BERRIEN BERENDS, (20th-century) U.S. author. *Whole Child/Whole Parent,* ch. 2 (rev. 1987).

2 When autonomy is respected, the two-year-old does not carry this unfinished task into later stages of growth. In adolescence, the youngster will again concentrate on independence, but he won't have to blast the roof off the second time around if it is already well established.

DOROTHY CORKVILLE BRIGGS, (20th-century) U.S. parent educator. *Your Child's Self-Esteem,* ch. 15 (1975).

3 Children, even infants, are capable of sympathy. But only after adolescence are we capable of compassion.

LOUISE KAPLAN, (20th-century) U.S. psychologist and author. *Adolescence,* ch. 12 (1984).

4 The toddler must say "no" in order to find out who she is. The adolescent says "no" to assert who she is not.

LOUISE KAPLAN, (20th-century) U.S. psychologist and author. *Adolescence,* ch. 9 (1984).

5 Unless your baby becomes uncomfortable and tries to push away, don't worry that you're cuddling too much. That way, when she reaches adolescence and goes through a normal period of being terribly embarrassed even to be seen with you in public, you'll have some memories to tide you over until she comes around again.

LAWRENCE KUTNER, (20th-century) U.S. child psychologist and author. *Pregnancy and Your Baby's First Year,* ch. 7 (1993).

6 Toddlerhood resembles adolescence because of the rapidity of physical growth and because of the impulse to break loose of parental boundaries. At both ages, the struggle for independence exists hand in hand with the often hidden wish to be contained and protected while striving to move forward in the world. How parents and toddlers negotiate their differences sets the stage for their ability to remain partners during childhood and through the rebellions of the teenage years.

ALICIA F. LIEBERMAN, (20th-century) U.S. psychologist and author. *The Emotional Life of the Toddler,* conclusion (1993).

7 For parents, the terrible twos are a psychological preview of puberty. . . . At the age of two or three, children eat only bananas and refuse to get a haircut. Ten years later, they eat only bananas and refuse to get a haircut.

CARIN RUBENSTEIN, (20th-century) U.S. social psychologist and author. "The Trying, Tedious, Treacherous, Truly Terrible 2's," *Working Mother* (February 1988).

Adolescents' Friendships and Peer Groups

1 A really tight friendship is when you start to really care about the person. If he gets sick, you kind of start worrying about him—or if he gets hit by a car. An everyday friend, you say, I know that kid, he's all right, and you don't really think much of him. But a close friend you worry about more than yourself. Well, maybe not more, but about the same.

ANONYMOUS FIFTEEN-YEAR-OLD BOY, as quoted in *Children's Friendships,* Zick Rubin, ch. 3 (1980).

2 You have known your friend so long and loved him so much, and then all of a sudden you are so mad at him, you say, I could just kill you and you still like each other, because you have always been friends and you know in your mind you are going to be friends in a few seconds anyway.

ANONYMOUS TWELVE-YEAR-OLD, as quoted in *Children's Friendships,* Zick Rubin, ch. 3 (1980).

3 Most literature on the culture of adolescence focuses on peer pressure as a negative force. Warnings about the "wrong crowd" read like

tornado alerts in parent manuals. . . . It is a relative term that means different things in different places. In Fort Wayne, for example, the wrong crowd meant hanging out with liberal Democrats. In Connecticut, it meant kids who weren't planning to get a Ph.D. from Yale.

MARY KAY BLAKELY, (20th-century) U.S. journalist and author. *American Mom,* ch. 10 (1994).

4 You just can't predict the course of friendship among girls at this age [9–12]. There's a need—varying in intensity according to the individual—for Gibraltar-like attachments in this betwixt-and-between period. Impressive sophistication and maturity exist side by side with fearsome anxiety about the changing body, the person-to-be. The "best friends" are anchors against these tides of confusion. . . . Girls need the support and backing of a group to relieve their anxieties about who they are and who they're going to be.

STELLA CHESS, (20th-century) U.S. psychiatrist and author. *Daughters,* ch. 6 (1978).

5 The conflict between the need to belong to a group and the need to be seen as unique and individual is the dominant struggle of adolecence.

JEANNE ELIUM AND DON ELIUM, (20th-century) U.S. family counselors and authors. *Raising a Daughter,* ch. 11 (1994).

6 Friendships in childhood are usually a matter of chance, whereas in adolescence they are most often a matter of choice.

DAVID ELKIND, (20th-century) U.S. child psychologist and author. *Parenting Your Teenager in the 90's,* ch. 2 (1993).

7 It is through friendships that teenagers learn to take responsibility, provide support, and give their loyalty to non-family members. It is also in teenage friendships that young people find confidants with whom to share thoughts and feelings that they are not comfortable sharing with their parents. Such sharing becomes one of the elements of true intimacy, which will be established later.

DAVID ELKIND, (20th-century) U.S. child psychologist and author. *Parenting Your Teenager in the 90's,* ch. 2 (1993).

8 We often overestimate the influence of a peer group on our teenager. While the peer group is most influential in matters of taste and preference, we parents are most influential in more abiding matters of standards, beliefs, and values.

DAVID ELKIND, (20th-century) U.S. child psychologist and author. *Parenting Your Teenager in the 90's,* ch. 2 (1993).

9 Remember that the peer group is important to young adolescents, and there's nothing wrong with that. Parents are often just as important, however. Don't give up on the idea that you can make a difference.

THE LIONS CLUBS INTERNATIONAL AND THE QUEST NATION, *The Surprising Years,* I, ch.5 (1985).

10 Peer pressure is not a monolithic force that presses adolescents into the same mold. . . . Adolescents generally choose friends whose values, attitudes, tastes, and families are similar to their own. In short, good kids rarely go bad because of their friends.

LAURENCE STEINBERG, (20th-century) U.S. professor of psychology and author. *You and Your Adolescent,* introduction (1990).

11 If you think about it, a peer group is nothing but an empathic envelope without adults around. It has the same three characteristics of a family. It has its own type of empathy ("We understand you, even if no one else does"); it has clear expectations ("Break rules and you're out"); and it offers kids a chance to spend time with one another.

RON TAFFEL, (20th-century) U.S. psychologist and author. *Parenting by Heart,* ch. 1 (1991).

Adulthood/Adult Development

1 When I was a child, I spake as a child, I understood as a child; but when I became a man, I put away childish things.

BIBLE: NEW TESTAMENT, *1 Corinthians* 13:11.

2 The twenties are tryout years and what motivates young people are two contradictory impulses. The urge to create a structure that will serve their needs into the (barely) foreseeable future and the fear of being locked into a life pattern that will ultimately prove unsatisfying or limited.

JANE ADAMS, (20th-century) U.S. author. *I'm Still Your Mother,* ch. 3 (1994).

3 It is not however, adulthood itself, but parenthood that forms the glass shroud of memory. For there is an interesting quirk in the memory of women. At 30, women see their adolescence quite clearly. At 30 a woman's adolescence remains a facet fitting into her current self.... At 40, however, memories of adolescence are blurred. Women of this age look much more to their earlier childhood for memories of themselves and of their mothers. This links up to her typical parenting phase.

TERRI APTER, (20th-century) British psychologist and author. *Altered Loves,* ch. 1 (1990).

4 We are all adult learners. Most of us have learned a good deal more out of school than in it. We have learned from our families, our work, our friends. We have learned from problems resolved and tasks achieved but also from mistakes confronted and illusions unmasked.... Some of what we have learned is trivial: some has changed our lives forever.

LAURENT A. DALOZ, (20th-century) U.S. educator. *Effective Teaching and Mentoring,* ch. 1 (1986).

5 Sigmund Freud was once asked to describe the characteristics of maturity, and he replied: *lieben un arbeiten* ("loving and working"). The mature adult is one who can love and allow himself or herself to be loved and who can work productively, meaningfully, and with satisfaction.

DAVID ELKIND, (20th-century) U.S. child psychologist and author. *The Hurried Child,* ch. 1 (1988).

6 During our twenties . . . we act toward the new adulthood the way sociologists tell us new waves of immigrants acted on becoming Americans: we adopt the host culture's values in an exaggerated and rigid fashion until we can rethink them and make them our own. Our idea of what adults are and what we're supposed to be is composed of outdated childhood concepts brought forward.

ROGER GOULD, (20th-century) U.S. psychotherapist and author. *Transformations,* sec. 4, ch. 2 (1978).

7 In many ways, life becomes simpler [for young adults]. . . . We are expected to solve only a finite number of problems within a limited range of possible solutions. . . . It's a mental vacation compared with figuring out who we are, what we believe, what we're going to do with our talents, how we're going to solve the social problems of the globe . . . and what the perfect way to raise our children will be.

ROGER GOULD, (20th-century) U.S. psychotherapist and author. *Transformations,* sec. 3 (1978).

8 The four stages of man are infancy, childhood, adolescence and obsolescence.

ART LINKLETTER, (20th-century) U.S. broadcaster and humorist. *A Child's Garden of Misfortune,* ch. 8 (1965).

9 We have two lives—the one we learn with and the life we live after that.

BERNARD MALAMUD, (20th-century) U.S. novelist and author. *The Natural.*

10 Life has a tendency to obfuscate and bewilder,
Such as fating us to spend the first part of our lives
being embarrassed by our parents and the last part
being embarrassed by our childer.

OGDEN NASH, (20th-century) U.S. poet. "What I Know About Life," *Versus,* 1949.

11 Maturity involves being honest and true to oneself, making decisions based on a conscious internal process, assuming responsibility for one's decisions, having healthy relationships with others and developing one's own true gifts. It involves thinking about one's environment and deciding what one will and won't accept.

MARY PIPHER, (20th-century) U.S. psychologist and author. *Reviving Ophelia,* ch. 13 (1994).

12 But one of the great misconceptions of modern life is the assumption that by the magic age of twenty-one we are jelled, dreams in place, ready to tackle the adult world and leave childhood behind. All we lack, according to this myth, is experience. The reality is that many of us lack quite a bit more: a psychic passport to adulthood.

VICTORIA SECUNDA, (20th-century) U.S. psychologist and author. *When You and Your Mother Can't Be Friends,* ch. 10 (1990).

13 The fundamental steps of expansion that will open a person, over time, to the full flowering of his or her individuality are the same for both genders. But men and women are rarely in the same place struggling with the same questions at the same age.

GAIL SHEEHY, (20th-century) U.S. author. *Passages,* ch. 1 (1976).

14 The work of adult life is not easy. As in childhood, each step presents not only new tasks of development but requires a letting go of the techniques that worked before. With each passage some magic must be given up, some cherished illusion of safety and comfortably familiar sense of self must be cast off, to allow for the greater expansion of our distinctiveness.

GAIL SHEEHY, (20th-century) U.S. author. *Passages,* ch. 1 (1976).

15 We must be willing to change chairs if we want to grow. There is no permanent compatibility between a chair and a person. And there is no one right chair. What is right at one stage may be restricting at another or too soft. During the passage from one stage to another, we will be between two chairs. Wobbling no doubt, but developing.

Gail Sheehy, (20th-century) U.S. author. *Passages,* ch. 1 (1976).

16 Somewhere slightly before or after the close of our second decade, we reach a momentous milestone—childhood's end. We have left a safe place and can't go home again. We have moved into a world where life isn't fair, where life is rarely what it should be.

Judith Viorst, (20th-century) U.S. novelist and poet. *Necessary Losses,* ch. 10 (1986).

Middle Age

1 The children despise their parents until the age of 40, when they suddenly become just like them—thus preserving the system.

Quentin Crewe, (20th-century) British author. *Saturday Evening Post* (Dec. 1, 1962).

2 The time passes so quickly during these full and active middle years that most people arrive at the end of middle age and the beginning of later maturity with surprise and a sense of having finished the journey while they were still preparing to commence it.

Robert Havinhurst, (20th-century) U.S. psychologist. *Developmental Tasks and Education,* ch. 7 (1948).

3 We live a pleasant life shopping at the Food Shoppe . . . taking the kids to the Weinery-Beanery, . . . and eating bran flakes . . . and then, with no warning, we wake up one morning stricken with middle age, full of loneliness, dumb, in pain. Our work is useless, our vocation is lost, and nobody cares about us at all. This is not bearable. In despair, we go do something spectacularly dumb, like run away with Amber the cocktail waitress, and suddenly all the women in our life look at us with unmitigated disgust.

Garrison Keillor, (20th-century) U.S. humorist and author. *The Book of Guys,* introduction (1993).

4 Middle age is when you've met so many people that every new person you meet reminds you of someone else. . . .

Ogden Nash, (20th-century) U.S. poet. "Let's Not Climb the Washington Monument Tonight," *Versus* (1949).

5 Middle age is a period when a man, for the first time, may be plumbing his "feminine" side—the part that cries easily at movies, that needs to hold tenderly and to be held by the people he most loves, the part that is aware of his emotional losses. In a way he may be making room for the daddy he never was, the daddy he now longs to be—and the daddy he may never have had.

Victoria Secunda, (20th-century) U.S. psychologist and author. *Women and Their Fathers,* ch. 4 (1992).

6 One of the few graces of getting old—and God knows there are few graces—is that if you've worked hard and kept your nose to the grindstone, something happens: The

body gets old but the creative mechanism is refreshed, smoothed and oiled and honed. That is the grace. That is what's happening to me.

MAURICE SENDAK, (20th-century) U.S. children's author and illustrator. As quoted in an interview with Leonard S. Marcus, *Parenting* (October 1993).

7 Age becomes reality when you hear someone refer to "that attractive young woman standing next to the woman in the green dress," and you find that you're the one in the green dress.

LOIS WYSE, (20th-century) U.S. author. *Funny, You Don't Look Like a Grandmother,* "Age-Old Conversations" (1990).

8 I am continually amazed at how old young has become. Didn't we, like our grandchildren, begin with a childhood we thought would never end? Now, all of a sudden, I'm older than my parents were when I thought *they* were old.

LOIS WYSE, (20th-century) U.S. author. *Funny, You Don't Look Like a Grandmother,* "Age-Old Conversations" (1990).

Adult Friendships

1 Men talk, but rarely about anything personal. Recent research on friendship . . . has shown that male relationships are based on *shared activities*: men tend to *do* things together rather than simply *be* together. . . . Female friendships, particularly close friendships, are usually based on self-disclosure, or on talking about intimate aspects of their lives.

BETTINA ARNDT, (20th-century) Australian journalist and author. *Private Lives,* ch. 2 (1986).

2 Friendship is by its very nature freer of deceit than any other relationship we can know because it is the bond least affected by striving for power, physical pleasure, or material profit, most liberated from any oath of duty or of constancy.

FRANCINE DU PLESSSIX GRAY, (20th-century) U.S. author and critic. Commencement speech at Barnard College, May 17, 1978.

3 To insult a friend implies that you respect his masculinity enough to know he can take it without acting like a crybaby. The swapping of insults, like the fighting between brothers, becomes the seal of the male bonding.

FRANK PITTMAN, (20th-century) U.S. psychiatrist and family therapist. *Man Enough,* ch. 8 (1993).

4 A friend and I flew south with our children. During the week we spent together I took off my shoes, let down my hair, took apart my psyche, cleaned the pieces, and put them together again in much improved condition. I feel like a car that's just had a tune-up. Only another woman could have acted as the mechanic.

ANNA QUINDLEN, (20th-century) U.S. journalist and novelist. *Living Out Loud,* "The Company of Woman" (1988).

5 What I expect from my male friends is that they are polite and clean. What I expect from my female friends is unconditional love, the ability to finish my sentences for me when I am sobbing, a complete and total willingness to pour their hearts out to me, and the ability to tell me why the meat ther-

mometer isn't supposed to touch the bone.

ANNA QUINDLEN, (20th-century) U.S. journalist and novelist. *Living Out Loud,* "Being a Woman" (1988).

6 Close friends contribute to our personal growth. They also contribute to our personal pleasure, making the music sound sweeter, the wine taste richer, the laughter ring louder because they are there.

JUDITH VIORST, (20th-century) U.S. novelist and poet. *Necessary Losses,* ch. 12 (1986).

7 Friends broaden our horizons. They serve as new models with whom we can identify. They allow us to be ourselves—and accept us that way. They enhance our self-esteem because they think we're okay, because we matter to them. And because they matter to us—for various reasons, at various levels of intensity—they enrich the quality of our emotional life.

JUDITH VIORST, (20th-century) U.S. novelist and poet. *Necessary Losses,* ch. 12 (1986).

Adults/Inner Children

1 Every adult, whether he is a follower or a leader, a member of a mass or of an elite, was once a child. He was once small. A sense of smallness forms a substratum in his mind, ineradicably. His triumphs will be measured against this smallness, his defeats will substantiate it. The questions as to who is bigger and who can do or not do this or that, and to whom—these questions fill the adult's inner life far beyond the necessities and the desirabilities which he understands and for which he plans.

ERIK H. ERIKSON, (20th-century) German-born U.S. psychoanalyst and author. *Childhood and Society,* ch. 11 (1950).

2 To brew up an adult, it seems that some leftover childhood must be mixed in; a little unfinished business from the past periodically intrudes on our adult life, confusing our relationships and disturbing our sense of self.

ROGER GOULD, (20th-century) U.S. psychotherapist and author. *Transformations,* sec. 1 (1978).

3 Children bring us a sense of intimacy which cannot be replicated in adult relationships. . . . Being attentive to physical comfort, hurt feelings, the ability to play with total concentration and joy . . . the nakedness of childhood preoccupations helps us to keep in touch with ourselves, with the child imprisoned within each adult.

GRETA HOFMANN NEMIROFF, (20th-century) U.S. author. *Mother Journeys,* ed. Maureen T. Reddy, Martha Roth, Amy Sheldon, sec. 3 (1994).

4 Another potentiality of our irrepressible juvenility is a capacity to maintain until the onset of senility an active creative interaction with our environment. We persist in exploring, investigating, inventing, discovering. In these respects humans of all eras, in all societies, all ages of life, are more like baby chimps and not at all like the sedate and rigidly conforming adult chimpanzee, who hasn't

changed much since she was five or six years old.

LOUISE KAPLAN, (20th-century) U.S. psychologist and author. *Adolescence,* ch. 4 (1984).

5 In every adult human there still lives a helpless child who is afraid of aloneness. . . . This would be so even if there were a possibility for perfect babies and perfect mothers.

LOUISE J. KAPLAN, (20th-century) U.S. psychologist and author. *Oneness and Separateness: From Infant to Individual,* ch. 7 (1978).

6 It especially helps if you know that we're all faking our adulthood—even your parents and their parents. Beneath these adult trappings—in our president, in our parents, in you and me—lurk the emotions of a child. If we know that only about ourselves, we become infantile; if we understand that about everybody, then we have nothing to be ashamed of—unless, of course, we go around acting like a child and expecting everyone else to act like grownups.

FRANK PITTMAN, (20th-century) U.S. psychiatrist and family therapist. "How to Manage Mom and Dad," *Psychology Today* (November/December 1994).

7 Personal change, growth, development, identity formation—these tasks that once were thought to belong to childhood and adolescence alone now are recognized as part of adult life as well. Gone is the belief that adulthood is, or ought to be, a time of internal peace and comfort, that growing pains belong only to the young; gone the belief that these are marker events—a job, a mate, a child—through which we will pass into a life of relative ease.

LILLIAN BRESLOW RUBIN, (20th-century) U.S. sociologist and family therapist. *Intimate Strangers,* ch. 1 (1983).

8 Growing up means letting go of the dearest megalomaniacal dreams of our childhood. Growing up means knowing they can't be fulfilled. Growing up means gaining the wisdom and skills to get what we want within the limitations imposed by reality—a reality which consists of diminished powers, restricted freedoms and, with the people we love, imperfect connections.

JUDITH VIORST, (20th-century) U.S. novelist and poet. *Necessary Losses,* ch. 11 (1986).

9 Our ego ideal is precious to us because it repairs a loss of our earlier childhood, the loss of our image of self as perfect and whole, the loss of a major portion of our infantile, limitless, ain't-I-wonderful narcissism which we had to give up in the face of compelling reality. Modified and reshaped into ethical goals and moral standards and a vision of what at our finest we might be, our dream of perfection lives on—our lost narcissism lives on—in our ego ideal.

JUDITH VIORST, (20th-century) U.S. novelist and poet. *Necessary Losses,* ch. 9 (1986).

10 My heart leaps up when I behold
A rainbow in the sky:
So was it when my life began;
So is it now I am a man;
So be it when I shall grow old,
Or let me die!
The Child is father of the Man;
And I could wish my days to be

Bound each to each by natural
piety.

William Wordsworth, (1770–1850) British poet. "My Heart Leaps Up" (1807).

Adult Children, Parents on their

1 To depend on one's own child is
blindness in one eye;
To depend on a stranger, blindness
in both eyes.

Malaysian proverb.

2 If we focus mostly on how we might have been partly or wholly to blame for what might have been less than a perfect, problem-free childhood, our guilt will overwhelm their pain. It becomes a story about us, not them. . . . When we listen, accept, and acknowledge, we feel regret instead, which is simply guilt without neurosis.

Jane Adams, (20th-century) U.S. author. *I'm Still Your Mother,* ch. 2 (1994).

3 Our [adult] children have an adult's right to make their own choices and have the responsibility of living with the consequences. If we make their problems ours, they avoid that responsibility, and we are faced with problems we can't and shouldn't solve.

Jane Adams, (20th-century) U.S. author. *I'm Still Your Mother,* ch. 3 (1994).

4 Even though I had let them choose their own socks since babyhood, I was only beginning to learn to trust their adult judgment. . . . I had a sensation very much like the moment in an airplane when you realize that even if you stop holding the plane up by gripping the arms of your seat until your knuckles show white, the plane will stay up by itself. . . . To detach myself from my children . . . I had to achieve a condition which might be called loving objectivity.

Anonymous Parent of Adult Children, as quoted in *Ourselves and Our Children,* the Boston Women's Health Book Collective, ch. 5 (1978).

5 I would hope that parents and grown children could be friends. When a friend confides in you that she's going to do something that you think is most inappropriate, foolhardy or even dangerous, wouldn't you as a friend say so—in a calm, supportive way? Yet I have to be so careful what I say to my children. I have to walk on eggs to be sure I'm not hurting their feelings or interfering with their lives.

Anonymous Parent of Adult Children, as quoted in *Ourselves and Our Children,* the Boston Women's Health Book Collective, ch. 5 (1978).

6 Never lend your car to anyone to whom you have given birth.

Erma Bombeck, (20th-century) U.S. humorist and author. As quoted in *Woman to Woman,* Julia Gilden and Mark Riedman (1994).

7 When a child becomes an adult . . . the elders are fearful. And for good reason . . . not we but they are the germinators of future generations. Will they leave us behind as we did our parents? Consign us to neatly paved retirement villages? Trample us in the dust as they go flying out to their new galaxies? We had better tie them down, flagellate them, isolate them in the family cocoon, . . .

indoctrinate them into the tribal laws and make sure they kneel before the power of the elders.

Louise Kaplan, (20th-century) U.S. psychologist and author. *Adolescence,* ch. 5 (1984).

8 The power we exert over the future behavior of our children is enormous. Even after they have left home, even after we have left the world, there will always be part of us that will remain with them forever.

Neil Kurshan, (20th-century) U.S. rabbi and author. *Raising Your Child to Be a Mensch,* ch. 5 (1987).

9 It helps parents to feel better if we remind them of our failures with them! And how they turned out just fine despite our imperfections. . . . We never get over needing nurturing parents. The more we comfort our own adult children, the more they can comfort our grandchildren.

Eda Le Shan, (20th-century) U.S. educator and author. *Grandparenting in a Changing World,* ch. 3 (1993).

10 "Hello, Arthur. This is your mother. Do you remember me? . . . Someday you'll get married and have children of your own and Honey, when you do, I only pray that they'll make you suffer the way you're making me. That's a Mother's Prayer."

Mike Nichols, (20th-century) U.S. director and screenwriter. "Mother and Son," as quoted in Frank Pittman, "How to Manage Mom and Dad," *Psychology Today* (November/December 1994).

11 A son is a son till he gets him a wife,
But a daughter's a daughter the rest
of your life.

Modern Proverb.

Adult Children on their Parents, General

1 Children rarely want to know who their parents were before they were parents, and when age finally stirs their curiosity, there is no parent left to tell them.

Russell Baker, (20th-century) American journalist and author. *Growing Up,* ch. 1 (1982).

2 Whoever inquires about our childhood wants to know something about our soul. If the question is not just a rhetorical one and the questioner has the patience to listen, he will come to realize that we love with horror and hate with an inexplicable love whatever caused us our greatest pain and difficulty.

Erika Burkart, (20th-century) Swiss author. As quoted in "Poisonous Pedagogy," *For Your Own Good,* Alice Miller (1983).

3 But psychoanalysis has taught that the dead—a dead parent, for example—can be more alive for us, more powerful, more scary, than the living. It is the question of ghosts.

Jacques Derrida, (20th-century) French philosopher. As quoted in "Jacques Derrida," Mitchell Stephens, *New York Times Magazine* (January 23, 1994).

4 Somewhere between the overly intrusive parent and the parent who forgets about us after we're out of the house is the ideally empathetic parent who recognizes the relativity of choice, the errors of his or her own way, and our need to find our own way and who can stay with us at a respectful distance while we do it.

Roger Gould, (20th-century) U.S. psychotherapist and author. *Transformations,* sec. 4, ch. 2 (1978).

5 One of the final challenges for human beings is to get old with as much verve and gumption as possible. Old parents who keep on being interested in life give a subtle kind of sustenance to their children; they are givers of hope and affirmers of life.

Alison Judson Ryerson, (20th-century) U.S. author As quoted in *Ourselves and Our Children,* the Boston Women's Health Book Collective, ch. 5 (1978).

6 We are intensely loyal to our parents. In spite of the pain we experienced at our parent's hands, we cling tenaciously to their views of life; and their examples of what it is to be a man or a woman follow us throughout life. Acknowledging the power of our loyalty to them, and especially our loyalty to our same-sex parent, is only the beginning of our journey to improve upon their model; but it is at least a first step.

Augustus Y. Napier, (20th-century) U.S. family therapist. *The Fragile Bond,* ch. 4 (1988).

7 Like children, the elders are a burden. But unlike children, they offer no hope or promise. They are a weight and an encumbrance and a mirror of our own mortality. It takes a person of great heart to see past this fact and to see the wisdom the elders have to offer, and so serve them out of gratitude for the life they have passed on to us.

Kent Nerburn, (20th-century) U.S. theologian and author. *Letters to My Son,* ch. 26 (1994).

8 No one, however powerful and successful, can function as an adult if his parents are not satisfied with him.

Frank Pittman, (20th-century) U.S. psychiatrist and family therapist. "How to Manage Mom and Dad," *Psychology Today* (November/December 1994).

9 One of the most highly valued functions of used parents these days is to be the villains of their children's lives, the people the child blames for any shortcomings or disappointments. But if your identity comes from your parents' failings, then you remain forever a member of the child generation, stuck and unable to move on to an adulthood in which you identify yourself in terms of what you do, not what has been done to you.

Frank Pittman, (20th-century) U.S. psychiatrist and family therapist. "How to Manage Mom and Dad," *Psychology Today* (November/December 1994).

10 Parents can fail to cheer your successes as wildly as you expected, pointing out that you are sharing your Nobel Prize with a couple of other people, or that your Oscar was for supporting actress, not really for a starring role. More subtly, they can cheer your successes too wildly, forcing you into the awkward realization that your achievement of merely graduating or getting the promotion did not warrant the fireworks and brass band.

Frank Pittman, (20th-century) U.S. psychiatrist and family therapist. "How to Manage Mom and Dad," *Psychology Today* (November/December 1994).

11 Parents can make us distrust ourselves. To them, we seem always to be works-in-progress.

Frank Pittman, (20th-century) U.S. psychiatrist and family therapist. "How to Manage Mom and Dad," *Psychology Today* (November/December 1994).

12 Parents have subtle ways of humbling you, of reminding you of your

origins, perhaps by showing up at the moment of your greatest glory and reminding you where you came from and demonstrating that you still have some of it between your toes.

FRANK PITTMAN, (20th-century) U.S. psychiatrist and family therapist. "How to Manage Mom and Dad," *Psychology Today* (November/December 1994).

13 Parents vary in their sense of what would be suitable repayment for creating, sustaining, and tolerating you all those years, and what circumstances would be drastic enough for presenting the voucher. Obviously there is no repayment that would be sufficient . . . but the effort to call in the debt of life is too outrageous to be treated as anything other than a joke.

FRANK PITTMAN, (20th-century) U.S. psychiatrist and family therapist. "How to Manage Mom and Dad," *Psychology Today* (November/December 1994).

14 Some parents were awful back then and are awful still. The process of raising you didn't turn them into grown-ups. Parents who were clearly imperfect can be helpful to you. As you were trying to grow up despite their fumbling efforts, you had to develop skills and tolerances other kids missed out on. Some of the strongest people I know grew up taking care of inept, invalid, or psychotic parents—but they know the parents weren't normal, healthy, or whole.

FRANK PITTMAN, (20th-century) U.S. psychiatrist and family therapist. "How to Manage Mom and Dad," *Psychology Today* (November/December 1994).

15 The child who would be an adult must give up any lingering childlike sense of parental power, either the magical ability to solve your problems for you or the dreaded ability to make you turn back into a child. When you are no longer hiding from your parents, or clinging to them, and can accept them as fellow human beings, then they may do the same for you.

FRANK PITTMAN, (20th-century) U.S. psychiatrist and family therapist. "How to Manage Mom and Dad," *Psychology Today* (November/December 1994).

16 The problem is simply this: no one can feel like CEO of his or her life in the presence of the people who toilet trained her and spanked him when he was naughty. We may have become Masters of the Universe, accustomed to giving life and taking it away, casually ordering people into battle or out of their jobs . . . and yet we may still dirty our diapers at the sound of our mommy's whimper or our daddy's growl.

FRANK PITTMAN, (20th-century) U.S. psychiatrist and family therapist. "How to Manage Mom and Dad," *Psychology Today* (November/December 1994).

17 We never really are the adults we pretend to be. We wear the mask and perhaps the clothes and posture of grown-ups, but inside our skin we are never as wise or as sure or as strong as we want to convince ourselves and others we are. We may fool all the rest of the people all of the time, but we never fool our parents. They can see behind the mask of adulthood. To her mommy and daddy, the empress never has on any clothes—and knows it.

FRANK PITTMAN, (20th-century) U.S. psychiatrist and family therapist. "How to Manage Mom and Dad," *Psychology Today* (November/December 1994).

18 To lose one parent may be regarded as a misfortune . . . to lose both seems like carelessness.

Oscar Wilde, (19th-century) Anglo-Irish playwright and author. Lady Bracknell in *The Importance of Being Earnest,* act 1.

Adult Childern Comparing their Mothers and Fathers

1 My mother protected me from the world and my father threatened me with it.

Quentin Crisp, (20th-century) British author. *The Naked Civil Servant,* ch. 5 (1968).

2 You don't have to deserve your mother's love. You have to deserve your father's. He is more particular. . . . The father is always a Republican towards his son, and his mother's always a Democrat.

Robert Frost, (1874–1963) U.S. poet. As quoted in *Writers at Work,* Second Series, ed. George Plimpton (1963).

3 We perversely see mother love as the problem—when it is all we have to sustain us—rather than blaming the fathers who have run out on our mothers and on us. We seem willing to forgive fathers for loving too little even as we still shrink in terror from mothers who love too much.

Frank Pittman, (20th-century) U.S. psychiatrist and family therapist. *Man Enough,* ch. 7 (1993).

4 Our mother gives us our earliest lessons in love—and its partner, hate. Our father—our "second other"—elaborates on them. Offering us an alternative to the mother-baby relationship . . . presenting a masculine model which can supplement and contrast with the feminine. And providing us with further and perhaps quite different meanings of lovable and loving and being loved.

Judith Viorst, (20th-century) U.S. novelist and poet. *Necessary Losses,* ch. 5 (1986).

5 All women become like their mothers. That is their tragedy. No man does. That's his.

Oscar Wilde, (19th-century) Anglo-Irish playwright and author. *The Importance of Being Earnest,* act I (1895).

Femininity/The Female Experience

1 Women are taught that their main goal in life is to serve others—first men, and later, children. This prescription leads to enormous problems, for it is supposed to be carried out as if women did not have needs of their own, as if one could serve others without simultaneously attending to one's own interests and desires. Carried to its "perfection," it produces the martyr syndrome or the smothering wife and mother.

Jean Baker Miller, (20th-century) U.S. psychiatrist. *Toward a New Psychology of Women,* ch. 6 (1976).

2 Diamonds may have been a girl's best friend in an era when a woman's only hope of having a high family income was to marry a man who was well-off, but today, marketable skills that will enable a woman to command a good income over her lifetime are a better investment.

Grace Baruch, U.S. developmental psychologist. **Rosalind Barnett,** U.S. psychologist, and **Caryl Rivers,** U.S. journalist (20th-century). *Life Prints,* ch. 3 (1983).

3 The myth of motherhood as martyrdom has been bred into women, and behavioral scientists have helped embellish the myth with their ideas of correct "feminine" behavior. If women understand that they do not have to ignore their own needs and desires when they become mothers, that to be self-interested is not to be selfish, it will help them to avoid the trap of overattachment.

GRACE BARUCH, U.S. developmental psychologist, **ROSALIND BARNETT,** U.S. psychologist, and **CARYL RIVERS,** U.S. journalist (20th-century). *Life Prints,* ch. 5 (1983).

4 The next generation of women will enter a world in which they are perceived to have more opportunities for creating fulfilling lives than women have ever had before.

ELIZABETH DEBOLD, IDELISSE MALAYE, AND MARIE WILSON, (20th-century) U.S. psychologists and authors. *Mother Daughter Revolution, Mother Daughter Revolution,* ch. 1 (1993).

5 A girl must allow others to share the responsibility for care, thus enabling others to care for her. She must learn how to care in ways appropriate to her age, her desires, and her needs; she then acts with authenticity. She must be allowed the freedom not to care; she then has access to a wide range of feelings and is able to care more fully.

JEANNE ELIUM AND DON ELIUM, (20th-century) U.S. family counselors and authors. *Raising a Daughter,* ch. 9 (1994).

6 Because relationships are a primary source of self-esteem for girls and women, daughters need to know they will not lose our love if they speak up for what they want to tell us about how they feel things. . . . Teaching girls to make specific requests, rather than being indirect and agreeable, will help them avoid the pitfalls of having to be manipulative and calculating to get what they want.

JEANNE ELIUM AND DON ELIUM, (20th-century) U.S. family counselors and authors. *Raising a Daughter,* ch. 4 (1994).

7 From infancy, a growing girl creates a tapestry of ever-deepening and ever-enlarging relationships, with her self at the center. . . . The feminine personality comes to define itself within relationship and connection, where growth includes greater and greater complexities of interaction.

JEANNE ELIUM AND DON ELIUM, (20th-century) U.S. family counselors and authors. *Raising a Daughter,* ch. 2 (1994).

8 Somehow we have been taught to believe that the experiences of girls and women are not important in the study and understanding of human behavior. If we know men, then we know all of humankind. These prevalent cultural attitudes totally deny the uniqueness of the female experience, limiting the development of girls and women and depriving a needy world of the gifts, talents, and resources our daughters have to offer.

JEANNE ELIUM AND DON ELIUM, (20th-century) U.S. family counselors and authors. *Raising a Daughter,* ch. 4 (1994).

9 To begin to use cultural forces for the good of our daughters we must first shake ourselves awake from the cultural trance we all live in. This is no small matter, to untangle our

true beliefs from what we have been taught to believe about who and what girls and women are.

Jeanne Elium and Don Elium, (20th-century) U.S. family counselors and authors. *Raising a Daughter,* ch. 4 (1994).

10 An accurate charting of the American woman's progress through history might look more like a corkscrew tilted slightly to one side, its loops inching closer to the line of freedom with the passage of time—but like a mathematical curve approaching infinity, never touching its goal. . . . Each time, the spiral turns her back just short of the finish line.

Susan Faludi, (20th-century) U.S. author. *Backlash: The Undeclared War Against American Women,* ch. 3 (1993).

11 The great question that has never been answered and which I have not get been able to answer, despite my thirty years of research into the feminine soul, is "What does a women want?"

Sigmund Freud, (1856–1939) Austrian psychiatrist and originator of psychoanalysis. As quoted from a letter to Marie Bonaparte in *Sigmund Freud: Life and Work* by Ernest Jones, vol. 2, pt. 3, ch. 16 (1955).

12 It is certainly not new or startling to find that women feel the desire to take care of their children. What is new is the number of women who are startled by such feelings.

Elaine Heffner, (20th-century) U.S. psychiatrist and author. *Mothering,* ch. 1 (1978).

13 Recently we've been hearing a lot about women "having it all." Myself, I think that is not really an accurate description of female lives today. It seems to me that what we have been up to is *doing* it all.

Sylvia Ann Hewlett, (20th-century) U.S. economist. *A Lesser Life,* ch. 17 (1987).

14 I figure that if I'm confused, you are, too, After all, we are the Whiplash Generation (patent pending): raised to be Doris Day, traversing our twenties yearning to be Gloria Steinem, then doomed to raise our midlife daughters in the age of Nancy Reagan and Princess Di. Now it's Hillary Rodham Clinton, thank goodness.

Erica Jong, (20th-century) U.S. author. *Fear of Fifty: A Middle Life Memoir,* reprinted in *Barnard Magazine* (summer 1994).

15 In a world where women work three times as hard for half as much, our achievement has been denigrated, both marriage and divorce have turned against us, our motherhood has been used as an obstacle to our success, our passion as a trap, our empathy for others as an excuse to underpay us.

Erica Jong, (20th-century) U.S. author. *Fear of Fifty: A Middle Life Memoir,* reprinted in *Barnard Magazine* (summer 1994).

16 We found ourselves always torn between the mothers in our heads and the women we needed to become simply to stay alive.With one foot in the past and another in the future, we hobbled through first love, motherhood, marriage, divorce, careers, menopause, widowhood—never knowing what or who we were supposed to be, staking out new emotional territory at every turn—like pioneers.

Erica Jong, (20th-century) U.S. author. *Fear of Fifty: A Middle Life Memoir,* reprinted in *Barnard Magazine* (summer 1994).

17 Girls face two major sexual issues in America in the 1990s. One is an old issue of coming to terms with their own sexuality, defining a sexual self, making sexual choices and learning to enjoy sex. The other issue concerns the dangers girls face of being sexually assaulted. By late adolescence, most girls today either have been traumatized or know girls who have. They are fearful of males even as they are trying to develop intimate relations with them.

MARY PIPHER, (20th-century) U.S. psychologist and author. *Reviving Ophelia,* ch. 11 (1994).

18 Girls have long been evaluated on the basis of appearance and caught in myriad double binds: achieve, but not too much, be polite, but be yourself, be feminine and adult; be aware of our cultural heritage, but don't comment on the sexism. . . . Girls are trained to be less than who they really are. They are trained to be what the culture wants of its young women, not what they themselves want to become.

MARY PIPHER, (20th-century) U.S. psychologist and author. *Reviving Ophelia,* ch. 2 (1994).

19 It's important to remember that feminism is no longer a group of organizations or leaders. It's the expectations that parents have for their daughters, and their sons, too. It's the way we talk about and treat one another. It's who makes the money and who makes the compromises and who makes the dinner. It's a state of mind. It's the way we live now.

ANNA QUINDLEN, (20th-century) U.S. journalist and novelist. "And Now, Babe Feminism," *New York Times* (January 19, 1994).

20 Most of us don't have mothers who blazed a trail for us—at least, not all the way. Coming of age before or during the inception of the women's movement, whether as working parents or homemakers, whether married or divorced, our mothers faced conundrums—what should they be? how should they act?—that became our uncertainties.

ANNE ROIPHE, (20th-century) U.S. author. "Raising Daughters," *Working Women* (April 1994).

21 They want to play at being mothers. So let them. Expressing tenderness in their own way will not prevent girls from enjoying a successful career in the future; indeed, the ability to nurture is as valuable a skill in the workplace as the ability to lead.

ANNE ROIPHE, (20th-century) U.S. author. "Raising Daughters," *Working Women* (April 1994).

22 We also have to make sure our children know the history of women. Tell them the rotten truth: it wasn't always possible for women to become doctors or managers or insurance people. Let them be armed with a true picture of the way we want it to be.

ANNE ROIPHE, (20th-century) U.S. author. "Raising Daughters," *Working Women* (April 1994).

23 Indeed, it is that ambiguity and ambivalence which often is so puzzling in women—the quality of shifting from child to woman, the seeming helplessness one moment and the utter self-reliance the next that baffle us, that seem most difficult to understand. These are the qualities that make her a mystery,

the qualities that provoked Freud to complain, "What does a woman want?"

LILLIAN BRESLOW RUBIN, (20th-century) U.S. sociologist and family therapist. *Women of a Certain Age,* ch. 3 (1979).

24 That myth—that image of the madonna-mother—has disabled us from knowing that, just as men are more than fathers, women are more than mothers. It has kept us from hearing their voices when they try to tell us their aspirations . . . kept us from believing that they share with men the desire for achievement, mastery, competence—the desire to do something for themselves.

LILLIAN BRESLOW RUBIN, (20th-century) U.S. sociologist and family therapist. *Women of a Certain Age,* ch. 2 (1979).

25 Women have learned the language of power, an add-on to their emotional fluency and a skill required for the financial survival of the family—but the cultural rewards for their twin efforts are slim indeed.

VICTORIA SECUNDA, (20th-century) U.S. psychologist and author. *Women and Their Fathers,* ch. 3 (1992).

26 No one—man or woman—can have it all without support from the workplace and genuine help at home. Women, regardless of how they have chosen to lead their lives, can now breathe a collective sigh of relief that superwoman is dead.

DEBORAH J. SWISS, (20th-century) U.S. educator and author. *Women and the Work Family Dilemma,* introduction (1993).

27 It was a lot to carry out of a childhood—all those textured layers of thwarted dreams rumbling under the fifties patina—but a lot of us did it. In those manicured lives and choreographed marriages there was an often-pronounced loneliness, an emptiness that we would try to fill with our own accomplishments. And our role, the one we would have so much trouble trying to shed later, was simply to be the best little girls in the world, the high-achieving, make-no-waves, properly behaved little kittens.

ANNE TAYLOR FLEMING, (20th-century) U.S. author and essayist. *Motherhood Deferred,* ch. 4 (1994).

Masculinity/The Male Experience

1 The ubiquitous and acutely conscious presence of our adolescents is a major problem, especially since much of their consciousness seems to be focused on sexuality—ours and theirs. They expect us to ignore them if they are kissing their dates in the family room; but let us so much as wink at one another, and they whistle loudly.

AUGUSTUS Y. NAPIER, (20th-century) U.S. family therapist. *The Fragile Bond,* ch. 15 (1988).

2 Acknowledge your male characteristics. Celebrate them. Honor them. Turn them into a manhood that serves the world around you. But do not let them overwhelm you and do not let those who confuse maleness and manhood take your manhood from you. Most of all, do not fall prey to the false belief that mastery and domination are synonymous with manliness.

KENT NERBURN, (20th-century) U.S. theologian and author. *Letters to My Son,* ch. 2 (1994).

3 I want you to consider this distinction as you go forward in life. Being male is not enough; being a man is a right to be earned and an honor to be cherished. I cannot tell you how to earn that right or deserve that honor. . . but I can tell you that the formation of your manhood must be a conscious act governed by the highest vision of the man you want to be.

KENT NERBURN, (20th-century) U.S. theologian and author. *Letters to My Son*, ch. 2 (1994).

4 In times past there were rituals of passage that conducted a boy into manhood, where other men passed along the wisdom and responsibilities that needed to be shared. But today we have no rituals. We are not conducted into manhood; we simply find ourselves there.

KENT NERBURN, (20th-century) U.S. theologian and author. *Letters to My Son*, ch. 2 (1994).

5 We are born male. We must learn to be men.

KENT NERBURN, (20th-century) U.S. theologian and author. *Letters to My Son* (1994).

6 You have a chance to define a new kind of manhood. If you do it well, it will be a manhood in which men do not cheapen themselves and the women around them by the kind of casual, brittle talk that turns women into objects and sex into sport. It will be a manhood in which men see the effects of their gestures and words and most well-intentioned actions. . . . It will be a world where we can love together, laugh together, and work together without fear and without judgment; a world of celebration, not a world of accusation and apology and unexamined assumptions.

KENT NERBURN, (20th-century) U.S. theologian and author. *Letters to My Son*, ch. 18 (1994).

7 You were born into a different world that will present you with different gifts and challenges. A new vision of manhood will be called for that does not tie so closely into the more aggressive and competitive residues of our male character. You will need to search out new ways of expressing strength, showing mastery, and exhibiting courage—ways that do not depend upon confronting the world before you as an adversary.

KENT NERBURN, (20th-century) U.S. theologian and author. *Letters to My Son*, ch. 2 (1994).

8 All those tough guys who want to scare the world into seeing them as men . . . who don't know how to be a man with a woman, only a brute or a boy, who fill up the divorce courts; all those corporate raiders and rain-forest burners and war starters who want more in hopes that will make them feel better; . . . are suffering from Father Hunger. They go through their puberty rituals day after day for a lifetime, waiting for a father to anoint them and say "Attaboy," to treat them as good enough to be considered a man.

FRANK PITTMAN, (20th-century) U.S. psychiatrist and family therapist. *Man Enough*, ch. 6 (1993).

9 But after the intimacy-inducing rituals of puberty, boys who would be

men are told we must go it alone, we must achieve our heroism as the Lone Ranger, we must see the other men as threats to our masculine mastery, as objects of competition.

FRANK PITTMAN, (20th-century) U.S. psychiatrist and family therapist. *Man Enough,* ch. 8 (1993).

10 In time, after a dozen years of centering their lives around the games boys play with one another, the boys' bodies change and that changes everything else. But the memories are not erased of that safest time in the lives of men, when their prime concern was playing games with guys who just wanted to be their friendly competitors. Life never again gets so simple.

FRANK PITTMAN, (20th-century) U.S. psychiatrist and family therapist. *Man Enough,* ch. 3 (1993).

11 Masculinity varies from time to time and place to place. But it doesn't exist just in the mind of a single guy: it is shared with the other guys. It is a code of conduct that requires men to maintain masculine postures and attitudes (however they are defined) at all times and in all places. Masculinity includes the symbols, uniforms, chants, and plays that make this the boys' team rather than the girls' team.

FRANK PITTMAN, (20th-century) U.S. psychiatrist and family therapist. *Man Enough,* introduction (1993).

12 The great passion in a man's life may not be for women or men or wealth or toys or fame, or even for his children, but for his masculinity, and at any point in his life he may be tempted to throw over the things for which he regularly lays down his life for the sake of that masculinity. He may keep this passion secret from women, and he may even deny it to himself, but the other boys know it about themselves and the wiser ones know it about the rest of us as well.

FRANK PITTMAN, (20th-century) U.S. psychiatrist and family therapist. *Man Enough,* ch.1 (1993).

13 The men who are messing up their lives, their families, and their world in their quest to feel man enough are not exercising true masculinity, but a grotesque exaggeration of what they think a man is. When we see men overdoing their masculinity, we can assume that they haven't been raised by men, that they have taken cultural stereotypes literally, and that they are scared they aren't being manly enough.

FRANK PITTMAN, (20th-century) U.S. psychiatrist and family therapist. *Man Enough,* introduction (1993).

14 We become male automatically because of the Y chromosome and the little magic peanut, but if we are to become men we need the help of other men—we need our fathers to model for us and then to anoint us, we need our buddies to share the coming-of-age rituals with us and to let us join the team of men, and we need myths of heroes to inspire us and to show us the way.

FRANK PITTMAN, (20th-century) U.S. psychiatrist and family therapist. *Man Enough,* ch. 9 (1993).

Youth

1 Good habits formed at youth make all the difference.

ARISTOTLE, (384–322 B.C.) Greek philosopher.

2 Jane Addams, founder of Hull House, once asked, "How shall we respond to the dreams of youth?" It is a dazzling and elegant question, a question that demands an answer—a range of answers, really, spiraling outward in widening circles.

WILLIAM AYERS, (20th-century) U.S. educator and author. *To Teach: The Journey of a Teacher,* ch. 7 (1993).

3 Alas that Spring should vanish with the rose,
That youth's sweet manuscript should close.

OMAR KHAYYAM, (1048?–1122) Persian poet and astronomer. *The Rubiyat of Omar Khayyam.*

4 Youth is a perpetual intoxication; it is a fever of the mind.

FRANÇOIS, DUC DE LA ROCHEFOUCAULD, (17th-century) French author and moralist.

5 Oh high is the price of parenthood,
And daughters may cost you double.
You dare not forget, as you thought you could,
That youth is a plague and a trouble.

PHYLLIS MCGINLEY, (20th-century) U.S. poet and author. "Homework for Anabelle," *Times Three* (1960).

6 A young person is a person with nothing to learn
One who already knows that ice does not chill and fire does not burn . . .
It knows it can spend six hours in the sun on its first
day at the beach without ending up a skinless beet,
And it knows it can walk barefoot through the barn
without running a nail in its feet
. . . . . .
Meanwhile psychologists grow rich
Writing that the young are ones' should not
undermine the self-confidence of which.

OGDEN NASH, (20th-century) U.S. poet. "Fortunately," *Versus* (1949).

7 But no matter how they make you feel, you should always watch elders carefully. They were you and you will be them. You carry the seeds of your old age in you at this very moment, and they hear the echoes of their childhood each time they see you.

KENT NERBURN, (20th-century) U.S. theologian and author. *Letters to My Son,* ch. 26 (1994).

8 It is easy to see how adolescence becomes so frustrating, and old age so abhorrent, to many people. The life line is disempowered at two major points: at the beginning and at the end. The only acceptable place is in the middle. Power is conferred only on adults. It is denied to youth and seniors.

VIRGINIA SATIR, (20th-century) U.S. family therapist and author. *The New Peoplemaking,* ch. 19 (1988).

9 Keep true to the dreams of thy youth.

(JOHANN CHRISTOPH) FRIEDRICH VON SCHILLER, (18th-century) German poet and dramatist.

Youth and Old Age, Compared

1 Our youth we can have but today,
We may always find time to grow old.

Chinese proverb.

2 Young people don't know what age is, and old people forget what youth was.

Irish Proverb.

3 Youth looks forward but age looks back.

British Proverb.

4 Credulity is the man's weakness, but the child's strength.

Charles Lamb, (1775–1834) English essayist and critic. *Essays of Elia, Witches and other Night Fears* (1823).

5 The great man is he who does not lose his child's-heart.

Mencius, (372–289 B.C.) Chinese sage. *Book IV,* ch. 2.

Stages of Parenthood

1 The trouble with being a parent is that by the time you are experienced, you are unemployed.

Anonymous.

2 Parenthood has really changed for me. It's much more than taking care of my son; more than saying yes and no. Now I have to figure out what I think and what I know so that I can answer his questions and explain things to him.

Anonymous Parent, as quoted in *Between Generations,* Ellen Galinsky, ch. 4 (1981).

3 The family is constantly changing, as each member changes. Some changes we recognize as developments, and the pleasure they bring usually makes us more adaptable. Some changes threaten, or disappoint other members, who may try to resist the change, or punish someone for changing.

Terri Apter, (20th-century) British psychologist and author. *Altered Loves,* ch. 4 (1990).

4 The mortgage is still in our name but, increasingly, the house is theirs. One diaper, one vote.

Fred G. Gosman, (20th-century) U.S. author. *How to Be a Happy Parent . . . in Spite of Your Children,* ch. 3 (1995).

5 Hopefulness is the heartbeat of the relationship between a parent and child. Each time a child overcomes the next challenge of his life, his triumph encourages new growth in his parents. In this sense a child is parent to his mother and father.

Louise J. Kaplan, (20th-century) U.S. psychologist and author. *Oneness and Separateness: From Infant to Individual,* ch. 1 (1978).

6 The middle years of childhood arrive just as your own are getting uncomfortably close.

Marguerite Kelly, (20th-century) U.S. author. *The Mothers Almanac II . . . Your Child From Six to Twelve,* pt. I (1989).

7 The lifelong process of caregiving is the ultimate link between caregivers of all ages. You and I are not just in a phase we will outgrow. This is life—birth, death, and everything in between. . . . The care continuum is the cycle of life turning full circle in each of our lives. And what we

learn when we spoon-feed our babies will echo in our ears as we feed our parents. The point is not to be done. The point is to be ready to do again.

PAULA C. LOWE, (20th-century) U.S. family educator and author. *Care Pooling,* ch. 3 (1993).

8 Only the family, society's smallest unit, can change and yet maintain enough continuity to rear children who will not be "strangers in a strange land," who will be rooted firmly enough to grow and adapt.

SALVADOR MINUCHIN, (20th-century) U.S. child psychiatrist and family therapist. *Families and Family Therapy,* ch. 3 (1974).

9 Parenting is a profoundly reciprocal process: we, the shapers of our children's lives, are also being shaped. As we struggle to be parents, we are forced to encounter ourselves; and if we are willing to look at what is happening between us and our children, we may learn how we came to be who we are.

AUGUSTUS Y. NAPIER, (20th-century) U.S. family therapist. *The Fragile Bond,* ch. 13 (1988).

10 Parents who expect change in themselves as well as in their children, who accept it and find in it the joy as well as the pains of growth, are likely to be the happiest and most confident parents.

FRED ROGERS, (20th-century) U.S. children's television personality and author. *Mister Rogers Talks With Parents,* ch. 6 (1983).

11 It's sad that children cannot know their parents when they were younger; when they were loving, courting, and being nice to one another. By the time children are old enough to observe, the romance has all too often faded or gone underground.

VIRGINIA SATIR, (20th-century) U.S. family therapist and author. *The New Peoplemaking,* ch. 9 (1988).

12 Middle-aged and older people today can expect to spend more time caring for their parents than they did caring for their children.

CHARLES D. SCHEWE, (20th-century) U.S. professor of marketing. "Playing the Part," *American Demographics* (1990).

13 No matter how old a mother is she watches her middle-aged children for signs of improvement.

FLORIDA SCOTT MAXWELL, (20th-century) Scottish-born U.S. author and suffragist. As quoted in *The Last Word,* ed. Carolyn Warner, ch. 16 (1992).

14 One is not the same parent at forty-five that one was at twenty-five. Personalities and emotional rhythms are buffeted not simply by internal forces but by external pressures as well: an economic slump, the death of a spouse, sudden illness—all sharpen or soften the contours of our lives.

VICTORIA SECUNDA, (20th-century) U.S. psychologist and author. *Women and Their Fathers,* ch. 4 (1992).

15 Thou art thy mother's glass, and
she in thee
Calls back the lovely April of her
prime.

WILLIAM SHAKESPEARE, (1564–1616) English playwright and poet. *Sonnet 3.*

16 Any balance we achieve between adult and parental identities,

between children's and our own needs, works only for a time—because, as one father says, "It's a new ball game just about every week." So we are always in the process of learning to be parents.

JOAN SHEINGOLD DITZION, (20th-century) U.S. parent educator. As quoted in *Ourselves and Our Children,* the Boston Women's Health Book Collective, ch. 2 (1978).

17 Once you have a child, you change so much along the way, you don't even recognize yourself by the time they're ready to move out!

RON TAFFEL, (20th-century) U.S. psychologist and author. *Parenting by Heart,* ch. 4 (1991).

Parents Letting Go/ Empty Nesters

1 I had heard so much about how hard it was supposed to be that, when they were little, I thought it would be horrible when they got married and left. But that's silly you know. . . . By the time they grow up, they change and you change. Eventually, they're not the same little kids and you're not the same mother. It's as if everything just falls into a pattern and you're ready.

ANONYMOUS MOTHER, as quoted in *Women of a Certain Age,* Lillian B. Rubin, ch. 2 (1979).

2 Lonesome? God, no! From the day the kids are born, if it's not one thing, it's another. After all those years of being responsible for them, you finally get to the point where you want to scream: "Fall out of the nest already, you guys, will you? It's time."

ANONYMOUS MOTHER OF FOUR, as quoted in *Women of a Certain Age,* Lillian B. Rubin, ch. 2 (1979).

3 For me, it's enough! They've been here long enough—maybe too long. It's a funny thing, though. All these years Fred was too busy to have much time for the kids, now he's the one who's depressed because they're leaving. He's really having trouble letting go. He wants to gather them around and keep them right here in this house.

ANONYMOUS PARENT, as quoted in *Women of a Certain Age,* Lillian B. Rubin, ch. 2 (1979).

4 It isn't that I want to hold the children here, it's just that I worry about what our life will be like. I don't know what we'll talk about, just the two of us, after all these years.

ANONYMOUS PARENTS, as quoted in *Women of a Certain Age,* Lillian B. Rubin, ch. 2 (1979).

5 You see much more of your children once they leave home.

LUCILLE BALL, (20th-century) U.S. comedian. As quoted in *The Last Word,* ed. Carolyn Warner, ch. 16 (1992).

6 However painful the process of leaving home, for parents and for children, the really frightening thing for both would be the prospect of the child never leaving home.

ROBERT NEELLY BELLAH, (20th-century) U.S. sociologist and author. *Habits of the Heart,* pt. 1, ch. 3 (1985).

7 Leaving home in a sense involves a kind of second birth in which we give birth to ourselves.

Robert Neelly Bellah, (20th-century) U.S. sociologist and author. *Habits of the Heart,* pt. 1, ch. 3 (1985).

8 Human beings are the only creatures on earth that allow their children to come back home.

Bill Cosby, (20th-century) U.S. comedian and author. *Fatherhood,* ch. 1 (1986).

9 Long before your child sets foot in his dorm, you'll begin the transition to college-style parent. It's a transition fraught with misgivings and exuberance, with self-doubt and bursts of confidence, with joyful letting go and tearful hanging on. And in case you think these refer only to your child's feelings, they don't. These [emotions] besiege just about every parent along about second semester of junior year in high school. That's when the reality sets in that your child—not someone else's this time—will be going off to college.

Norman Giddan, (20th-century) U.S. psychiatrist and author. *Parenting through the College Years,* ch. 1 (1988).

10 For parents the grown-up child's leave-taking from the family nest is a time for reexamining their own lives. . . . They reminisce about the birth of this marvelous child, her first smile, her first words, her first steps. . . . They look back . . . to their mothers and fathers as they seemed then—so strong, so marvelous—to the schoolyard games, to the springtime of youth when the energies of growth propelled them into the future and everything still seemed possible.

Louise Kaplan, (20th-century) U.S. psychologist and author. *Adolescence,* ch. 6 (1984).

11 Contrary to all we hear about women and their empty-nest problem, it may be fathers more often than mothers who are pained by the children's imminent or actual departure—fathers who want to hold back the clock, to keep the children in the home for just a little longer. Repeatedly women compare their own relief to their husband's distress.

Lillian Breslow Rubin, (20th-century) U.S. sociologist and family therapist. *Women of a Certain Age,* ch. 2 (1979).

12 How then can we account for the persistence of the myth that inside the empty nest lives a shattered and depressed shell of a woman—a woman in constant pain because her children no longer live under her roof? Is it possible that a notion so pervasive is, in fact, just a myth?

Lillian Breslow Rubin, (20th-century) U.S. sociologist and family therapist. *Women of a Certain Age,* ch. 2 (1979).

13 The greatest gifts you can give your children are the roots of responsibility and the wings of independence.

Denis Waitly, (20th-century) as quoted, from a patchwork quilt, in *The Winning Family,* ch. 25, Louise Hart (1987).

Parents on the Decision to Have Children

1 Birth control that really works: every night before we go to bed we spend an hour with our kids.

Roseanne, (20th-century) U.S. actor and comedian. As quoted in *Woman to Woman,* Julia Gilden and Mark Riedman (1994).

2 I guess the real reason that my wife and I had children is the same rea-

son that Napoleon had for invading Russia: it seemed like a good idea at the time.

BILL COSBY, (20th-century) U.S. comedian and author. *Fatherhood,* ch. 3 (1986).

3 Yes, having a child is surely the most beautifully irrational act that two people in love can commit.

BILL COSBY, (20th-century) U.S. comedian and author. *Fatherhood,* ch. 1 (1986).

4 The decision to have a child is both a private and a public decision, for children are our collective future.

SYLVIA ANN HEWLETT, (20th-century) U.S. economist. *A Lesser Life,* ch. 6 (1986).

5 In the past the intrinsic pleasures of parenthood for most American families were increased by the extrinsic economic return that children brought. Today, parents have children despite their economic cost. This is a major, indeed a revolutionary, change.

KENNETH KENISTON, (20th-century) U.S. professor of human development. As quoted in *All Our Children,* ch. 1, The Carnegie Council on Children (1977).

6 Each of us enters the world because hope for the future preceded us.

MARGE KENNEDY, (20th-century) U.S. author. *100 Things You Can Do to Keep Your Family Together . . .,* introduction to pt. 1 (1994).

7 When we choose to be parents, we accept another human being as part of ourselves, and a large part of our emotional selves will stay with that person as long as we live. From that time on, there will be another person on this earth whose orbit around us will affect us as surely as the moon affects the tides, and affect us in some ways more deeply than anyone else can. Our children are extensions of ourselves in ways our parents are not, nor our brothers and sisters, nor our spouses.

FRED ROGERS, (20th-century) U.S. children's television personality and author. *Mister Rogers Talks With Parents,* ch. 1 (1983).

Pregnancy and Childbirth

1 At last I feel the equal of my parents. Knowing you are going to have a child is like extending yourself in the world, setting up a tent and saying "Here I am, I am important." Now that I'm going to have a child it's like the balance is even. My hand is as rich as theirs, maybe for the first time. I am no longer just a child.

ANONYMOUS FATHER, as quoted in *Ourselves and Our Children,* the Boston Women's Health Book Collective, ch. 5 (1978).

2 I think that carrying a baby inside of you is like running as fast as you can. It feels like finally letting go and filling yourself up to the widest limits.

ANONYMOUS MOTHER, as quoted in *Ourselves and Our Children,* the Boston Women's Health Book Collective, ch. 2 (1978).

3 My whole outlook on life changed with those three little words, "The rabbit died."

ANONYMOUS MOTHER, as quoted in *When Men Are Pregnant,* ch. 5, Jerrold Lee Shapiro (1987).

4 I have come, Sire, to complain of one of your subjects who has

been so audacious as to kick me in the belly.

MARIE ANTOINETTE, (1755–1793) French royalty, wife of King Louis XVI of France. As quoted in *The Mother Book,* Liz Smith. This line was used to inform her husband that she was pregnant with their first child.

5 Because humans are not alone in exhibiting such behavior—bees stockpile royal jelly, birds feather their nests, mice shred paper—it's possible that a pregnant woman who scrubs her house from floor to ceiling [just before her baby is born] is responding to a biological imperative . . . . Of course there are those who believe that . . . the burst of energy that propels a pregnant woman to clean her house is a perfectly natural response to their mother's impending visit.

MARY ARRIGO, (20th-century) U.S. author. "The Whole 9 Months," *Parenting* (October 1993).

6 Our Lamaze instructor . . . assured our class . . . that our cervix muscles would become "naturally numb" as they swelled and stretched, and deep breathing would turn the final explosions of pain into "manageable discomfort." This descriptions turned out to be as accurate as, say a steward advising passengers aboard the Titanic to prepare for a brisk but bracing swim.

MARY KAY BLAKELY, (20th-century) U.S. journalist and author. *American Mom,* ch. 1 (1994).

7 A pregnant woman and her spouse dream of three babies—the perfect four-month-old who rewards them with smiles and musical cooing, the impaired baby, who changes each day, and the mysterious real baby whose presence is beginning to be evident in the motions of the fetus.

T. BERRY BRAZELTON, (20th-century) U.S. pediatrician and author. *Touchpoints,* ch. 1 (1992).

8 If you want to know the feeling [of labor pain], just take your bottom lip and pull it over your head.

CAROL BURNETT, (20th-century) U.S. comedian. As quoted in *Fatherhood,* Bill Cosby, ch. 2 (1986).

9 When I had reached my term, I looked like a rat dragging a stolen egg.

COLETTE [SIDONIE GABRIELLE COLETTE], (1873–1954) French novelist and author. As quoted in *Woman to Woman,* Julia Gilden and Mark Riedman (1994).

10 If pregnancy were a book they would cut the last two chapters.

NORA EPHRON, (20th-century) U.S. author. As quoted in *Woman to Woman,* Julia Gilden and Mark Riedman, 1994.

11 You do a lot of growing up when you're pregnant. It's suddenly like, "Yikes. Here it is, folks. Playtime is over."

CONNIE FIORETTO, (20th-century) U.S. mother. As quoted in *Between Generations,* Ellen Galinsky, ch. 1 (1981).

12 There's an African story of birth where the women gather and send you across the river, and as you walk across this log across the river you head out with these women. As you go across on the narrowest part you're alone. No one can be there with you, and as you emerge onto the other side of the river, all the women who have ever given birth are there to greet you.

LIZ KOCH, (20th-century) U.S. editor and author. As quoted in *Mothering the New Mother,* ch. 2 (1994).

13 Pregnancy represents one of the great unknowns in life. Everyone's at least a little worried about how it will turn out.

LAWRENCE KUTNER, (20th-century) U.S. child psychologist and author. *Pregnancy and Your Baby's First Year,* ch. 1 (1993).

14 The frequency of personal questions grows in direct proportion to your increasing girth. . . . No one would ask a man such a personally invasive question as "Is your wife having natural childbirth or is she planning to be knocked out?" But someone might ask that of you. No matter how much you wish for privacy, your pregnancy is a public event to which everyone feels invited.

JEAN MARZOLLO, (20th-century) U.S. author. *Your Maternity Leave,* ch. 1 (1989).

New Parents, General

1 When that kid looks into your eyes and you know it's yours, you know what it means to be alive.

ANONYMOUS FATHER, as quoted in *When Men are Pregnant,* Jerrold Lee Shapiro, ch. 15 (1987).

2 The first year was critical to my assessment of myself as a person. It forced me to realize that, like being married, having children is not an end in itself. You don't at last arrive at being a parent and suddenly feel satisfied and joyful. It is a constantly reopening adventure.

ANONYMOUS MOTHER, as quoted in *The Joys of Having a Child,* Bill and Gloria Adler (1993).

3 Most of us would do more for our babies than we have ever been willing to do for anyone, even ourselves.

POLLY BERRIEN BERENDS, (20th-century) U.S. author. *Whole Child/Whole Parent,* ch. 2 (rev. 1987).

4 Cultural expectations shade and color the images that parents-to-be form. The baby product ads, showing a woman serenely holding her child, looking blissfully and mysteriously contented, or the television parents, wisely and humorously solving problems, influence parents-to-be.

ELLEN GALINSKY, (20th-century) U.S. child development specialist and author. *Between Generations,* ch. 1 (1981).

5 Having a child is the great divide between one's own childhood and adulthood. All at once someone is totally dependent upon you. You are no longer the child of your mother but the mother of your child. Instead of being taken care of, you are responsible for taking care of someone else.

ELAINE HEFFNER, (20th-century) U.S. psychiatrist and author. *Mothering,* ch. 2 (1978).

6 A baby changes your dinner party conversation from politics to poops.

MAURICE JOHNSTONE, (20th-century) U.S. father. As quoted in *What Is a Baby?,* Richard and Helen Exley.

7 A baby is a full time job for three adults. Nobody tells you that when you're pregnant, or you'd probably jump off a bridge. Nobody tells you how all-consuming it is to be a mother—how reading goes out the window and thinking too.

ERICA JONG, (20th-century) U.S. author. *Fear of Fifty,* ch. 2 (1994).

8 It's so easy during those first few months to think that the problems will never end. You feel as if your son will never sleep through the night, will always spit up food after eating, and will never learn to smile—even though you don't know any adults or even older children who still act this way.

LAWRENCE KUTNER, (20th-century) U.S. child psychologist and author. *Pregnancy and Your Baby's First Year,* ch. 8 (1993).

9 With all the attention paid to your new baby, it's easy for your own feelings and needs to get lost in the shuffle. Although all parents engage in some self-sacrifice for their children, keep in mind that your goal isn't just to raise a happy, healthy child. You want that child to be part of a happy, healthy family as well.

LAWRENCE KUTNER, (20th-century) U.S. child psychologist and author. *Pregnancy and Your Baby's First Year,* ch. 8 (1993).

10 As new working parents, we all go from being couples who finish each other's sentences to being people who never even heard the first half of the sentence.

LOUISE LAGUE, (20th-century) U.S. editor and author. *The Working Mom's Book of Hints, Tips, and Everyday Wisdom,* ch. 3 (1995).

11 To be perfectly, brutally honest, those of us who are still carrying diapers everywhere we go are not at our most scintillating time of life . . .We need to remember that at one time in our lives, we all had senses of humor and knew things thÂt were going on in the world. And if we just keep our social networks open, there will be people ready to listen when we once again have intelligent things to say.

LOUISE LAGUE, (20th-century) U.S. editor and author. *The Working Mom's Book of Hints, Tips, and Everyday Wisdom,* ch. 2.

12 Nothing ever prepares a couple for having a baby, especially the first one. And even baby number two or three, the surprises and challenges, the cosmic curve balls, keep on coming. We can't believe how much children change everything—the time we rise and the time we go to bed; the way we fight and the way we get along. Even when, and if, we make love.

SUSAN LAPINSKI, (20th-century) U.S. journalist. "Parenting Passages," *Child Magazine* (June/July 1992).

13 *First*
Let the rockets flash and the cannon thunder,
This child is a marvel, a matchless wonder.
A staggering child, a child astounding,
Dazzling, diaperless, dumfounding,
Stupendous, miraculous, unsurpassed,
A child to stagger and flabbergast,
Bright as a button, sharp as a thorn,
And the only perfect one ever born.
Second
Arrived this evening at half-past nine.
Everybody is doing fine.
Is it a boy, or quite the reverse?
You can call in the morning and ask the nurse.

OGDEN NASH, (20th-century) U.S. poet. "First Child . . . Second Child," *Versus,* 1949.

14 The myths about what we're supposed to feel as new mothers run strong and deep. . . . While joy and elation are surely present after a

new baby has entered our lives, it is also within the realm of possibility that other feelings might crop up: neediness, fear, ambivalence, anger.

SALLY PLACKSIN, (20th-century) U.S. producer and author. *Mothering the New Mother,* ch. 1 (1994).

15 While you are nurturing your newborn, you need someone to nurture you, whether it is with healthful drinks while you're nursing, or with words of recognition and encouragement as you talk about your feelings. In this state of continual giving to your infant—whether it is nourishment or care or love—you are easily drained, and you need to be replenished from sources outside yourself so that you will have reserves to draw from.

SALLY PLACKSIN, (20th-century) U.S. producer and author. *Mothering the New Mother,* ch. 3 (1994).

16 Men have their own questions, and they differ from those of mothers. New mothers are more interested in nutrition and vulnerability to illness while fathers tend to ask about when they can take their babies out of the house or how much sleep babies really need.

KYLE D. PRUETT, (20th-century) U.S. child psychiatrist and author. *The Nurturing Father,* ch. 15 (1987).

17 A woman can get married and her life does change. And a man can get married and his life changes. But nothing changes life as dramatically as having a child. . . . In this country, it is a particular experience, a rite of passage, if you will, that is unsupported for the most part, and rather ignored. Somebody will send you a couple of presents for the baby, but people do not acknowledge the massive experience to the parents involved.

DANA RAPHAEL, (20th-century) U.S. anthropologist. As quoted in *Mothering the New Mother,* Sally Placksin, ch. 1 (1994).

18 The addition of a helpless, needy infant to a couple's life limits freedom of movement, changes role expectancies, places physical demands on parents, and restricts spontaneity.

JERROLD LEE SHAPIRO, (20th-century) U.S. family therapist. *When Men Are Pregnant,* ch. 13 (1987).

19 In our first year with children we cross from adulthood to parenthood. . . . We share a history with our children, come to know our partner also as a parent, see how our society really treats families. Maybe more important, we get some handle on who we are as parents—different from our parents, from common stereotypes of fathers and mothers, from peers who were parents before us. Our parenthood is not at all finished—it's fragile, a "work in progress"—but it's much more than we had before.

JOAN SHEINGOLD DITZION AND DENNIE PALMER, (20th-century) *Ourselves and Our Children,* the Boston Women's Health Book Collective, ch. 2 (1978).

20 This [new] period of parenting is an intense one. Never will we know such responsibility, such productive and hard work, such potential for isolation in the caretaking role and such intimacy and close involvement in the growth and development of another human being.

JOAN SHEINGOLD DITZION AND DENNIE PALMER, (20th-century) *Our-*

selves and Our Children, the Boston Women's Health Book Collective, ch. 2 (1978).

21 Much that is urged on us new parents is useless, because we didn't really choose it. It was pushed on us. It—whether it be Raffi videos, French lessons, or the complete works of Brazelton—might be just right for you and your particular child. But it is only right when you feel that it is. You know your family best; you decide.

SONIA TAITZ, (20th-century) U.S. journalist and author. *Mothering Heights,* introduction (1992).

22 You may be used to a day that includes answering eleven phone calls, attending two meetings, and writing three reports; when you are at home with an infant you will feel you have accomplished quite a lot if you have a shower and a sit-down meal in the same day.

ANNE C. WEISBERG, (20th-century) U.S. attorney. *Everything a Working Mother Needs to Know,* ch. 4 (1994).

New Parents, Dealing with Inexperience

1 Parenthood always comes as a shock. Postpartum blues? Postpartum panic is more like it. We set out to have a baby; what we get is a total take-over of our lives.

POLLY BERRIEN BERENDS, (20th-century) U.S. author. *Whole Child/Whole Parent,* ch. 2 (rev. 1987).

2 The absolute dependence of a newborn infant inspired many things in me, but it did not activate any magical knowledge about what to do for the next twenty years.

MARY KAY BLAKELY, (20th-century) U.S. journalist and author. *American Mom,* ch. 1 (1994).

3 The naive notion that a mother naturally acquires the complex skills of childrearing simply because she has given birth now seems as absurd to me as enrolling in a nine-month class in composition and imagining that at the end of the course you are now prepared to begin writing *War and Peace.*

MARY KAY BLAKELY, (20th-century) U.S. journalist and author. *American Mom,* ch. 1 (1994).

4 You can read the best experts on child care. You can listen to those who have been there. You can take a whole childbirth and child-care course without missing a lesson. But you won't really know a thing about yourselves and each other as parents, or your baby as a child, until you have her in your arms. That's the moment when the lifelong process of bringing up a child into the fold of the family begins.

STELLA CHESS, (20th-century) U.S. psychiatrist and author. *Daughters,* ch. 1 (1978).

5 The first time many women hold their tiny babies, they are apt to feel as clumsy and incompetent as any man. The difference is that our culture tells them they're not supposed to feel that way. Our culture assumes that they will quickly learn how to be a mother, and that assumption rubs off on most women—so they learn.

PAMELA PATRICK NOVOTNY, (20th-century) U.S. journalist and author. *The Joy of Twins,* ch. 6 (1988 rev. 1994).

6 After your baby arrives, you yourself may feel like something of a

present, albeit clumsy, wrapped in unmatched ribbons and bows, but new. Untried. Untested.

SALLY PLACKSIN, (20th-century) U.S. producer and author. *Mothering the New Mother,* ch. 1 (1994).

7 If you are a new mother or about to become one, has anyone told you that much parenting is a learned behavior, not—as we have been led to believe—all instinct and mother-wit?

SALLY PLACKSIN, (20th-century) U.S. producer and author. *Mothering the New Mother,* ch. 1 (1994).

8 A healthy newborn has been delivered in a more or less satisfying fashion. The baby is feeding well, has short nails and a clean bottom, and has not drowned. What now?

SANDRA SCARR, (20th-century) U.S. developmental psychologist and author. *Mother Care/Other Care,* pt. 3, ch. 7 (1984).

9 "It's hard enough to adjust [to the lack of control] in the beginning," says a corporate vice president and single mother. "But then you realize that everything keeps changing, so you never regain control. I was just learning to take care of the belly-button stump, when it fell off. I had just learned to make formula really efficiently, when Sarah stopped using it."

ANNE C. WEISBERG, (20th-century) U.S. attorney. *Everything a Working Mother Needs to Know,* ch. 4 (1994).

New Parents and Sex

1 Afterwards, when the bombshell of early motherhood first hit, I remember wondering how any woman could possibly entertain erotic thoughts while sleepwaking through the chaos of feeds, nappies, stress and fatigue. I assume my husband and I *must* have had sex at least a few times in that two year period . . . but I must say I can't remember it happening. Perhaps I dozed through it, who knows.

BETTINA ARNDT, (20th-century) Australian journalist and author. *Private Lives,* ch. 1 (1986).

2 From three to six months, most babies have settled down enough to be fun but aren't mobile enough to be getting into trouble. This is the time to pay some attention to your relationship again. Otherwise, you may spend the entire postpartum year thinking you married the wrong person and overlooking the obvious—that parenthood can create rough spots even in the smoothest marriage.

ANNE CASSIDY, (20th-century) U.S. journalist and author. "We Are Three . . . .," *Working Mother* (September 1989).

3 A couple's relationship often moves to the back burner as they focus on the new baby and temporarily prefer sleep over sex.

SUSAN LAPINSKI, (20th-century) U.S. journalist. "Parenting Passages," *Child* (June–July 1992).

4 In the best of all possible worlds, childbirth enriches a marriage. In the worst, it harms it. No matter how good their marriage is, most couples find that having a baby challenges their relationship.

JEAN MARZOLLO, (20th-century) U.S. author. *Your Maternity Leave,* ch. 5 (1989).

Parents on Living with Toddlers

1 In the range of things toddlers have to learn and endlessly review—why you can't put bottles with certain labels in your mouth, why you have to sit on the potty, why you can't take whatever you want in the store, why you don't hit your friends—by the time we got to why you can't drop your peas, well, I was dropping a few myself.

MARY KAY BLAKELY, (20th-century) U.S. journalist and author. *American Mom,* ch. 4 (1994).

2 I often think about the opening words of Charles Dickens's *A Tale of Two Cities*: "It was the best of times, it was the worst of times." I know Dickens wasn't talking about one- to three-year-olds, but his words do capture the extremes of emotion that toddlers and their parents experience every day. Can there be a creature on earth as adorable—and as trying—as a toddler?

ANNE CASSIDY, (20th-century) U.S. journalist and author. "Don't Let Your Good Baby Turn into a Terrible Toddler!" *Working Mother* (November 1990).

3 Your well-tempered guiding effort keeps your adventurous, enthusiastic, active ever-learning toddler from becoming passive, docile, and limp, without drive, will to learn, or interest in your company. Your skillful handling keeps her from turning into a bundle of rebellion and unfocused negativism, getting her kicks out of grownups' anger rather than their pleasure and approval. And with experience and growing understanding she gradually learns how to operate relatively easily and peacefully in the world.

STELLA CHESS, (20th-century) U.S. psychiatrist and author. *Daughters,* ch. 6 (1978).

4 They are not long, the days of construction paper and gilded rigatoni. That's why we save those things so relentlessly, why the sisterhood of motherhood, those of us who can instantly make friends with a stranger by discussing colic and orthodonture, have as our coat of arms a sheet of small handprints executed in finger paint.

ANNA QUINDLEN, (20th-century) U.S. journalist and novelist. *Thinking Out Loud,* "The Days of Gilded Rigatoni, May 12, 1991" (1993).

5 I tell parents . . . when they are the recipients of public humiliation inflicted by their irrational toddlers or preschoolers, and they are being stared at by clucking strangers, to repeat this mantra: "I do not know these people. They are not my friends. I will never see them again."

NANCY SAMALIN, (20th-century) U.S. parent educator and author. *Love and Anger: The Parental Dilemma,* ch. 1 (1991).

Parents on Living with Children in the Middle Years

1 One of the most difficult aspects of being a parent during the middle years is feeling powerless to protect our children from hurt. However "growthful" it may be for them to experience failure, disappointment and rejection, it is nearly impossible to maintain an intellectual perspective when our sobbing child or rageful child comes in to us for

help. . . . We can't turn the hurt around by kissing the sore spot to make it better. We are no longer the all-powerful parent.

Ruth Davidson Bell, (20th-century) U.S. author. *Ourselves and Our Children,* the Boston Women's Health Book Collective, ch. 3 (1978).

2 The middle years of parenthood are characterized by ambiguity. Our kids are no longer helpless, but neither are they independent. We are still active parents but we have more time now to concentrate on our personal needs. Our children's world has expanded. It is not enclosed within a kind of magic dotted line drawn by us. Although we are still the most important adults in their lives, we are no longer the only significant adults.

Ruth Davidson Bell, (20th-century) U.S. author. *Ourselves and Our Children,* the Boston Women's Health Book Collective, ch. 3 (1978).

3 I had let preadolescence creep up on me without paying much attention—and I seriously underestimated this insidious phase of child development. You hear about it, but you're not a true believer until it jumps out at you in the shape of your own, until recently quite companionable child.

Susan Ferraro, (20th-century) U.S. journalist. "My 11-year-old Knows Just How to Get to Me," *Working Mother* (August 1988).

4 I call the years when our children are between six and twelve the "golden years," not because everything's perfect . . . but because the kids are capable and independent. . . . They're becoming fascinating human beings who continually astound us and make us laugh. And they build our self-esteem. They still adore us for the most part, not yet having reached that age of thinking everything we do is dumb, old-fashioned and irrelevant.

Vicki Lansky, (20th-century) U.S. author. *Practical Parenting Tips,* introduction (1985).

5 If there is a price to pay for the privilege of spending the early years of child-rearing in the driver's seat, it is our reluctance, our inability, to tolerate being demoted to the backseat. Spurred by our success in programming our children during the preschool years, we may find it difficult to forgo in later states the level of control that once afforded us so much satisfaction.

Melinda M. Marshall, (20th-century) U.S. editor and author. *Good Enough Mothers,* ch. 3 (1993).

6 Each day we move a little closer to the sidelines of their lives, which is where we belong, if we do our job right.

Anna Quindlen, (20th-century) U.S. journalist and novelist. *Thinking Out Loud,* "The Days of Gilded Rigatoni, May 12, 1991" (1993).

Parents on Living with Teenagers

1 No one ever promised me it would be easy and it's not. But I also get many rewards from seeing my children grow, make strong decisions for themselves, and set out on their own as independent, strong, likeable human beings. And I like who I am becoming, too. Having teenagers has made me more human, more flexible, more humble, more questioning—and, finally

it's given me a better sense of humor!

ANONYMOUS FATHER, as quoted in *Ourselves and Our Children,* the Boston Women's Health Book Collective, ch. 4 (1978).

2 I became the Incredible Shrinking Mother the year they started junior high. If our relationship today depended on physical clout, I would have about the same influence with them that the republic of Liechtenstein has on world politics.

MARY KAY BLAKELY, (20th-century) U.S. journalist and author. *American Mom,* ch. 4 (1994).

3 Spooky things happen in houses densely occupied by adolescent boys. When I checked out a four-inch dent in the living room ceiling one afternoon, even the kid still holding the baseball bat looked genuinely baffled about how he possibly could have done it.

MARY KAY BLAKELY, (20th-century) U.S. journalist and author. *American Mom,* ch. 9 (1994).

4 With girls, everything looks great on the surface. But beware of drawers that won't open. They contain a three-month supply of dirty underwear, unwashed hose, and rubber bands with blobs of hair in them.

ERMA BOMBECK, (20th-century) U.S. humorist and author. *Motherhood, the Second Oldest Profession,* ch. 8 (1983).

5 Odors from decaying food wafting through the air when the door is opened, colorful mold growing between a wet gym uniform and the damp carpet underneath, and the complete supply of bath towels scattered throughout the bedroom can become wonderful opportunities to help your teenager learn once again that the art of living in a community requires compromise, negotiation, and consensus.

BARBARA COLOROSO, (20th-century) U.S. parent educator and author. *Kids Are Worth It,* ch. 9 (1994).

6 Teenagers who are never required to vacuum are living in one.

FRED G. GOSMAN, (20th-century) U.S. author. *How to Be a Happy Parent . . . in Spite of Your Children,* ch. 8 (1995).

7 The fellow parent you are scared to call is as appalled by the clique's plans as you are. . . . The other parent is as happy to hear from you as you would be to hear from him.

FRED G. GOSMAN, (20th-century) U.S. author. *How to Be a Happy Parent . . . in Spite of Your Children,* ch. 11 (1995).

8 In the continual enterprise of trying to guide appropriately, renegotiate with, listen to and just generally coexist with our teenage children, we ourselves are changed. We learn even more clearly what our baseline virtues are. We listen to our teenagers and change our minds about some things, stretching our own limits. We learn our own capacity for flexibility, firmness and endurance.

JEAN JACOBS SPEIZER, as quoted in *Ourselves and Our Children,* the Boston Women's Health Collective, ch. 4 (1978).

9 The years when we are parenting teenagers are the high point, the crest when everything seems to be in bright colors and in ten-foot letters.

JEAN JACOBS SPEIZER, as quoted in *Ourselves and Our Children,* the Boston Women's Health Collective, ch. 4 (1978).

10 The long discussions and painful arguments of adolescence and the

fierce loyalties to teachers, heroes, and gurus during the teenage years are simply our children's struggles to ensure that the lifestyles and values they adopt are worthy of their allegiance.

NEIL KURSHAN, (20th-century) U.S. rabbi and author. *Raising Your Child to Be a Mensch,* ch. 4 (1987).

11 There is no magic decoding ring that will help us read our young adolescent's feelings. Rather, what we need to do is hold out our antennae in the hope that we'll pick up the right signals.

THE LIONS CLUBS INTERNATIONAL AND THE QUEST NATION, *The Surprising Years,* III, ch. 4 (1985).

12 It isn't easy to see the formerly loving child who once curled up in our laps turn into a surly stranger who cannot spare us a kind word. One mother . . . was taken aback when she called, as her daughter was going out the door, "Have a good time," and her daughter angrily replied, "Stop telling me what to do!"

NANCY SAMALIN, (20th-century) U.S. parent educator and author. *Love and Anger: The Parental Dilemma,* ch. 3 (1991).

13 Negotiating the adolescent stage is neither quick nor easy. . . . I have often said to parents, "If it isn't illegal, immoral, or fattening, give it your blessing." We do much better . . . if we find and support all the places we can appropriately say yes, and say only the no's that really matter.

VIRGINIA SATIR, (20th-century) U.S. family therapist and author. *The New Peoplemaking,* ch. 20 (1988).

14 The upbeat lawyer/negotiator of preadolescence has become a real pro by now—cynical, shrewd, a tough cookie. You're constantly embroiled in a match of wits. You're exhausted.

RON TAFFEL, (20th-century) U.S. psychologist and author. *Parenting by Heart,* ch. 4 (1991).

The Family in Society

Caregiving

1 The caretaking has to be done. "Somebody's got to be the mommy." Individually, we underestimate this need, and as a society we make inadequate provision for it. Women take up the slack, making the need invisible as we step in to fill it.

MARY CATHERINE BATESON, (20th-century) U.S. author. *Composing a Life,* ch. 8 (1989).

2 In the United States, it is now possible for a person eighteen years of age, female as well as male, to graduate from high school, college, or university without ever having cared for, or even held, a baby; without ever having comforted or assisted another human being who really needed help. . . . No society can long sustain itself unless its members have learned the sensitivities, motivations, and skills involved in assisting and caring for other human beings.

URIE BRONFENBRENNER, (20th-century) U.S. psychologist and author. *The Ecology of Human Development,* ch. 3 (1979).

3 Who we are has been sidetracked by labels for who we aren't. Phrase names have divided us. Stay-at-home mom, new dad, parent of special needs child, working mother, job sharer, non-custodial parent, single parent, empty nesters, spouse caring for spouse, parent with teens, teenage parent, elder caregiver—these and so many other titles have put us in little niches and kept us thinking that we can't help each other because . . . we are so different. But we are not a collection of separate sub-species. We caregivers are more like one another than not, no matter how we spend our days.

PAULA C. LOWE, (20th-century) U.S. family educator and author. *Care Pooling,* ch. 1 (1993).

4 Of course, some men are very effective caregivers [of elderly parents]. But this situation occurs far less frequently for males than females, because it is a role reversal. For women, caregiving is an expected duty; for men, it is an unexpected expression of love or devotion.

TISH SOMMERS, (20th-century) U.S. author. "Who Takes Care of Our Parents?" as quoted in *The Utne Reader* (April 1990).

5 The duty of caring for failing elderly relatives is more than a fam-

ily matter, a personal dilemma, or a sex equity issue. Basically, it is a problem of how our society views old and disabled people. With the growing numbers of chronically ill, it can no longer be some other family's tragedy. Eventually we must face hard questions, as individuals and as a nation.

TISH SOMMERS, (20th-century) U.S. author. "Who Takes Care of Our Parents?" as quoted in *The Utne Reader* (April 1990).

Childcare

1 To deny the need for comprehensive child care policies is to deny a reality—that there's been a revolution in American life. Grandma doesn't live next door anymore, Mom doesn't work just because she'd like a few bucks for the sugar bowl.

EDITORIAL, *The New York Times* (September 6, 1983).

2 The question is still asked of women: "How do you propose to answer the need for child care?" That is an obvious attempt to structure conflict in the old terms. The questions are rather: "If we *as a human community want* children, how does the total society propose to provide for them?"

JEAN BAKER MILLER, (20th-century) U.S. psychiatrist. *Toward a New Psychology of Women,* ch. 11 (1976).

3 Even today . . . experts, usually male, tell women how to be mothers and warn them that they should not have children if they have any intention of leaving their side in their early years. . . . Children don't need parents' full-time attendance or attention at any stage of their development. Many people will help take care of their needs, depending on who their parents are and how they chose to fulfill their roles.

STELLA CHESS, (20th-century) U.S. psychiatrist and author. *Daughters,* ch. 1 (1978).

4 Mothers don't put their children in daycare because they don't love them.

ALISON CLARKE-STEWART, (20th-century) U.S. child development specialist and author. *Daycare,* ch. 2 (1982).

5 Your child should feel entitled to cry when you leave; crying is a natural thing for a child to do when she feels bad. The fact that your child cries when you go doesn't mean she will never like day care. It just means she wants you to stay.

AMY LAURA DOMBRO, (20th-century) U.S. early childhood educator and author. *The Ordinary Is Extraordinary,* ch. 13 (1988).

6 A commonplace of political rhetoric has it that the quality of a civilization may be measured by how it cares for its elderly. Just as surely, the future of a society may be forecast by how it cares for its young.

DANIEL PATRICK MOYNIHAN, (20th-century) U.S. senator and historian. *Family and Nation,* ch. 3 (1986).

7 Day care poses no risk for children, provided that it is high quality. . . . Poor quality day care is risky for children everywhere. . . . The cost of poor quality day care is measured in children's lives. High quality day care costs only money.

SANDRA SCARR, (20th-century) U.S. developmental psychologist and author. As quoted in *Childhood,* Robert H. Wozniak (1991), a viewer's guide produced in collaboration with Thirteen WNET

Childcare Workers

1 About children's caregivers . . . you want someone who is loving but not so loving you're displaced.

Kathleen Christensen, (20th-century) U.S. professor of environmental psychology. *Wall Street Journal* (May 21, 1993).

2 A new talker will often call her caregiver "mommy," which makes parents worry that the child is confused about who is who. She isn't. This is a case of limited vocabulary rather than mixed-up identities. When a child has only one word for the female person who takes care of her, calling both of them "mommy" is understandable.

Amy Laura Dombro, (20th-century) U.S. early childhood educator and author. *Sharing the Caring,* ch. 6 (1991).

3 By sharing the information and observations with the caregiver, you have a chance to see your child through another pair of eyes. Because she has some distance and objectivity, a caregiver often sees things that a parent's total involvement with her child doesn't allow.

Amy Laura Dombro, (20th-century) U.S. early childhood educator and author. *Sharing the Caring,* conclusion (1991).

4 Your child has the capacity to care for more than one person at a time. The affection she feels for her caregiver doesn't diminish the love she feels for you. Your caregiver isn't your competition. She is your ally.

Amy Laura Dombro, (20th-century) U.S. early childhood educator and author. *Sharing the Caring,* conclusion (1991).

5 It is not only their own need to mother that takes some women by surprise; there is also the shock of discovering the complexity of alternative childcare arrangements that have been made to sound so simple. Those for whom the intended solution is equal parenting have found that some parents are more equal than others.

Elaine Heffner, (20th-century) U.S. psychiatrist and author. *Mothering,* ch. 1 (1978).

6 Other people—grandparents, sisters and brothers, the mother's best friend, the next-door neighbor—get to be familiar to the baby. If the mother communicates her trust in these people, the baby will regard them as delicious novelties. Anybody the mother trusts whom the baby sees often enough partakes a bit of the presence of the mother.

Louise J. Kaplan, (20th-century) U.S. psychologist and author. *Oneness and Separateness: From Infant to Individual,* ch. 4 (1978).

7 Often, we expect too much [from a nanny]. We want someone like ourselves—bright, witty, responsible, loving, imaginative, patient, well-mannered, and cheerful. Also, we want her to be smart, but not so smart that she's going to get bored in two months and leave us to go to medical school.

Louise Lague, (20th-century) U.S. editor and author. *The Working Mom's Book of Hints, Tips, and Everyday Wisdom,* ch. 4 (1995).

8 If the child-caregiver relationship is nurturing, reliable and often even joyous, the child's confidence in human relationships as a source of comfort and reciprocity will be

strengthened and expanded in spite of the parent's absence. The child will learn that not only are the parents to be trusted but that other people are trustworthy as well.

Alicia F. Lieberman, (20th-century) U.S. psychologist and author. *The Emotional Life of the Toddler,* ch. 10 (1993).

9 Bad childcare is the nightmare from which no mother can escape. The professional who can run a business or save a life . . . the mother who can organize a community fund-raiser while entertaining two toddlers and nursing a baby—no matter how thoroughly they've investigated a nanny, no matter how many years they've known their sitter, all walk out the door haunted by the specter that the sitter or staff member to whom they've entrusted their most precious responsibility is a Hyde masquerading as a Jekyll, or otherwise not the woman they thought her to be.

Melinda M. Marshall, (20th-century) U.S. editor and author. *Good Enough Mothers,* pt. II (1993).

10 Most of us don't have the option of quitting work, even if our care situation drove us to consider it in desperation. . . . It's having no choice but to beat the bushes, having no choice but to "settle" on someone or some institution, having no choice but to hand over our child and hope for the best (or, at least, hope to avoid the worst) that gnaws away at even the most unflappable among us.

Melinda M. Marshall, (20th-century) U.S. editor and author. *Good Enough Mothers,* pt. II (1993).

11 The best protection parents can have against the nightmare of a day care arrangement where someone might hurt their child is to choose a place that encourages parents to drop in at any time and that facilitates communication among parents using the program. If parents are free to drop in and if they exercise this right, it is not likely that adults in that place are behaving in ways that harm children.

Gwen Morgan, (20th-century) U.S. early childhood advocate. *In Support of Families,* ed. Michael W. Yogman and T. Berry Brazelton, ch. 9 (1986).

12 It is hard to find someone who will give your children a feeling of security while it lasts and not wound them too much when it is finished, who will treat those children as if they were her own, but knows—and never forgets—that they are yours.

Anna Quindlen, (20th-century) U.S. journalist and novelist. *Living Out Loud,* "Understanding" (1988).

13 Given Freudian assumptions about the nature of children and the biological predestination of mothers, it is unthinkable for mothers voluntarily to leave their babies in others' care, without guilt about the baby's well-being and a sense of self-deprivation. Mothers need their babies for their own mental health, and babies need their mothers for their mental health—a reciprocal and symbiotic relationship.

Sandra Scarr, (20th-century) U.S. developmental psychologist and author. *Mother Care/Other Care,* pt. 2, ch. 4 (1984).

14 We know that babies develop as well in nonmaternal as in maternal

care, *as long as the care is of good quality*. The issue is not who gives the care but the quality of that care, . . . The guilt trip is, in my view, a hangover of another era and of unacknowledged tactics to keep women in their proper place—at home full-time.

Sandra Scarr, (20th-century) U.S. developmental psychologist and author. *Mother Care/Other Care,* pt. 2, ch. 4 (1984).

15 Part of the pain in leaving our children to go to work is that we miss them, wish we could be with them. We also hate to turn them over to someone who is not identical to us, who will do things, at best, differently—at worst, in ways we don't believe are good for children. We are up against this whenever we share the care of our children with others—even grandparents or trusted and loved ones.

Joan Sheingold Ditzion, (20th-century) author. *Ourselves and Our Children,* the Boston Women's Health Book Collective, ch. 2 (1978).

16 Treat your child-care worker as you want your boss to treat you—with respect, professionalism, adherence to policies and prompt payments.

Candyce H. Stapen, (20th-century) U.S. journalist. "Treating Your Provider as a Professional," *Working Woman* (March 1988).

Childrearing Across Cultures

1 In the Native American tradition . . . a man, if he's a mature adult, nurtures life. He does rituals that will help things grow, he helps raise the kids, and he protects the people. His entire life is toward balance and cooperativeness. The ideal of manhood is the same as the ideal of womanhood. You are autonomous, self-directing, and responsible for the spiritual, social and material life of all those with whom you live.

Paula Gunn Allen, (20th-century) U.S. author. As quoted in *The Winning Family,* Louise Hart (1987).

2 If the Russians have gone too far in subjecting the child and his peer group to conformity to a single set of values imposed by the adult society, perhaps we have reached the point of diminishing returns in allowing excessive autonomy and in failing to utilize the constructive potential of the peer group in developing social responsibility and consideration for others.

Urie Bronfenbrenner, (20th-century) U.S. psychologist and author. *Two Worlds of Childhood: U.S. and U.S.S.R.,* ch. 6 (1973).

3 Normal children of both sexes and all cultures will follow a more or less standard and universal developmental pattern and timetable, and reach approximately the same level of development at maturity. While a particular culture's need and expectations and teaching will shape the course of development and affect adult capabilities to some degree, normal individuals, whatever their native culture, if transplanted and taught, could learn to meet the normal demands of their adapted cultures.

Stella Chess, (20th-century) U.S. psychiatrist and author. *Daughters,* ch. 2 (1978).

4 The thing that impresses me most about America is the way parents obey their children.

EDWARD, DUKE OF WINDSOR, (1894–1972) British royalty, King Edward VIII. *Look* (March 5, 1957). Said more than twenty years after his abdication.

5 The American adolescent, then, is faced, as are the adolescents of all countries who have entered or are entering the machine age, with the question: freedom from what and at what price? The American feels so rich in his opportunities for free expression that he often no longer knows what it is he is free from. • Neither does he know where he is not free; he does not recognize his native autocrats when he sees them.

ERIK H. ERIKSON, (20th-century) German-born U.S. psychoanalyst and author. *Childhood and Society,* ch. 8 (1950).

6 The fact remains that the human being in early childhood learns to consider one or the other aspect of bodily function as evil, shameful, or unsafe. There is not a culture which does not use a combination of these devils to develop, by way of counterpoint, its own style of faith, pride, certainty, and initiative.

ERIK H. ERIKSON, (20th-century) German-born U.S. psychoanalyst and author. *Childhood and Society,* ch. 11 (1950).

7 Japanese mothers credit "effort" as the key determinant of a child's achievement in school, while American mothers name "ability" as the more important factor.

PERRY GARFINKEL, (20th-century) U.S. educator and journalist. "The Best 'Jewish Mother' in the World," *Psychology Today* (September 1983).

8 My grandfathers, my grandmothers and my mother hardly ever spanked at all. My grandfather said that if you spanked the little ones, you made them scared and they couldn't think. My great great-grandfathers used to use the double rope, but they never hit you; they would just barely miss you with that rope. Afterwards, they would go easy. They would take this boy or girl and talk very softly and kindly to them, and these youngsters would listen.

MAX HANLEY, (20th-century) U.S. Navajo educator. As quoted in *Respect for Life,* ed. by Sylvester M. Morey and Olivia L. Gilliam, ch. 7 (1975).

9 In most other modern societies working mothers are not put under these special and exaggerated pressures. For example, French and English mothers often prefer to breast-feed their babies, but they do not feel that their womanhood is at stake if they fail to do so. Nor does anyone else.

SYLVIA ANN HEWLETT, (20th-century) U.S. economist. *A Lesser Life,* ch. 2 (1986).

10 Until her child goes to school, the Japanese mother devotes herself to the rearing of the child. In verbal and nonverbal ways, she reminds the child of her deep, deep, warm feelings and that the child is the most important thing in the world to her. Then she says, "After all I've done for you, don't disappoint me." She's like the Jewish mother who says, "What do you mean you're not hungry—after I've slaved all day over a hot stove for you."

JEROME KAGAN, (20th-century) U.S. professor of developmental psychology. As quoted in "The Best 'Jewish Mother' in the World," by Perry Garfinkel, *Psychology Today* (September 1983).

11 In all times and in all places—in Constantinople, northwestern Zambia, Victorian England, Sparta, Arabia, . . . medieval France, Babylonia, . . . Carthage, Mahenjo-Daro, Patagonia, Kyushu, . . . Dresden—the time span between childhood and adulthood, however fleeting or prolonged, has been associated with the acquisition of virtue as it is differently defined in each society. A child may be good and morally obedient, but only in the process of arriving at womanhood or manhood does a human being become capable of virtue—that is, the qualities of mind and body that realize society's ideals.

Louise Kaplan, (20th-century) U.S. psychologist and author. *Adolescence,* ch. 1 (1984).

12 In a cross-cultural study of 173 societies (by Herbert Barry and L. M. Paxson of the University of Pittsburgh) 76 societies typically had mother and infant sharing a bed; in 42 societies they shared a room but not a bed; and in the remaining 55 societies they shared a room with a bed unspecified. There were *no* societies in which infants routinely slept in a separate room.

Melvin Konner, (20th-century) U.S. professor of psychiatry and anthropology. *Childhood,* ch. 3 (1991).

13 Navajo infants get so attached to cradleboard that they cry to be tied into it. Kikuyu infants in Kenya get handed around several "mothers," all wives to one man. . . . Mothers in rural Guatemala keep their infants quiet, in dark huts. Middle-class American mothers talk a blue streak at them. Israeli kibbutz mothers give them over to a communal caretaker . . . Japanese mothers sleep with them. . . . All these tactics are compatible with normal health—physical and mental—and development in infancy. So one lesson for parents so far seems to be: Let a hundred flowers bloom.

Melvin Konner, (20th-century) U.S. professor of psychiatrisy and anthropology, *Childhood,* ch. 2 (1991).

14 Teasing is universal. Anthropologists have found the same fundamental patterns of teasing among New Zealand aborigine children and inner-city kids on the playgrounds of Philadelphia.

Lawrence Kutner, (20th-century) U.S. child psychologist and author. *Parent and Child,* ch. 9 (1991).

15 In Japan, mothers insist on achievement and accomplishment as a sign of love and respect. Thus to fail places children in a highly shamed situation.

Michael Lewis, (20th-century) U.S. professor of pediatrics and psychiatry. *Shame, The Exposed Self,* ch. 11 (1992).

16 The Indians feel that each stage is crucial and that the child should be allowed to dwell in each for the appropriate period of time so that every aspect of his being can evolve, just as a plant evolves in the proper time and sequence of the seasons. Otherwise, the child never has a chance to master himself in any one phase of his life.

ALAN QUETONE, (20th-century) U.S. government official and member of the Kiowa tribe. As quoted in *Respect for Life,* ed. Sylvester M. Morey and Olivia L. Gilliam, ch. 14 (1975).

17 All in all, the communally reared children of Israel are far from the emotional disasters that psychoanalytic theory predicted. Neither have they been saved from all personality problems, as the founders of the kibbutz movement had hoped when they freed children from their parents. In any reasonable environment, children seem to grow up to be themselves. There is no evidence that communal rearing with stimulating, caring adults is either the ruination or the salvation of children.

SANDRA SCARR, (20th-century) U.S. developmental psychologist and author. *Mother Care/Other Care,* pt. 4, ch. 8 (1984).

Children in Society

1 Children need people in order to become human. . . . It is primarily through observing, playing, and working with others older and younger than himself that a child discovers both what he can do and who he can become—that he develops both his ability and his identity. . . . Hence to relegate children to a world of their own is to deprive them of their humanity, and ourselves as well.

URIE BRONFENBRENNER, (20th-century) U.S. psychologist and author. *Two Worlds of Childhood: U.S. and U.S.S.R.,* preface (1973).

2 If the children and youth of a nation are afforded the opportunity to develop their capacities to the fullest, if they are given the knowledge to understand the world and the wisdom to change it, then the prospects for the future are bright. In contrast, a society which neglects its children, however well it may function in other respects, risks eventual disorganization and demise.

URIE BRONFENBRENNER, (20th-century) U.S. psychologist and author. *Two Worlds of Childhood: U.S. and U.S.S.R.,* introduction (1973).

3 America is a nation fundamentally ambivalent about its children, often afraid of its children, and frequently punitive toward its children.

LETTY COTTIN POGREBIN, (20th-century) U.S. editor and author. *Family and Politics,* ch. 3 (1983).

4 The country is fed up with children and their problems. For the first time in history, the differences in outlook between people raising children and those who are not are beginning to assume some political significance. This difference is already a part of the conflicts in local school politics. It may spread to other levels of government. Society has less time for the concerns of those who raise the young or try to teach them.

JOSEPH FEATHERSTONE, (20th-century) U.S. social critic. "Family Matters," *Harvard Educational Review,* (February 1979).

5 It can be fairly argued that the highest priority for mankind is to save itself from extinction. However, it can also be argued that a society that neglects its children and robs them of their human potential can extinguish itself without an external enemy.

SELMA FRAIBERG, (20th-century) U.S. child psychoanalyst and author. *Every Child's*

Birthright: In Defense of Mothering, ch. 5 (1977).

6 It's a failure of national vision when you regard children as weapons, and talents as materials you can mine, assay, and fabricate for profit and defense.

JOHN HERSEY, (20th-century) U.S. author. *The Child Buyer,* "Friday, October 25" (1960).

7 If in the earlier part of the century, middle-class children suffered from overattentive mothers, from being "mother's only accomplishment," today's children may suffer from an underestimation of their needs. Our idea of what a child needs in each case reflects what parents need. The child's needs are thus a cultural football in an economic and marital game.

ARLIE HOCHSCHILD, (20th-century) U.S. sociologist and author. *The Second Shift,* ch. 15 (1989).

8 No society can survive without children. The rhetoric that holds children to be our greatest national resource is true, but the reality is that we do little to demonstrate any conviction of its truth. Becoming a parent and being a "good," concerned, and attentive parent may be the most significant contribution any adult can make to our society—and ultimately to the gross national product and to the future of the society. . . . Surely, it is time to acknowledge the contribution parents make in bearing, caring for, and rearing future generations of citizens, workers, and parents—even if they share personally in the rewards of having children. Surely, parenting is a life cycle stage warranting support at its inception and as an ongoing process by a society that needs and wants children.

SHEILA B. KAMERMAN, (20th-century) U.S. professor of social policy and author. *Parenting in an Unresponsive Society,* epilogue (1980).

9 For Americans the contradiction between national ideal and social fact required explanation and correction. Ultimately this contradiction did not lead to the abandonment of the ideal of equal opportunity but rather to its postponement: to the notion of achieving for the next generation what could not be achieved for the current one. And the chief means to this end was a brilliant American invention: universal, free, compulsory public education. This "solution" was especially important for children and families because it gave children a central role in achieving the national ideal.

KENNETH KENISTON, (20th-century) U.S. professor of human development. *All Our Children,* ch. 2, The Carnegie Council on Children (1977).

10 Consider children as a beat. Clearly not an institution of power, children don't vote and they don't pass taxes. They have no money, and they don't buy newspapers or watch the news on television. Consequently, children are one of the most neglected segments of society in the news, except as a subtopic of other power beats such as education, family, and crime. Children are in serious trouble in this society, which means the foundation of our society is in trouble, which means the future is in trouble, and that is news.

JOAN KONNER, (20th-century) U.S. journalist. "Readers Don't Always Know What

They Want," *ASNE (American Association of Editors) Bulletin* (September 1992).

11 Any beast can cry over the misfortunes of its own child. It takes a mensch to weep for others' children.

Sam Levenson, (20th-century) U.S. humorist. As quoted in *Raising Your Child to Be a Mensch,* Neil Kurshan, ch. 2 (1987).

12 Everywhere, everywhere, children are the scorned people of the earth.

Toni Morrison, (20th-century) U.S. novelist and author. As quoted in *Woman to Woman,* Julia Gilden and Mark Riedman (1994).

13 It is fair to assume that the United States has become the first society in history in which a person is more likely to be poor if young rather than old.

Daniel Patrick Moynihan, (20th-century) U.S. senator and historian. *Family and Nation,* ch. 3 (1986).

14 Nor did the world have to await scientific progress to save the bulk of its children. The highest levels of infant mortality were never necessary. Children have always been something of an option. The only revolutionary change which modern medicine has offered us, very recently, is the expectation that all our children will survive and the confidence to invest our affections in them. But whether this will ensure that they will stand higher among our values will also prove to be a matter of attitude.

C. John Sommerville, (20th-century) U.S. historian and author. *The Rise and Fall of Childhood,* ch. 14 (rev. 1990).

15 It is perverse that a nation so rich should neglect its children so shamefully. Our attitude toward them is cruelly ambivalent. We are sentimental about children but in our actions do not value them. We say we love them but give them little honor.

Richard B. Stolley, (20th-century) U.S. editor and child advocate. "Our Future Depends on How We Treat America's Children," *Money* (May 1995).

Children in Society, Historical Perspectives

1 Courtin's manual of etiquette of 1671 explains: "These little people are allowed to amuse themselves without anyone troubling to see whether they are behaving well or badly; they are permitted to do as they please; nothing is forbidden them; they laugh when they ought to cry, they cry when they ought to laugh, they talk when they ought to be silent, and they are mute when good manners require them to replay. It is cruelty to allow them to go on living in this way. The parents say that when they are bigger they will be corrected. Would it not be better to deal with them in such a way that there was nothing to correct?"

Philippe Aries, (20th-century) French historian. *Centuries of Childhood,* pt. 1, ch. 5 (1962).

2 In 1600 the specialization of games and pastimes did not extend beyond infancy; after the age of three or four it decreased and disappeared. From then on the child played the same games as the adult, either with other children or with adults. . . . Conversely, adults used

to play games which today only children play.

PHILIPPE ARIES, (20th-century) French historian. *Centuries of Childhood,* pt. 1, ch. 4 (1962).

3 In medieval society the idea of childhood did not exist; this is not to suggest that children were neglected, forsaken or despised. The idea of childhood is not to be confused with affection for children; it corresponds to an awareness of the particular nature of childhood, that particular nature which distinguishes the child from the adult, even the young adult. . . . That is why, as soon as the child could live without the constant solicitude of his mother, his nanny or his cradle-rocker, he belonged to adult society.

PHILIPPE ARIES, (20th-century) French historian. *Centuries of Childhood,* pt. 1, conclusion (1962).

4 It is as if, to every period of history, there corresponded a privileged age and a particular division of human life: "youth" is the privileged age of the seventeenth century, childhood of the nineteenth, adolescence of the twentieth.

PHILIPPE ARIES, (20th-century) French historian. *Centuries of Childhood,* pt. 1, ch. 1 (1962).

5 Nothing in medieval dress distinguished the child from the adult. In the seventeenth century, however, the child, or at least the child of quality, whether noble or middle-class, ceased to be dressed like the grown-up. This is the essential point: henceforth he had an outfit reserved for his age group, which set him apart from the adults. These can be seen from the first glance at any of the numerous child portraits painted at the beginning of the seventeenth century.

PHILIPPE ARIES, (20th-century) French historian. *Centuries of Childhood,* pt. 1, ch. 3 (1962).

6 The Abbé Goussault, a counsellor at High Court, writes [at the end of the 17th century]: "Familiarizing oneself with one's children, getting them to talk about all manner of things, treating them as sensible people and winning them over with sweetness, is an infallible secret for doing what one wants with them. . . . A few caresses, a few little presents, a few words of cordiality and trust make an impression on their minds, and they are few in number that resist these sweet and easy methods of making them persons of honour and probity."

PHILIPPE ARIES, (20th-century) French historian. *Centuries of Childhood,* pt. 1, conclusion (1962).

7 The general feeling was, and for a long time remained, that one had several children in order to keep just a few. As late as the seventeenth century . . . people could not allow themselves to become too attached to something that was regarded as a probable loss. This is the reason for certain remarks which shock our present-day sensibility, such as Montaigne's observation, "I have lost two or three children in their infancy, not without regret, but without great sorrow."

PHILIPPE ARIES, (20th-century) French historian. *Centuries of Childhood,* pt. 1, ch. 2 (1962).

8 Until the end of the Middle Ages, and in many cases afterwards too, in order to obtain initiation in a trade of any sort whatever—whether that of courtier, soldier, administrator, merchant or workman—a boy did not amass the knowledge necessary to ply that trade before entering it, but threw himself into it; he then acquired the necessary knowledge.

PHILIPPE ARIES, (20th-century) French historian. *Centuries of Childhood,* pt. 1, ch. 4 (1962).

9 In proper English households . . . one writer remembered the 1630s as a time when, "The child perfectly loathed the sight of his parents, as the slave his Torturer. Gentlemen of thirty or forty years old, fitt for any employment in the commonwealth, were to stand like great mutes and fools bare headed before their parents; and the Daughters (grown women) were to stand at the Cupboard's side during the whole time of the proud mothers visit, unless (as the fashion was) 'twas desired that leave (forsooth) should be given to them to kneele upon cushions brought them by the servingman, after they had done sufficient Penance standing."

JOHN AUBREY, (20th-century) British historian. As quoted in *The Rise and Fall of Childhood,* C. John Sommerville, ch. 11 (rev. 1990).

10 In former times and in less complex societies, children could find their way into the adult world by watching workers and perhaps giving them a hand; by lingering at the general store long enough to chat with, and overhear conversations of, adults. . . by sharing and participating in the tasks of family and community that were necessary to survival. They were in, and of, the adult world while yet sensing themselves apart as children.

DOROTHY H. COHEN, (20th-century) U.S. educator and child development specialist. *The Learning Child,* "What Changes Do We Need" (1972).

11 The idea of childhood as a social invention, in retrospect, is hardly credible. In the Bible, in writings of the Greeks and Romans, and in the works of the first great educat or of the modern era, Comenius, children were recognized as being both different from adults and different from one another with respect to their stages of development. To be sure, the scientific study of children and the increased length of life in modern times have enhanced our understanding of age differences, but they have always been acknowledged.

DAVID ELKIND, (20th-century) U.S. child psychologist and author. *Miseducation,* ch. 3 (1987).

12 Reprehension is a kind of middle thing betwixt admonition and correction: it is sharpe admonition, but a milde correction. It is rather to be used because it may be a meanes to prevent strokes and blowes, especially in ingenuous and good natured children. [Blows are] the last remedy which a parent can use: a remedy which may doe good when nothing else can.

WILLIAM GOUGE, (17th-century) Puritan writer. As quoted in *The Rise and Fall of Childhood,* C. John Sommerville, ch. 11 (rev. 1990). Originally from *Of Domestical Duties,* William Gouge, 1622.

13 John B. Watson, the most influential child-rearing expert [of the 1920s], warned that doting mothers could retard the development of children . . . Demonstrations of affection were therefore limited. "If you must, kiss them once on the forehead when they say goodnight. Shake hands with them in the morning."

SYLVIA ANN HEWLETT, (20th-century) U.S. economist. *A Lesser Life,* ch. 11 (1986).

14 Within forty years of their arrival in the Plymouth colony, the first white settlers were afraid their children had lost the dedication and religious conviction of the founding generation. Ever since, Americans have looked to the next generation not only with love and solicitude but with a good measure of anxiety, worrying whether they themselves were good parents, fearful that their children would not turn out well.

KENNETH KENISTON, (20th-century) U.S. professor of human development. *All Our Children,* ch. 1, The Carnegie Council on Children (1977).

15 Archaeologists have uncovered six-thousand-year-old clay tablets from southern Babylonia that describe in great detail how the adults of that community found the younger generation to be insolent and disobedient.

LAWRENCE KUTNER, (20th-century) U.S. child psychologist and author. *Parent and Child,* ch. 6 (1991).

16 The first duty of a state is to see that every child born therein shall be well housed, clothed, fed and e ducated till it attains years of discretion.

JOHN RUSKIN, (19th-century) English social critic. *Time and Tide,* letter 13 (1867).

17 Each era invents its own child. Over the past five hundred years, conceptions of the child changed gradually from an ill-formed adult who must be subjugated to society's goals to a precious being who must be protected from unreasonable social demands. Childhood has come to be seen as a special period of life, rather than as a temporary state of no lasting importance for adulthood.

SANDRA SCARR, (20th-century) U.S. developmental psychologist and author. *Mother Care/Other Care,* pt. 2, ch. 3 (1984).

18 [17th-century] Puritans were the first modern parents. Like many of us, they looked on their treatment of children as a test of their own self-control. Their goal was not to simply to ensure the child's duty to the family, but to help him or her make personal, individual commitments. They were the first authors to state that children must obey God rather than parents, in case of a clear conflict.

C. JOHN SOMMERVILLE, (20th-century) U.S. historian and author. *The Rise and Fall of Childhood,* ch. 11 (rev. 1990).

19 Ambivalence reaches the level of schizophrenia in our treatment of violence among the young. Parents do not encourage violence, but neither do they take up arms against the industries which encourage it. Parents hide their eyes from the books and comics, slasher films, videos and lyrics which form the texture of an adolescent culture. While all successful societies have

inhibited instinct, ours encourages it. Or at least we profess ourselves powerless to interfere with it.

C. JOHN SOMMERVILLE, (20th-century) U.S. historian and author. *The Rise and Fall of Childhood,* ch. 1 (rev. 1990).

20 Children became an obsessive theme in Victorian culture at the same time that they were being exploited as never before. As the horrors of life multiplied for some children, the image of childhood was increasingly exalted. Children became the last symbols of purity in a world which was seen as increasingly ugly.

C. JOHN SOMMERVILLE, (20th-century) U.S. historian and author. *The Rise and Fall of Childhood,* ch. 15 (rev. 1990).

21 In the years of the Roman Republic, before the Christian era, Roman education was meant to produce those character traits that would make the ideal family man. Children were taught primarily to be good to their families. To revere gods, one's parents, and the laws of the state were the primary lessons for Roman boys. Cicero described the goal of their child-rearing as "self-control, combined with dutiful affection to parents, and kindliness to kindred."

C. JOHN SOMMERVILLE, (20th-century) U.S. historian and author. *The Rise and Fall of Childhood,* ch. 4 (rev. 1990).

22 "Our earth is degenerate in these latter days. Bribery and corruption are common. Children no longer obey their parents. . . . The end of the world is evidently approaching." Sound familiar? It is, in fact, the lament of a scribe in one of the earliest inscriptions to be unearthed in Mesopotamia, where Western civilization was born.

C. JOHN SOMMERVILLE, (20th-century) U.S. historian and author. *The Rise and Fall of Childhood,* ch. 2 (rev. 1990).

23 Quintilian [educational writer in Rome about A.D. 100] hoped that teachers would be sensitive to individual differences of temperament and ability. . . . Beating, he thought, was usually unnecessary. A teacher who had made the effort to understand his pupil's individual needs and character could probably dispense with it: "I will content myself with saying that children are helpless and easily victimized, and that therefore no one should be given unlimited power over them."

C. JOHN SOMMERVILLE, (20th-century) U.S. historian and author. *The Rise and Fall of Childhood,* ch. 4 (rev. 1990).

24 What is clear is that Christianity directed increased attention to childhood. For the first time in history it seemed important to decide what the moral status of children was. In the midst of this sometimes excessive concern, a new sympathy for children was promoted. Sometimes this meant criticizing adults. . . . So far as parents were put on the defensive in this way, the beginning of the Christian era marks a revolution in the child's status.

C. JOHN SOMMERVILLE, (20th-century) U.S. historian and author. *The Rise and Fall of Childhood,* ch. 5 (rev. 1990).

25 If you are not willing to lose all the labour you have been at to break the will of your child, to bring his will into subjection to yours that it may be afterward subject to the will

of God, there is one advice which, though little known, should be particularly attended. . . . It is this; never, on any account, give a child anything that it cries for. . . . If you give a child what he cries for, you pay him for crying: and then he will certainly cry again.

John Welsley, (18th century) Puritan author. As quoted in *The Rise and Fall of Childhood,* C. John Sommerville, ch. 12 (rev. 1990).

Special Concerns of Modern Children

1 Some parents feel that if they introduce their children to alcohol gradually in the home environment, the children will learn to use alcohol in moderation. I'm not sure that's such a good idea. First of all, alcohol is not healthy for the growing child. Second, introducing alcohol to a child suggests that you condone drinking—even to the point where you want to teach your child how to drink.

Lawrence Balter, (20th-century) U.S. psychologist and author. *Who's In Control?* ch. 6 (1989).

2 One of the most significant effects of age-segregation in our society has been the isolation of children from the world of work. Whereas in the past children not only saw what their parents did for a living but even shared substantially in the task, many children nowadays have only a vague notion of the nature of the parent's job, and have had little or no opportunity to observe the parent, or for that matter any other adult, when he is fully engaged in his work.

Urie Bronfenbrenner, (20th-century) U.S. psychologist and author. *Two Worlds of Childhood: U.S. and U.S.S.R.,* preface (1973).

3 Many more children observe attitudes, values and ways different from or in conflict with those of their families, social networks, and institutions. Yet today's young people are no more mature or capable of handling the increased conflicting and often stimulating information they receive than were young people of the past, who received the information and had more adult control of and advice about the information they did receive.

James P. Comer, (20th-century) U.S. psychiatrist and author. *School Power,* ch. 1 (1980).

4 While most of today's jobs do not require great intelligence, they do require greater frustration tolerance, personal discipline, organization, management, and interpersonal skills than were required two decades and more ago. These are precisely the skills that many of the young people who are staying in school today, as opposed to two decades ago, lack.

James P. Comer, (20th-century) U.S. psychiatrist and author. *School Power,* ch. 1 (1980).

5 Many older wealthy families have learned to instill a sense of public service in their offspring. But newly affluent middle-class parents have not acquired this skill. We are using our children as symbols of leisure-class standing without building in safeguards against an overweening sense of entitlement—a sense of entitlement that may incline some young people more toward the

good life than toward the hard work that, for most of us, makes the good life possible.

David Elkind, (20th-century) U.S. child psychologist and author. *Miseducation,* ch. 4 (1987).

6 Modern children were considerably less innocent than parents and the larger society supposed, and post-modern children are less competent than their parents and the society as a whole would like to believe. . . . The perception of childhood competence has shifted much of the responsibility for child protection and security from parents and society to children themselves.

David Elkind, (20th-century) U.S. child psychologist and author. *Ties That Stress,* ch. 6 (1994).

7 So while it is true that children are exposed to more information and a greater variety of experiences than were children of the past, it does not follow that they automatically become more sophisticated. We always know much more than we understand, and with the torrent of information to which young people are exposed, the gap between knowing and understanding, between experience and learning, has become even greater than it was in the past.

David Elkind, (20th-century) U.S. child psychologist and author. *Miseducation,* ch. 1 (1987).

8 The shift from the perception of the child as innocent to the perception of the child as competent has greatly increased the demands on contemporary children for maturity, for participating in competitive sports, for early academic achievement, and for protecting themselves against adults who might do them harm. While children might be able to cope with any one of those demands taken singly, taken together they often exceed children's adaptive capacity.

David Elkind, (20th-century) U.S. child psychologist and author. *Ties That Stress,* ch. 6 (1994).

9 In the end, the fate of children depends on our ability to use technology constructively and carefully. The connection of children and technology is not simply a matter of seat belts, safe toys, safe air, water and food, additive-free baby foods, or improved television programming. These are all important issues, but to stop here is to forget that today's children will soon be adults. Technological decisions made today will determine, perhaps irrevocably, the kind of physical and social world we bequeath them and the kind of people they become.

Kenneth Keniston, (20th-century) U.S. professor of human development. *All Our Children,* ch. 3, The Carnegie Council on Children (1977).

10 Today's children are living a childhood of firsts. They are the first day care generation; the first truly multicultural generation; the first generation to grow up in the electronic bubble, the environment defined by computers and new forms of television; the first post-sexual revolution generation; the first generation for which nature is more abstraction than reality; the first generation to grow up in new kinds of dispersed, deconcentrated cities, not quite urban, rural, or suburban.

RICHARD LOUV, (20th-century) U.S. journalist and author. *Childhood's Future,* introduction (1991).

11 In our country today, very few children are raised to believe that their principal destiny is to serve their family, their country, or God.

BENJAMIN SPOCK, (20th-century) U.S. pediatrician and author. *Dr. Spock's Baby and Child Care* (1985).

12 A decline in supervision is not the entire story. Even in the fifties there were undersupervised children . . . who nevertheless did not become pregnant at thirteen . . . and who did not smoke anything stronger than an occasional Camel or Lucky Strike. . . . It took a combination of unsupervised children and a permissive, highly charged sexual atmosphere and an influx of easily acquired drugs and the wherewithal to buy them to bring about precocious experimentation by young and younger children. This occurred in the mid-seventies.

MARIE WINN, (20th-century) U.S. author. *Children Without Childhood,* ch. 1 (1981).

13 Perhaps an understanding that early childhood is not the only important stage of childhood, that the middle years are equally important, may lead parents to . . . devote more time and attention, more care and supervision, to their post-toddler children, capable and unchildlike though they may seem. . . . Perhaps an understanding of the importance of play in children's lives . . . will provoke parents to take a stronger stand in controlling their children's television viewing, television being the greatest replacement of play among today's children. . . . Perhaps an understanding . . . that children do not prosper when treated as equal, will encourage parents to take a more authoritative, not authoritarian—position in the family. . . . Perhaps the recognition that a highly complicated civilization cannot afford the period of nurture and protection of its immature members will restore a real childhood to the children of coming generations.

MARIE WINN, (20th-century) U.S. author. *Children Without Childhood,* afterword (1981).

14 The widespread fear among today's parents that their manageable children will turn overnight into dope fiends, school dropouts, or voracious sexual voluptuaries reflects a certain anger and animosity towards the young, a fear and loathing that helps turn the myth into a self-fulfilling prophecy. After all, there were "bad" children and uncontrolled teenagers in the past; nevertheless, parents expected their own children to be good, to grow up well. . . . The fact that today's parents are amazed if their children do not turn into black sheep makes it clear that a less than optimistic, indeed a deeply distrustful and negative, attitude towards children exists today.

MARIE WINN, (20th-century) U.S. author. *Children Without Childhood,* ch. 1 (1981).

Rushed Children/Hurried Childhoods

1 It's a hurried world out there. But kids still need time just to be kids. They need time to enjoy their immaturity.

DAVID BJORKLUND, (20th-century) U.S. child development expert. As quoted by Leslie Dreyfous, The Associated Press (February 9, 1992).

2 A child is nothing like a racing car. . . . Souping up babies doesn't work that way. The child is what she is. There is a certain irreducible if elusive core. Pushing, pulling, stretching, and shrinking will not really change it. There may be spectacular interim results. The baby may say the alphabet before she walks, master two-times or even ten-times table at three. In the long run, however, this forced precocity tends to be irrelevant. . . . Whatever gains there are become unimportant. The losses can be irrevocable.

STELLA CHESS, (20th-century) U.S. psychiatrist and author. *Daughters,* ch. 2 (1978).

3 Adults understandably assume that the level of verbal proficiency a five-year-old displays represents his level of proficiency in all areas of functioning—if he *talks* like an adult, he must *think* and *feel* like one. However, five-year-olds . . . belie the promise of adult-like behavior with their child-like, impulsive actions.

DOROTHY H. COHEN, (20th-century) U.S. educator and child development specialist. *The Learning Child,* "Developmental Aspects of Five-year-olds" (1972).

4 Even assuming the possibility of greater knowledge among responsive young children of a mass media age, it is questionable whether an increase in verbal knowledge and expression has much effect on the capacity for understanding in depth or on the style of behavior of children with no more than five years of living and growing behind them. . . . The drawings of contemporary fives are no more complex, the capacity for judgment no sharper, the feelings of helplessness when they get sick or into trouble no less painful than they have ever been, as far as we know.

DOROTHY H. COHEN, (20th-century) U.S. educator and child development specialist. *The Learning Child,* "Developmental Aspects of Five-year-olds" (1972).

5 [Children] need time to stare at a wall, daydream over a picture book, make mud pies, kick a ball around, whistle a tune or play the kazoo—to do the things today's adults had time to do when they were growing up.

LESLIE DREYFOUS, (20th-century) U.S. journalist, The Asssociated Press (February 9, 1992).

6 Much of the pressure contemporary parents feel with respect to dressing children in designer clothes, teaching young children academics, and giving them instruction in sports derives directly from our need to use our children to impress others with our economic surplus. We find "good" rather than real reasons for letting our children go along with the crowd.

DAVID ELKIND, (20th-century) U.S. child psychologist and author. *Miseducation,* ch. 4 (1987).

7 Preschoolers sound much brighter and more knowledgeable than they really are, which is why so many parents and grandparents are so sure their progeny are gifted and

super-bright. Because children's questions sound so mature and sophisticated, we are tempted to answer them at a level of abstraction far beyond the child's level of comprehension. That is a temptation we should resist.

DAVID ELKIND, (20th-century) U.S. child psychologist and author. *Miseducation,* ch. 6 (1987).

8 Today's pressures on middle-class children to grow up fast begin in early childhood. Chief among them is the pressure for early intellectual attainment, deriving from a changed perception of precocity. Several decades ago precocity was looked upon with great suspicion. The child prodigy, it was thought, turned out to be a neurotic adult; thus the phrase "early ripe, early rot!"

DAVID ELKIND, (20th-century) U.S. child psychologist and author. *The Hurried Child,* ch. 1 (1988).

9 Just as the archetype of the supermom—the woman who can do it all—minimizes the real needs of women, so too the archetype of the "superkid" minimizes the real needs of children. It makes it all right to treat a young child as if he or she were older.

ARLIE HOCHSCHILD, (20th-century) U.S. sociologist and author. *The Second Shift,* ch. 15 (1989).

10 Children who are pushed into adult experience do not become precociously mature. On the contrary, they cling to childhood longer, perhaps all their lives.

PETER NEUBAUER, (20th-century) U.S. psychoanalyst. As quoted in *Children Without Childhood,* Marie Winn, 1981, ch. 13.

11 As today's children impress adults with their sophisticated ways, adults begin to change their ideas about children and their needs. . . . No longer need adults withhold information about the harsh realities of life from children. . . . Rather, they begin to feel it is their duty to prepare children for the exigencies of modern life. . . . As adults act less protectively . . . and as they expose children to the formerly secret underside of their lives—adult sexuality, violence, injustice—those former innocents grow tougher, perforce, less playful and trusting, more skeptical—in short, more like adults. We have come full circle.

MARIE WINN, (20th-century) U.S. author. *Children Without Childhood,* introduction (1981).

12 The new concept of the child as equal and the new integration of children into adult life has helped bring about a gradual but certain erosion of these boundaries that once separated the world of children from the word of adults, boundaries that allowed adults to treat children differently than they treated other adults because they understood that children are different.

MARIE WINN, (20th-century) U.S. author. *Children Without Childhood,* ch. 13 (1981).

Community

1 Practically everyone now bemoans Western man's sense of alienation, lack of community, and inability to find ways of organizing society for human ends. We have reached the end of the road that is built on the

set of traits held out for male identity—advance at any cost, pay any price, drive out all competitors, and kill them if necessary.

JEAN BAKER MILLER, (20th-century) U.S. psychiatrist. *Toward a New Psychology of Women,* ch. 8 (1976).

2 In an ideal society, mothers and fathers would produce potty-trained, civilized, responsible new citizens while government and corporate leaders would provide a safe, healthy, economically just community.

MARY KAY BLAKELY, (20th-century) U.S. journalist and author. *American Mom,* prologue (1994).

3 In the planning and designing of new communities, housing projects, and urban renewal, the planners both public and private need to give explicit consideration to the kind of world that is being created for the children who will be growing up in these settings. Particular attention should be given to the opportunities which the environment presents or precludes for involvement of children with persons both older and younger than themselves.

URIE BRONFENBRENNER, (20th-century) U.S. psychologist and author. *Two Worlds of Childhood: U.S. and U.S.S.R.,* preface (1973).

4 In most nineteenth-century cities, both large and small, more than 50 percent—and often up to 75 percent—of the residents in any given year were no longer there ten years later. People born in the twentieth century are much more likely to live near their birthplace than were people born in the nineteenth century.

STEPHANIE COONTZ, (20th-century) U.S. historian. *The Way We Were,* ch. 1 (1992).

5 Commitment, by its nature, frees us from ourselves and, while it stands us in opposition to some, it joins us with others similarly committed. Commitment moves us from the mirror trap of the self absorbed with the self to the freedom of a community of shared values.

MICHAEL LEWIS, (20th-century) Professor of pediatrics and psychiatry. *Shame, The Exposed Self,* ch. 11 (1992).

6 If we desire a kinder nation, seeing it through the eyes of children is an eminently sensible endeavor: A city that is pro-child, for example, is also a more humane place for adults.

RICHARD LOUV, (20th-century) U.S. journalist and author. *Childhood's Future,* pt. 1, ch. 3 (1991).

7 Because it's not only that a child is inseparable from the family in which he lives, but that the lives of families are determined by the community in which they live and the cultural tradition from which they come.

BERNICE WEISSBOURD, (20th-century) U.S. family advocate and author. Excerpts from the speech delivered to the Family Resource Coalition Conference (October 1988).

Role Models in the Community

1 The situation of our youth is not mysterious. Children have never been very good at listening to their elders, but they have never failed to imitate them. They must, they have no other models.

JAMES BALDWIN, (1924–1987) U.S. novelist and author. "Fifth Avenue, Uptown: A letter from Harlem," *Nobody Knows My Name* (1961).

2 We as a nation need to be reeducated about the necessary and sufficient conditions for making human beings human. We need to be reeducated not as parents—but as workers, neighbors, and friends; and as members of the organizations, committees, boards—and, especially, the informal networks that control our social institutions and thereby determine the conditions of life for our families and their children.

URIE BRONFENBRENNER, (20th-century) U.S. psychologist and author. "Who Needs Parent Education?" Position paper for the Working Conference on Parent Education (1977).

3 Many of us carry memories of an influential teacher who may scarcely know we existed, yet who said something at just the right time in our lives to snap a whole world into focus.

LAURENT A. DALOZ, (20th-century) U.S. educator. *Effective Teaching and Mentoring,* ch. 2 (1986).

4 Whether or not you have children yourself, you are a parent to the next generation. If we can only stop thinking of children as individual property and think of them as the next generation, then we can realize we all have a role to play.

CHARLOTTE DAVIS KASL, (20th-century) U.S. psychologist and author. *Finding Joy,* ch. 71 (1994).

5 A few [women] warrant our attention not because they have the answer but because they have rejected the mentality that insists there must be one answer. What makes them role models is not how much or how little they work, how many or how few hats they wear, but rather how well they understand, and accept, that for all rewards there will be commensurate sacrifice; for all gains, some loss; for any pleasure, some pain.

MELINDA M. MARSHALL, (20th-century) U.S. editor and author. *Good Enough Mothers,* ch. 1 (1993).

6 Whatever we're doing, whoever we are, it isn't enough. . . . Little wonder we have trouble finding role models to guide us through these shoals. No one less than God Herself could be all the things we'd like to be to all the people we'd like to feel approval from.

MELINDA M. MARSHALL, (20th-century) U.S. editor and author. *Good Enough Mothers,* ch. 2 (1993).

7 I believe, as Maori people do, that children should have more adults in their lives than just their mothers and fathers. Children need more than one or two positive role models. It is in your children's best interest that you help them cultivate a support system that extends beyond their immediate family.

STEPHANIE MARSTON, (20th-century) U.S. family therapist and author. *The Divorced Parent,* ch. 1 (1994).

8 For most of us, the word *family* carries very personal and emotional connotations, but it is essential that we learn to view all of humanity as part of the earth's family. While we have no trouble cherishing our own children, we must also appreciate our broader responsibility to the world's children. Only when we learn to value other people's children as our own will all children

have the opportunity to reach their full potential. And only then can we be assured of our own future and the future of our planet.

MARIANNE E. NEIFERT, (20th-century) U.S. pediatrician and author. *Dr. Mom's Parenting Guide,* ch. 1 (1991).

9 Those of us who are in this world to educate—to care for—young children have a special calling: a calling that has very little to do with the collection of expensive possessions but has a lot to do with the worth inside of heads and hearts. In fact, that's our domain: the heads and hearts of the next generation, the thoughts and feelings of the future.

FRED ROGERS, U.S. children's television personality and author. "That Which is Essential Is Invisible to the Eye," *Young Children* (July 1994).

10 It is the responsibility of every adult—especially parents, educators and religious leaders—to make sure that children hear what we have learned from the lessons of life and to hear over and over that we love them and they are not alone.

MARIAN WRIGHT EDELMAN, (20th-century) U.S. child advocate and author. *The Measure of Our Success: A Letter to My Child and Yours,* II, p. 15 (1992).

Cultural Identity

1 My smiling child
Named for a noble ancestor
Great hunter or warrior
You will be one day.
Which will give your papa pride
But always I will remember you
thus.

AFRICAN LULLABY, as quoted in *Roots,* Alex Haley (1976).

2 My parents were very Old World. They come from Brooklyn, which is the heart of the Old World. Their values in life are God and carpeting.

WOODY ALLEN, (20th-century) U.S. comedian, film director, and author. *Woody Allen: Clown Prince of American Humor,* ch. 1.

3 As blacks, we need not be afraid that encouraging moral development, a conscience and guilt will prevent social action. Black children without the ability to feel a normal amount of guilt will victimize their parents, relatives and community first. They are unlikely to be involved in social action to improve the black community. Their self-centered personalities will cause them to look out for themselves without concern for others, black or white.

JAMES P. COMER, (20th-century) U.S. psychiatrist and author. *Raising Black Children,* ch. 4 (rev. 1992).Originally published as *Black Child Care* (1975)

4 I think I see her sitting bowed and
black,
Stricken and seared with slavery's
mortal scars,
Reft of her children, lonely,
anguished, yet
Still looking at the stars.

JESSIE FAUSET, (20th-century) U.S. poet and novelist. "I Think I See Her," *Golden Slippers,* ed. Arna Bontemps (1941).

5 The term "mensch" literally means a "person" or "man," but it represents a moral ideal for all people, men and women alike. . . . It means being sensitive to other people's needs and seeking out ways to help them. It is acquired by living close to family and extending one's sense of obligation beyond the family to

the broader community. In the Jewish culture of Eastern Europe where the term arose, to call someone a mensch was the highest compliment that could be given.

NEIL KURSHAN, (20th-century) U.S. rabbi and author. *Raising Your Child to Be a Mensch,* ch. 1 (1987).

6 A Jewish man with parents alive is a fifteen-year-old boy, and will remain a fifteen-year-old boy till they die.

PHILIP ROTH, (20th-century) U.S. novelist and author. *Portnoy's Complaint* (1967).

7 It's a family joke that when I was a tiny child I turned from the window out of which I was watching a snowstorm, and hopefully asked, 'Momma, do we believe in winter?'

PHILIP ROTH, (20th-century) U.S. novelist and author. *Portnoy's Complaint* (1967).

8 It is not always possible to predict the response of a doting Jewish mother. Witness the occasion on which the late piano virtuoso Oscar Levant telephoned his mother with some important news. He had proposed to his beloved and been accepted. Replied Mother Levant: "Good, Oscar, I'm happy to hear it. But did you practice today?"

LIZ SMITH, (20th-century) U.S. columnist and author. *The Mother Book* (1978).

9 The legacies that parents and church and teachers left to my generation of Black children were priceless but not material: a living faith reflected in daily service, the discipline of hard work and stick-to-itiveness, and a capacity to struggle in the face of adversity.

MARIAN WRIGHT EDELMAN, (20th-century) U.S. child advocate and author. *The Measure of Our Success: A Letter to My Child and Yours,* I, p. 6 (1992).

Education

1 Plato—who may have understood better what forms the mind of man than do some of our contemporaries who want their children exposed only to "real" people and everyday events—knew what intellectual experience made for true humanity. He suggested that the future citizens of his ideal republic begin their literary education with the telling of myths, rather than with mere facts or so-called rational teachings.

BRUNO BETTELHEIM, (20th-century) Austrian-born U.S. child psychologist and author. *The Uses of Enchantment,* "Fairy Tales Vs. Myth" (1975).

2 The liberally educated person is one who is able to resist the easy and preferred answers, not because he is obstinate but because he knows others worthy of consideration.

ALLAN BLOOM, (20th-century) U.S. educator. *The Closing of the American Mind,* preface (1987).

3 Education must, then, be not only a transmission of culture but also a provider of alternative views of the world and a strengthener of the will to explore them.

JEROME S. BRUNER, (20th-century) U.S. psychologist and educator. "After John Dewey, What?" *Bank Street College of Education Publication* (March 1961).

4 I would urge that the yeast of education is the idea of excellence, and the idea of excellence comprises as

many forms as there are individuals, each of whom develops his own image of excellence. The school must have as one of its principal functions the nurturing of images of excellence.

JEROME S. BRUNER, (20th-century) U.S. psychologist and educator. "After John Dewey, What?" *Bank Street College of Education Publication* (March 1961).

5 Surely knowledge of the natural world, knowledge of the human condition, knowledge of the nature and dynamics of society, knowledge of the past so that one may use it in experiencing the present and aspiring to the future—all of these, it would seem reasonable to suppose, are essential to an educated man. To these must be added another—knowledge of the products of our artistic heritage that mark the history of our aesthetic wonder and delight.

JEROME S. BRUNER, (20th-century) U.S. psychologist and educator. "After John Dewey, What?" *Bank Street College of Education Publication* (March 1961).

6 At the heart of the educational process lies the child. No advances in policy, no acquisition of new equipment have their desired effect unless they are in harmony with the child, unless they are fundamentally acceptable to him.

CENTRAL ADVISORY COUNCIL FOR EDUCATION, *Children and Their Primary Schools* (The Plowden Report), Her Majesty's Stationery Office (1967).

7 Those who first introduced compulsory education into American life knew exactly why children should go to school and learn to read: to save their souls. . . . Consistent with this goal, the first book written and printed for children in America was titled *Spiritual Milk for Boston Babes in either England, drawn from the Breasts of both Testaments for their Souls' Nourishment.*

DOROTHY H. COHEN, (20th-century) U.S. educator and child development specialist. *The Learning Child,* "What Does Innovation Mean" (1972).

8 We must abandon completely the naive faith that school automatically liberates the mind and serves the cause of human progress; in fact, we know that it may serve any cause. [It] may serve tyranny as well as truth, war as well as peace, death as well as life . . . whether it is good or evil depends, not on the laws of learning, but on the conception of life and civilization that gives it substance and direction. In the course of history, education has served every purpose and doctrine contrived by man. If it is to serve the cause of human freedom, it must be explicitly designed for that purpose.

GEORGE S. COUNTS, as quoted in *The Moral and Spiritual Crisis in Education,* David E. Purpel (1989).

9 A good education ought to help people to become both more receptive to and more discriminating about the world: seeing, feeling, and understanding more, yet sorting the pertinent from the irrelevant with an ever finer touch, increasingly able to integrate what they see and to make meaning of it in ways that enhance their ability to go on growing.

LAURENT A. DALOZ, (20th-century) U.S. educator. *Effective Teaching and Mentoring,* ch. 9 (1986).

10 The proper aim of education is to promote significant learning. Significant learning entails development. Development means successively asking broader and deeper questions of the relationship between oneself and the world. This is as true for first graders as graduate students, for fledging artists as graying accountants.

LAURENT A. DALOZ, (20th-century) U.S. educator. *Effective Teaching and Mentoring,* ch. 9 (1986).

11 Experiences in order to be educative must lead out into an expanding world of subject matter, a subject matter of facts or information and of ideas. This condition is satisfied only as the educator views teaching and learning as a continuous process of reconstruction of experience.

JOHN DEWEY, (1859–1952) U.S. philosopher and educator. *Experience and Education,* ch. 7 (1938).

12 It is part of the educator's responsibility to see equally to two things: first, that the problem grows out of the conditions of the experience being had in the present, and that it is within the range of the capacity of students; and, secondly, that it is such that it arouses in the learner an active quest for information and for production of new ideas. The new facts and new ideas thus obtained become the ground for further experiences in which new problems are presented.

JOHN DEWEY, (1859–1952) U.S. philosopher and educator. *Experience and Education,* ch. 7 (1938).

13 The belief that all genuine education comes about through experience does not mean that all experiences are genuinely or equally educative.

JOHN DEWEY, (1859–1952) U.S. philosopher and educator. *Experience and Education,* ch. 2 (1938).

14 There is, I think, no point in the philosophy of progressive education which is sounder than its emphasis upon the importance of the participation of the learner, in the formation of the purposes which direct his activities in the learning process, just as there is no defect in traditional education greater than its failure to secure the active cooperation of the pupil in construction of the purposes involved in his studying.

JOHN DEWEY, (1859–1952) U.S. philosopher and educator. *Experience and Education,* ch. 6 (1938).

15 Now what I want is facts. Teach these boys and girls nothing but facts. Facts alone are wanted in life. Plant nothing else and root out everything else. You can only form the minds of reasoning animals upon Facts: nothing else will ever be of any service to them.

CHARLES DICKENS, (19th-century) English novelist. *Hard Times* (1854).

16 Do your children view themselves as successes or failures? Are they being encouraged to be inquisitive or passive? Are they afraid to challenge authority and to question assumptions? Do they feel comfortable adapting to change? Are they easily discouraged if they cannot arrive at a solution to a problem? The answers to those questions will give you a better appraisal of their education than any list of courses, grades, or test scores.

LAWRENCE KUTNER, (20th-century) U.S. child psychologist and author. *Parent and Child,* ch. 8 (1991).

17 The only fence against the world is a thorough knowledge of it.

JOHN LOCKE, (17th-century) English philosopher. *Some Thoughts Concerning Education,* sec. 88 (1693).

18 If you educate a man you educate a person, but if you educate a woman you educate a family.

RUBY MANIKAN, (20th-century) Indian church leader. "Sayings of the Week," *Observer* (March 30, 1947).

19 The principle goal of education in the schools should be creating men and women who are capable of doing new things, not simply repeating what other generations have done; men and women who are creative, inventive and discoverers, who can be critical and verify, and not accept, everything they are offered.

JEAN PIAGET, (20th-century) as quoted in *Education for Democracy, Proceedings from the Cambridge School Conference on Progressive Education,* ed. Kathe Jervis and Arthur Tobier (1988).

20 Education is for improving the lives of others and for leaving your community and world better than you found it.

MARIAN WRIGHT EDELMAN, (20th-century) U.S. child advocate and author. *The Measure of Our Success: A Letter to My Child and Yours,* I, p. 10 (1992).

21 [How] the young . . . can grow from the primitive to the civilized, from emotional anarchy to the disciplined freedom of maturity without losing the joy of spontaneity and the peace of self-honesty is a problem of education that no school and no culture have ever solved.

LEONTINE YOUNG, (20th-century) U.S. social worker and author. *Life Among the Giants,* ch. 1 (1965).

Early Childhood Education

1 Although good early childhood programs can benefit all children, they are not a quick fix for all of society's ills—from crime in the streets to adolescent pregnancy, from school failure to unemployment. We must emphasize that good quality early childhood programs can help change the social and educational outcomes for many children, but they are not a panacea; they cannot ameliorate the effects of all harmful social and psychological environments.

BARBARA BOWMAN, (20th-century) U.S. early childhood educator. "Birthday Thoughts," *Young Children* (January 1986).

2 The academic expectations for a child just beginning school are minimal. You want your child to come to preschool feeling happy, reasonably secure, and eager to explore and learn.

BETTYE CALDWELL, (20th-century) U.S. child development specialist. "What Every Preschooler Needs to Know," *Child* (June-July 1992).

3 Certainly, young children can begin to practice making letters and numbers and solving problems, but this should be done without workbooks. Young children need to learn initiative, autonomy, industry, and competence before

they learn that answers can be right or wrong.

DAVID ELKIND, (20th-century) U.S. child psychologist and author. *Miseducation,* ch. 8 (1987).

4 Infants and young children are not just sitting twiddling their thumbs, waiting for their parents to teach them to read and do math. They are expending a vast amount of time and effort in exploring and understanding their immediate world. Healthy education supports and encourages this spontaneous learning.

DAVID ELKIND, (20th-century) U.S. child psychologist and author. *Miseducation,* ch. 1 (1987).

5 No authority in the field of child psychology, pediatrics, or child psychiatry advocates the formal instruction, in any domain, of infants and young children. In fact, the weight of solid professional opinion opposes it and advocates providing young children with a rich and stimulating environment that is, at the same time, warm, loving, and supportive of the child's own learning priorities and pacing. It is within this supportive, non-pressured environment that infants and young children acquire a solid sense of security, positive self-esteem, and a long-term enthusiasm for learning.

DAVID ELKIND, (20th-century) U.S. child psychologist and author. *Miseducation,* ch. 1 (1987).

6 The conviction that the best way to prepare children for a harsh, rapidly changing world is to introduce formal instruction at an early age is wrong. There is simply no evidence to support it, and considerable evidence against it. Starting children early academically has not worked in the past and is not working now.

DAVID ELKIND, (20th-century) U.S. child psychologist and author. *Miseducation,* ch. 9 (1987).

7 Young children learn in a different manner from that of older children and adults, yet we can teach them many things if we adapt our materials and mode of instruction to their level of ability. But we miseducate young children when we assume that their learning abilities are comparable to those of older children and that they can be taught with materials and with the same instructional procedures appropriate to school-age children.

DAVID ELKIND, (20th-century) U.S. child psychologist and author. *Miseducation,* ch. 3 (1987).

8 A positive learning climate in a school for young children is a composite of many things. It is an attitude that respects children. It is a place where children receive guidance and encouragement from the responsible adults around them. It is an environment where children can experiment and try out new ideas without fear of failure. It is an atmosphere that builds children's self-confidence so they dare to take risks. It is an environment that nurtures a love of learning.

CAROL B. HILLMAN, (20th-century) U.S. early childhood educator. *Creating a Learning Climate for the Early Childhood Years,* Fastback Series (1989).

9 Early education can only promise to help make the third and fourth

and fifth years of life good ones. It cannot insure without fail that any tomorrow will be successful. Nothing "fixes" a child for life, no matter what happens next. But exciting, pleasing early experiences are seldom sloughed off. They go with the child, on into first grade, on into the child's long life ahead.

JAMES L. HYMES, JR., (20th-century) U.S. child psychologist and author. *Teaching the Child Under Six,* ch. 1 (1968).

10 Every day care center, whether it knows it or not, is a school. The choice is never between custodial care and education. The choice is between unplanned and planned education, between conscious and unconscious education, between bad education and good education.

JAMES L. HYMES, JR., (20th-century) U.S. child psychologist and author. *Teaching the Child Under Six,* ch. 1 (1968).

11 Too many existing classrooms for young children have this overriding goal: To get the children ready for first grade. This goal is unworthy. It is hurtful. This goal has had the most distorting impact on five-year-olds. It causes kindergartens to be merely the handmaidens of first grade.... Kindergarten teachers cannot look at their own children and plan for their present needs as five-year-olds.

JAMES L. HYMES, JR., (20th-century) U.S. child psychologist and author. *Teaching the Child Under Six,* ch. 1 (1968).

12 As you consider whether to move a child into formal academic training, remember that we want our children to do more than just learn how to read and write; we want them to learn in such a way that they become lifelong readers and writers. If we push our children to start learning these skills too far ahead of their own spontaneous interest and their capacity, we may sacrifice the long-range goal of having them enjoy such pursuits.

LILIAN G. KATZ, (20th-century) U.S. early childhood educator. "Should Preschoolers Learn the Three R's?" *Parents Magazine* (October 1990).

13 If we focus exclusively on teaching our children to read, write, spell, and count in their first years of life, we turn our homes into extensions of school and turn bringing up a child into an exercise in curriculum development. We should be parents first and teachers of academic skills second.

NEIL KURSHAN, (20th-century) U.S. rabbi and author. *Raising Your Child to Be a Mensch,* ch. 3 (1987).

14 Quintilian [educational writer in Rome around A.D. 100] thought that the earliest years of the child's life were crucial. Education should start earlier than age seven, within the family. It should not be so hard as to give the child an aversion to learning. Rather, these early lessons would take the form of play—that embryonic notion of kindergarten.

C. JOHN SOMMERVILLE, (20th-century) U.S. historian and author. *The Rise and Fall of Childhood,* ch. 4 (rev. 1990).

Parent Education, General

1 Most advice on child-rearing is sought in the hope that it will con-

firm our prior convictions. If the parent had wished to proceed in a certain way but was made insecure by opposing opinions of neighbors, friends, or relatives, then it gives him great comfort to find his ideas seconded by an expert.

Bruno Bettelheim, (20th-century) Austrian-born U.S. child psychologist and author. *A Good Enough Parent,* ch. 2 (1987).

2 The only effective way to help well-intentioned, intelligent persons to do the best they can in raising children is to encourage and guide them always to do their own thinking in their attempts at understanding and dealing with child-rearing situations and problems, and not to rely blindly on the opinions of others.

Bruno Bettelheim, (20th-century) Austrian-born U.S. child psychologist and author. *A Good Enough Parent,* ch. 1 (1987).

3 After I discovered the real life of mothers bore little resemblance to the plot outlined in most of the books and articles I'd read, I started relying on the expert advice of other mothers—especially those with sons a few years older than mine. This great body of knowledge is essentially an oral history, because anyone engaged in motherhood on a daily basis has no time to write an advice book about it.

Mary Kay Blakely, (20th-century) U.S. journalist and author. *American Mom,* prologue (1994).

4 Our basic ideas about how to parent are encrusted with deeply felt emotions and many myths. One of the myths of parenting is that it is always fun and games, joy and delight. Everyone who has been a parent will testify that it is also anxiety, strife, frustration, and even hostility. Thus most major parenting-education formats deal with parental emotions and attitudes and, to a greater or lesser extent, advocate that the emotional component is more important than the knowledge.

Bettye M. Caldwell, (20th-century) U.S. child development specialist. *In Support of Families,* ed. Michael W. Yogman and T. Berry Brazelton, ch. 13 (1986).

5 In spite of the six thousand manuals on child raising in the bookstores, child raising is still a dark continent and no one really knows anything. You just need a lot of love and luck—and, of course, courage.

Bill Cosby, (20th-century) U.S. comedian and author. *Fatherhood,* ch. 1 (1986).

6 The childless experts on child raising also bring tears of laughter to my eyes when they say, "I love children because they're so honest." There is not an agent in the CIA or the KGB who knows how to conceal the theft of food, how to fake being asleep, or how to forge a parent's signature like a child.

Bill Cosby, (20th-century) U.S. comedian and author. *Fatherhood,* ch. 5 (1986).

7 You know the only people who are always sure about the proper way to raise children? Those who've never had any.

Bill Cosby, (20th-century) U.S. comedian and author. *Fatherhood,* ch. 5 (1986).

8 The cohort that made up the population boom is now grown up; many are in fact middle-aged. They

are one reason for the enormous current interest in such topics as child-rearing and families. The articulate and highly educated children of the baby boom form a huge, literate market for books on various issues in parenting and child-rearing, and, as time goes on, adult development, divorce, midlife crisis, old age, and of course, death.

JOSEPH FEATHERSTONE, (20th-century) U.S. social critic. "Family Matters," *Harvard Educational Review* (February 1979).

9 All of the assumptions once made about a parent's role have been undercut by the specialists. The psychiatric specialists, the psychological specialists, the educational specialists, all have mystified child development. They have fostered the idea that understanding children and promoting their intellectual well-being is too complex for mothers and requires the intervention of experts.

ELAINE HEFFNER, (20th-century) U.S. psychiatrist and author. *Mothering*, ch. 2 (1978).

10 Mothers and others who work with children each have their own special expertise; each has something to contribute to a child's well-being. The opinion of each needs to be respected. Together they can work more effectively on behalf of the child. It is not that one is right, the other wrong, that one is good, the other bad. There are no certain answers and all the information available is needed. It is time to stop looking for a villain—and it is certainly time to stop casting mothers in that role.

ELAINE HEFFNER, (20th-century) U.S. psychiatrist and author. *Mothering*, ch. 10 (1978).

11 Staying in charge as a mother means exercising one's own judgment about what is best for one's child. It means, at times, disregarding the advice of experts. It means fighting one's way into institutional decision making in an effort to make it responsive to the needs of one's own child. It means trusting one's own point of view. Most of all, it means developing the ability to tolerate both the internal anxiety and the external hostility that are generated when one tries to stay in charge.

ELAINE HEFFNER, (20th-century) U.S. psychiatrist and author. *Mothering*, ch. 10 (1978).

12 The belief that there are final and immutable answers, and that the professional expert has them, is one that mothers and professionals tend to reinforce in each other. They both have a need to believe it. They both seem to agree, too, that if the professional's prescription doesn't work it is probably because of the mother's inadequacy.

ELAINE HEFFNER, (20th-century) U.S. psychiatrist and author. *Mothering*, ch. 2 (1978).

13 The relationship between mother and professional has not been a partnership in which both work together on behalf of the child, in which the expert helps the mother achieve her own goals for her child. Instead, professionals often behave as if they alone are advocates for the child; as if they are the guardians of

the child's needs; as if the mother left to her own devices will surely damage the child and only the professional can rescue him.

ELAINE HEFFNER, (20th-century) U.S. psychiatrist and author. *Mothering,* ch. 2 (1978).

14 The degree to which the child-rearing professionals continue to be out of touch with reality is astounding. For example, a widely read manual on breast-feeding devotes fewer than two pages to the working mother.

SYLVIA ANN HEWLETT, (20th-century) U.S. economist. *A Lesser Life,* ch. 2 (1986).

15 Parents still have primary responsibility for raising children, but they must have the power to do so in ways consistent with their children's needs and their own values. . . . We must address ourselves less to the criticism and reform of parents themselves than to the criticism and reform of the institutions that sap their self-esteem and power.

KENNETH KENISTON, (20th-century) U.S. professor of human development. *All Our Children,* ch. 1, The Carnegie Council on Children (1977).

16 In spite of our worries to the contrary, children are still being born with the innate ability to learn spontaneously, and neither they nor their parents need the sixteen-page instructional manual that came with a rattle ordered for our baby boy!

NEIL KURSHAN, (20th-century) U.S. rabbi and author. *Raising Your Child to Be a Mensch,* ch. 3 (1987).

17 It is easy to lose confidence in our natural ability to raise children. The true techniques for raising children are simple: Be with them, play with them, talk to them. You are not squandering their time no matter what the latest child development books say about "purposeful play" and "cognitive learning skills."

NEIL KURSHAN, (20th-century) U.S. rabbi and author. *Raising Your Child to Be a Mensch,* ch. 3 (1987).

18 Parents ought to feel more comfortable about the care of their children than some experts would seem to permit. If children were so fragile and parenting so difficult to learn, where would we all be as adults?

SANDRA SCARR, (20th-century) U.S. developmental psychologist and author. *Mother Care/Other Care,* ch. 1 (1984).

19 The very fact that there are experts may be intimidating; we hate to think that there must be one best way to handle any situation as parents and that we don't know what it is. So as we get more and more advice we seem less and less sure of what we ought to do for our children.

C. JOHN SOMMERVILLE, (20th-century) U.S. historian and author. *The Rise and Fall of Childhood,* ch. 1 (rev. 1990).

20 You know more than you think you do.

BENJAMIN SPOCK, (20th-century) U.S. pediatrician and author. *Dr. Spock's Baby and Child Care,* "The Parent's Part" (1945 rev. 1985).

21 We can glut ourselves with how-to-raise children information . . . strive to become more mature and aware but none of this will spare us from the . . . inevitability that some of the

time we are going to fail our children. Because there is a big gap between knowing and doing. Because mature, aware people are imperfect too. Or because some current event in our life may so absorb or depress us that when our children need us we cannot come through.

JUDITH VIORST, (20th-century) U.S. novelist and poet. *Necessary Losses,* ch. 14 (1986).

22 If mothers are told to do this or that or the other, . . . they lose touch with their own ability to act. . . . Only too easily they feel incompetent. If they must look up everything in a book, they are always too late even when they do the right things, because the right things have to be done immediately. It is only possible to act at exactly the right point when the action is intuitive or by instinct, as we say. The mind can be brought to bear on the problem afterwards.

D. W. WINNICOTT, (20th-century) British child psychiatrist. *Health Education Through Broadcasting,* ch. 1 (1993).

Parent Education, Historical Perspectives

1 We are better advised and more educated than any other generation of parents. Yet this deluge of literature and advice can also leave us feeling overwhelmed and inadequate. Where is the joy of bringing a child into the world if we are always afraid of making a mistake?

NEIL KURSHAN, (20th-century) U.S. rabbi and author. *Raising Your Child to Be a Mensch,* ch. 3 (1987).

2 "Never hug and kiss your children! Mother love may make your children's infancy unhappy and prevent them from pursuing a career or getting married!" That's total hogwash, of course. But it shows an extreme example of what state-of-the-art "scientific" parenting was supposed to be in early twentieth-century America. After all, that was the heyday of efficiency experts, time-and-motion studies, and the like.

LAWRENCE KUTNER, (20th-century) U.S. child psychologist and author. *Pregnancy and Your Baby's First Year,* ch. 12 (1993).

3 Our species successfully raised children for tens of thousands of years before the first person wrote down the word "psychology." The fundamental skills needed to be a parent are within us. All we're really doing is fine-tuning a process that's already remarkably successful.

LAWRENCE KUTNER, (20th-century) U.S. child psychologist and author. *Pregnancy and Your Baby's First Year,* introduction (1993).

4 The conscientious mother of this age approaches the birth of her first baby with two ideas firmly in mind. One is that she will raise the baby by schedule. The other, that she will not let it suck its thumb.

GLADYS D. SCHULTZ, (20th-century) as quoted in *Mothering,* Elaine Heffner, ch. 11 (1978).

5 I think that parents ought to get some idea of how the so-called "experts" have changed their advice over the decades, so that they won't take them deadly seriously, and so that if the parent has the strong feeling, "I don't like this advice,"

the parent won't feel compelled to follow it. . . . So don't worry about trying to do a perfect job. There is no perfect job. There is no one way of raising your children.

Benjamin Spock, (20th-century) U.S. pediatrician and author. As quoted in *Childhood,* Melvin Konner, ch. 3 (1991).

Parent Education, The Need for

1 There is evidence that all too many people are approaching parenthood with a dangerous lack of knowledge and skill. The result is that many children are losing out on what ought to be an undeniable right—the right to have parents who know how to be good parents, parents skilled in the art of "parenting."

T. H. Bell, (20th-century) U.S. educator. "The Child's Right to Have a Trained Parent," *Elementary School Guidance and Counseling* (May 1975).

2 The fear of failure is so great, it is no wonder that the desire to do right by one's children has led to a whole library of books offering advice on how to raise them.

Bruno Bettelheim, (20th-century) Austrian-born U.S. child psychologist and author. *A Good Enough Parent,* ch. 2 (1987).

3 Someday soon, we hope that all middle and high schools will have required courses in child-rearing for girls and boys to help prepare them for one of the most important and rewarding tasks of their adulthood: being a parent. Most of us become parents in our lifetime and it is not acceptable for young people to be steeped in ignorance or questionable folklore when they begin their critical journey as mothers and fathers.

James P. Comer, (20th-century) U.S. psychiatrist and author. *Raising Black Children,* ch. 9 (rev. 1992). Originally published as *Black Child Care* (1975)

4 Every society consists of men in the process of developing from children into parents. To assure continuity of tradition, society must early prepare for parenthood in its children; and it must take care of the unavoidable remnants of infantility in its adults. This is a large order, especially since a society needs many beings who can follow, a few who can lead, and some who can do both, alternately or in different areas of life.

Erik H. Erikson, (20th-century) German-born U.S. psychoanalyst and author. *Childhood and Society,* ch. 11 (1950).

5 Many people operate under the assumption that since parenting is a natural adult function, we should instinctively know how to do it—and do it well. The truth is, effective parenting requires study and practice like any other skilled profession. Who would even consider turning an untrained surgeon loose in an operating room? Yet we "operate" on our children every day.

Louise Hart, (20th-century) U.S. community psychologist and author. *The Winning Family,* ch. 1 (1987).

6 Recognizing that family self-sufficiency is a false myth, we also need to acknowledge that all today's families need help in raising children. The problem is not so much to reeducate parents but to make available the help they need and to give them enough power so that

they can be effective advocates with and coordinators of the other forces that are bringing up their children.

KENNETH KENISTON, (20th-century) U.S. professor of human development. *All Our Children,* ch. 1, The Carnegie Council on Children (1977).

7 Everything from airplanes to kitchen blenders—and even chopsticks—comes with an instruction manual. Children, despite all their complexity, do not.

LAWRENCE KUTNER, (20th-century) U.S. child psychologist and author. *Parent and Child,* introduction (1991).

Parent Education, Problem Solving

1 The trouble with most problem-solving books for parents is that they start with the idea that the child has a problem. Then they try to tell us how to fix the child, or else, after blaming the parent, they suggest how we can fix ourselves.

POLLY BERRIEN BERENDS, (20th-century) U.S. author. *Whole Child/Whole Parent,* ch. 2 (rev. 1987).

2 One year, I'd completely lost my bearings trying to follow potty training instruction from a psychiatric expert. I was stuck on step one, which stated without an atom of irony: "Before you begin, remove all stubbornness from the child." . . . I knew it only could have been written by someone whose suit coat was still spotless at the end of the day, not someone who had any hands-on experience with an actual two-year-old.

MARY KAY BLAKELY, (20th-century) U.S. journalist and author. *American Mom,* prologue (1994).

3 One current reaction to change in families, for example, is the proposal for more "education for parenthood," on the theory that this training will not only teach specific skills such as how to change diapers or how to play responsively with toddlers, but will raise parents' self-confidence at the same time. The proposed cure, in short, is to reform and educate the people with the problem.

KENNETH KENISTON, (20th-century) U.S. professor of human development. *All Our Children,* ch. 1, The Carnegie Council on Children (1977).

4 Theories of child development and guidelines for parents are not cast in stone. They are constantly changing and adapting to new information and new pressures. There is no "right" way, just as there are no magic incantations that will always painlessly resolve a child's problems.

LAWRENCE KUTNER, (20th-century) U.S. child psychologist and author. *Parent and Child,* ch. 1 (1991).

5 Particularly in the early years of the child's development, parents may get different opinions from professionals who view the child in different settings. A pediatrician seeing the child in a busy office diagnoses "attention deficit disorder"; a nursery school teacher who observes the child in an unruly classroom calls him "hyperactive" . . . a psychologist or psychiatrist . . . decides he's very active but not "hyper" and talks of emotional and family prob-

lems; while a neurologist, meeting with the child on a one-to-one basis . . . says he is "normal."

STANLEY TURECKI, (20th-century) U.S. psychiatrist and author. *The Difficult Child,* ch. 4 (1985).

School

1 Placing too much importance on where a child goes rather than what he does there . . . doesn't take into account the child's needs or individuality, and this is true in college selection as well as kindergarten.

NORMAN GIDDAN, (20th-century) U.S. psychiatrist and author. *Parenting Through the College Years,* ch. 2 (1988).

2 School success is not predicted by a child's fund of facts or a precocious ability to read as much as by emotional and social measures; being self-assured and interested; knowing what kind of behavior is expected and how to rein in the impulse to misbehave; being able to wait, to follow directions, and to turn to teachers for help; and expressing needs while getting along with other children.

DANIEL GOLEMAN, (20th-century) U.S. psychologist and author. *Emotional Intelligence,* ch. 12 (1995).

3 Good schools are schools for the development of the *whole child.* They seek to help children develop to their maximum their social powers and their intellectual powers, their emotional capacities, their physical powers.

JAMES L. HYMES, JR., (20th-century) U.S. child psychologist and author. *Teaching the Child Under Six,* ch. 1 (1968).

4 We need to nurture uniqueness and independence. . . . Ours must be schools for ego-strength—the child's ego, not the teacher's. "You can do it!" has to be the teacher's consistent, over-and-over steady slogan: "You can hang up your own coat. . . ." "You can pour your own juice. . . ." "You can climb to the top. . . ." "You can figure it out." We have no stake in schools where children learn to color within the lines. No stake in pushing for unnecessary conformity, no stake in children submerging themselves in the group, no stake in everlasting lessons in obediently following the directions.

JAMES L. HYMES, JR., (20th-century) U.S. child psychologist and author. *Teaching the Child Under Six,* ch. 3 (1968).

5 Schools, the institutions traditionally called upon to correct social inequality, are unsuited to the task; without economic opportunity to follow educational opportunity, the myth of equality can never become real. Far more than a hollow promise of future opportunity for their children, parents need jobs, income, and services. And children whose backgrounds have stunted their sense of the future need to be taught by example that they are good for more than they dared dream.

KENNETH KENISTON, (20th-century) U.S. professor of human development. *All Our Children,* ch. 2, The Carnegie Council on Children (1977).

6 We measure the success of schools not by the kinds of human beings they promote but by whatever increases in reading scores they

chalk up. We have allowed quantitative standards, so central to the adult economic system, to become the principal yardstick for our definition of our children's worth.

Kenneth Kenniston, (20th-century) U.S. professor of human development. As quoted in *The Hurried Child,* David Elkind, ch. 3 (1988).

7 Children learn and remember at least as much from the context of the classroom as from the content of the coursework.

Lawrence Kutner, (20th-century) U.S. child psychologist and author. *Parent and Child,* ch. 8 (1991).

8 It is cheering to note that [Martin] Luther (1524) did not see why schools should not be fun as well: "Now since the young must leap and jump, or have something to do, because they have a natural desire for it which should not be restrained (for it is not well to check them in everything) why should we not provide for them such schools, and lay before them such studies?"

Martin Luther, (1483–1546) German theologist and leader of the Protestant reformation. As quoted in *The Rise and Fall of Childhood,* C. John Sommerville, ch. 9 (rev. 1990).

9 There is absolutely no evidence—developmental or otherwise—to support separating twins in school as a general policy. . . . The best policy seems to be no policy at all, which means that each year, you and your children need to decide what will work best for you.

Pamela Patrick Novotny, (20th-century) U.S. journalist and author. *The Joy of Twins,* ch. 8 (1988, rev. 1994).

School and Parent Interaction

1 Parental attitudes have greater correlation with pupil achievement than material home circumstances or variations in school and classroom organization, instructional materials, and particular teaching practices.

Central Advisory Council for Education, *Children and Their Primary Schools,* (The Plowden Report), Her Majesty's Stationery Office (1967).

2 Nevertheless, no school can work well for children if parents and teachers do not act in partnership on behalf of the children's best interests. Parents have every right to understand what is happening to their children at school, and teachers have the responsibility to share that information without prejudicial judgment. . . . Such communication, which can only be in a child's interest, is not possible without mutual trust between parent and teacher.

Dorothy H. Cohen, (20th-century) U.S. educator and child development specialist. *The Learning Child,* "Beyond the Home to School and Community" (1972).

3 Parents can offer their help by suggesting and locating resources likely to be unfamiliar to children, such as people, books, and materials that can be useful.

Dorothy H. Cohen, (20th-century) U.S. educator and child development specialist. *The Learning Child,* "Parent and Child During the Intermediate Years" (1972).

4 Parents do not give up their children to strangers lightly. They wait in uncertain anticipation for an expression of awareness and inter-

est in their children that is as genuine as their own. They are subject to ambivalent feelings of trust and competitiveness toward a teacher their child loves and to feelings of resentment and anger when their child suffers at her hands. They place high hopes in their children and struggle with themselves to cope with their children's failures.

DOROTHY H. COHEN, (20th-century) U.S. educator and child development specialist. *The Learning Child,* "Beyond the Home to School and Community" (1972).

5 They [parents] can help the children work out schedules for homework, play, and television that minimize the conflicts involved in what to do first. They can offer moral support and encouragement to persist, to try again, to struggle for understanding and mastery. And they can share a child's pleasure in mastery and accomplishment. But they must not do the job for the children.

DOROTHY H. COHEN, (20th-century) U.S. educator and child development specialist. *The Learning Child,* "Parent and Child During the Intermediate Years" (1972).

6 Children in home-school conflict situations often receive a double message from their parents: "The school is the hope for your future, listen, be good and learn" and "the school is your enemy. . . ." Children who receive the "school is the enemy" message often go after the enemy—act up, undermine the teacher, undermine the school program, or otherwise exercise their veto power.

JAMES P. COMER, (20th-century) U.S. psychiatrist and author. *School Power,* ch. 2 (1980).

7 Children who grow up in stimulating, emotionally supportive, highly verbal, and protective environments where the caretaker teaches and models skill development are usually ready for school. When the child is able to meet expectations, he or she receives praise or a positive feedback in school. This also compliments the caretaker—a child-rearing job well done. The caretaker or parent and school people feel good about each other. The child receives a message from parents that the school program is good. The positive emotional bond between parents and child is extended to the school. The school staff can then serve as parent surrogates. This facilitates learning.

JAMES P. COMER, (20th-century) U.S. psychiatrist and author. *School Power,* ch. 2 (1980).

8 Often low-income parents give their children every other thing they need for successful participation in school and the world of work except the planning and organizing skills and habit patterns needed to operate in complex settings. Many intelligent and able college students from low-income backgrounds confront these deficits when faced with a heavy assignment load. . . . These patterns are best acquired at an early age and need to be quite well developed by late elementary school or twelve or thirteen years of age.

JAMES P. COMER, (20th-century) U.S. psychiatrist and author. *School Power,* ch. 8 (1980).

9 We are now a nation of people in daily contact with strangers.

Thanks to mass transportation, school administrators and teachers often live many miles from the neighborhood schoolhouse. They are no longer in daily informal contact with parents, ministers, and other institution leaders . . . [and are] no longer a natural extension of parental authority.

JAMES P. COMER, (20th-century) U.S. psychiatrist and author. *School Power,* ch. 1 (1980).

10 Dissonance between family and school, therefore, is not only inevitable in a changing society; it also helps to make children more malleable and responsive to a changing world. By the same token, one could say that absolute homogeneity between family and school would reflect a static, authoritarian society and discourage creative, adaptive development in children.

SARA LAWRENCE LIGHTFOOT, (20th-century) U.S. educator and author. *Worlds Apart,* ch. 1 (1978).

11 For those parents from lower-class and minority communities . . . [who] have had minimal experience in negotiating dominant, external institutions or have had negative and hostile contact with social service agencies, their initial approaches to the school are often overwhelming and difficult. Not only does the school feel like an alien environment with incomprehensible norms and structures, but the families often do not feel *entitled* to make demands or force disagreements.

SARA LAWRENCE LIGHTFOOT, (20th-century) U.S. educator and author. *Worlds Apart,* ch. 5 (1978).

12 Mothers seem to be in subtle competition with teachers. There is always an underlying fear that teachers will do a better job than they have done with their child. . . . But mostly mothers feel that their areas of competence are very much similar to those of the teacher. In fact they feel they know their child better than anyone else and that the teacher doesn't possess any special field of authority or expertise.

SARA LAWRENCE LIGHTFOOT, (20th-century) U.S. educator and author. *Worlds Apart,* ch. 2 (1978).

13 Productive collaborations between family and school, therefore, will demand that parents and teachers recognize the critical importance of each other's participation in the life of the child. This mutuality of knowledge, understanding, and empathy comes not only with a recognition of *the child* as the central purpose for the collaboration but also with a recognition of the need to maintain roles and relationships with children that are comprehensive, dynamic, and *differentiated.*

SARA LAWRENCE LIGHTFOOT, (20th-century) U.S. educator and author. *Worlds Apart,* ch. 5 (1978).

14 The ambiguous, gray areas of authority and responsibility between parents and teachers exacerbate the distrust between them. The distrust is further complicated by the fact that it is rarely articulated, but usually remains smoldering and silent.

SARA LAWRENCE LIGHTFOOT, (20th-century) U.S. educator and author. *Worlds Apart,* ch. 1 (1978).

15 Sure, you can love your child when he or she has just brought home a report card with straight "A's." It's a lot harder, though, to show the same love when teachers call you from school to tell you that your child hasn't handed in any homework since the beginning of the term.

THE LIONS CLUBS INTERNATIONAL AND THE QUEST NATION, *The Surprising Years,* II, ch.3 (1985).

16 Teachers . . . were not much appreciated. As one Englishman put it (in 1678): "Were the particular salaries of school-masters throughout the Land set forth in a table, it is not to be feared that their amply patrimony would excite the covetousness or envy of the reader."

C. JOHN SOMMERVILLE, (20th-century) U.S. historian and author. As quoted in *The Rise and Fall of Childhood,* ch. 8 (rev. 1990).

Schoolteachers and Teaching

1 In Rousseau's view (1762) . . . most of the problems of education are problems of motivation, as teachers try to rush things. They talk of geography before the child knows the way around his own backyard. They teach history before the child understands anything about adult motivation. . . . It would be far better, to let questions arise naturally. . . . When a child is self-motivated, the teacher cannot keep him from learning.

C. JOHN SOMMERVILLE, (20th-century) U.S. historian and author. As quoted in *The Rise and Fall of Childhood,* ch. 12 (rev. 1990).

2 How a child is taught affects his image of himself, which in turn, influences what he will dare and care to try to learn. The interdependence of the two is inescapable.

BARBARA BIBER, (20th-century) U.S. developmental psychologist. "Learning and Personality Development: A Point of View," introduction, *Bank Street College of Education Publication* (March 1961).

3 It is sentimentalism to assume that the teaching of life can always be fitted to the child's interests, just as it is empty formalism to force the child to parrot the formulas of adult society. Interests can be created and stimulated.

JEROME S. BRUNER, (20th-century) U.S. psychologist and educator. "After John Dewey, What?" *Bank Street College of Education Publication* (March 1961).

4 One seeks to equip the child with deeper, more gripping, and subtler ways of knowing the world and himself.

JEROME S. BRUNER, (20th-century) U.S. psychologist and educator. "After John Dewey, What?" *Bank Street College of Education Publication* (March 1961).

5 I hear and I forget;
I see and I remember;
I do and I understand.

CHINESE PROVERB.

6 Learning without thought is labor lost.

CONFUCIUS, (551–479 B.C.) Chinese philosopher.

7 For good teaching rests neither in accumulating a shelf-full of knowledge nor in developing a repertoire of skills. In the end, good teaching lies in a willingness to attend and care for what happens in our students, ourselves, and the space between us. Good teaching is a cer-

tain kind of stance, I think. It is a stance of receptivity, of attunement, of listening.

LAURENT A. DALOZ, (20th-century) U.S. educator. *Effective Teaching and Mentoring,* ch. 9 (1986).

8 It makes little sense to spend a month teaching decimal fractions to fourth-grade pupils when they can be taught in a week, and better understood and retained, by sixth-grade students. Child-centeredness does not mean lack of rigor or standards; it does mean finding the best match between curricula and children's developing interests and abilities.

DAVID ELKIND, (20th-century) U.S. child psychologist and author. *Ties That Stress,* ch. 6 (1994).

9 If you are truly serious abut preparing your child for the future, don't teach him to subtract—teach him to deduct.

FRAN LEBOWITZ, (20th-century) U.S. humorist and author. *The Fran Lebowitz Reader,* "Parental Guidance" (1994).

10 Learning and teaching should not stand on opposite banks and just watch the river flow by; instead, they should embark together on a journey down the water. Through an active, reciprocal exchange, teaching can strengthen learning how to learn.

LORIS MALAGUZZI, (20th-century) Italian early childhood education specialist. As quoted in *The Hundred Languages of Children,* ch. 3, Carolyn Edwards (1993).

11 The wider the range of possibilities we offer children, the more intense will be their motivations and the richer their experiences. We must widen the range of topics and goals, the types of situations we offer and their degree of structure, the kinds and combinations of resources and materials, and the possible interactions with things, peers, and adults.

LORIS MALAGUZZI, (20th-century) Italian early education specialist. As quoted in *The Hundred Languages of Children,* ch. 3, Carolyn Edwards (1993).

12 Teach a child to play solitaire, and she'll be able to entertain herself when there's no one around. Teach her tennis, and she'll know what to do when she's on a court. But raise her to feel comfortable in nature, and the whole planet is her home.

JOYCE MAYNARD, (20th-century) U.S. journalist. "The Call of the Wild," *Parenting Magazine* (August 1994).

13 Experience is not always the kindest of teachers, but it is surely the best.

SPANISH PROVERB.

Families and Society

1 We did not inherit this land from our fathers. We are borrowing it from our children.

AMISH PROVERB, as quoted in *The Winning Family,* ch. 26, Louise Hart (1987).

2 The family is in flux, and signs of trouble are widespread. Expectations remain high. But realities are disturbing.

ROBERT NEELLY BELLAH, (20th-century) U.S. sociologist and author. *The Good Society,* ch. 1 (1991).

3 One theme links together these new proposals for family policy—the idea that the family is exceedingly

durable. Changes in structure and function and individual roles are not to be confused with the collapse of the family. Families remain more important in the lives of children than other institutions. Family ties are stronger and more vital than many of us imagine in the perennial atmosphere of crisis surrounding the subject.

JOSEPH FEATHERSTONE, (20th-century) U.S. social critic. "Family Matters," *Harvard Educational Review* (February 1979).

4 Whatever else American thinkers do, they psychologize, often brilliantly. The trouble is that psychology only takes us so far. The new interest in families has its merits, but it will have done us all a disservice if it turns us away from public issues to private matters. A vision of things that has no room for the inner life is bankrupt, but a psychology without social analysis or politics is both powerless and very lonely.

JOSEPH FEATHERSTONE, (20th-century) U.S. social critic. "Family Matters," *Harvard Educational Review* (February 1979).

5 In brief, we have no explicit family policy but instead have a haphazard patchwork of institutions and programs designed mostly under crisis conditions, whether the crisis is national in scope (such as a recession) or personal (such as a breakup of a particular family).

KENNETH KENISTON, (20th-century) U.S. professor of human development. *All Our Children*, ch. 4, The Carnegie Council on Children (1977).

6 Put together all the existing families and you have society. It is as simple as that. Whatever kind of training took place in the individual family will be reflected in the kind of society that these families create.

VIRGINIA SATIR, (20th-century) U.S. family therapist and author. *The New Peoplemaking*, ch. 24 (1988).

7 Awareness has changed so that every act for children, every piece of legislation recognizes that children are part of families and that it is within families that children grow and thrive—or don't.

BERNICE WEISSBOURD, (20th-century) U.S. family advocate and author. Excerpts from the speech delivered to the Family Resource Coalition Conference (October 1988).

8 We have fought too much rhetoric and red tape to be lulled and comforted by a paid political advertisement showing a candidate tossing his grandchild in the air while a disembodied voice espouses "family values" in the background.

BERNICE WEISSBOURD, (20th-century) U.S. family advocate and author. Excerpts from the speech delivered to the Family Resource Coalition Conference (October 1988).

9 The value of a family is that it cushions and protects while the individual is learning ways of coping. And a supportive social system provides the same kind of cushioning for the family as a whole.

MICHAEL W. YOGMAN, (20th-century) U.S. author. *In Support of Families*, introduction (1986).

Families and Society, Historical Perspectives

1 Extended families have never been the norm in America; the highest

figure for extended-family households ever recorded in American history is 20 percent. Contrary to the popular myth that industrialization destroyed "traditional" extended families, this high point occurred between 1850 and 1885, during the most intensive period of early industrialization. Many of these extended families, and most "producing" families of the time, depended on the labor of children; they were held together by dire necessity and sometimes by brute force.

STEPHANIE COONTZ, (20th-century) U.S. historian. *The Way We We·e*, ch. 1 (1992).

2 For every nineteenth-century middle-class family that protected its wife and child within the family circle, there was an Irish or a German girl scrubbing floors in that home, a Welsh boy mining coal to keep the home-baked goodies warm, a black girl doing the family laundry, a black mother and child picking cotton to be made into clothes for the family, and a Jewish or an Italian daughter in a sweatshop making "ladies" dresses or artificial flowers for the family to purchase.

STEPHANIE COONTZ, (20th-century) U.S. historian. *The Way We Were*, ch. 1 (1992).

3 In the supposedly enlightened eighteenth and nineteenth centuries, parental indifference, child neglect, and raw cruelty appeared among Europeans of all classes.... In mid-nineteenth-century France, families abandoned their children at the rate of thirty-three thousand a year. ... It took sixty years after the criminalization of cruelty to animals for cruelty to children to be made punishable under English law.... Industrialized America added brutalizing child labor to the oppressions of the young.

LETTY COTTIN POGREBIN, (20th-century) U.S. editor and author. *Family and Politics*, ch. 3 (1983).

4 Many Americans imagine simpler times even as a storm of social change swirls about, blowing parents here and children there. Sure, the 1950s ideal world would be wonderful. But knock on the nation's doors: Ozzie and Harriet are seldom at home.

LESLIE DREYFOUS, (20th-century) U.S. journalist, The Asssociated Press (October 25,1992).

5 Families suffered badly under industrialization, but they survived, and the lives of men, women, and children improved. Children, once marginal and exploited figures, have moved to a position of greater protection and respect ... The historic decline in the overall death rates for children is an astonishing social fact, notwithstanding the disgraceful infant mortality figures for the poor and minorities. Like the decline in death from childbirth for women, this is a stunning achievement.

JOSEPH FEATHERSTONE, (20th-century) U.S. social critic. "Family Matters," *Harvard Educational Review* (February 1979).

6 Nostalgia is one of the great enemies of clear thinking about the family. The disruption of families in the nineteenth century through

death, separation, and other convulsions of an industrializing economy was much more catastrophic than we imagine.

Joseph Featherstone, (20th-century) U.S. social critic. "Family Matters," *Harvard Educational Review* (February 1979).

7 The "family" has clearly emerged anew in the late 1970s as a central subject for discussion, debate, research and writing in both scholarly and popular arenas. Anxiety over whether or not the family as a basic social institution is dying has diminished. In its stead has emerged a fairly broad consensus around the position that the family is "here to stay," but that it certainly is changing.

Sheila B. Kamerman, (20th-century) U.S. professor of social policy and author. *Parenting in an Unresponsive Society,* ch. 1 (1980).

8 In the early nineteenth century, the doctrine of self-sufficiency came to apply to families as well as individuals. . . . The family became a special protected place, the repository of tender, pure, and generous feelings (embodied by the mother) and a bulwark and bastion against the raw, competitive, aggressive, and selfish world of commerce (embodied by the father). . . . In performing this protective task, the good family was to be as self-sufficient as the good man.

Kenneth Keniston, (20th-century) U.S. professor of human development. *All Our Children,* ch. 1, The Carnegie Council on Children (1977).

9 Not all the family functions that seem to have been transferred outside the family—or that romantics sometimes yearn to bring back—were there in the first place. It is often claimed that "extended families" (with three generations at home, aunts and uncles included) were the rule, and that they have now been replaced by "nuclear" families. But actually most Americans have always lived in families consisting only of parents and children, and in colonial days, just as today, most children moved away from their parents' homes to set up households of their own. Nor is the mobility that scatters kinfolk to widely separated regions a new thing; historical studies indicate that frequent moves to new places have always been the rule in American life.

Kenneth Keniston, (20th-century) U.S. professor of human development. *All Our Children,* ch. 1, The Carnegie Council on Children (1977).

10 The most important difference between these early American families and our own is that early families constituted economic units in which all members, from young children on up, played important productive roles within the household. The prosperity of the whole family depended on how well husband, wife, and children could manage and cultivate the land. Children were essential to this family enterprise from age six or so until their twenties, when they left home.

Kenneth Keniston, (20th-century) U.S. professor of human development. *All Our Children,* ch. 1, The Carnegie Council on Children (1977).

11 To be sure, changes in American family structure have been fairly

continuous since the first European settlements, but today these changes seem to be occurring so rapidly that the shift is no longer a simple extension of long-term trends. We have passed a genuine watershed: this is the first time in our history that the typical school-age child has a mother who works outside the home.

KENNETH KENISTON, (20th-century) U.S. professor of human development. *All Our Children,* ch. 1, The Carnegie Council on Children (1977).

12 American family life has never been particularly idyllic. In the nineteenth century, nearly a quarter of all children experienced the death of one of their parents. . . . Not until the sixties did the chief cause of separation of parents shift from death to divorce.

RICHARD LOUV, (20th-century) U.S. journalist and author. *Childhood's Future,* pt. 1, ch. 3 (1991).

13 Family life in Western society since the time of the Old Testament has been a struggle to maintain patriarchy, male domination, and double standards in the face of a natural drift towards monogamous bonding. Young men have been called upon to prove their masculinity by their willingness to die in warfare, and young women have been called upon to prove their femininity by their willingness to die for their man. Women have been asked to appear small, dumb, and helpless so men would feel big and strong, brave, and clever. It's been a trick.

FRANK PITTMAN, (20th-century) U.S. psychiatrist and family therapist. *Man Enough,* ch. 6 (1993).

14 Once women invented farming, and began to keep and breed animals, they discovered the crucial function of the rooster and the henhouse. Fathers suddenly gained a function, and could do what only women had been able to do for all those millions of years—point at a child and say, "That is my son," "That is my daughter." Patriarchy quickly followed, beginning about five thousand years ago; a very short time in the development of our species, but covering all of recorded history.

FRANK PITTMAN, (20th-century) U.S. psychiatrist and family therapist. *Man Enough,* ch. 6 (1993).

15 Until the Second World War, it was unthinkable for a married woman of the working or middle class to disgrace her husband by working after marriage, because her employment indicated that he was a poor provider.

SANDRA SCARR, (20th-century) U.S. developmental psychologist and author. *Mother Care/Other Care,* ch. 2 (1984).

16 For my part, I have no hesitation in saying that although the American woman never leaves her domestic sphere and is in some respects very dependent within it, nowhere does she enjoy a higher station . . . if anyone asks me what I think the chief cause of the extraordinary prosperity and growing power of this nation, I should answer that it is due to the superiority of their woman.

ALEXIS DE TOCQUEVILLE, (19th-century) French social philosopher. As quoted in *Habits of the Heart,* by Robert Neelly Bellah, pt. 1, ch. 4 (1985).

Families and Society and the Needs for Social Supports

1 Families need families. Parents need to be parented. Grandparents, aunts, and uncles are back in fashion because they are necessary. Stresses on many families are out of proportion to anything two parents can handle.

T. BERRY BRAZELTON, (20th-century) U.S. pediatrician and author. *Touchpoints,* ch. 44 (1992).

2 We urgently need a debate about the best ways of supporting families in modern America, without blinders that prevent us from seeing the full extent of dependence and interdependence in American life. As long as we pretend that only poor or abnormal families need outside assistance, we will shortchange poor families, overcompensate rich ones, and fail to come up with effective policies for helping families in the middle.

STEPHANIE COONTZ, (20th-century) U.S. historian. *The Way We Were,* ch. 4 (1992).

3 The ideal of the self-sufficient American family is a myth, dangerous because most families, especially affluent families, do in fact make use of a range of services to survive. Families needing one or another kind of help are not morally deficient; most families do need assistance at one time or another.

JOSEPH FEATHERSTONE, (20th-century) U.S. social critic "Family Matters," *Harvard Educational Review* (February 1979).

4 There is growing consensus that new parents need help—information, advice, practical assistance—and that infants and toddlers need stimulation as well as care and nurture.

SHEILA KAMERMAN, (20th-century) U.S. professor of social policy and author. *Starting Right,* ch. 7 (1995).

5 Despite the long-term reduction in familial roles and functions, we believe that parents are still the world's greatest experts about the needs of their own children. Virtually any private or public program that supports parents effectively supports children. This principle of supporting family vitality seems to us preferable to any policy that would have the state provide children directly with what it thinks they need.

KENNETH KENISTON, (20th-century) U.S. professor of human development. *All Our Children,* ch. 4, The Carnegie Council on Children (1977).

6 The myth of self-sufficiency blinds us to the workings of other forces in family life. For families are not now, nor were they ever, the self-sufficient building blocks of society, exclusively responsible, praiseworthy, and blamable for their own destiny. They are deeply influenced by broad social and economic forces over which they have little control.

KENNETH KENISTON, (20th-century) U.S. professor of human development. *All Our Children,* ch. 1, The Carnegie Council on Children (1977).

7 The myth of the self-sufficient individual and of the self-sufficient, protected, and protective family . . . tells us that those who need help are ultimately inadequate. And it

tells us that for a family to need help—or at least to admit it publicly—is to confess failure. Similarly, to give help, however generously, is to acknowledge the inadequacy of the recipients and indirectly to condemn them, to stigmatize them, and even to weaken what impulse they have toward self-sufficiency.

KENNETH KENISTON, (20th-century) U.S. professor of human development. *All Our Children,* ch. 1, The Carnegie Council on Children (1977).

8 American families, however, without exception, experience a double message in our society, one that claims a commitment to families and stresses the importance of raising bright, stable, productive citizens, yet remains so bound by an ideal of "rugged individualism" that parents receive little support in their task from the public or private sectors.

BERNICE WEISSBOURD, (20th-century) U.S. family advocate and author. "Family Focus," *Children Today* (March/April 1981).

9 Parents need all the help they can get. The strongest as well as the most fragile family requires a vital network of social supports.

BERNICE WEISSBOURD, (20th-century) U.S. family advocate and author. Excerpts from the speech delivered to the Family Resource Coalition Conference (October 1988).

Special Concerns of Modern Families

1 While there are practical and sometimes moral reasons for the decomposition of the family, it coincides neither with what most people in society say they desire nor, especially in the case of children, with their best interests.

ROBERT NEELLY BELLAH, (20th-century) U.S. sociologist and author. *The Good Society,* ch. 1 (1991).

2 A "snapshot" feature in *USA Today* listed the five greatest concerns parents and teachers had about children in the '50s: talking out of turn, chewing gum in class, doing homework, stepping out of line, cleaning their rooms. Then it listed the five top concerns of parents today: drug addiction, teenage pregnancy, suicide and homicide, gang violence, anorexia and bulimia. We can also add AIDS, poverty, and homelessness.... Between my own childhood and the advent of my motherhood—one short generation—the culture had gone completely mad.

MARY KAY BLAKELY, (20th-century) U.S. journalist and author. *American Mom,* prologue (1994).

3 The U.S. is becoming an increasingly fatherless society. A generation ago, an American child could reasonably expect to grow up with his or her father. Today an American child can reasonably expect not to. Fatherlessness is now approaching a rough parity with fatherhood as a defining feature of American childhood.

DAVID BLANKENHORN, (20th-century) U.S. editor and author. *Fatherless America,* introduction (1995).

4 In today's world parents find themselves at the mercy of a society which imposes pressures and priorities that allow neither time nor place for meaningful activities and

relations between children and adults, which downgrade the role of parents and the functions of parenthood, and which prevent the parent from doing things he wants to do as a guide, friend, and companion to his children.

URIE BRONFENBRENNER, (20th-century) U.S. psychologist and author. *Two Worlds of Childhood: U.S. and U.S.S.R.,* preface (1973).

5 Today's fathers and mothers—with only the American dream for guidance—extend and overextend themselves, physically, emotionally, and financially, during the best years of their lives to ensure that their children will grow up prepared to do better and go further than they did.

STELLA CHESS, (20th-century) U.S. psychiatrist and author. *Daughters,* ch. 7 (1978).

6 Families have always been in flux and often in crisis; they have never lived up to nostalgic notions about "the way things used to be." But that doesn't mean the malaise and anxiety people feel about modern families are delusions, that everything would be fine if we would only realize that the past was not all it's cracked up to be. . . . Even if things were not always right in families of the past, it seems clear that some things have newly gone wrong.

STEPHANIE COONTZ, (20th-century) U.S. historian. *The Way We Were,* introduction (1992).

7 Even healthy families need outside sources of moral guidance to keep those tensions from imploding—and this means, among other things, a public philosophy of gender equality and concern for child welfare. When instead the larger culture aggrandizes wife beaters, degrades women or nods approvingly at child slappers, the family gets a little more dangerous for everyone, and so, inevitably, does the larger world.

BARBARA EHRENREICH, (20th-century) U.S. essayist and author. *The Snarling Citizen,* "Oh, Those Family Values," (1995).

8 Simply because our times are complex, does it follow that our parenting must also be? Must we reject the common sense that worked so well in the past just because our times are high-tech? We live in such fear of being called "old-fashioned" that we are cutting ourselves off from that which is proven.

FRED G. GOSMAN, (20th-century) U.S. author. *How to Be a Happy Parent . . . in Spite of Your Children,* introduction (1995).

9 We have become unsure of the rules and unsure of our roles. Parenting, like brain surgery, is now all-consuming, fraught with anxiety, worry, and self-doubt. We have allowed what used to be simple and natural to become bewildering and intimidating.

FRED G. GOSMAN, (20th-century) U.S. author. *How to Be a Happy Parent . . . in Spite of Your Children,* introduction (1995).

10 It is misleading to discuss recent changes in family life without emphasizing the fact that for generations some Americans have had to raise children under particularly appalling pressures. Although much of what is worrying American parents is shared by them all, the most grievous problems are those that especially afflict a large minority—the poor, the nonwhite

and, in various ways, the parents of handicapped children.

KENNETH KENISTON, (20th-century) U.S. professor of human development. *All Our Children,* ch. 2, The Carnegie Council on Children (1977).

11 There is nothing to be gained by blaming ourselves and other individuals for family changes. We need to look instead to the broader economic and social forces that shape the experience of children and parents. Parents are not abdicating—they are being dethroned, by forces they cannot influence, much less control. Behind today's uncertainty among parents lies a trend of several centuries toward the transformation and redefinition of family life. We see no possibility—or desirability—of reversing this trend and turning the clock back to the "good old days," for the price then was high in terms of poverty and drudgery, of no education in today's sense at all, and of community interference in what we today consider private life.

KENNETH KENISTON, (20th-century) U.S. professor of human development. *All Our Children,* ch. 1, The Carnegie Council on Children (1977).

12 Today's parents have little authority over those others with whom they share the task of raising their children. On the contrary, most parents deal with those others from a position of inferiority or helplessness. Teachers, doctors, social workers, or television producers possess more status than most parents. . . . As a result, the parent today is . . . a maestro trying to conduct an orchestra of players who have never met and who play from a multitude of different scores, each in a notation the conductor cannot read.

KENNETH KENISTON, (20th-century) U.S. professor of human development. *All Our Children,* ch. 1, The Carnegie Council on Children (1977).

13 The family environment in which your children are growing up is different from that in which you grew up. The decisions our parents made and the strategies they used were developed in a different context from what we face today, even if the "content" of the problem is the same. It is a mistake to think that our own experience as children and adolescents will give us all we need to help our children. The rules of the game have changed.

LAWRENCE KUTNER, (20th-century) U.S. child psychologist and author. *Parent and Child,* ch. 1 (1991).

14 I do not mean to imply that the good old days were perfect. But the institutions and structure—the web—of society needed reform, not demolition. To have cut the institutional and community strands without replacing them with new ones proved to be a form of abuse to one generation and to the next. For so many Americans, the tragedy was not in dreaming that life could be better; the tragedy was that the dreaming ended.

RICHARD LOUV, (20th-century) U.S. journalist and author. *Childhood's Future,* pt. 1, ch. 3 (1991).

15 The rebellion is against time pollution, the feeling that the essence of what makes life worth living—the

small moments, the special family getaways, the cookies in the oven, the weekend drives, the long dreamlike summers —so much of this has been taken from us, or we have given it up. For what? Hitachi stereos? Club Med? Company cars? Racquetball? For fifteen-hour days and lousy day care?

RICHARD LOUV, (20th-century) U.S. journalist and author. *Childhood's Future,* pt. 1, ch. 1 (1991).

16 We do not raise our children alone. . . . Our children are also raised by every peer, institution, and family with which they come in contact. Yet parents today expect to be blamed for whatever results occur with their children, and they expect to do their parenting alone.

RICHARD LOUV, (20th-century) U.S. journalist and author. *Childhood's Future,* pt. 1, ch. 3 (1991).

17 Through a series of gradual power losses, the modern parent is in danger of losing sight of her own child, as well as her own vision and style. It's a very big price to pay emotionally. Too bad it's often accompanied by an equally huge price financially.

SONIA TAITZ, (20th-century) U.S. journalist and author. *Mothering Heights,* introduction (1992).

18 The community and family networks which helped sustain earlier generations have become scarcer for growing numbers of young parents. Those who lack links to these traditional sources of support are hard-pressed to find other resources, given the emphasis in our society on providing treatment services, rather than preventive services and support for health maintenance and well-being.

BERNICE WEISSBOURD, (20th-century) U.S. family advocate and author. *Children Today* (March/April 1981).

Hopes for the Future

1 I long for a land that does not yet exist, a place where women are valued both for their intellects and their motherhood and where choices between career and nurturing are somehow less stark.

GABRIELLE GLASER, (20th-century) U.S. journalist. "Where Mothers Matter," *The New York Times Magazine* (February 20, 1994).

2 It will be a great day when our schools get all the money they need and the Air Force has to hold a bake sale to buy a bomber.

ADVERTISING POSTER, New York City School (1983).

3 I believe that if we are to survive as a planet, we must teach this next generation to handle their own conflicts assertively and nonviolently. If in their early years our children learn to listen to all sides of the story, use their heads and then their mouths, and come up with a plan and share, then, when they become our leaders, and some of them will, they will have the tools to handle global problems and conflict.

BARBARA COLOROSO, (20th-century) U.S. parent educator and author. *Kids Are Worth It,* ch. 8 (1994).

4 We need to encourage members of this next generation to become all that they can become, not try to force them to become what we

want them to become. . . . You and I can't even begin to dream the dreams this next generation is going to dream, or answer the questions that will be put to them.

BARBARA COLOROSO, (20th-century) U.S. parent educator and author. *Kids Are Worth It,* epilogue (1994).

5 What a wise and good parent will desire for his own children a nation must desire for all children.

CONSULTATIVE COMMITTEE ON THE PRIMARY SCHOOLS, *Report of the Consultative Committee on the Primary School* (Hadow), H.M.S.O. (1931).

6 The modern world needs people with a complex identity who are intellectually autonomous and prepared to cope with uncertainty; who are able to tolerate ambiguity and not be driven by fear into a rigid, single-solution approach to problems, who are rational, foresightful and who look for facts; who can draw inferences and can control their behavior in the light of foreseen consequences, who are altruistic and enjoy doing for others, and who understand social forces and trends.

ROBERT HAVIGHURST, (20th-century) U.S. psychologist. As quoted in *The Learning Child,* "Beyond the Home to School and Community," Dorothy H. Cohen (1972).

7 Just as we are learning to value and conserve the air we breathe, the water we drink, the energy we use, we must learn to value and conserve our capacity for nurture. Otherwise, in the name of human potential we will slowly but surely erode the source of our humanity.

ELAINE HEFFNER, (20th-century) U.S. psychiatrist and author. *Mothering,* ch. 1 (1978).

8 Hold fast to dreams
For if dreams die
Life is a broken-winged bird
That cannot fly.

LANGSTON HUGHES, (20th-century). U.S. poet and author. "Dreams," *Golden Slippers,* ed. Arna Bontemps (1941).

9 The family that prays together stays together.

AL SCALPONE, (20th-century). Slogan devised for the Roman Catholic Family Rosary Crusade (1947).

10 We reiterate the values [of the family support movement]. We believe that we cannot exist each unto ourselves, that commitment and a sense of obligation to the welfare of others, to the community, and to the nation are ingredients of being human. We believe that our obligation as members of the community and nation include caring about the next generation. If we care about our own children, we need to care about all children because all will be citizens of this country. We believe that parents want to be good parents. When a child is born, each new mother and father begin their most important life's work, and it is our job to ensure those parents have the concrete and emotional support to be the best parents they can be.

BERNICE WEISSBOURD, (20th-century) U.S. family advocate and author. Excerpts from the speech delivered to the Family Resource Coalition Conference (October 1988).

11 The future which we hold in trust for our own children will be shaped by our fairness to other people's children.

MARIAN WRIGHT EDELMAN, (20th-century) U.S. child advocate and author. As quoted in "Our Future Depends on How We

Treat America's Children," Richard B. Stolley, *Money* (May 1995).

Media

1 I wouldn't be above brainwashing your child about which shows you think are good and which you think are just awful. Nor would I hesitate to enlighten a child about products that are advertised on TV. If you watch a commercial with your child, say to him, "Remember when we saw that toy at the store and it was just a piece of junk? You can't always tell when you see it on TV, because there are ways of filming it at different angles to make it look bigger and more powerful. Keep that in mind when you think you want all those toys they advertise."

LAWRENCE BALTER, (20th-century) U.S. psychologist and author. *Who's In Control?* Ch. 5 (1989).

2 We cannot spare our children the influence of harmful values by turning off the television any more than we can keep them home forever or revamp the world before they get there. Merely keeping them in the dark is no protection and, in fact, can make them vulnerable and immature.

POLLY BERRIEN BERENDS, (20th-century) U.S. author. *Whole Child/Whole Parent,* ch. 7 (rev. 1987).

3 With all of its bad influences, T.V. is not to be feared.... It can be a fairly safe laboratory for confronting, seeing through, and thus being immunized against unhealthy values so as to be "in the world but not of it."

POLLY BERRIEN BERENDS, (20th-century) U.S. author. *Whole Child/Whole Parent,* ch. 7 (rev. 1987).

4 Television programming for children need not be saccharine or insipid in order to give to violence its proper balance in the scheme of things.... But as an endless diet for the sake of excitement and sensation in stories whose plots are vehicles for killing and torture and little more, it is not healthy for young children. Unfamiliar as yet with the full story of human response, they are being misled when they are offered perversion before they have fully learned what is sound.

DOROTHY H. COHEN, (20th-century) U.S. educator and child development specialist. *The Learning Child,* "Beyond the Home to School and Community," (1972).

5 At times it seems that the media have become the mainstream culture in children's lives. Parents have become the alternative. Americans once expected parents to raise their children in accordance with the dominant cultural messages. Today they are expected to raise their children in opposition to it.

ELLEN GOODMAN, (20th-century) U.S. journalist. *Value Judgments* (1993).

6 Television thus illustrates the mixed blessings of technological change in American society. It is a new medium, promising extraordinary benefits: great educational potential, a broadening of experience, enrichment of daily life, entertainment for all. But it teaches children the uses of violence, offers material consumption as the answer to life's problems, sells

harmful products, habituates viewers to constant stimulation, and undermines family interaction and other forms of learning such as play and reading.

KENNETH KENISTON, (20th-century) U.S. professor of human development. *All Our Children,* ch. 3, The Carnegie Council on Children (1977).

7 Isn't it odd that networks accept billions of dollars from advertisers to *teach* people to use products and then proclaim that children aren't *learning* about violence from their steady diet of it on television!

TONI LIEBMAN, (20th-century) U.S. early childhood educator. "A Call to Action," *NYSAEYC Reporter* (Fall 1993).

8 Not too many years ago, a child's experience was limited by how far he or she could ride a bicycle or by the physical boundaries that parents set. Today . . . the real boundaries of a child's life are set more by the number of available cable channels and videotapes, by the simulated reality of videogames, by the number of megabytes of memory in the home computer. Now kids can go anywhere, as long as they stay inside the electronic bubble.

RICHARD LOUV, (20th-century) U.S. journalist and author. *Childhood's Future,* pt. 8, ch. 4 (1991).

9 Never before has a generation of parents faced such awesome competition with the mass media for their children's attention. While parents tout the virtues of premarital virginity, drug-free living, nonviolent resolution of social conflict, or character over physical appearance, their values are daily challenged by television soaps, rock music lyrics, tabloid headlines, and movie scenes extolling the importance of physical appearance and conformity.

MARIANNE E. NEIFERT, (20th-century) U.S. pediatrician and author. *Dr. Mom's Parenting Guide,* ch. 1 (1991).

10 Some television programs are made very attractive to young children by presenting short, rapidly moving sequences and ever-changing episodes. . . . Some experts now argue that slower-paced television fare that allows children time to think about the material is more valuable than the faster-paced programs that merely capture their attention.

SANDRA SCARR, (20th-century) U.S. developmental psychologist and author. *Mother Care/Other Care,* pt. 3, ch. 6 (1984).

11 Parents everywhere, trying to bring up kids in a plugged-in, supercharged, high-tech world, need all the information and support we can give each other.

RON TAFFEL, (20th-century) U.S. psychologist and author. *Parenting by Heart,* preface (1991).

12 The children [on TV] are too well behaved and are reasonable beyond their years. All the children pop in with exceptional insights. On many of the shows the children's insights are apt to be unexpectedly philosophical. The lesson seems to be, "Listen to little children carefully and you will learn great truths."

G. WEINBERG, (20th-century) as quoted in *The Hurried Child,* ch. 4, David Elkind (1988).

13 It is among the ranks of school-age children, those six- to twelve-year-

olds who once avidly filled their free moments with childhood play, that the greatest change is evident. In the place of traditional, sometimes ancient childhood games that were still popular a generation ago, in the place of fantasy and make-believe play . . . today's children have substituted television viewing and, most recently, video games.

MARIE WINN, (20th-century) U.S. author. *Children Without Childhood,* ch. 4 (1981).

Mental Health

1 Mental health data from the 1950's on middle-aged women showed them to be a particularly distressed group, vulnerable to depression and feelings of uselessness. This isn't surprising. If society tells you that your main role is to be attractive to men and you are getting crow's feet, and to be a mother to children and yours are leaving home, no wonder you are distressed.

GRACE BARUCH, U.S. developmental psychologist, ROSALIND BARNETT, U.S. psychologist, and CARYL RIVERS, U.S. journalist (20th-century). *Life Prints,* ch. 12 (1983).

2 Psychiatric enlightenment has begun to debunk the superstition that to manage a machine you must become a machine, and that to raise masters of the machine you must mechanize the impulses of childhood.

ERIK H. ERIKSON, (20th-century) German-born U.S. psychoanalyst and author. *Childhood and Society,* ch. 8 (1950).

3 Mental health depends upon the maintenance of a balance within the personality between the basic human urges and egocentric wishes on the one hand and the demands of conscience and society on the other hand.

SELMA H. FRAIBERG, (20th-century) U.S. child psychoanalyst and author. *The Magic Years,* ch. 1 (1959).

4 In our great concern about the mental health of children, however, we have overlooked the mental health of mothers. They have been led to believe that their children's needs must not be frustrated, and therefore all of their own normal angers, the normal ambivalences of living, are not permissible. The mother who has "bad" feelings toward her child is a bad mother.

ELAINE HEFFNER, (20th-century) U.S. psychiatrist and author. *Mothering,* ch. 2 (1978).

5 The fact that the mental health establishment has equated separation with health, equated women's morality with soft-heartedness, and placed mothers on the psychological hot seat has taken a toll on modern mothers.

RON TAFFEL, (20th-century) U.S. psychologist and author. *Parenting by Heart,* ch. 1 (1991).

Power and Politics

1 When any relationship is characterized by difference, particularly a disparity in power, there remains a tendency to model it on the parent-child-relationship. Even protectiveness and benevolence toward the poor, toward minorities, and especially toward women

have involved equating them with children.

Mary Catherine Bateson, (20th-century) U.S. author. *Composing a Life,* ch. 6 (1989).

2 We have imagined ourselves a special creation, set apart from other humans. In the last twentieth century, we see that our poverty is as absolute as that of the poorest nations. We have attempted to deny the human condition in our quest for power after power. It would be well for us to rejoin the human race, to accept our essential poverty as a gift, and to share our material wealth with those in need.

Robert Neelly Bellah, (20th-century) U.S. sociologist and author. *Habits of the Heart,* conclusion (1985).

3 People whose integrity has not been damaged in childhood, who were protected, respected, and treated with honesty by their parents, will be—both in their youth and in adulthood—intelligent, responsive, empathic, and highly sensitive. They will take pleasure in life and will not feel any need to kill or even hurt others or themselves. They will use their power to defend themselves, not to attack others. They will not be able to do otherwise than respect and protect those weaker than themselves, including their children, because this is what they have learned from their own experience.

Alice Miller, (20th-century) German-born psychoanalyst and author. *For Your Own Good,* afterword to second edition (1984).

4 The father receives his power from God (and from his own father). The teacher finds the soil already prepared for obedience, and the political leader has only to harvest what has been sown.

Alice Miller, (20th-century) German-born psychoanalyst and author. *For Your Own Good,* "Poisonous Pedagogy" (trans. 1983).

5 We all participate in weaving the social fabric; we should therefore all participate in patching the fabric when it develops holes—mismatches between old expectations and current realities.

Anne C. Weisberg, (20th-century) U.S. attorney. *Everything a Working Mother Needs to Know,* ch. 3 (1994).

Social Problems

1 We can teach prevention. For little kids, the best protection is that they should not be alone in public places. All children should be conscious of strangers, and be discriminating and wary of them. This won't make them grow up suspicious as long as they have adults around whom they know and can trust: relatives, friends of their parents, parents of friends.

David Elkind, (20th-century) U.S. child psychologist and author. As quoted in "How Parents Can Talk to Their Kids," Jean Sehgman, *Newsweek* (January 10, 1994).

2 Pessimists say that the family is eroding. Optimists say the family is diversifying. Both points of view are right. Families are more diverse and they are more in trouble—but not because of their diversity. The families of today—whatever their size or shape—are in crisis because our economy is failing, our national resources are shrinking, and our

governmental policies to support them are inadequate.

CONSTANCE R. AHRONS, (20th-century) U.S. sociologist and family therapist. *The Good Divorce*, ch. 2 (1994).

3 The young love and cherish people and places from which they receive the skills and the emotional support which enable them to make it in the world or to meet their basic human needs. The same people and places are often the first recipients of the frustration and anger—violence, vandalism, disrespect—of young people who are not making it well in the world. I suspect that this is the reason that personal and school property violence is increasing more rapidly than school burglary and dropout rates.

JAMES P. COMER, (20th-century) U.S. psychiatrist and author. *School Power*, ch. 1 (1980).

4 The mother's battle for her child—with sickness, with poverty, with war, with all the forces of exploitation and callousness that cheapen human life—needs to become a common human battle, waged in love and in the passion for survival.

ADRIENNE RICH, (20th-century) U.S. poet and author. *Of Women Born: Motherhood as Experience and Institution* (1976).

5 Social and demographic changes have combined to diminish the likelihood that families can assure their children's healthy growth and development without help from outside the family—at the very time that there is a growing skepticism about the desirability and workability of societal action to provide the supports that families require.

LISBETH B. SCHORR, (20th-century) U.S. economist. *In Support of Families*, ed. Michael W. Yogman and T. Berry Brazelton, ch. 14 (1986).

6 Being dismantled before our eyes are not just individual programs that politicians cite as too expensive but the whole idea that society has a stake in the well-being of children down the block and the security of families on the other side of town. Whether or not kids eat well, are nurtured and have a roof over their heads is not just a consequence of how their parents behave. It is also a responsibility of society—but now apparently a diminishing one.

RICHARD B. STOLLEY, (20th-century) U.S. editor and child advocate. "Our Future Depends on How We Treat America's Children," *Money* (May 1995).

7 Do we honestly believe that hopeless kids growing up under the harsh new rules will turn out to be chaste, studious, responsible adults? On the contrary, by limiting welfare, job training, education and nutritious food, won't we plant the seeds for another bumper crop of out-of-wedlock moms, deadbeat dads and worse?

RICHARD B. STOLLEY, (20th-century) U.S. editor and child advocate. "Our Future Depends on How We Treat America's Children," *Money* (May 1995).

Social Problems: Poverty

1 Sustained unemployment not only denies parents the opportunity to meet the food, clothing, and shelter needs of their children but also denies them the sense of adequacy, belonging, and worth which being able to do so provides. This

increases the likelihood of family problems and decreases the chances of many children to be adequately prepared for school.

JAMES P. COMER, (20th-century) U.S. psychiatrist and author. *School Power,* ch. 1 (1980).

2 Like many another romances, the romance of the family turns sour when the money runs out. If we really cared about families, we would not let "born again" patriarchs send up moral abstractions as a smokescreen for the scandal of American family economics.

LETTY COTTIN POGREBIN, (20th-century) U.S. editor and author. *Family and Politics,* ch. 3 (1983).

3 The ultra-right would have us believe that families are in trouble because of humanism, feminism, secular education, or sexual liberation, but the consensus of Americans is that what tears families apart is unemployment, inflation, and financial worries.

LETTY COTTIN POGREBIN, (20th-century) U.S. editor and author. *Family and Politics,* ch. 4 (1983).

4 What exacerbates the strain in the working class is the absence of money to pay for services they need, economic insecurity, poor day care, and lack of dignity and boredom in each partner's job. What exacerbates it in upper-middle class is the instability of paid help and the enormous demands of the career system in which both partners become willing believers. But the tug between traditional and egalitarian models of marriage runs from top to bottom of the class ladder.

ARLIE HOCHSCHILD, (20th-century) U.S. sociologist and author. *The Second Shift,* ch. 13 (1989).

5 Children cannot start right in life without some protection against the risk of being born into poverty or into families with grossly inadequate incomes.

SHEILA KAMERMAN, (20th-century) U.S. professor of social policy and author. *Starting Right,* ch. 3 (1995).

6 Parents who are stressed or disturbed will have more difficulty in meeting their children's needs. Parents who have little support—from friends, relatives, neighbors, or the community—are more likely to be overburdened by the demands of their babies and to be unable to respond to them adequately. Parents who experience severe poverty or economic insecurity, who cannot satisfy their own basic needs, are likely to have difficulty in responding to their children's needs.

SHEILA KAMERMAN, (20th-century) U.S. professor of social policy and author. *Starting Right,* ch. 1 (1995).

7 Poor children live in a particularly dangerous world—an urban world of broken stair railings, of busy streets serving as playgrounds, of lead paint, rats and rat poisons, or a rural world where families do not enjoy the minimal levels of public health accepted as standard for nearly a century. Whether in city or country, this is a world where cavities go unfilled and ear infections threatening permanent deafness go untreated. It is world where even a small child learns to be ashamed of the way he or she lives.

KENNETH KENISTON, (20th-century) U.S. professor of human development. *All Our Children,* ch. 2, The Carnegie Council on Children (1977).

8 The psychological pain—and the ethical shame—of American poverty are made greater by the fact that this country possesses the wealth and the energy to raise all children to a minimally decent standard of living.

KENNETH KENISTON, (20th-century) U.S. professor of human development. *All Our Children,* ch. 2, The Carnegie Council on Children (1977).

Social Problems: Racism

1 I cannot be soft because it will make her soft, I thought, and soft black children cannot survive in this world. I do not know if this is true, but it was (and is) for me an undying truism.

GERALD EARLY, (20th-century) U.S. author. *Daughters,* pt. 1 (1994).

2 It was common practice for me to take my children with me whenever I went shopping, out for a walk in a white neighborhood, or just felt like going about in a white world. The reason was simple enough: if a black man is alone or with other black men, he is a threat to whites. But if he is with children, then he is harmless, adorable.

GERALD EARLY, (20th-century) U.S. author. *Daughters,* pt. 2 (1994).

3 Confronted with the unhappy facts of exclusion, we sometimes reassure ourselves by telling stories: the poor boys who made it, the blacks who became a "credit to their race," the women elected to high office, the handicapped who made "useful contributions" to our society.... Just as we believe in the self-sufficient family, we also believe that any child with enough grit and ability can escape poverty and make a rewarding life. But these stories and beliefs clearly reflect the exceptions.

KENNETH KENISTON, (20th-century) U.S. professor of human development. *All Our Children,* ch. 2, The Carnegie Council on Children (1977).

Social Problems: Sexism

1 Some of the things ... sound like things our grandmothers would have told us: "Men will be boys. We let them play their little games with each other. We know it isn't about the important things, but they think so. So we let them. We take care of them so that they can go on playing." What grandma did not tell us is that men are capable of something altogether different.... But even though men are untapped wells of potential, they will not move forward if women continue to subsidize the status quo.

JEAN BAKER MILLER, (20th-century) U.S. psychiatrist. *Toward a New Psychology of Women,* ch. 7 (1976).

2 The man, or the boy, in his development is psychologically deterred from incorporating serving characteristics by an easily observable fact: there are already people around who are clearly meant to serve and they are girls and women. To perform the activities these people are doing is to risk being, and being thought of, and thinking of oneself, as a woman. This has been made a

terrifying prospect and has been made to constitute a major threat to masculine identity.

Jean Baker Miller, (20th-century) U.S. psychiatrist. *Toward a New Psychology of Women,* ch. 6 (1976).

3 Women have acquired equal place to man in society, but the double standard has really never been relinquished; certainly not by men. Modern man's fear of passivity or of the active woman proves to be as eternal as modern woman's struggle to come to terms with her femininity.

Peter Blos, (20th-century) U.S. psychoanalyst. *On Adolescence,* ch. 6 (1962).

4 I find it profoundly symbolic that I am appearing before a committee of fifteen men who will report to a legislative body of one hundred men because of a decision handed down by a court comprised of nine men—on an issue that affects millions of women. . . . I have the feeling that if men could get pregnant, we wouldn't be struggling for this legislation. If men could get pregnant, maternity benefits would be as sacrosanct as the G.I. Bill.

Letty Cottin Pogrebin, (20th-century) U.S. editor and author. *Family and Politics,* ch. 6 (1983). Excerpted from a speech before the U.S. Senate subcommittee on labor in 1977.

5 American feminists have generally stressed the ways in which men and women should be equal and have therefore tried to put aside differences. . . . Social feminists [in Europe] . . . believe that men and society at large should provide systematic support to women in recognition of their dual role as mothers and workers.

Sylvia Ann Hewlett, (20th-century) U.S. economist. *A Lesser Life,* ch. 6 (1986).

6 As long as the "woman's work" that some men do is socially devalued, as long as it is defined as woman's work, as long as it's tacked onto a "regular" work day, men who share it are likely to develop the same jagged mouth and frazzled hair as the coffee-mug mom. The image of the new man is like the image of the supermom: it obscures the strain.

Arlie Hochschild, (20th-century) U.S. sociologist and author. *The Second Shift,* ch. 3 (1989).

7 As motherhood as a "private enterprise" declines and more mothers rely on the work of lower-paid specialists, the value accorded the work of mothering (not the value of children) has declined for women, making it all the harder for men to take it up.

Arlie Hochschild, (20th-century) U.S. sociologist and author. *The Second Shift,* ch. 15 (1989).

8 The "female culture" has shifted more rapidly than the "male culture"; the image of the go-get 'em woman has yet to be fully matched by the image of the let's take-care-of-the-kids-together man. More important, over the last thirty years, men's underlying feelings about taking responsibility at home have changed much less than women's feelings have changed about forging some kind of identity at work.

Arlie Hochschild, (20th-century) U.S. sociologist and author. *The Second Shift,* ch. 14 (1989).

9 Views of women, on one side, as inwardly directed toward home and family and notions of men, on the other, as outwardly striving toward fame and fortune have resounded throughout literature and in the texts of history, biology, and psychology until they seem uncontestable. Such dichotomous views defy the complexities of individuals and stifle the potential for people to reveal different dimensions of themselves in various settings.

SARA LAWRENCE LIGHTFOOT, (20th-century) U.S. educator and author. *Worlds Apart,* ch. 2 (1978).

10 As boys without bonds to their fathers grow older and more desperate about their masculinity, they are in danger of forming gangs in which they strut their masculinity for one another, often overdo it, and sometimes turn to displays of fierce, macho bravado and even violence.

FRANK PITTMAN, (20th-century) U.S. psychiatrist and family therapist. *Man Enough,* ch. 5 (1993).

11 In the U.S. for instance, the value of a homemaker's productive work has been imputed mostly when she was maimed or killed and insurance companies and/or the courts had to calculate the amount to pay her family in damages. Even at that, the rates were mostly pink collar and the big number was attributed to the husband's pain and suffering.

GLORIA STEINEM, (20th-century) U.S. feminist and author. *Moving Beyond Words,* pt. 5 (1994).

12 Anthropologists have found that around the world whatever is considered "men's work" is almost universally given higher status than "women's work." If in one culture it is men who build houses and women who make baskets, then that culture will see housebuilding as more important. In another culture, perhaps right next door, the reverse may be true, and basket-weaving will have higher social status than housebuilding.

MARY STEWART VAN LEEUWEN, "A View from Other Cultures: Must Men Fear 'Women's Work?' " As quoted in *The Utne Reader* (April 1990).

Social Problems: Violence and Abuse

1 Children are extraordinarily precious members of society; they are exquisitely alert, sensitive, and conscious of their surroundings; and they are extraordinarily vulnerable to maltreatment or emotional abuse by adults who refuse to give them the profound respect and affection to which they are unconditionally entitled.

BARBARA COLOROSO, (20th-century) U.S. parent educator and author. As quoted in *Kids Are Worth It,* ch. 1 (1994).

2 Spare the rod and spoil the child.

BIBLE: HEBREW.

3 The unjustifiable severity of a parent is loaded with this aggravation, that those whom he injures are always in his sight.

JOSEPH ADDISON, (1672–1719) English essayist. *Interesting Anecdotes, Memoirs, Allegories, Essays, and Poetical Fragments,* "The Cruelty of Parental Tyranny" (1794).

4 Certainly, words can be as abusive as any blow. . . . When a three-year-old yells, "You're so stupid! What a dummy!" it doesn't carry the same weight as when a mother yells those words to a child. . . . Even if you don't physically abuse young children, you can still drive them nuts with your words.

MARY KAY BLAKELY, (20th-century) U.S. journalist and author. *American Mom,* ch. 4 (1994).

5 If family violence teaches children that might makes right at home, how will we hope to cure the futile impulse to solve worldly conflicts with force?

LETTY COTTIN POGREBIN, (20th-century) U.S. editor and author. *Family and Politics,* ch. 1 (1983).

6 Much is made of the accelerating brutality of young people's crimes, but rarely does our concern for dangerous children translate into concern for children in danger. We fail to make the connection between the use of force on children themselves, and violent antisocial behavior, or the connection between watching father batter mother and the child deducing a link between violence and masculinity.

LETTY COTTIN POGREBIN, (20th-century) U.S. editor and author. *Family and Politics,* ch. 5 (1983).

7 When a family is free of abuse and oppression, it can be the place where we share our deepest secrets and stand the most exposed, a place where we learn to feel distinct without being "better," and sacrifice for others without losing ourselves.

LETTY COTTIN POGREBIN, (20th-century) U.S. editor and author. *Family and Politics,* ch. 2 (1983).

8 We now recognize that abuse and neglect may be as frequent in nuclear families as love, protection, and commitment are in non-nuclear families.

DAVID ELKIND, (20th-century) U.S. child psychologist and author. *Ties That Stress,* ch. 2 (1994).

9 While violent families often suffer from the stresses of poverty, family violence occurs at all levels of the social class structure. Researchers have repeatedly found violent families, whether rich or poor, to be characterized by high levels of social isolation, rigid sex-role stereotyping, poor communication, and extreme inequalities in the distribution of power among family members. These characteristics are consistently noted, whether the studies are wife battering, child abuse, or abuse of the elderly.

MARY FIELD BELENKY, (20th-century) U.S. psychologist. *Women's Ways of Knowing,* pt. 2, ch. 8 (1986).

10 Can we not teach children, even as we protect them from victimization, that for them to become victimizers constitutes the greatest peril of all, specifically the sacrifice—physical or psychological—of the well-being of other people? And that destroying the life or safety of other people, through teasing, bullying, hitting or otherwise, "putting them down," is as destructive to themselves as to their victims.

LEWIS P. LIPSITT, (20th-century) U.S. professor of psychology and medical science. "Us and Them," *Child and Adolescent Behavior Letter,* Brown University (May 1995).

11 The hearts of small children are delicate organs. A cruel beginning in this world can twist them into

curious shapes. The heart of a hurt child can shrink so that forever afterward it is hard and pitted as the seed of a peach. Or, again, the heart of such a child may fester and swell until it is misery to carry within the body, easily chafed and hurt by the most ordinary things.

CARSON MCCULLERS, (20th-century) U.S. author and playwright. As quoted in *The Last Word,* ed. Carolyn Warner, ch. 26 (1992).

12 Punishment followed on a grand scale. For ten days, an unconscionable length of time, my father blessed the palms of his child's outstretched, four-year-old hands with a sharp switch. Seven strokes a day on each hand; that makes one hundred forty strokes and then some. This put an end to the child's innocence.

CHRISTOPH MECKEL, (20th-century) German author. As quoted in *For Your Own Good,* Alice Miller, "Poisonous Pedagogy" (trans. 1983).

13 Almost everywhere we find . . . the use of various coercive measures, to rid ourselves as quickly as possible of the child within us—i.e., the weak, helpless, dependent creature—in order to become an independent competent adult deserving of respect. When we reencounter this creature in our children, we persecute it with the same measures once used in ourselves.

ALICE MILLER, (20th-century) German-born psychoanalyst and author. *For Your Own Good,* "Poisonous Pedagogy" (trans. 1983).

14 For some years now, there has been proof that the devastating effects of the traumatization of children take their inevitable toll on society—a fact that we are still forbidden to recognize. This knowledge concerns every single one of us, and—if disseminated widely enough—should lead to fundamental changes in society; above all, to a halt in the blind escalation of violence.

ALICE MILLER, (20th-century) German-born psychoanalyst and author. *For Your Own Good,* afterword to second edition (1984).

15 It is unlikely that someone could proclaim "truths" that are counter to physical laws for very long (for example, that it is healthy for children to run around in bathing suits in winter and in fur coats in summer) without appearing ridiculous. But it is perfectly normal to speak of the necessity of striking and humiliating children and robbing them of their autonomy, at the same time using such high-sounding words as chastising, upbringing, and guiding onto the right path.

ALICE MILLER, (20th-century) German-born psychoanalyst and author. *For Your Own Good,* "Poisonous Pedagogy" (trans. 1983).

16 It is very difficult for people to believe the simple fact that every persecutor was once a victim. Yet it should be very obvious that someone who was allowed to feel free and strong from childhood does not have the need to humiliate another person.

ALICE MILLER, (20th-century) German-born psychoanalyst and author. *For Your Own Good,* "Unintentional Cruelty Hurts, Too" (trans. 1983).

17 Sadism is not an infectious disease that strikes a person all of a sudden. It has a long prehistory in childhood and always originates in the desperate fantasies of a child who is

searching for a way out of a hopeless situation.

ALICE MILLER, (20th-century) German-born psychoanalyst and author. *For Your Own Good,* "Unlived Anger," (trans. 1983).

18 Those children who are beaten will in turn give beatings, those who are intimidated will be intimidating, those who are humiliated will impose humiliation, and those whose souls are murdered will murder.

ALICE MILLER, (20th-century) German-born psychoanalyst and author. *For Your Own Good* (trans. 1983).

19 Till now, society has protected the adult and blamed the victim. It has been abetted in its blindness by theories, still in keeping with the pedagogical principles of our great-grandparents, according to which children are viewed as crafty creatures, dominated by wicked drives, who invent stories and attack their innocent parents or desire them sexually. In reality, children tend to blame themselves for their parents' cruelty and to absolve the parents, whom they invariably love, of all responsibility.

ALICE MILLER, (20th-century) German-born psychoanalyst and author. *For Your Own Good,* afterword to second edition (1984).

20 We are still barely conscious of how harmful it is to treat children in a degrading manner. Treating them with respect and recognizing the consequences of their being humiliated are by no means intellectual matters; otherwise, their importance would long since have been generally recognized.

ALICE MILLER, (20th-century) German-born psychoanalyst and author. *For Your Own Good,* "The War of Annilihation against the Self," (trans. 1983).

21 Men who have been raised violently have every reason to believe it is appropriate for them to control others through violence; they feel no compunction over being violent to women, children, and one another.

FRANK PITTMAN, (20th-century) U.S. psychiatrist and family therapist. *Man Enough,* ch. 4 (1993).

22 Whether the child is the father's or someone else's, if a man is involved in the physical care of his child before the age of three, there is a dramatic reduction in the probability that that man will be involved later in life in sexual abuse of children in general as well as his own.

KYLE D. PRUETT, (20th-century) U.S. child psychiatrist and author. *The Nurturing Father,* ch. 2 (1987).

23 When it comes to evil, there are no gray areas. Fathers who abuse their children by battering or starving or raping them automatically relinquish any entitlement to mitigation or sympathy. They commit the unpardonable moral offense of betraying their children. It matters not what their own histories were; millions of people with childhood horror stories to tell do not repeat them with their own children.

VICTORIA SECUNDA, (20th-century) U.S. psychologist and author. *Women and Their Fathers,* ch. 4 (1992).

24 Research has convincingly demonstrated that using the "rod" creates children who are not more obedient but who are instead simply more angry and aggressive than other kids. Parents who routinely slap or strike their children are actually handing them a model of

violence to imitate—and many do indeed grow to be abusive, some even murderously so.

JULIUS SEGAL, (20th-century) U.S. pediatrician. "10 Myths About Child Development," *Parents Magazine* (July 1989).

Work and Family Life, General

1 The problem, thus, is not whether or not women are to combine marriage and motherhood with work or career but how they are to do so—concomitantly in a two-role continuous pattern or sequentially in a pattern involving job or career discontinuities.

JESSIE BERNARD, (20th-century) U.S. sociologist and author. "Women's Educational Needs," ch. 11, *The Modern American College*, ed. Arthur W. Chickering (1981).

2 Parenting, as an unpaid occupation outside the world of public power, entails lower status, less power, and less control of resources than paid work.

NANCY CHODOROW, (20th-century) U.S. psychologist and author. *The Reproduction of Mothering Psychoanalysis and the Sociology of Gender*, ch. 2 (1978).

3 Choose a job you love, and you will never have to work a day in your life.

CONFUCIUS, (551–479 B.C.) Chinese philosopher.

4 The all-American work ethic, destructive enough by itself, also packs a gender double standard that strip-mines the natural resources of both parents. It has taught us that as their earnings and success increase, men become "more manly," while women become "less feminine." This perverse cultural dynamic gives fathers an incentive to stay away from their families and kill themselves at work, while coercing mothers to limit their career commitment, which in turn limits their wages and shortchanges their families.

LETTY COTTIN POGREBIN, (20th-century) U.S. editor and author. *Family and Politics*, ch. 6 (1983).

5 Freud was once asked what he thought a normal person should be able to do well. The questioner probably expected a complicated answer. But Freud, in the curt way of his old days, is reported to have said: "Lieben und arbeiten" (to love and to work). It pays to ponder on this simple formula; it gets deeper as you think about it.

ERIK H. ERIKSON, (20th-century) German-born U.S. psychoanalyst and author. *Childhood and Society*, ch. 7 (1950).

6 Being a member of the labor force and a full-time parent means trying to manage against overwhelming odds in an unresponsive society.

SHEILA B. KAMERMAN, (20th-century) U.S. professor of social policy and author. *Parenting in an Unresponsive Society*, ch. 7 (1980).

7 Work though we must, our jobs do not automatically determine our priorities concerning our marriages, our children, our social life, or even our health. It's still life, constrained as it may be by limited disposable income or leisure time, and we're still responsible for making it something we enjoy or endure.

MELINDA M. MARSHALL, (20th-century) U.S. editor and author. *Good Enough Mothers*, ch. 4 (1993).

8 Welcome to the great American two-career family and pass the aspirin please.

ANASTASIA TOUFEXIS, (20th-century) U.S. journalist. "The Perils of Dual Careers," *Time* (May 13, 1985).

9 No one on his deathbed ever said, "I wish I had spent more time on my business."

PAUL E. TSONGAS, (20th-century) U.S. politician. *"Blind Ambition,"* as quoted in *Living Out Loud,* Anna Quindlen (1988).

Work and Family Life, Corporate Response to

1 "Which is more important to you, your field or your children?" the department head asked. She replied, "That's like asking me if I could walk better if you amputated my right leg or my left leg."

ANONYMOUS PARENT, as quoted in *Women and the Work Family Dilemma,* Deborah J. Swiss and Judith P. Walker, ch. 2 (1993).

2 All of the valuable qualities . . . like helping in the development of others—will not get you to the top at General Motors, were that path open to women. . . . The characteristics most highly developed in women and perhaps most essential to human beings are *the* very characteristics that are specifically dysfunctional for success in the world as it is. . . . They may, however, be the important ones for making the world different.

JEAN BAKER MILLER, (20th-century) U.S. psychiatrist. *Toward a New Psychology of Women,* ch. 10 (1976).

3 Perhaps one reason that many working parents do not agitate for collective reform, such as more governmental or corporate childcare, is that the parents fear, deep down, that to share responsibility for child-rearing is to abdicate it.

FAYE J. CROSBY, (20th-century) U.S. psychologist and author. *Juggling,* ch. 1 (1991).

4 It is ultimately in employers' best interests to have their employees' families functioning smoothly. In the long run, children who misbehave because they are inadequately supervised or marital partners who disapprove of their spouse's work situation are productivity problems. Just as work affects parents and children, parents and children affect the workplace by influencing the employed parents' morale, absenteeism, and productivity.

ANN C. CROUTER, (20th-century) U.S. researcher. *In Support of Families,* ed. Michael W. Yogman and T. Berry Brazelton, ch. 6 (1986).

5 Corporate America will likely be motivated to support childcare when it can be shown to have positive effects on that which management is concerned about—recruitment, retention and productivity. Indeed, employers relate to childcare as a way to provide growth fostering environments for young managers.

DANA E. FRIEDMAN, (20th-century) U.S. researcher and educator. "The Potential for Employer Supported Childcare to Create Growth Fostering Environments for Young Children," paper prepared for MacArthur Foundation's Conference on Childcare (November 1982).

6 What we have seen in the way of adaptation and adjustment seems to indicate that families are adjusting parenting to the world of work,

rather than the labor markets and industries responding to the parenting and family needs of their employees.

SHEILA B. KAMERMAN, (20th-century) U.S. professor of social policy and author. *Parenting in an Unresponsive Society,* ch. 5 (1980).

7 Unfortunately, we cannot rely solely on employers seeing that it is in their self-interest to change the workplace. Since the benefits of family-friendly policies are long-term, they may not be immediately visible or quantifiable; companies tend to look for success in the bottom line. On a deeper level, we are asking those in power to change the rules by which they themselves succeeded and with which they identify.

ANNE C. WEISBERG, (20th-century) U.S. attorney. *Everything a Working Mother Needs to Know,* ch. 9 (1994).

Work and Family Life Conflicts

1 Q: What would have made a family and career easier for you?
A: Being born a man.

ANONYMOUS MOTHER, (20th-century) U.S. physician and mother of four. As quoted in *Women and the Work Family Dilemma,* Deborah J. Swiss and Judith P. Walker, ch. 2 (1993).

2 Q: Have you made personal sacrifices for the sake of your career?
A: Leaving a three-month-old infant in another person's house for nine hours, five days a week is a personal sacrifice.

ALICE CORT, (20th-century) U.S. doctor and mother of two. As quoted in *Women and the Work Family Dilemma,* Deborah J. Swiss and Judith P. Walker, ch. 2 (1993).

3 Although Freud said happiness is composed of love and work, reality often forces us to choose love or work.

LETTY COTTIN POGREBIN, (20th-century) U.S. editor and author. *Family and Politics,* ch. 6 (1983).

4 Work-family conflicts—the trade-offs of your money or your life, your job or your child—would not be forced upon women with such sanguine disregard if men experienced the same career stalls caused by the-buck-stops-here responsibility for children.

LETTY COTTIN POGREBIN, (20th-century) U.S. editor and author. *Family and Politics,* ch. 6 (1983).

5 Anyone who wishes to combine domestic responsibilities and paid employment with the least stress and most enjoyment might start by pondering this paradox: the first step to better functioning is to stop blaming herself for not functioning well enough.

FAYE J. CROSBY, (20th-century) U.S. psychologist and author. *Juggling,* ch. 1 (1991).

6 We can paint unrealistic pictures of the juggler—displaying her now as a problem-free paragon of glamour and now as a modern hag. Or we can see in the juggler a real person who strives to overcome the obstacles that nature and society put in her path and who does so with vigor and determination.

FAYE J. CROSBY, (20th-century) U.S. psychologist and author. *Juggling,* ch. 7 (1991).

7 The influx of women into paid work and her increased power raise a woman's aspirations and hopes for equal treatment at home. Her

lower wage and status at work and the threat of divorce reduce what she presses for and actually expects.

ARLIE HOCHSCHILD, (20th-century) U.S. sociologist and author. *The Second Shift,* ch. 16 (1989).

8 Certainly we expect to maintain both a career and a family, but we expect excellence in one role will come at some cost to the other. Certainly we would like to think we're entitled to . . . Caribbean vacations, but we're chastened by our minimal savings and the specter of our husbands losing their jobs. Certainly we want issues such as child care and family leave to be perceived as problems affecting all of us, not just women—but we recognize, too, that we must then all bear the burden of paying for them and making them work for the businesses upon which our economic survival is based.

MELINDA M. MARSHALL, (20th-century) U.S. editor and author. *Good Enough Mothers,* ch. 1 (1993).

9 I acknowledge that the balance I have achieved between work and family roles comes at a cost, and every day I must weigh whether I live with that cost happily or guiltily, or whether some other lifestyle entails trade-offs I might accept more readily. It is always my choice: to change what I cannot tolerate, or tolerate what I cannot—or will not—change.

MELINDA M. MARSHALL, (20th-century) U.S. editor and author. *Good Enough Mothers,* Introduction (1993).

10 A "super person" is one who expects to manage a career, home, and family with complete ease, expecting to maintain a perfect job, a perfect marriage, a perfect house, and perfect control of the children.

JOYCE PORTNER, (20th century) U.S. author. *Stress and Family,* ch. 11 (1983).

11 Current conflicts and guilt about being a woman who is a mother and a person in her own right are a socially defined malaise, not an individual problem. . . . The conflict is not between being a mother and having a career; it is between nineteenth-century ideas about children and today's ideas about women.

SANDRA SCARR, (20th-century) U.S. developmental psychologist and author. *Mother Care/Other Care,* pt. 2, ch. 3 (1984).

12 Employees from families where all adults work are still coping with rules and conditions of work designed, as one observer put it, to the specifications of Ozzie and Harriet. These conditions include rigid adherence to a 40-hour workweek, a concept of career path inconsistent with the life cycle of a person with serious family responsibilities, notions of equity formed in a different era, and performance evaluation systems that confuse effort with results by equating hours of work with productivity.

FRAN SUSSNER RODGERS, (20th-century) U.S. educator. "Business and the Facts of Family Life," *Harvard Business Review* (November/December 1989).

13 Many women are surprised by the intensity of their maternal pull and the conflict it brings to their competing roles. This is the precise point at which many women feel the stress of the work/family dilemma most keenly. They realize that they may have a price to pay

for wanting to be both professionals and mothers. They feel guilty for not being at work, and angry for being manipulated into feeling this guilt. . . . They don't quite fit at home. They don't quite fit at work.

Deborah J. Swiss, (20th-century) U.S. educator and author. *Women and the Work Family Dilemma,* ch. 1 (1993).

14 Realistic about how much one person can accomplish in a given day, women expect to have to make some trade-offs between work and family. Families, however, have absorbed all the stress and strain they possibly can. The entire responsibility for accommodation is taking place on the home side of the equation.

Deborah J. Swiss, (20th-century) U.S. educator and author. *Women and the Work Family Dilemma,* introduction (1993).

15 The first full-fledged generation of women in the professions did not talk about their overbooked agenda or the toll it took on them and their families. They knew that their position in the office was shaky at best. . . . If they suffered self-doubt or frustration . . . they blamed themselves—either for expecting too much or for doing too little.

Deborah J. Swiss, (20th-century) U.S. educator and author. *Women and the Work Family Dilemma,* Introduction (1993).

16 The myth of superwoman has hung on long after the media stopped airing fantasy-based commercials about working women's lives: here she comes, home from the office after 12 hours of high-powered negotiations in the executive suite. Her designer suit is still fresh and unwrinkled, her face radiant and unlined as she opens her arms to greet her two adorable children—and sends a seductive glance toward her handsome husband, beaming proudly in the background. Watch her as, with one smooth motion, she slips off her jacket and into a dainty apron as she glides toward the spotless kitchen to create a three-course meal for her beloved family. After dinner she will check the children's French homework and read them a chapter of *Jane Eyre* before tucking the little cherubs into bed. While her husband watches the late-night news, she will disappear into the den to make an overseas call that will clinch a multinational deal for her company.

Deborah J. Swiss, (20th-century) U.S. educator and author. *Women and the Work Family Dilemma,* ch. 3 (1993).

Work and Family Life, Positive Aspects of

1 The truth is despite the hard work and juggling required to keep the different facets of the frantic life afloat, the "superwoman" has one marvelous compensation. Being busy and being seen to be busy lets you off the hook. Buys you a way out of all aspects of your many roles you secretly despise ... like cleaning cupboards . . . or entertaining your husband's business friends. When you combine wife, mother, career and all, each role becomes the perfect excuse for avoiding the worst aspects of the other.

Bettina Arndt, (20th-century) Australian journalist and author. *Private Lives,* ch. 2 (1986).

2 One of the most important findings to come out of our research is that being where you want to be is good for you. We found a very strong correlation between preferring the role you are in and well-being. The homemaker who is at home because she likes that "job," because it meets her own desires and needs, tends to feel good about her life. The woman at work who wants to be there also rates high in well-being.

GRACE BARUCH, U.S. developmental psychologist, **ROSALIND BARNETT,** U.S. psychologist, and **CARYL RIVERS,** U.S. journalist (20th-century). *Life Prints,* ch. 2 (1983).

3 The knowledge that for women in middle adulthood, multiple roles can tie in with well-being should help younger women who are struggling with the pressures of small children and a job, and who may be tempted to abandon or severely curtail their career goals. . . . The woman who manages to hang onto her career may be in for some stress in her younger years when the pulls and tugs of family and career can be intense, but if she can persist, her chances for much smoother sailing in her mature years seem very good.

GRACE BARUCH, U.S. developmental psychologist, **ROSALIND BARNETT,** U.S. psychologist, and **CARYL RIVERS,** U.S. journalist (20th-century). *Life Prints,* ch. 8 (1983).

4 The more a woman likes her job, the better her self-image and the more she enjoys her life.

GRACE BARUCH, U.S. developmental psychologist, **ROSALIND BARNETT,** U.S. psychologist, and **CARYL RIVERS,** U.S. journalist (20th-century). *Life Prints,* ch. 6 (1983).

5 Combining paid employment with marriage and motherhood creates safeguards for emotional well-being. Nothing is certain in life, but generally the chances of happiness are greater if one has multiple areas of interest and involvement. To juggle is to diminish the risk of depression, anxiety, and unhappiness.

FAYE J. CROSBY, (20th-century) U.S. psychologist and author. *Juggling,* ch. 3 (1991).

6 Having an identity at work separate from an identity at home means that the work role can help absorb some of the emotional shock of domestic distress. Even a mediocre performance at the office can help a person repair self-esteem damaged in domestic battles.

FAYE J. CROSBY, (20th-century) U.S. psychologist and author. *Juggling,* ch. 4 (1991).

7 If we confine ourselves to one life role, no matter how pleasant it seems at first, we starve emotionally and psychologically. We need a change and balance in our daily lives. We need sometimes to dress up and sometimes to lie around in torn jeans. . . . Even a grimy factory can afford some relief from a grimy kitchen and vice versa.

FAYE J. CROSBY, (20th-century) U.S. psychologist and author. *Juggling,* ch. 4 (1991).

8 Juggling produces both practical and psychological benefits. . . . A woman's involvement in one role can enhance her functioning in another. Being a wife can make it easier to work outside the home. Being a mother can facilitate the activities and foster the skills of the efficient wife or of the effective worker. And employment outside

the home can contribute in substantial, practical ways to how one works within the home, as a spouse and as a parent.

Faye J. Crosby, (20th-century) U.S. psychologist and author. *Juggling,* ch. 4 (1991).

9 When men and women across the country reported how happy they felt, researchers found that jugglers were happier than others. By and large, the more roles, the greater the happiness. Parents were happier than nonparents, and workers were happier than nonworkers. Married people were much happier than unmarried people. Married people were generally at the top of the emotional totem pole.

Faye J. Crosby, (20th-century) U.S. psychologist and author. *Juggling,* ch. 3 (1991).

10 True balance requires assigning realistic performance expectations to each of our roles. True balance requires us to acknowledge that our performance in some areas is more important than in others. True balance demands that we determine what accomplishments give us honest satisfaction as well as what failures cause us intolerable grief.

Melinda M. Marshall, (20th-century) U.S. editor and author. *Good Enough Mothers,* ch. 4 (1993).

11 Work is a responsibility most adults assume, a burden at times, a complication, but also a challenge that, like children, requires enormous energy and that holds the potential for qualitative, as well as quantitative, rewards. Isn't this the only constructive perspective for women who have no choice but to work? And isn't it a more healthy attitude for women writhing with guilt because they choose to compound the challenges of motherhood with work they enjoy?

Melinda M. Marshall, (20th-century) U.S. editor and author. *Good Enough Mothers,* introduction (1993).

12 It is undeniable that a woman's ability to stretch and pursue her total competence outside the home and get paid what she's worth for it makes for happier and more fulfilled women.

Kyle D. Pruett, (20th-century) U.S. child psychiatrist and author. *The Nurturing Father,* ch. 13 (1987).

13 One other contradiction or paradox that I've discovered as a working mother is that children, despite having obviously curtailed my freedom, have also brought me a new freedom that I hadn't anticipated. They've liberated me from the sorts of petty career or work anxieties that formerly were capable of obsessing me, especially the need for approval from those in authority.

Barbara Schapiro, (20th-century) U.S. author. As quoted in *Mother Journeys,* ed. Maureen T. Reddy, Martha Roth, Amy Sheldon, sec. 3 (1994).

Working Mothers

1 The things women find rewarding about work are, by and large ,the same things that men find rewarding and include both the inherent nature of the work and the social relationships.

Grace Baruch, U.S. developmental psychologist, **Rosalind Barnett,** U.S. psychologist, and **Caryl Rivers,** U.S. journalist (20th-century). *Life Prints,* ch. 6 (1983).

2 Working women today are trying to achieve in the work world what men have achieved all along—but men have always had the help of a woman at home who took care of all the other details of living! Today the working woman is also that woman at home, and without support services in the workplace and a respect for the work women do within and outside the home, the attempt to do both is taking its toll—on women, on men, and on our children.

JEANNE ELIUM AND DON ELIUM, (20th-century) U.S. family counselors and authors. *Raising a Daughter*, ch. 3 (1994).

3 Modern women are squeezed between the devil and the deep blue sea, and there are no lifeboats out there in the form of public policies designed to help these women combine their roles as mothers and as workers.

SYLVIA ANN HEWLETT, (20th-century) U.S. economist. *A Lesser Life*, ch. 2 (1986).

4 She isn't harassed. She's busy, and it's glamorous to be busy. Indeed, the image of the on-the-go working mother is very like the glamorous image of the busy top executive. The scarcity of the working mother's time seems like the scarcity of the top executive's time. . . . The analogy between the busy working mother and the busy top executive obscures the wage gap between them at work, and their different amounts of backstage support at home.

ARLIE HOCHSCHILD, (20th-century) U.S. sociologist and author. *The Second Shift*, ch. 3 (1989).

5 The only difference between men and women is that women are able to create new little human beings in their bodies while simultaneously writing books, driving tractors, working in offices, planting crops—in general, doing everything men do.

ERICA JONG, (20th-century) U.S. novelist and poet. As quoted in *Necessary Losses*, Judith Viorst, ch. 8 (1986).

6 Knowing how beleaguered working mothers truly are—knowing because I am one of them—I am still amazed at how one need only say "I work" to be forgiven all expectation, to be assigned almost a handicapped status that no decent human being would burden further with demands. "I work" has become the universally accepted excuse, invoked as an all-purpose explanation for bowing out, not participating, letting others down, or otherwise behaving inexcusably.

MELINDA M. MARSHALL, (20th-century) U.S. editor and author. *Good Enough Mothers*, ch. 4 (1993).

7 Working mothers are just as likely to want to conform to a standard of perfection—and just as likely to suffer from their failure to meet it—as their stay-at-home counterparts.

MELINDA M. MARSHALL, (20th-century) U.S. editor and author. *Good Enough Mothers*, ch. 4 (1993).

8 There is no reason why parents who work hard at a job to support a family, who nurture children during the hours at home, and who have searched for and selected the best [daycare] arrangement possible for their children need to feel anxious and guilty. It almost seems

as if our culture wants parents to experience these negative feelings.

GWEN MORGAN, (20th-century) U.S. childcare advocate. *In Support of Families,* ed. Michael W. Yogman and T. Berry Brazelton, ch. 9 (1986).

9 It was almost two years ago, while awaiting the imminent birth of my second child, that I decided to start working part-time. This would have been unthinkable to me when I was younger. At twenty-five I should have worn a big red A on my chest; it would have stood for ambition, an ambition so brazen and burning that it would have reduced Hester Prynne's transgression to pale pink.

ANNA QUINDLEN, (20th-century) U.S. journalist and novelist. *Living Out Loud,* "Blind Ambition" (1988).

10 Little has been written about the role of the jane, as I prefer to call the female john, in the life of the contemporary career woman. . . . In some ways it has replaced the old consciousness-raising group as a setting for the free exchange of ideas about men, work, children, personal development, and the ridiculous price of pantyhose. In most offices, it is one of the few spots in which a woman employee can pause, throw back her head, and say, loudly, "Men are so stupid sometimes I want to shoot all of them."

ANNA QUINDLEN, (20th-century) U.S. journalist and novelist. *Living Out Loud,* "The Jane" (1988).

11 It's true, as Marya Mannes says: "No one believes [a woman's] time to be sacred. A man at his desk in a room with a closed door is a man at work. A woman at a desk in any room is available."

LILLIAN BRESLOW RUBIN, (20th-century) U.S. sociologist and family therapist. *Women of a Certain Age,* ch. 1 (1979).

12 [In answer to the question, "How can you be both a lawmaker and a mother?"] I have a brain and a uterus, and I use both.

PAT SCHROEDER, (20th-century) U.S. Congresswoman. As quoted in *Family and Politics,* Letty Cottin Pogrebin ch. 6 (1983).

13 "Working mother" is a misnomer. . . . It implies that any mother without a definite career is lolling around eating bon-bons, reading novels, and watching soap operas. But the word "mother" is already a synonym for some of the hardest, most demanding work ever shouldered by any human. . . . It is one she cannot easily give up for several decades. It can be slavery, joy in work, a magnificent career. It can be failure or triumph, but it can never be insignificant or unimportant since it is one "job" affecting the outcome of another's life.

LIZ SMITH, (20th-century) U.S. columnist and author. *The Mother Book,* "Work, Work, Work!" (1978).

14 Most fathers will admit that having children does not change perceptibly the way they are treated or perceived in the workplace, even if their wives work. Everyone at his workplace assumes that she will take on the responsibilities of the children and the home, even if she too is in the office all day.

ANNE C. WEISBERG, (20th-century) U.S. attorney. *Everything a Working Mother Needs to Know,* ch. 1 (1994).

15 We felt often that we were perceived as mothers trying to be lawyers, while a male colleague of ours who had a young child was perceived as a lawyer who also happened to be a father.

Anne C. Weisberg, (20th-century) U.S. attorney. *Everything a Working Mother Needs to Know,* ch. 1 (1994).

16 Americans have internalized the value that mothers of young children should be mothers first and foremost, and not paid workers. The result is that a substantial amount of confusion, ambivalence, guilt, and anxiety is experienced by working mothers. Our cultural expectations of mother and realities of female participation in the labor force are directly contradictory.

Ruth E. Zambrana, U.S. researcher. "The Working Mother in Contemporary Perspectives: A Review of Literature," *Pediatrics* (December 1979).

Working Mothers, The Effects on Children

1 The working woman may be quick to see any problems with children as her fault because she isn't as available to them. However, the fact that she is employed is rarely central to the conflict. And overall, studies show, being employed doesn't have negative effects on children; carefully done research consistently makes this clear.

Grace Baruch, U.S. developmental psychologist. **Rosalind Barnett,** U.S. psychologist, and **Caryl Rivers,** U.S. journalist (20th-century). *Life Prints,* ch. 5 (1983).

2 What stunned me was the regular assertion that feminists were "anti-family." . . . It was motherhood that got me into the movement in the first place. I became an activist after recognizing how excruciatingly personal the political was to me and my sons. It was the women's movement that put self-esteem back into "just a housewife," rescuing our intelligence from the junk pile of "instinct" and making it human, deliberate, powerful.

Mary Kay Blakely, (20th-century) U.S. journalist and author. *American Mom,* ch. 3 (1994).

3 Recent studies that have investigated maternal satisfaction have found this to be a better prediction of mother-child interaction than work status alone. More important for the overall quality of interaction with their children than simply whether the mother works or not, these studies suggest, is how satisfied the mother is with her role as worker or homemaker. Satisfied women are consistently more warm, involved, playful, stimulating and effective with their children than unsatisfied women.

Alison Clarke-Stewart, (20th-century) U.S. child development specialist and author. *Daycare,* ch. 7 (1982).

4 Adults empathize so readily with a clinging child because all of us (including those who were raised by doting mothers who stayed home) have felt abandoned at some time or other as children: it's part of growing up. . . . But you can't stop working because your child doesn't want you to leave her—and you needn't think it would be better if you could.

Amy Laura Dombro, (20th-century) U.S. early childhood educator and author. *The Ordinary Is Extraordinary,* ch. 13 (1988).

5 Your children get a lot of good stuff out of your work . . . They benefit from the tales you tell over dinner. They learn from the things you explain to them about what you do. They brag about you at school. They learn that work is interesting, that it has dignity, that it is necessary and pleasing, and that it is a perfectly natural thing for both mothers and fathers to do . . . Your work enriches your children more than it deprives them.

Louise Lague, (20th-century) U.S. editor and author. *The Working Mom's Book of Hints, Tips, and Everyday Wisdom,* ch. 1 (1995).

6 I'm always on the lookout for research "proving" that women who work are a) in the majority (because misery loves company); b) raising more, not fewer Nobel Prize winners or Olympic medalists; and c) not handicapping children for life, because they need or want to work.

Melinda M. Marshall, (20th-century) U.S. editor and author. *Good Enough Mothers,* ch. 3 (1993).

7 After your baby is born, guilt can grow into a monster that sits on your shoulder and whispers into your ear, "Mirror, mirror on the wall—who's the guiltiest of them all?" The answer is working mothers. Every time you can't calm your screaming baby, the guilt monster will tell you that if you were a true mom, an at-home mom, you would know what to do. . . . Everytime something goes wrong at work, it will tell you that it's your fault for trying to be a "supermom."

Jean Marzollo, (20th-century) U.S. author. *Your Maternity Leave,* ch. 3 (1989).

8 If work is part of your identity, think very carefully before you give it up. Giving it up won't make you a better mother; it will make you less of the person you are; and that will make you less of a mother.

Jean Marzollo, (20th-century) U.S. author. *Your Maternity Leave,* ch. 9 (1989).

9 You have a lifetime to work, but children are only young once.

Polish Proverb.

10 Many working mothers feel guilty about not being at home. And when they are there, they wish it could be perfect. . . . This pressure to make every minute happy puts working parents in a bind when it comes to setting limits and modifying behavior.

Cathy Rindner Tempelsman, (20th-century) U.S. journalist and author. *Child-Wise,* ch. 11 (1994).

11 All we know is that the school achievement, IQ test score, and emotional and social development of working mothers' children are every bit as good as that of children whose mothers do not work.

Sandra Scarr, (20th-century) U.S. developmental psychologist and author. *Mother Care/Other Care,* ch. 1 (1984).

12 It is not only a question of who is responsible for very young children. There is no longer anyone home to care for adolescents and the elderly. There is no one around to take in the car for repair or to let the plumber in. Working families are faced with daily dilemmas: Who will take care of a sick child? Who will go to the big soccer game? Who will attend the teacher conference?

FRAN SUSSNER RODGERS, (20th-century) U.S. educator. "Business and the Facts of Family Life," *Harvard Business Review* (November/December 1989).

13 Looking back as an adult on his mother's decision to be a career woman, Nicholas has this to say about Anna L. Bruenn, D.D.S.: " . . . what really made her such a good parent was the serenity that came from her self-realization as a woman. . . . She knew who she was, she was satisfied with the person she'd made herself into, and therefore she was absolutely unintimidated by how anybody else thought she should live. That was an enormous help to me. It meant she was strong enough to allow me freedom."

NICHOLAS VON HOFFMAN, (20th-century) U.S. columnist. As quoted in *The Mother Book,* "Work, Work, Work!" Liz Smith. (1978).

14 All studies have found that daughters of working mothers have a less sex-stereotyped self concept, and both sons and daughters have a less traditional concept of sex roles in general.

RUTH E. ZAMBRANA, U.S. researcher. "The Working Mother in Contemporary Perspectives: A Review of Literature," *Pediatrics* (December 1979).

15 Generally there is no consistent evidence of significant differences in school achievement between children of working and nonworking mothers, but differences that do appear are often related to maternal satisfaction with her chosen role, and the quality of substitute care.

RUTH E. ZAMBRANA, U.S. researcher. "The Working Mother in Contemporary Perspectives: A Review of Literature," *Pediatrics* (December 1979).

Working Mothers, Reasons for Working

1 Women have entered the work force . . . partly to express their feelings of self-worth . . . partly because today many families would not survive without two incomes, partly because they are not at all sure their marriages will last. The day of the husband as permanent meal-ticket is over, a fact most women recognize, however they feel about "women's liberation."

ROBERT NEELLY BELLAH, (20th-century) U.S. sociologist and author. *Habits of the Heart,* pt. 1, ch. 4 (1985).

2 Mothers work outside the home for many reasons; one of them is almost always because their families need their income to live up to their standards for their children.

KENNETH KENISTON, (20th-century) U.S. professor of human development. *All Our Children,* ch. 1, The Carnegie Council on Children (1977).

3 Whether outside work is done by choice or not, whether women seek their identity through work, whether women are searching for pleasure or survival through work, the integration of motherhood and the world of work is a source of ambivalence, struggle, and conflict for the great majority of women.

SARA LAWRENCE LIGHTFOOT, (20th-century) U.S. educator and author. *Worlds Apart,* ch. 2 (1978).

4 Love and work are viewed and experienced as totally separate

activities motivated by separate needs. Yet, when we think about it, our common sense tells us that our most inspired, creative acts are deeply tied to our need to love and that, when we lack love, we find it difficult to work creatively; that work without love is dead, mechanical, sheer competence without vitality, that love without work grows boring, monotonous, lacks depth and passion.

Marta Zahaykevich, Ukranian-born U.S. psychiatrist. *Critical Perspectives on Adult Women's Development,* Columbia university Monograph (1980).

Working Mothers and At-home Mothers

1 In different life prints, stress will be felt intensely at different times. The woman who is trying to juggle young children and a demanding job may feel the most pressure in her late twenties and early thirties, but by her forties her investment in the job will be paying off and the demands of the family will be lessening. The woman who has been a homemaker in a very traditional pattern may experience a great deal of stress around the issue of redefining her life as the active role of mothering comes to an end.

Grace Baruch, U.S. developmental psychologist, **Rosalind Barnett,** U.S. psychologist, and **Caryl Rivers,** U.S. journalist (20th-century). *Lifeprints,* ch. 8 (1983).

2 By now, legions of tireless essayists and op-ed columnists have dressed feminists down for making such a fuss about entering the professions and earning equal pay that everyone's attention has been distracted from the important contributions of mothers working at home. This judgment presumes, of course, that prior to the resurgence of feminism in the 70s, housewives and mothers enjoyed wide recognition and honor. This was not exactly the case.

Mary Kay Blakely, (20th-century) U.S. journalist and author. *American Mom,* ch. 2 (1994).

3 It's an old trick now, God knows, but it works every time. At the very moment women start to expand their place in the world, scientific studies deliver compelling reasons for them to stay home.

Mary Kay Blakely, (20th-century) U.S. journalist and author. *American Mom,* ch. 1 (1994).

4 I'm real ambivalent about [working mothers]. Those of use who have been in the women's movement for a long time know that we've talked a good game of "go out and fulfill your dreams" and "be everything you were meant to be." But by the same token, we want daughters-in-law who are going to stay home and raise our grandchildren.

Erma Bombeck, (20th-century) U.S. humorist and author. As quoted in *The Last Word,* ed. Carolyn Warner, ch. 39 (1992).

5 Most baby books also tend to romanticize the mother who stays at home, as if she really spends her entire day doing nothing but beaming at the baby and whipping up educational toys from pieces of string, rather than balancing cooing time with laundry, cleaning, shopping and cooking.

Susan Chira, (20th-century) U.S. journalist. "Still Guilty After All These Years: A Bouquet of Advice Books for the Working Mom," *New York Times Book Review* (May 8, 1994).

6 Many women who used to be full-time mothers are discovering that outside work gives them friends, challenges, variety, money, independence; it makes them feel better about themselves, and therefore lets them be better parents.

WENDY COPPEDGE SANFORD, (20th-century) U.S. editor and author. *Ourselves and Our Children*, the Boston Women's Health Book Collective, introduction (1978).

7 Just as we need to encourage women to test life's many options, we need to acknowledge real limits of energy and resources. It would be pointless and cruel to prescribe role combinations for every woman at each moment of her life. Life has its seasons. There are moments when a woman ought to invest emotionally in many different roles, and other moments when she may need to conserve her psychological energies.

FAYE J. CROSBY, (20th-century) U.S. psychologist and author. *Juggling*, ch. 3 (1991).

8 For women the wage gap sets up an infuriating Catch-22 situation. They do the housework because they earn less, and they earn less because they do the housework.

SYLVIA ANN HEWLETT, (20th-century) U.S. economist. *A Lesser Life*, ch. 4 (1986).

9 There is a striking dichotomy between the behavior of many women in their lives at work and in their lives as mothers. Many of the same women who are battling stereotypes on the job, who are up against unspoken assumptions about the roles of men and women, seem to accept—and in their acceptance seem to reinforce—these roles at home with both their sons and their daughters.

ELLEN LEWIS, (20th-century) U.S. television producer. "Making a Difference," *New York Times Magazine* (December 1993).

10 For the mother who has opted to stay home, the question remains: Having perfected her role as a caretaker, can she abdicate control to less practiced individuals? Having put all her identity eggs in one basket, can she hand over the basket freely? Having put aside her own ambitions, can she resist imposing them on her children? And having set one example, can she teach another?

MELINDA M. MARSHALL, (20th-century) U.S. editor and author. *Good Enough Mothers*, ch. 3 (1993).

11 Stay-at-home mothers, . . . their self-esteem constantly assaulted, . . . are ever more fervently concerned that their offspring turn out better so they won't have to stoop to say "I told you so." Working mothers . . . their self-esteem corroded by guilt . . . are praying their kids turn out functional so they can stop being defensive and apologetic and instead assert "See? I did do it all."

MELINDA M. MARSHALL, (20th-century) U.S. editor and author. *Good Enough Mothers*, ch. 3 (1993).

12 The problem of invisibility, the incredible deficit of self-esteem that full-time mothers describe, seems to come with the territory. Day in and day out, the feedback from their spouse and kids suggests they are part of the woodwork, with no

intelligence to illuminate a homework question or share any insights on politics. . . . When no one recognizes or applauds their amazing juggling act, they perforce derive their sense of self-worth from being ringmaster—someone not necessarily talented but indisputably in charge.

Melinda M. Marshall, (20th-century) U.S. editor and author. *Good Enough Mothers,* ch. 3 (1993).

13 Both at-home *and* working mothers can overmeet their mothering responsibilities. In order to justify their jobs, working mothers can overnurture, overconnect with, and overschedule their children into activities and classes. Similarly, some at-home mothers . . . can make at-home mothering into a bigger deal than it is, over stimulating, overeducating, and overwhelming their children with purposeful attention.

Jean Marzollo, (20th-century) U.S. author. *Your Maternity Leave,* ch. 3 (1989).

14 Women find ways to give sense and meaning to daily life—ways to be useful in the community, to keep mind active and soul growing even while they change diapers and cook vegetables.

Lillian Breslow Rubin, (20th-century) U.S. sociologist and family therapist. *Women of a Certain Age,* ch. 3 (1979).

15 The time-use studies also show that employed women spend as much time as nonworking women in *direct* interactions with their children. Employed mothers spend as much time as those at home reading to and playing with their young children, although they do not, of course, spend as much time simply in the same room or house with the children.

Sandra Scarr, (20th-century) U.S. developmental psychologist and author. *Mother Care/Other Care,* ch. 1 (1984).

16 Every mother is a working mother.

Modern Proverb.

17 Some of the smartest women in the country said that they're too embarrassed to attend their reunions at Harvard Business School if they have dropped out of the work force, left the fast track by choosing part-time work, or decided to follow anything other than the standard male career path.

Deborah J. Swiss, (20th-century) U.S. educator and author. *Women and the Work-Family Dilemma,* ch. 2 (1993).

18 Many people will say to working mothers, in effect, "I don't think you can have it all." The phrase for "have it all" is code for "have your cake and eat it too." What these people really mean is that achievement in the workplace has always come at a price—usually a significant personal price; conversely, women who stayed home with their children were seen as having sacrificed a great deal of their own ambition for their families.

Anne C. Weisberg, (20th-century) U.S. attorney. *Everything a Working Mother Needs to Know,* ch. 1 (1994).

Women and Women's Work Choices

1 They [women] can use their abilities to support each other, even as

they develop more effective and appropriate ways of dealing with power. . . . Women do not need to diminish other women . . . [they] need the power to advance their own development, but they do not "need" the power to limit the development of others.

JEAN BAKER MILLER, (20th-century) U.S. psychiatrist. *Toward a New Psychology of Women,* ch. 10 (1976).

2 Women will not advance except by joining together in cooperative action. . . . Unlike other groups, women do not need to set affiliation and strength in opposition one against the other. We can readily integrate the two, search for more and better ways to use affiliation to enhance strength—and strength to enhance affiliation.

JEAN BAKER MILLER, (20th-century) U.S. psychiatrist. *Toward a New Psychology of Women,* ch. 8 (1976).

3 I have the strong impression that contemporary middle-class women do seem prone to feelings of inadequacy. We worry that we do not measure up to some undefined level, some mythical idealized female standard. When we see some women juggling with apparent ease, we suspect that we are grossly inadequate for our own obvious struggles.

FAYE J. CROSBY, (20th-century) U.S. psychologist and author. *Juggling,* ch. 7 (1991).

4 Is it impossible not to wonder why a movement which professes concern for the fate of all women has dealt so unkindly, contemptuously, so destructively, with so significant a portion of its sisterhood. Can it be that those who would reorder society perceive as the greater threat not the chauvinism of men or the pernicious attitudes of our culture, but rather the impulse to mother within women themselves?

ELAINE HEFFNER, (20th-century) U.S. psychiatrist and author. *Mothering,* ch. 1 (1978).

5 One might imagine that a movement which is so preoccupied with the fulfillment of human potential would have a measure of respect for those who nourish its source. But politics make strange bedfellows, and liberated women have elected to become part of a long tradition of hostility to mothers.

ELAINE HEFFNER, (20th-century) U.S. psychiatrist and author. *Mothering,* ch. 1 (1978).

6 Women do not have to sacrifice personhood if they are mothers. They do not have to sacrifice motherhood in order to be persons. Liberation was meant to expand women's opportunities, not to limit them. The self-esteem that has been found in new pursuits can also be found in mothering.

ELAINE HEFFNER, (20th-century) U.S. psychiatrist and author. *Mothering,* ch. 1 (1978).

7 Women of my age in America are at the mercy of two powerful and antagonistic traditions. The first is the ultradomestic fifties with its powerful cult of motherhood; the other is the strident feminism of the seventies with its attempt to clone the male competitive model. . . . Only in America are these ideologies pushed to extremes.

SYLVIA ANN HEWLETT, (20th-century) U.S. economist. *A Lesser Life,* ch. 2 (1986).

8 Some days your hat's off to the full-time mothers for being able to endure the relentless routine and incessant policing seven days a week instead of two. But on other days, merely the image of this woman crafting a brontosaurus out of sugar paste and sheet cake for her two-year-old's birthday drives a stake through your heart.

MELINDA M. MARSHALL, (20th-century) U.S. editor and author. *Good Enough Mothers,* ch. 3 (1993).

9 The generation of women before us who rushed to fill the corporate ranks altered our expectations of what working motherhood could be, tempered our ambition, and exploded the supermom myth many of us held dear.

MELINDA M. MARSHALL, (20th-century) U.S. editor and author. *Good Enough Mothers,* ch. 1 (1993).

Index of Sources